THE OXFORD IBSEN

Volume VIII

LITTLE EYOLF
JOHN GABRIEL BORKMAN
WHEN WE DEAD AWAKEN

THE OXFORD
IBSEN

Volume VIII

LITTLE EYOLF
JOHN GABRIEL BORKMAN
WHEN WE DEAD AWAKEN

Edited and translated by
JAMES WALTER McFARLANE

Oxford   London   New York
OXFORD UNIVERSITY PRESS
1977

Oxford University Press, Walton Street, Oxford OX2 6DP

OXFORD LONDON GLASGOW NEW YORK
TORONTO MELBOURNE WELLINGTON CAPE TOWN
IBADAN NAIROBI DAR ES SALAAM LUSAKA ADDIS ABABA
KUALA LUMPUR SINGAPORE JAKARTA HONG KONG TOKYO
DELHI BOMBAY CALCUTTA MADRAS KARACHI

British Library Cataloguing in Publication Data

Ibsen, Henrik
　The Oxford Ibsen.
　Vol. 8.
　I. Title　II. McFarlane, James Walter
　839.8'2'26　　PT8851
　ISBN 0-19-211387-9

PRINTED IN GREAT BRITAIN BY
THE CAMELOT PRESS LTD, SOUTHAMPTON

For

J.M.†, F.E.M., L.K.M., I.A.M., G.M.M., and A.E.R.M.

CONTENTS

PREFACE

The publication of this eighth and final volume of the *Oxford Ibsen* marks the completion of an undertaking, the beginnings of which go back twenty years to 1957. In that year the Publisher, and through him the Delegates, of the Oxford University Press received from me a scheme for bringing out in English translation a newly edited and collected edition of Ibsen's letters. (At the time I was motivated by the knowledge that these letters were available to an English reader only in a selected edition; the situation remains the same today.) The considered response at the time from the publishers was that Ibsen was not held to be among the world's most exciting correspondents; and that a complete edition of the letters was not timely. But, it was added, what about a new edition of the dramas? With ill-concealed enthusiasm, I submitted what I now rather more clearly recognize to have been a distinctly audacious scheme for a complete and scholarly edition in eight volumes, with newly translated texts, a full and carefully edited account of the draft and other manuscript material, a series of critical introductions, and a generous measure of supporting scholarly apparatus. With a faith one can only hope now they feel not to have been misplaced, the Delegates approved the scheme.

Initially the tempo of publication was brisk, and the first four volumes appeared at yearly intervals: vol. VI in 1960, vol. V in 1961, vol. II in 1962, and vol. IV in 1963. With this, half the edition was complete. Thereupon the rhythm of publication slackened. At the end of 1963 came my move from King's College, Newcastle in the University of Durham to the new University of East Anglia as founding Dean of its School of European Studies; in 1968 there followed, without interval, a three-year tour of duty until 1971 as the University's Pro-Vice-Chancellor. The intervals between the volumes inevitably grew longer: vol. VII appeared in 1966, vol. I in 1970, vol. III in 1972, and now, finally, vol. VIII in 1977 to complete the project as originally planned.

As was the case with all the earlier volumes, the translations here of the final definitive text of the dramas are based on the Norwegian texts as printed in the Centenary Edition (*Hundreårsutgave*, Oslo, 1928–57), edited by Francis Bull, Halvdan Koht, and Didrik Arup

Seip. The manuscript drafts have been edited and translated direct
from the extant manuscripts, all of which are in the University
Library, Oslo: *Little Eyolf*, U.B.Mss. 1941, 8° and 1117, 4°; *John
Gabriel Borkman*, U.B.Ms. 1118, 4°; and *When We Dead Awaken*,
U.B.Ms. 1119, 4°.

Since this is the final volume of the series, it is perhaps appropriate
that I should reiterate here some of the points I have made in earlier
prefaces. Of first importance is the fact that the plays themselves have
not been in any way cut, condensed, or in any other respect altered. For
purposes of study, the need for a complete text is of course obvious;
and when it comes to the theatre, I find myself recalling what Shaw
once wrote about the cutting of Shakespeare: 'The simple thing to do
with a Shakespeare play is to perform it. The alternative is to let it
alone. If Shakespeare made a mess of it, it is unlikely that Smith or
Robinson will succeed where he failed.' Even in circles where this is
felt to be too stern or perfectionist a doctrine, there is still likely to be
wide support for the view that cutting is in any case not the *translator's*
job.

The best translation, says the man with no knowledge of the original,
is one that does not read like a translation; for anybody familiar with
the original, on the other hand, it is imperative that he should be
reminded of it at every stage, and in every possible particular. If I
have had any definable policy in shaping the present versions, it was
to reconcile as far as I was able these two factors—making something
that to the knowledgeable was recognizably a 'translation' and not a
'free-rendering' or 'adaptation' or something equally undisciplined,
and yet at the same time making the lines 'sayable'. If the translations
of the drafts (as distinct from the plays proper) seem by comparison
less 'sayable', the reason is twofold: since the lines in this context
perhaps more obviously claim the attention of the student rather than
the actor, this particular element in the translation could afford to be
given less weighting in the general scheme of things; and since the
dialogue in them had not been subjected to Ibsen's meticulous final
revision, they were already less 'sayable' even in the original. Where
Ibsen has taken over into his final version phrases from an earlier
draft, I have wherever possible attempted to retain that identity at the
appropriate points in the English version. One other point may be
referred to here: in deciding whether characters should address each
other by first name or surname, I have chosen what seemed appropriate
to the equivalent English context of situation, rather than follow the

Norwegian conventions mechanically; titles such as 'Adjunkt',
'Frøken', and so on, have been similarly treated; and I have also tried
to exploit this device to the point where it would, I hoped, deal
relatively unobtrusively with the perennial problem of 'De' and 'du',
the formal and familiar modes of address.

   Much of the draft material presented in this edition has not been
available in English before; and what was earlier available was not
always presented in a form that offered a coherent account of the
development of the individual plays. What I have tried to do with the
fuller material now available is to fit it into a proper chronological
framework, so that the enthralling story of a play's growth from
initial conception to finished version is adequately documented.
Clearly what is offered here does not pretend to account for *all* the
details of the various revisions; indeed it is doubtful whether any
translated text could sustain the enormous weight of scholarly apparatus that would in that case be necessary—although it must be admitted
that P. G. la Chesnais's French edition has tried it. Instead I have
ventured to describe certain parallel passages as 'not greatly dissimilar'.
Inevitably with such a coarse-meshed device as this, some seemingly
negligible but—for particular and specialized inquiries—potentially
significant details will have slipped through; this is the price I have had
to pay for reducing the mass of detail to manageable proportions.
Moreover, the plan I have adopted is to a large extent only an
acknowledgement of the fact that, beyond a certain point, the
scholarly study of Ibsen is possible only by addressing oneself to the
original Norwegian text.

   In connection with the staging of Ibsen's plays, there is one point of
some interest: 'left' and 'right' in the stage directions mean 'as seen
from the point of view of the audience'. In a letter of 22 November
1884 to the Swedish actor-manager, August Lindberg, Ibsen wrote:
'In answer to your question, I hasten to inform you that *The Wild
Duck* is disposed from the auditorium and not from the stage, as indeed
all my plays are. I position everything as I see it in my mind's eye as
I am writing it down.'

   To attempt any full catalogue of those individuals and insti-
tutions to whom the edition owes in sum a deep debt of gratitude is
to embark on an impossibly large task. Nevertheless, even at the risk
of invidiousness, certain names must be mentioned. First, surely, must
come the publishers. Now that the thing is complete, it can be admitted
that it must have taken strong nerves and a stiff (and, in retrospect, to

its editor flattering) measure of confidence to give the scheme its initial approval. And my thanks as editor go unreservedly to those who were and have continued to be concerned with the edition, not only for their vision in initiating the enterprise but also for the impressive skills, both editorial and publishing, which they have brought to each succeeding volume: to John (now Sir John) Brown who took the main responsibility for the initial decisions; to John Bell who as Chief Editor and presiding genius has more than anyone been responsible for the smooth navigation of the edition over the years; and to Miss Ena Sheen who, associated with the project from its earliest days, has brought a sustained editorial ability of the highest order to bear on the successive volumes.

A second identifiable group is formed by those who have contributed directly to the edition as translators, as editors, or in some other more immediate capacity. The earlier individual volumes of the edition acknowledge in their various prefaces the preciser details, but it is fitting here to record in more consolidated form the larger debts: to Professor Glynne Wickham and the late Evelyn Ramsden for their translation of *The Pretenders*; to Christopher Fry and his collaborator Johan Fillinger for the brilliant translation of *Peer Gynt*; to James Kirkup for his spirited and moving version of *Brand* based on a literal translation supplied by me; to Jens Arup both for his verse translation of *Love's Comedy* and for his work as translator and editor of *Hedda Gabler*; and, supremely, to the late Graham Orton, sometime Reader in German in the University of Durham, whose linguistic and scholarly abilities contributed so markedly to volumes I and IV, and whose untimely death in 1969 was such a sad blow to German and Scandinavian scholarship in general, and to the *Oxford Ibsen* in particular.

It is a pleasure also to acknowledge with gratitude the valuable services of Miss Enid Self in preparing the typescripts of the later volumes.

The third group is formed by those who, corporately or individually, have assisted the progress of the edition either by material subvention or by scholarly or other professional assistance. I gratefully acknowledge a measure of financial assistance over the years from the British Academy, from the Leverhulme Trust (for their generous award of a European Faculty Fellowship in 1971–72), from the Research Fund of King's College, Newcastle, and from the University of East Anglia (which, in addition to a measure of financial support, also granted me a period of sabbatical leave at a stage crucial for the completion of the edition). Libraries and centres of documentation in many parts of Europe have given generously of their professional help; and if I select for particular mention the librarians and staff of the University Libraries of Oslo and Bergen, the Royal Library of Copenhagen, and the University Libraries of Newcastle upon Tyne and of East Anglia (Norwich), it is because the assistance I have had from them has been beyond conventional expectation. (Through their ready co-operation, I have for instance been able to assemble a virtually complete collection in photocopy of the extant Ibsen manuscript material.) I am also grateful to the BBC's Information Services, in particular the members of the Written Archives Centre, Caversham Park, and of the Play Library.

Last but in no sense least come those whose initials appear on the dedication page of this volume. Without their loving support, their loyalty and their understanding, this edition would never have been possible; and my debt to them is beyond measure.

SCHOOL OF EUROPEAN STUDIES   J.W.McF.
UNIVERSITY OF EAST ANGLIA
NORWICH

INTRODUCTION

It took time and the onset of illness to persuade Ibsen of the inescapable finality of *When We Dead Awaken*, to bring him to a recognition that with this 'dramatic epilogue' (as he sub-titled it on its publication in December 1899) all was now said and done. His first reaction, when he saw the critics reading the term as a declaration that he was now finished with writing, was to protest: 'What I intended . . . by "Epilogue",' he is reported to have said, 'is merely to indicate that the play forms the epilogue to that series of my dramas which starts with *A Doll's House* and is now complete with *When We Dead Awaken*. This last work belongs to those experiences I have sought to describe in the series as a whole. It forms a unity, an entity, and it is with this I am now finished. If after this . . . I write anything else, it will all be in a completely different context, perhaps also in a different form.'

When, only a few weeks later, he notably reduced the span of authorship for which he felt this latest play properly served as 'the epilogue'—from eleven works to four—it was doubtless an index of even stronger optimism about what his pen might still be capable of. On 5 March 1900 he wrote significantly to his French translator, Moritz Prozor: 'In essence you are right when you say that the series for which the "epilogue" is the completion actually began with *The Master Builder*.' But the perspectives were soon to change. After a brief but worrying illness, in consequence of which his doctor had temporarily forbidden him to put pen to paper, Ibsen was moved to take a more sombre view of his chances of ever again doing serious writing. The phrases he used at the end of April 1900 when discussing with his literary agent how this 'epilogue' could most appropriately be incorporated into the collected edition of his works dwelt on the overriding sense of finality with which he felt the play should now be read: 'Most acceptable for me would be to see an arrangement whereby *When We Dead Awaken* was taken as a concluding item into the collected works, where it organically belongs as a finale to the series.'

It is therefore with endorsement from Ibsen himself that *When We Dead Awaken* presents itself as a possibly triple culmination: to the 'series' of four plays written between 1892 and 1899; to the eleven or twelve 'contemporary plays' extending back over nearly quarter of a

century; and to the totality of his life's work since the publication of
his first drama in 1850.

To trace—in obedience to the first of these three recognitions—the
deeper origins of *Little Eyolf* (1894), *John Gabriel Borkman* (1896), and
When We Dead Awaken (1899) to a common inspiration which found
its initial expression in *The Master Builder* is to award crucial significance to the short poem 'There they sat, those two':

> De sad der, de to, i så lunt et hus
> ved høst og i vinterdage.
> Så brændte huset. Alt ligger i grus.
> De to får i asken rage.
>
> For nede i den er et smykke gemt, —
> et smykke, som aldri kan brænde.
> Og leder de trofast, hænder det nemt,
> at det findes af ham eller hende.
>
> Men finder de end, de brandlidte to,
> det dyre, ildfaste smykke, —
> aldri hun finder sin brændte tro,
> han aldri sin brændte lykke.
>
> They sat there, those two, in so snug a house
> in autumn and in winter days.
> Then the house burnt. All lies in ruins.
> Those two must rake in the ashes.
>
> For down among them a jewel is hidden,
> a jewel that can never burn.
> And if they search diligently, it might perhaps
> be found by him or her.
>
> But even if this fire-scarred pair ever do find
> that precious fireproof jewel, —
> She will never find her burnt faith,
> he never his burnt happiness.

Best known by Ibsen's own identification of it as 'the first piece of
preliminary work for *The Master Builder*', it was precisely dated by
him '16 March 1892'. Whether or not it was initially conceived as an
organic component of *The Master Builder* itself is uncertain, for in the

spring of 1892 Ibsen is believed to have cast aside (and possibly destroyed) the working notes and drafts of the play he was then currently engaged on, and he started anew. (His letters of these months to Hildur Andersen, then studying music in Vienna, would doubtless have shed light here had they survived.) Not in dispute, however, is that this same poem (with two small amendments) was again in the forefront of his mind in the July and August of 1894, in the period when he was deeply engrossed in the composition of *Little Eyolf*. In the draft version he was then working on, the grieving parents in Act III are faced with the anguish of adjusting to a life made desolate by the death of their son; at this juncture Alfred Allmers reads aloud to his wife Rita a poem he has written in his grief. It is 'They sat there, those two'. Alfred begins by assuming an obvious meaning: that it is about himself and Rita. She sees it very differently: as being about Alfred and his 'sister'. Name transference and overlapping identities introduce further ambiguity. And Alfred finally has to concede a complex multiple reference:

ALLMERS. . . . Did you understand that, Rita?

RITA [*rising*]. Yes. And I also understood that you didn't write those lines about me.

ALLMERS. Whom else . . .?

RITA. You wrote them about yourself and Asta.

ALLMERS. First and foremost about little Eyolf . . .

RITA. Oh, no, not about that little Eyolf who is lying deep deep out there. . . . You wrote them about that other one. About her whom you called little Eyolf when she was a child.

ALLMERS. Both to [*sic*] the big one and the little one. And also to you, Rita.

The poem with its ensuing dialogue tersely reinforces the recognition that central to the drama as a whole is a preoccupation with shifting human relationships as, merging and dissolving, they move through the stages of superimposition and reassertion, of conflict and resolution. Nevertheless, for reasons which were obviously important for Ibsen at the time, the poem was deleted from the play in the final stages of its revision and replaced by the much longer and more circumstantial account which Alfred gives of his ordeal in the mountains when he lost his way.

As an ingredient thus active in the formative stages of both *The Master Builder* and *Little Eyolf*, yet ultimately rejected from them both,

B1

the poem nevertheless retains a special significance. In its laconic account of a man and a woman, unidentified except as 'he' and 'she', who stand in close but undefined relationship to each other in a domestic context of the widest frame of reference (the 'house'), whose lives are struck by disaster and misfortune of an elementally symbolic kind (the 'fire'), in consequence of which the man's 'happiness' and the woman's 'faith/peace' are irrevocably lost, but where something both precious and indestructible (the 'jewel'), though now missing, might just conceivably by shared and patient endeavour be repossessed, the poem articulates in severely abstracted form a preoccupation which recurs in many different forms in Ibsen's work of these years. The world of Ibsen's last plays is the creation of a mind haunted by problems of personal relations in conditions of stress, and by the way these things bear on individual happiness and faith. With the same compulsive anguish that Alfred brings to his poem—'I had [he exclaims] to give expression to something which I cannot bear in silence any longer'— these dramas explore the complex interactions, the interdependencies, the shifts and dislocations, the endless conjoining and disjoining of multiple relationships which, though individually often deceptively simple and linear, combine into chains and patterns of daunting elaboration and subtlety. Each discrete relationship is discovered imposing its own peculiar imperatives, raising its own inhibitions, exerting its own special kind of attraction and compulsion. Within this containing structure of interlatticed relationships, this plexus of blood ties and family ties, of parenthood and childhood, of sex and marriage, of youth and age, the inhabitants of the Ibsenist world are subjected to close and intense scrutiny as they stumble in agonized pursuit of happiness and fulfilment.

The kinship links in these late plays—most conspicuously in *Little Eyolf* and *John Gabriel Borkman*—trace an elaborate geometry, an intricate interweaving of ties parental and filial, of sibling and other blood relationships, of affiliate and affinal connections of astonishing variety. Family and kinship obligations are seen occupying a wide band in the spectrum of 'pligt', that larger concept of duty which emerges as one of the dominant motivating forces in these later dramas, exacting from the individual—under pain of 'guilt'—the kind of conduct which convention or tradition or society's expectations impose. (How far Ibsen's preoccupation with 'in-law' relationships was prompted by the recent enlargement of his own affinal connections following his son's marriage to Bjørnson's daughter must of course remain conjectural.)

Prominent is the emphasis given to the obligations and aspirations of parenthood: the rights and duties of fatherhood, the demands and rewards of motherhood are repeatedly appealed to by characters who accord to them a distinctive importance in the business of living. For Alfred Allmers, fatherhood—if one is prepared to accept his protestations—has become the supremely defining element of his life, something with undisputed priority not only over any claims on him by his wife but also over those ambitions he cherished as a writer over the previous ten years: 'From now on it is a father to Eyolf I want to be. . . . Eyolf shall achieve the consummation of the family line. And my new life's work shall be that of bringing him to that consummation.' Borkman, though almost completely indifferent to his son for many years, ultimately comes to recognize in the relationship a formidable potential, an opportunity to appeal to Erhart's filial loyalty in the battle for his own rehabilitation: 'Listen, Erhart . . .' he says as his wife and his sister-in-law exert their competing claims on his son, 'What about coming with your father, then? . . . Erhart, will you join me and help me in this new life?' Rubek for his part is served with an affiliation order from his model Irene who insistently, almost hysterically, claims the sculpture 'Resurrection Day' as their 'child' and demands of Rubek that he display a father's solicitude towards it:

IRENE [*silently and swiftly draws a thin sharp knife from her bosom, and whispers hoarsely*]. Arnold . . . have you done harm to our child?

RUBEK [*evasively*]. Harm? I don't exactly know what you would call it.

IRENE [*breathlessly*]. Tell me, what have you done to the child?

RUBEK. If you'll sit down and listen calmly to what I have to say, I'll tell you.

IRENE [*puts the knife away*]. As calmly as ever a mother can who. . . .

Motherhood is awarded even greater prominence in these plays— natural motherhood, step-motherhood, foster-motherhood, adoptive motherhood, usurpative or surrogate motherhood, and of course metaphorical motherhood. Rita is as vociferous in repudiating the conventional role of mother as Gunhild is in asserting it. For Rita, motherhood means having *had* the child, not in continuing to minister to it; in her scheme of things, the child is merely an unwanted rival for her husband's affection, and her hostility and aggression mysteriously precipitate the catastrophic events. At the same time, she is also ruefully aware that her place as mother to Eyolf had long ago been usurped by her putative 'sister-in-law': 'Eyolf would never whole-heartedly give himself to me. . . . Somebody stood between us. . . . Asta, she possessed him. Right from the time that it happened . . . the accident.' Gunhild, in *John Gabriel Borkman*, had also been supplanted, in her case by a twin sister who took over as foster-mother to Erhart after the collapse of the family fortunes; but, in contrast to Rita, Gunhild had been stiffened in her resolve to bind her son to her: 'I alone shall be his mother,' she declares on learning of her sister's plan to adopt Erhart, 'I alone. My son's heart shall be mine—mine, and no one else's.' The force of the words is not lost upon Ella Rentheim who, only moments before, had accused Borkman of cheating her of a mother's joy and happiness: 'And of a mother's sorrows and tears, too. And that was perhaps my cruellest loss.' In *When We Dead Awaken*, Irene too is quick both to interpret and to assess her past life in terms of motherhood: the anguish of serving as 'mother' to the statue, and the pain she suffered from being deprived of real motherhood: 'I should have borne children. Many children. Real children. Not the kind that are preserved in tombs. That should have been my calling.'

The emphasis, once achieved, carries over to a range of other oblique or displaced or deviant parental relationships, which are then made to bear an important motivational burden within the drama. A surrogate mother/son relationship in *Little Eyolf*—Asta's past devotion to Eyolf—is itself reinforced by Borghejm's readiness to play surrogate father to Eyolf during Alfred's absence. A continuing influence on all the Allmers' present lives comes from the family's complex and confused past history of parenthood, legal and natural, from those emotionally intense parentless years which Alfred and Asta spent together when young, and from the fateful impact of the surviving novercal correspondence. In the Borkman household, alongside the natural mother/son relationship, there is also the past foster-mother/ foster-child relationship between Ella and Erhart, as well as the proposed adoptant mother/adoptive son relationship which provokes Gunhild to such vigorous reaction.

A large part of the continuing fascination which the family held for Ibsen doubtless lay in its function as a natural repository of inherited characteristics. It presented an obvious focus of inquiry for exploring how certain more contingent forces—chance encounter, or friendship and marriage, or the domestic environment generally—combine with factors transmitted through the blood, down the family 'line'.

Allmers' half-jesting 'We all have the same eyes' conceals a deep loyalty to the family and betrays a sense of pride in its distinctive features and characteristics, something which can prompt him to say: 'How good it is I have you, Asta. . . . Rita is not a blood relation. It's not like having a sister.' In *John Gabriel Borkman* the device of making the two Rentheim sisters twins—which, if one accepts them as 'identical twins', on a mathematical analogy reduces the variables in the situation—permits a dramatically more elegant demonstration of the forces at work within the infrastructure of the family. Even Mrs. Wilton is moved to comment on the relative merits of natural motherhood and foster-motherhood, on blood relationship and non-blood relationship in the domestic context:

MRS. WILTON. I think a good foster-mother often deserves more thanks than one's real mother.

MRS. BORKMAN. Has that been your experience?

MRS. WILTON. Bless you . . . I scarcely knew my mother. But if I'd had a good foster-mother, I might not have become as . . . as badly behaved as people say I am.

Sibling relationships, together with the more distant blood ties and affinal links which radiate out from these, also function as subtle determinants of individual conduct; and there is persuasive evidence in the extant draft material to indicate not only that Ibsen gave earnest and athletic attention to these matters, but also that the alterations he introduced under this rubric were often of the most far-reaching significance, affecting the plays at their deepest levels of meaning.

It facilitates the argument at this stage to take the plays out of their chronological order and consider the (in this respect) somewhat less complicated *John Gabriel Borkman* before the fearsomely convoluted *Little Eyolf.* Ibsen's early plans for *John Gabriel Borkman* did not intend that the two sisters should be twins. In the stage directions of the draft, the unmarried sister 'is older than her sister and resembles her, with traces of past beauty'. To intensify this relationship to twinship at a formative stage in the play's composition marks a deliberate (and, one must assume, purposeful) change of intent: to introduce a modulation, in the interests of the overall balance of motivating forces within the drama, of those expectations which audience and society normally attach to the sisterly relationship. Moreover there was a further knock-on effect transmitted down to a number of the other less

immediate relationships in the play: to the Ella–Borkman relation,
whereby an already elaborately compounded emotional and affinal
relationship—erstwhile lovers who become sister/brother-in-law—is
further complicated by the twinship nexus; and to what would otherwise have remained a simple aunt/nephew relationship between Ella
and Erhart, whereby the nephew is required to relate to a 'maternal
aunt' who is not a simple 'mother's sister' but the much more intense
'mother's twin sister', which when compounded with an additional
element of 'foster-motherhood' yields a total relationship of formidable
complexity.

The consequence for criticism of this degree of elaboration is that
any attempt to analyse the motivational forces at work in these late
dramas is confronted by patterns of interaction of great complexity.
Take, for example, the position of Erhart: not only is he at the climax
of the drama positioned at the intersection of five different forces
seeking to define his destiny—those of a dominating and hate-ridden
mother, an assertive and paranoid father, a mortally sick aunt, a
seductive divorcee, and the sexual compulsions of his own youth and
emergent manhood—but some of these individual lines of force are
also themselves (as we have seen) greatly distinctive in their nature and
trace out a highly individualistic pentagon of forces.

Already before this, however, *Little Eyolf* had exceeded in audacity
even such kinship complications as these by introducing the total
bouleversement, through the revelation of past sexual transgression, of
what was an apparently established, stable, and even defining relational
system. And in the extended attention which he gave to modifying the
relational pattern as one draft of the play succeeded another, Ibsen
gave convincing evidence of the importance he attached to these
factors as determinants of human conduct in the wider world.

Not unlike William and Fanny Price in *Mansfield Park*—of whose
relationship it is there remarked that 'children of the same family, the
same blood, with the same first associations and habits, have some
means of enjoyment in their power which no subsequent connection
can supply'—Alfred and Asta are powerfully drawn to each other. In
the surviving draft manuscripts, however, the earliest list of characters
shows Asta (at this preliminary stage somewhat confusingly called
Rita) as simply 'sister' to the character who was eventually to become
Alfred, and not (as in the final text) as 'half-sister'. When eventually the
change was made from full-sibling to half-sibling relationship—and
this may well have occurred at a quite early stage in the play's genesis,

possibly even before the opening pages of the surviving drafts were written—the effect was to create plausible pre-conditions for a later fateful denial of blood relationship between Alfred and Asta, and thus to permit a profound change in the basic course of the drama. Moreover when the evidence of Asta's mother's adultery was allowed to come to light, it not only had the result of releasing Alfred and Asta from any ties of blood relationship (with all the consequences which that had for their possible future life together), but it also destroyed any remnants of family affinity between Asta and Rita, and furthermore (posthumously) destroyed Asta's 'aunthood'—though, interestingly, not her usurpative motherhood—in respect of Eyolf.

Counterpointing this is the progressively diminishing degree of relationship between the Rat Wife and the Allmers family as the draft material took shape—changes in which can again be detected the extreme care Ibsen took to balance the various relationships one against the other. In the earliest plan, the Rat Wife is designated as *Rita's* (or, as it was at this early drafting stage, Johanne's) aunt; this was subsequently modified to make of her Eyolf's aunt (literally 'mother's sister'); and at a later stage still, this was qualified and still further reduced by Miss Varg's own comment in the draft on her situation: '. . . . Just send for Aunt Ellen. . . . Isn't it strange that everybody calls me Aunt Ellen? Despite the fact that I haven't any living relative—either in heaven or on earth.'

The immediate consequence of this overall revision of relationships was enormously to increase the play's power by admitting into the dramatic action the theme of incipient incest. When precisely this theme entered the play is difficult to determine on the evidence of the surviving manuscripts. Nevertheless, it is not implausible to see the play as having originally based itself on a relatively uncomplicated triangular pattern of husband, wife, and husband's sister, tracing the impact within this situation of certain stresses upon the destiny of the son. (If so, it would have quietly rehearsed the way in which *John Gabriel Borkman* operates with a triangular pattern of husband, wife, and wife's sister, and the way it too impinges on the destiny of the son.)

The progressive modifications to the structure of *Little Eyolf* following the introduction of the incest motif brought a number of new and disturbing elements. The reiterated Asta–Eyolf transferences, the reported transvestite practices of the earlier days, the association of Alfred's betrayal to Rita of these childhood secrets (as well as of

Eyolf's crippling accident) with a moment of highly charged sexual passion—all these and more were relatively late additions or adjustments to the play, and must have post-dated the decision to eliminate any blood relationship between Alfred and Asta. Such factors, by their deliberate and pondered introduction, draw attention to the weight of symbolic significance which Ibsen attached to the meta-relationship between kinship obligations and sexual compulsions in the business of daily living.

Running obliquely across kinship links and casual encounters alike is the sexual nexus. To catalogue the sexual relations in these last plays—interpreting the term widely in the sense of how men and women relate to each other—is to identify a very considerable range: marital, pre-marital, and extra-marital, consummated and unconsummated, promiscuous and abstinent, invited and withheld, sensualized and sublimated, overt and suppressed, deviant and incipiently incestuous.

Immediately from the stage directions, and before any word is uttered, it is made obvious that it is the women who are destined to take the sexual initiative, and who are the most obviously endowed physically for the role. By contrast, the men—with the obvious exception of Ulfheim—are for the most part conspicuously deficient in libido. The figure of the married woman of experience and maturity, no longer in her first youth but vital and attractive and strongly motivated sexually, appears in all three plays: Rita in *Little Eyolf*, the 'good-looking woman, blond, fairly tall and shapely (*yppig*), of about thirty'; Fanny Wilton in *John Gabriel Borkman*, the 'shapely (*yppig*) and strikingly beautiful woman in her thirties, (with) generous, smiling red lips, sparkling eyes, rich, dark hair'; and Maja in *When We Dead Awaken*, 'quite youthful, with a vivacious face and bright roguish eyes, though she has a slightly weary air'. Moreover, even those women on whom age or personal disaster has left a mark often still give evidence of an earlier physical appeal: Gunhild with her abundant hair and elegant but now shabby clothes; Ella with her thick wavy silver-white hair, who 'still retains some of the great and characterful beauty of her younger days'; and the one-time artist's model Irene, now reduced to 'a shadow'.

Not unexpectedly, in the *mélange* of personal relationships—sexual, marital, parental, affinal—it is the women who are most immediately exposed to the claims of loyalties which are generally multiple, often

competitive, frequently incompatible, and sometimes totally irrecon-
cilable. Faced in *Little Eyolf* with the competing claims of wifehood and
motherhood, Rita (as was seen above) declares herself totally for the
former, and in large measure repudiates the latter; Gunhild, by
contrast, is bleakly determined to be wife to Borkman in nothing but
name, and seeks her entire fulfilment in a mother's relationships with
Erhart. *Little Eyolf*, at one crucial moment, pivots about the choice
Asta is required to make between a life as wife and helpmeet to
Borghejm and a 'passionless' existence as 'sister' to Alfred. There is in
all these late plays a readiness to contemplate, sometimes even to adopt,
triangular relationships; and the admission in all three plays of the
possibility of a *ménage à trois* as a means of resolving a tangled
emotional situation is in itself quite striking. Mrs. Wilton, Frida and
Erhart go off as a threesome in order that Erhart may have a sexual
relationship in reserve; Rubek discusses with both Maja and Irene the
possibility of the latter's moving into the household in the villa on the
Taunitzer See; in *Little Eyolf*, both husband and wife appeal to Asta to
live her life with them, an appeal which is still further complicated by
what they individually know or do not know of the consanguinity
factor.

The men are much less easily moved to passion than the women.
Alfred Allmers found on his first encounter with Rita that her 'consuming loveliness' filled him with 'terror'; later he was to discover that
to yield to her attractions was—in a literal as well as a metaphorical
sense—fraught with crippling consequences, to his child and to his own
psyche. Borkman first finds sexual love a commodity easily convert-
ible into commercial currency, but then discovers that love invaded
and contaminated by shame turns to fierce hate: 'If Mrs. Borkman
had not loved her husband,' Ibsen is reported to have said, 'she would
have forgiven him long ago.' When Irene offered herself for cultural
congress, giving herself 'with such vibrant desire, such exalted passion'
to their aesthetic intercourse, serving him 'with all the throbbing
blood' of her youth, Rubek held back from touching her for fear (he
said) of profaning his artistic sensibilities, and called the whole thing
'an episode'.

The suppression of sexuality is seen by these men as a kind of
victory, a triumph of self-control, a defeat for those darker disruptive
forces which would otherwise subvert life's greater, nobler purposes:
a child's upbringing, the creation of social wealth, the achievement of
art. Their lives are conducted in the name of *duty*—a father's, an

entrepreneur's, an artist's—which offers them a double advantage: not only does it serve as plausible justification of their apparently insensitive conduct towards the women, but it also effectively cloaks their own deeper fears and inadequacies. But the imagery which accompanies them in the plays stamps them as 'cold'. The cold numbs them, deadens them, literally kills them. Either, like Allmers, they are recognized as having 'fish's blood' in their veins; or, like Borkman, they are destroyed by the grip of an icy hand; or, like Rubek, they toil at their art in cold, damp cellars away from the warmth of the sun.

One of the defining characteristics of the men, indeed, is that they tend—as much in obedience to society's expectations as to their own proclivities—to seek fulfilment outside the everyday range of personal and domestic relationships, that arena which is in fact the only one open to the women. Borghejm, perhaps the most naïvely ambitious in this direction, is not wholly typical of the late Ibsenist hero, for he is prepared to allow a positive role in his life for a personal relationship on the domestic level. But it is significant that even though his passion for road-building stops well short of obsession, even though his ambition is more a part of the joyous 'game' of life than it is a determined sacrificial undertaking, nevertheless his natural promptings are to see the wife essentially as helpmeet, as sharer of *his* joys and *his* sorrows: '. . . Nobody to help me in it . . .', he says in his unhappiness to Asta, 'Nobody. Nobody to share in the joy of it.' It is a role which Asta too would find wholly acceptable: 'Oh, if only I could be there with you! Help you in times of trouble. Share the joy of it with you . . .' In those instances where the men find it less easy to reconcile domestic and ambitional claims, ambition usually prevails; and even where this seems to require the savage sacrifice of the love (and even the sanity) of others, there is little hesitation. Borkman's slip of the tongue, which he somewhat shamefacedly but unconvincingly corrects, betrays the scheme of relative values by which these men lead their lives: 'You know very well it was higher motives . . . well, other motives, then . . . that forced my hand,' he says to Ella Rentheim in explanation of how it was he came to throw her over.

The world of these plays is one that virtually disqualifies women from holding ambitions of the order of Borkman's, Rubek's, or even Allmers'. No women artists, no women writers, certainly no women tycoons are thinkable. The most they can contemplate is public achievement by proxy, through the intermediacy or agency of a man—

a husband, perhaps, or a son, possibly a brother. Gunhild can only look to her son to achieve her vengeance and to achieve her reinstatement; Ella needs a man, her nephew, to prevent the disappearance of her family name. For a woman who was prepared to break with home and country and also with the prevailing moral code, it might just be possible—as with Frida—to achieve a career in which the male competition was not severe, like music. Otherwise, there is little for the women beyond a limited extension of motherhood into a more public domain, as when Rita contemplates a measure of social work by mothering the deprived village children.

With passion and ambition distributed in this fashion between the sexes, it is not unexpected to find at the heart of all three dramas a woman's humiliatingly unfulfilled sexuality. Rita, having prepared for her husband's return after weeks of absence by dressing seductively in white, letting down her long fragrant hair, turning the lights low and serving champagne, finds even as she begins to undress that Alfred is more concerned about the state of their child's digestion. Ella Rentheim, wringing from Borkman the monstrous admission that he had once as part of a squalid business deal traded her for a bank directorship, angrily indicts him of that 'truly monstrous crime . . . for which there is no forgiveness'. Irene reveals to Rubek how his self-control as he gazed day after day on her naked beauty had finally driven her to despair and flight and a life of debauchery and madness. Death by drowning, death from seizure, death by avalanche—the direct or oblique retribution which these acts of denial bring is dire.

Nevertheless, a simple affirmation of the more elemental life forces does not always hold out unambiguous promise of fulfilment. Admittedly Ulfheim, hunting his women with the same sporting instinct as he brought to his bear hunting, finds in this a source of pleasure uncomplicated by moral scruple, the pleasure of what Hilde Wangel had earlier called 'a robust conscience'; and Maja, for her part, is also stimulated to glad cries as he and she make their way off the mountain to the receptive valley below. Similarly Mrs. Wilton, though a more genteel seducer than Ulfheim, finds her pleasure—and again a pleasure uncontaminated by conscience—in running away with Erhart and Frida. At the same time, running counter to the idea that a straight surrender to sexual promptings brings simple contentment and as if to emphasize that the causalities of this world are never simple, there is Irene's deep ambivalence at the time of what Rubek called the 'episode' when, by her own confession, she had a sharp and deadly weapon concealed about her person ready to revenge any violation by Rubek of their purely aesthetic relationship.

Such a system of interpenetrating relationships, each with its own peculiar duties and loyalties, obligations and rewards, invaded by motives derived (in the main) from male endeavour—ambition, a sense of mission, the lust for power, the claims of art, the pursuit of status and esteem—provides the basic pattern by which the fictive life of these dramas is lived. Nevertheless there are two other important elements present to prevent the dramatic event from being a merely or largely predictable consequence of identifiable cause and effect.

The first is that at the deeper and less rationally accessible level of this world there can be seen at work a pervasive influence from mystic or quasi-mystic (or even mock-mystic) forces, a system of 'pulls' and 'currents' and 'undertows' of will and suggestion: forces of which the Rat Wife is the most explicit manifestation, and Mrs. Wilton's throw-away references to her 'spell-casting' the most ironic. The persistent attention which Ibsen had given in the immediately preceding plays— in *The Lady from the Sea*, in *Hedda Gabler*, and in *The Master Builder*— to the power of mind over mind, and the influence of mind over matter, is continued here. The subterranean spirits call to Borkman, stretching out to him their 'twisting, sinuous, beckoning arms' like a greeting from loyal subjects; Alfred and Rita look forward at the final curtain to a visitation by the spirits of those who have departed; Irene lives in a world of shades, herself a 'shadow' watched over by a shadow; the living dead—Borkman whom the cold had long ago killed, Gunhild and Ella existing as two shades over the dead man, Irene and Rubek who had died an earlier death—lead their zombie-like existences, living and partly living. And all the time the secret tides and currents of life are imperceptibly, ineluctably at work. Mysteriously, rationally inexplicable, they act to complement the surface forces of these last plays, and thus to complete a reverberant universe of motivation.

The second (and in its own way decisive) factor comes with the recognition that this is a thoroughly deceptive world. Deceit is endemic; self-deception commonplace; witnesses, particularly where their own motives and conduct are concerned, are frequently unreliable; dissimulation becomes a way of life. It is crucial to realize that one must constantly beware of accepting the characters and their version of events at face value.

The occasion when this most clearly surfaces is in that intensely moving and deeply betraying exchange between Borkman and Foldal, when circumstances finally compel them to admit that they have voluntarily practised mutual deception for as long as they have known each other. Their encounter is a clear invitation to see their two careers as a double melodic line, a two-part harmony in which the one supports, sustains, and complements the other. On the one side is the humble and inadequate clerk whose entire adult life has been sustained only by the dubious promise of an uncompleted play, a tragedy which—in itself a kind of analogue to its author's career—will never be consummated, but which, like Hjalmar Ekdal's invention in *The Wild Duck*, is enough to sustain the level of self-esteem at least at subsistence level. The counterpointing with Borkman's situation is deliberate. His belief in himself as a great captain of industry is underpinned by Foldal in exchange for favours received. An objectively reconstructed and dispassionate account of the events of Borkman's career could only reveal how flawed and inadequate it had been in reality: a simple squalid history of embezzlement, made nastier by his readiness to betray the woman he loved in the interests of sordid commercial gain, followed by a deserved prison sentence which had left him full of excuses and self-justification and illusions of grandeur.

Borkman's and Foldal's exasperated acknowledgement of the real truth about their relationship gives a pointer to the range of possible deception which the characters in these plays practise on each other and on themselves:

BORKMAN. So all this time you've lied to me.

FOLDAL [*shakes his head*]. Never lied, John Gabriel.

BORKMAN. Have you not sat there feeding my hopes and beliefs and confidence with lies?

FOLDAL. They weren't lies as long as *you* believed in *my* calling. As long as you believed in me, I believed in you.

BORKMAN. Then it's just been mutual deception. And perhaps self-deception too—on both sides.

FOLDAL. But isn't that what friendship really is, John Gabriel?

BORKMAN [*with a bitter smile*]. Yes. To deceive . . . that's what friendship is. You are right. . . .

One remarks a high incidence of those who, consciously or

unconsciously, rationalize their own conduct in deceptive terms, who designate as duty a course of action which at the deeper level is dictated by essentially selfish motives, who devise plausible altruisms in order to escape from situations which either they find distasteful or in which they sense themselves inadequate: Allmers, who ostentatiously addresses himself to his son's needs in order to give second priority to the (to him) alarming sexual advances of his wife; Borkman, who rationalizes his own desire for money and power as a duty to release the slumbering mineral deposits for the benefit of mankind at large; Rubek, who dresses up the 'episode' with his model Irene in sententious references to the holiness of art and the need to avoid profaning it with ordinary humanity. There are those who are blind to or afraid of the realities: pathetically so sometimes, like little Eyolf dreaming of learning to swim and with ambitions of becoming a soldier; culpably so, as with Borkman who refuses to see what is obvious to all, that his plans for a resumption of his business career are hopelessly doomed. Allmers is incapable of facing up to the realities of Eyolf's crippling, and drafts hopelessly unrealistic plans for his son's future. The key element is that in every case the ascription to 'duty' is seen (or at least offered) as a kind of victory, a triumph of self-control, and a defeat of those dark disruptive forces which threaten to subvert man's noble endeavours.

Occasionally it happens that one or another of the characters, generally a woman, will see through the pretence, see through the intellectual and emotional dishonesty, and have the courage to say so. In *Little Eyolf*, Rita indicates already in the draft that she is not deceived by Alfred's grand words when he speaks of his obligations towards Eyolf as representing his 'highest duty' and of having 'sacrificed' his career as a writer to this task. It was (she says) not really because Alfred loved his son: 'You were beginning to be consumed by doubts yourself,' Rita declares. 'All that happy confidence, all that hope that you had some great task to perform [as a writer]—this began to desert you. I saw it clearly enough. . . . You wanted to make a child prodigy out of him, Alfred. Because he was *your* child. But you never really loved him.' When Ibsen came to revise this exchange, he took the opportunity to work into the final version phrases which even more clearly indicated the disguised and concealed motives that had contributed to the situation: 'Look inside yourself!' Rita exhorts Alfred with some embarrassment. 'And examine carefully all those things lying under . . . and behind . . . the surface.' As the kind of instruction which might equally well have come from Ibsen to his reader, it hints at the restless complexity of the dramatist's intent.

In the case of *Little Eyolf*, there is a particularly high betrayal value attaching to those changes which Ibsen made both to the substance and to the detail of the drafts in order to achieve the final intricate orchestration of the work. As William Archer early saw: revision in the case of this play amounted almost to re-invention, and nearly everything that gives the play its depth, its horror, and its elevation came as what Archer—still perhaps not fully grasping the real significance—rather dismissively called 'an afterthought'. Hermann Weigand's confident italics some years later very properly corrected the balance: 'It is evident', he wrote in 1925, *'that a startling change of plan separates the finished play from Ibsen's original intention.'* The end-product was an artistic and technical *tour de force* without parallel in Ibsen's *œuvre*, a delicate fabric of nuance and suggestiveness, deeply enigmatic and shot through with the profoundest irony. The value of cataloguing in some detail the various shifts of meaning and displacements of emphasis through the different stages of the play's composition is that one thereby identifies a number of tracer elements which, when plotted, help to define the movement and the direction of the dramatist's basic purposes.

Caution in interpreting the surviving draft is nevertheless essential. As it stands, this draft is in no sense the product of a consistent and fully formed inspiration. Based—as, in accord with Ibsen's usual practice, it surely is—on some earlier set of notes, jottings, scenarios, and trial dialogue, it is the uneven product of a period of some eight weeks' work (from mid-June to early August 1894) at a time when the author's sense of the totality of the piece was still fluid and when substantial thematic changes were being introduced *passim* as they suggested themselves to him. In consequence a number of important new ideas are present on the later pages of the manuscript (for instance, the highly charged reference to the existence of *two* Eyolfs, one big and one little) which are inconsistent with the draft's earlier pages, but which Ibsen was clearly holding in suspense in his mind ready to build into the earlier stretches of the action when the moment came for consolidating revision of his material.

In a curious way the progressive changes to the draft anticipate the account which Rubek was later to give, in *When We Dead Awaken*, of the modifications which he had carried out between phase one and phase two of his statue 'Resurrection Day'. All the evidence suggests that in its first conception *Little Eyolf* was a considerably less ambiguous thing than the complex play it eventually became; and like Rubek's introduction of a great wealth of modifying complexities into a work which in its first stages had been a more unitary and uncomplicated sculptural statement, Ibsen's dramatic invention elaborately revised the motivational patterns in *Little Eyolf* until the new meaning represented a radical displacement of the old. The final version is only the 'same' drama as the earlier version in the sense that the revised 'Resurrection Day' remained the 'same'.

The characteristics which the draft assigned to Hakon Skjoldheim make of him an essentially different person from the Alfred Allmers he eventually became. Among other things it invested the former with a set of dramatic problems quite unlike those of the latter in a number of significant respects. Skjoldheim starts off as an already *successful* writer, the author of a number of published works which he feels were 'well written' and which he also claims were 'well received'. Of late he had been engaged on a book which seemingly had reasonable expectations of being his best yet, his 'masterpiece'. His motives (at this stage of the draft) for changing course now commend themselves as admirable and wholly selfless: he had been too much concerned with thinking and writing and not enough with *doing*, had been too much given to his own personal and selfish ambitions and indifferent to those of his child. At this stage of the draft, he will now renounce those blinkered, in-turned ideas; and, by devoting himself to his son's welfare, help him towards self-fulfilment and an understanding of 'the art of life'.

In the final text, by contrast, Alfred Allmers has seemingly been working away inconclusively for ten years on a book about 'human responsibility'. The transmutation went through an intermediate stage. At the first revise to the draft, Allmers is made to describe his work thus:

> There I sat writing day after day. And sometimes half the night. Writing that big book [*skrev på den store bogen*] on human responsibility.

For the final version, the phrasing was given a further slight but subtly important revision—the kind of revision which, by its wording, conveys to an alert audience a hint of the spurious:

> There I sat bent over my desk, writing, day after day. And sometimes half the night. Writing away at that great thick book [*skrev og skrev på den store tykke bogen*] on 'Human responsibility'.

As yet, the draft carries no reference to the briefcase full of old family letters which, in the later course of events, were to bear so importantly on the extra-marital adventures of Alfred's step-mother, and consequently on the kinship ties between Alfred and his supposed sister Asta. Nor, in this same connection, is there yet any reference to Asta's recent strange behaviour—a comment by Rita which, in the final text, finds its obvious explanation in the fact of Asta's having by then read the family letters and thus discovered the truth about her relationship to Alfred. Nor is there yet any reference to the orphaned childhood of Alfred and Asta being so evidently 'poverty-stricken'; nor any explicit emphasis on the fact that their subsequent comfortable existence stemmed from Rita's wealth, from her 'gold and green forests'. Furthermore, there is a complete absence of any open or declared hostility on the part of the wife for the 'sister' as a possible rival for Alfred's (or even Eyolf's) affection; indeed, in Act I of the draft at least, the sister is already openly betrothed to Borghejm, and to that extent therefore already emotionally committed elsewhere.

The emergent dramatic conflict at this stage of the drama's composition seems relatively uncomplicated; and when the wife demands her husband for herself unshared, the tensional pattern at this stage seems clearly foreshadowed by the brief exchange in the draft between husband and wife:

ALLMERS. You have a jealous nature. Previously you were jealous of my work. Now you are jealous of Eyolf.

MRS. ALLMERS. I cannot be different from what I am. If you parcel yourself out between us ... I'll be revenged on you, Alfred!

(The fact that the agent of 'possessiveness' in the marriage situation is now the wife and not the husband—as it was, for example, most obviously in *A Doll's House*—in itself marks a significant change of emphasis in Ibsen's authorship.) The above exchange would then be entirely consistent with the 'willing' of Eyolf's death via the Rat Wife— a member of the *dramatis personae* who is one of the earliest and most persistent in the entire play.

Thereafter, the introduction and the progressive enlargement of what has here been earlier called the incipient incest motif faced the dramatist with formidable structural problems; and it retroactively imposed important changes on a number of existing passages. By the time the draft had advanced as far as Act III, this theme had acquired a central importance. Nevertheless it seems as if certain ideas persisting from an earlier conception of the play continued to influence the shape of the action; and this led to serious psychological inconsistencies in the structure of the play. In the third Act of the draft, it is *Asta* who is anxious to reconstitute the chaste 'brother/sister' relationship. Although she of course knows the real truth about her relationship to Alfred, she still speaks to Borghejm of her 'brother', declaring that she cannot now let him go because she feels she can care for him 'as only a sister can care for a brother'. At this stage in the composition of the play, it is Alfred who sees menace in the proposed *ménage à trois*, a threat that comes from the possibility of his *own* loss of self-control:

ALLMERS. . . . Oh, Asta, I no longer have you. Not the way I had you before.

BORGHEJM [*looks at them in astonishment*]. But I don't understand . . .

ASTA. Oh, but you do, Alfred. Believe me . . . for you I will always be the same as I was.

ALLMERS. But not I.

ASTA [*shrinks back*]. Ah . . . !

She then evades his embrace as he comes forward to take his leave. Rita, as yet ignorant of their true relationship, urges Asta to remain in their household as their 'child': 'We must have a child who can bring us together. . . . Something calm, warm, passionless. . . . A child or a sister.' Asta, after her final appeal to Alfred to be allowed to stay has thus been peremptorily refused, thereupon leaves. Rita, from her detached point of observation, thinks she sees through the situation to what is the real but unacknowledged truth: that Alfred has sent Asta away because he fears that she (Asta) could not survive a situation where her own sexual promptings would conflict with her role as 'passionless' sister: 'She too wanted to be all things to you,' Rita declares in the draft. 'Same as me.' But, through ignorance of the real situation, she has read the signs wrongly; and Alfred has to confess that in reality *he* and *his* feelings were the sexually untrustworthy factors. Rita's immediate reaction is shock that he could even contemplate incestuous conduct: 'Alfred! You could think . . . desire . . . something criminal! Never in the world!' Her amazement when she learns the real truth is equally prompt, but for entirely different reasons: that Alfred, being thus freed of the prohibitions of sexual taboo, should not at once have seized the opportunity presented by the new situation. A mixture of disbelief and contempt that he could be so ineffectually sexless prompts her immediate response: 'How could you, Alfred? I'd never have been capable of anything like that . . . Oh, but it's just like I say—fish's blood. . . .' Then, quickly correcting herself, she compassionately says what she knows he wants her to say and to believe: 'No, no, I don't mean it. It is the great and pure side of you which has won the victory.' It is a clear instance of the readiness of Ibsen's characters to say what the immediate relationship expects of them, rather than what they really think. And once again it results in a kind of deception à la Foldal.

These shifts left a residue of implausibility in the draft of the drama as it was, and especially in the motivation of Alfred's behaviour. Was he or was he not the kind of man who could remain unmoved by the knowledge that his resident and dearly beloved 'sister' was no longer sexually protected from him by society's taboos? (Alfred and Asta of course represent a reversal of the earlier incestuous dilemma of Oswald and Regine in *Ghosts*, where in the earlier drama the exposure of past misbehaviour *imposes* a taboo on the relationship, whereas in the later one it eliminates it.) Was he or was he not really the kind of 'passionless' person Rita at times accuses him of being? There is some slight evidence to suggest that Ibsen himself momentarily wavered between the two possibilities; and the hesitant revisions to the stage directions which mark Alfred's first appearance seem to document this uncertainty. First, in the draft proper, he is 'a slim, slight figure with a serious expression on his face; thinning dark hair and beard'; after the first revise, his hair is thicker, he is clean-shaven, and his eyes 'sparkle'—clearly a much more assertive character; this was then again revised to restore his beard, to give him back his 'thinning' hair, and to attribute to him 'gentle eyes'—which is how it survived into the final text. The change is reflected in the final revisions to the draft of Act III. Now it is Alfred who begs Asta to stay, and Rita joins in his entreaty: to be sister to him, and to 'be Eyolf' to them. Now it is Asta who cannot trust herself in the altered situation: 'Yes, Alfred . . . it *is* running away. . . . From you—and from myself.' The changes mean that Rita is now not immediately let into the kinship secret; and in consequence the earlier contemptuous reference by her in the draft to Alfred's 'fish's blood' has now disappeared. Vanished also is her earlier (draft) remark that Asta 'wanted to be all things' to Alfred, and thus by implication usurp her wifely place. The irony of the situation is that now, in the drama's revised form, the remark would have been true.

Running like a thread through the entire sequence of exchanges at the start of Act III in its final formulation—in the first instance between

Asta and Borghejm and, subsequently, between Alfred and Rita—is a distinct but suppressed sense of the terror and the ecstasy of the forbidden as it announces itself to Asta, of her aching desire to be with Alfred and her fear of how life might inevitably develop, given the nature of her feelings. When Borghejm innocently—thinking of Eyolf's death—comments to Asta that 'this thing' had changed her whole position *vis-à-vis* the Allmers household, she gives a guilty start since that is precisely how she must have presented the new sexually orientated position to herself. And Rita, in ignorance of the real facts as they related to sexual and blood relationships, again misinterprets the signs. This time she simply assumes that Borghejm is the reason Asta cannot remain with them.

In its final shape, the play thus sets out to demarcate an arena of intricate and tightly drawn linear relationships of a sexual and familial nature. Then two things are allowed to happen: first, disaster, seemingly and mysteriously self-engendered by the situation, invades the scene, imposing one set of adjustments from those who compose it; second, revelations from the past indicate that the world of relationships is in one crucial respect not as it seems. And this requires a further set of adjustments from those concerned. Finally, superimposed on this groundwork of changing and disrupted relationships is an overlay of deception: deceptive appearances, self-deceiving attitudes, feigned motives, false feelings, defensive pretences. Only by paying the utmost attention not only to what is said, but also how it is said, can one begin to resolve the problems of who in these plays can be taken as a reliable witness of events, of whose testimony is suspect, or of what is behind the façade.

If, in those long hours of introspection after the death of Eyolf, Alfred had been able to be totally honest with himself, able to analyse dispassionately and even clinically the true sequence of events and his own part in them, his train of thought might well have run:

As a young man, I knew a great love for my younger half-sister, Asta. The basis of this love was (I now see) sexual, but society's taboos compelled me to subdue and repress my deeper feelings. Together, therefore, we pretended she was a boy. This left its residual effect on my own attitudes to sexual passion. When I first met Rita, who was both rich and very beautiful, my dominant feeling was terror; but marriage to her offered a solution to Asta's and my financial problems, and assured our continuing life close to each other. When my son was born, I called him Eyolf—the nickname I had earlier used for Asta as my pretended brother—in an effort to perpetuate that earlier idyllic relationship. The circumstances of his crippling accident a year later left me psycho-sexually even more reduced than I had been before. Ostentatious self-dedication to my writing protected me to some extent from Rita's passionate demands on my night hours; devotion to our son offered a new line of defence when the book began to lose conviction as a pretext. Both the book and the child inevitably drew Rita's hatred. Then in quick succession two of my defences against the inroads of passion were removed: Eyolf was drawn to his death by drowning; and the blood taboos which had kept my relations with Asta what they were were withdrawn. I tried for a 'passionless' solution: a triangular relationship based on what the world calls a 'brother and sister' relationship with both Rita and Asta. But in the new situation Asta feared for her own self-control. I am now left with a 'passionless' existence with Rita, a life in which we devote ourselves to good works, cling to the memories of past happiness, and try to salvage something of value (the 'jewel in the ashes'?) from the collapse.

Instead of this honesty, he pretends; pretends even to himself; pretends that he is sacrificing a writer's and scholar's career in the interests of his son, assigns the blame for Eyolf's death to Rita's unconsciously murderous thoughts, offers a great parade of his grief, does grotesque mental calculations for Asta's benefit to determine how far the currents have taken Eyolf's body out to sea, makes a pathetically inept and spurious suicide attempt, and cruelly torments Rita about her readiness to follow Eyolf into the next world. In short, Eyolf has already become for him what Relling in *The Wild Duck* prophesied Hedvig would soon become for Hjalmar: 'the theme of a pretty little party piece [*et vakkert deklamationstema*]'. Then he'll bring it all up, Relling declares: 'All about "the child so untimely torn from a loving father's heart". Then you'll see him wallowing deeper and deeper in sentimentality and self-pity.'

In a last appeal, Alfred tries by something approaching emotional blackmail to preserve a domestic situation where both women are still available to pander to him. Finally when this fails comes the greatly self-dramatizing account of his mountain encounter with Death; he lingers lugubriously on the notion of dying young, playing unmercifully on Rita's feelings:

ALLMERS.... I clambered along the precipitous cliffs ... and enjoyed the peace and serenity that comes from the nearness of death.

RITA [*jumps up*]. Oh, don't use such words about this dreadful thing.

ALLMERS. That was how I felt. Absolutely no fear. I felt that Death and I walked side by side like two good travelling companions. It all seemed so reasonable ... so obvious at the time. People in my family don't usually live till they are old....

RITA. Oh, please stop talking about these things, Alfred! You did come through all right, after all.

The viciousness of his attitude towards the village children and their feckless parents is translated by him, wholly in character, into 'a duty'; and in dressing up this duty in phrases of typical theatricality, he also at the same time manages to evade any possible personal commitment or responsibility for himself: 'I've a right to be hard from now on! A duty! My duty towards Eyolf! He must not die unavenged. Make it quick, Rita! That's what I say. Think it over. Have the whole place razed to the ground—when I am gone.'

The changes imposed upon Alfred in the course of the play's composition—who naturally as husband, 'brother', and father is positioned at the very centre of the cataclysmic events within the household—indicate a strongly marked shift towards the ineffectual, the impotent, the wordily pretentious, the self-delusory. The breast-beating, the choked sob, the histrionics, become progressively more evident as one follows Alfred from stage to stage in the draft; and the ostensible motives for his actions become more and more suspect. In contrast to Rita's impetuous, instinctively 'hot-blooded' but essentially generous reactions, Alfred is caught out striking attitudes, mouthing phrases, self-consciously acting a part even at moments of the greatest pathos. In its final form, the play is a technically audacious attempt to construct an action on the tensions between a suspect articulation and enactment of motives and causes and the reality of things inherent in the total situation.

John Gabriel Borkman is concerned to explore the dynamics of obsession and self-delusion within what is now a recognizably Ibsenist arena of complex interlocking personal relationships. Borkman himself lives in a private and solitary world, admission to which is given only to those who consent to share his fantasies. He designs a comprehensive personal myth, within which he casts himself for the central role: that of the *Übermensch* in close contact with those elemental and sub-terranean powers which inhabit the rich ore-bearing strata of the earth, and whose liberation he is convinced he can achieve. To see him as a great captain of commerce, a Napoleon of industry, is to accept him at his own valuation and to ignore the discrepancy between the portentousness of his phrases and the tawdry reality they conceal. In *his* testimony, a sordid and botched act of embezzlement becomes a heroic undertaking, and simple criminal ineptitude finds excuses for itself in an elaborate myth of betrayal. The spectacle is one of self-administered mythopoeic therapy.

The motives, real and imagined, which led him in the past to do what he did have now fused indistinguishably together in his mind. At one moment, it belongs to the myth that his crime was simply an act of obedience to the call of mystic mineral powers. He claims to have been conscious of a mysterious force of attraction, a 'pull', an inexplic-able and irresistible drawing power, a reaching out from the veins of metal ore like spirits of the earth 'stretching out their twisting, sinuous, beckoning arms' to him. At other moments, he traces his actions to their source in a Gynt-like pursuit of his deeper Self: 'Why did I do it?' he asks. 'Because I am me—John Gabriel Borkman.' In this mood, he is the Nietzschean '*Ausnahmemensch*', living by standards different from those that apply to his more 'average' fellow men. On other occasions still he is ready to acknowledge within himself the simple drive of ambition: '... My ambitions in life. ... I wanted to gain command of all the sources of power in this land. ... I wanted control.' Yet even before this particular utterance is complete, he has re-categorized this essentially personal ambition as an agency of social enrichment: 'I wanted to build myself an empire, and thereby create prosperity for thousands upon thousands of others.'

Borkman is clearly constituted as a latter-day 'pillar of society', whose misfortune it was this time not merely to be found out, but to suffer the penalties for his corrupt actions; and the way in which certain features of his conduct echo the earlier career of Bernick is surely designed to call attention to the parallel. Not only does he, like Bernick, callously throw over his betrothed for her sister (twin-sister in the one instance, step-sister in the other) for motives of crude commercial gain; not only does it come easily to him to justify this action by ascribing it to social or family 'duty'; but also the disparity between the real and the declared motives is extraordinarily similar in the two cases. Borkman's excuse that he was acting in the interests of the well-being of 'thousands upon thousands of others' is of the same brand of hypocrisy as Bernick's explanation of why he privately bought up the land over which the branch railway was to run:

> Don't you see what a boost it will give to our whole community? Just think of the huge tracts of forest it will open up! Think of all the rich mineral deposits that can be worked! Think of the river, with one waterfall after another! What about the industrial development that could be made there!... We, the practical men of business, will serve the community by bringing prosperity to as wide a circle as possible.

His obsession with the pursuit of power and wealth reduces everything to undifferentiated sustenance for his fantasies. In his mind, the motives coalesce: mystic inducement, willed desire, and public service. All things are judged, all values determined, by the one single obsessional criterion: how is thus ambition served? Of the multiple drives and imperatives which intersect within his own person, one alone counts; and in awarding an overriding precedence to this he brutally and insensitively repudiates all others. When he reviews the evidence for his guilt, he has no difficulty in finding total—and heroic— justification for his actions. Contemplating that moment of critical decision in the past when he abandoned Ella for a bank directorship, he is quick to use the standard phrases of the heroic: 'I had no choice. I had to conquer or fall.' But this is not heroic; it is only heroics. It is nothing more than, retrospectively and spuriously, putting things in a heroic light. Because he is who he is, because in his own estimate his talents are extraordinary and his objectives sublime, he feels immune to guilt, even though the bare details of his conduct show it to have been mean and sordid in the extreme. Palpably guilty, he acknowledges no guilt, no injury to anybody but himself; all he can see is a self-inflicted wound that cut short a Napoleonic career. His last refuge and defence is always that nobody ever did, or ever does, understand him.

The dreamer returns for his last moments of life to his dream landscape to re-people it and re-stock it with spinning wheels, smoking chimneys, and a toiling night-shift. He prides himself on being 'hard', like the iron ore he worships, and the metallic powers with which he claims allegiance. Even the last mortal pressure on his heart he endures with readier acceptance when he finds that he can correct his identification of the source of it: 'No. Not a hand of ice. A hand of iron.' Yet even this appeal to the values of the mines is suspect; he is himself not a miner (though at times he seems anxious to give the impression that he is) but a miner's son; and all the lyricism of his talk of the singing ore and the liberating hammerblows is largely secondhand, certainly romanticized, and part of the proliferating myth for which he works so assiduously. In the case of this superman *imaginaire*, only one thing is real, one thing great: his obsession. Held to resolutely, stubbornly, it becomes for him the one sustaining element in life. Only when that is destroyed—dismantled in the first instance by Foldal's denial of him, and then by Erhart's repudiation—is the life support gone.

Between the initial conception and the final realization of the sculptured 'Resurrection Day' in *When We Dead Awaken*, falls the loss of innocence. At the start, all was simplicity and idealism. Both the design of work and the early circumstances of its creation were serene, spontaneous, pure, and unsullied. It was to be a single unitary figure, a representation of 'the world's noblest, purest, most perfect woman', a vision of how 'the pure woman would wake on Resurrection Day, not wondering at things new and unfamiliar and unimagined, but filled with a holy joy at finding herself unchanged—a mortal woman— in those higher, freer, happier realms after the long and dreamless sleep of death'. An idealized, uncomplicated, direct expression born of exaltation, a positive vision. The circumstances were chaste, even reverential; the naked model was 'a sacred being, untouchable, something to worship in thought alone'. The pure simplicity of the artist's vision required a simple purity of conduct and setting. But, for Rubek, the passage of time brought new and disturbing insights into the real nature of life. Within the artist grew the realization that he had something much more complex to express, something more elaborate and ambiguous:

RUBEK. . . . . In the years that followed, Irene, the world taught me many things. I began to conceive 'Resurrection Day' as something bigger, something . . . something more complex. That little round plinth on which your statue stood, erect and lonely . . . no longer provided space for all the other things I now wanted to say . . .

IRENE [*reaches for the knife, then stops*]. What other things? Tell me!

RUBEK. Things I saw with my own eyes in the world around me. I had to bring them in. I had no choice, Irene. I extended the plinth . . . made it broad and spacious. And on it I created an area of cracked and heaving earth. And out of the cracks swarmed people, their faces animal beneath the skin. Men and women . . . as I knew them from life.

In the adjustments thus made to the overall design of the work, in the relegation of the once solitary sculptured figure to a congested middle-ground, in the elaborate additions and accretions of the second stage of composition, was embodied a newer and sadder honesty, a profounder and more penetrating yet at the same time more cynical view of the human condition. Behind its new wealth of de-idealized detail—just as also behind the 'speaking likenesses' of the new-style portrait busts to which Rubek turns his talents—is the artist's growing awareness of the brutalities, the stupidities, and the insensitivities of life as he increasingly came to see it, and of the soul's torment.

Within the context of the drama, the re-working of the sculpture—as hesitantly described by Rubek—marks a profound shift in the artist's view of life: from an earlier confident belief in simple pieties and a faith in his own capacity to communicate them through art, to a seriously uncertain, ambivalent, and complex view of things in which truth is elusive and where guilt and remorse and a sense of forfeited opportunity and wasted life occupy the central place. Truth and artistic integrity have insisted that these disturbing maturer recognitions be incorporated into the totality of the vision; and it is these later sophistications which have imposed the elaborate revision.

What the drama reveals as it plots this progression from innocence to experience, from simplicity to complexity, is that the work of art which embodies this change has demanded human sacrifice. The creative act had necessitated the exploitation of Irene's humanity, had required the draining of her life's essence, had exacted the death of her living soul. Art functions here as a life-destructive force; and the artist, serving as its agent, had left her disturbed, deranged, unfulfilled, a shadow of her former self, a zombie-like creature enduring a death-in-life existence. Nor was the artist himself exempt from the malignant and corrupting effects:

IRENE. And when I heard you say—cold as an icy grave—that I was nothing more than an episode in your life . . . I took out the knife. I was going to plunge it into your back.

RUBEK [*darkly*]. And why didn't you?

IRENE. Because I suddenly realized with horror that you were already dead. . . . Long, long dead. . . . Dead like me. We sat there by the Taunitzer See, two clammy corpses. . . .

Deprived of its sacrificial victim, art quickly becomes corrupt, and the artist impotent. Even Maja, who staunchly repudiates any claims that art might make on her, who remains unchangingly hostile to the whole ethos of 'cold figures in damp cellars', nevertheless feels threatened by the mere proximity of art, trapped by her association with Rubek, caged in her marriage. But she retains enough of her independence to be able finally to assert herself, to choose the frankly sensual existence offered by Ulfheim, and thus make good her escape to 'life'.

Not merely art reveals itself here as the enemy of 'life', however. Rubek's crisis of recognition, that moment of truth, of 'awakening' from a living death which is foreshadowed in the play's title, invokes a much wider frame of reference than merely that of artist and model:

RUBEK. I'll tell you what it was. I began to think that all this business about the artist's mission and the artist's vocation was all so much empty, hollow, meaningless talk.

MAJA. What would you put in its place?

RUBEK. Life, Maja. . . . Hasn't life in sunlight and beauty a value altogether different from toiling away to the end of your days in some cold, damp cellar, wrestling with lumps of clay and blocks of stone?

Art, poetry, an ideal, a mission, a vocation, a big business enterprise, anything which demands sacrificial dedication of the order Rubek has experienced and which is required to subjugate 'life' so ruthlessly to its purposes can by this token only be destructive of human happiness, chillingly death-dealing. Images of life, death, and resurrection, and the concepts of living death, death in life, and life after death recur throughout all these late plays—from Allmers' sense of impending 'resurrection' from the deadening pain of Eyolf's loss, and Gunhild's acknowledgement over the corpse of Borkman that 'the cold had killed him long ago', to the accretions to the statue of 'Resurrection Day' and the living-death existence of Rubek and Irene.

Rubek's account of the progressively elaborate remodelling of his statue, the counterweighting of idealism with scepticism, the super-imposition of anguished introspection and remorse upon the earlier confident and untroubled harmonies of the original design, thus clearly also has a significance transcending the context of the particular play to which it belongs. In the first place it offers itself as an image of the revisionary procedures to which Ibsen himself subjected his own indi-vidual dramas, in consequence of which what might have begun (as in *Little Eyolf*) as the relatively plain articulation of some 'observation' or

other he had made about life—to use the term (*iagtagelse*) he was fond
of using to describe the initial stimulus that gave life to his dramas—
was transformed into an elaborately orchestrated and counterpointed
statement embracing all those subsequent doubts and qualifications
which had forced themselves upon his attention at the secondary and
tertiary stages of composition. Nor, by extension, is it too fanciful to
see Rubek's account as a commentary on the totality of Ibsen's own
œuvre as it advanced from the relatively undifferentiated idealism and
optimism of his earliest dramas of the 1850s to the seemingly often
impenetrable ambiguities of the last works.

What these last plays set out to do from their starting point in the
poem 'They sat there, those two' was to conduct a rigorous exploration
of those sources of human conduct which the ageing dramatist, after
the experience of a lifetime, had come to recognize as belonging to the
essence of modern living; to communicate something of those forces
which he was now persuaded bore most significantly on contemporary
patterns of behaviour; and to dissect and lay bare those layers of
motivation, those insistent forces at work within and upon the
individual, which he, as a compulsive student of human nature and of
the fabric of society, felt he could now identify as among the more
powerful determinants of his own age. The result is a series of dramatic
analyses of extreme virtuosity and daunting complexity, subjecting to
scrutiny the dynamics of small and variously integrated and inter-
related social groups, and examining the complex interrelations of
the multiple factors that bear upon the members of these units:
the compulsions of individual will and desire, the obligations of
kinship and family, and the prevailing social and community expectations.

In sheerly technical terms, these dramas stretched the potentialities
of dramatic composition to new limits, vigorously exploiting drama's
capacity to communicate truths too elusive to be contained within any
purely analytical construction. For his purposes, Ibsen developed a
semiological system—to call it merely a 'dramatic language' ascribes
too heavy a *verbal* component to it to be entirely satisfactory—which
combined the qualities of stringent economy with the most delicate
subtlety. Into this sign system Ibsen incorporated not merely his own
powerful and idiosyncratic variants of drama's traditional elements—
speech, action, setting—but also a number of extra semantic devices of
a more uncommon kind: the indexing by kinship or relational descrip-

tors of particular imperatives; the encoding of meaning not so much into overt speech as covertly and more elusively into particular speech habits; the locating of action within a carefully defined symbolic topography of setting. The result was a succession of plays of a density and opaqueness resistant to simple analysis, but which in sum consti-tute a general declaration that great art is, and must inevitably be, destructive: destructive on the one hand of all that is spurious, inauthentic, meretricious, degenerate; destructive on the other of the lives and happiness of those who are sacrificed to it.

These plays establish a gallery of deeply flawed lives, of deficient achievement, of frustrated endeavour. Crippled, guilt-ridden, bank-rupt, mortally sick, frigid, impotent, ineffectual, mentally disturbed, these characters exemplify a wide variety of inauthentic living. What little there is in these plays of positive asseveration is generally either naïvely superficial or ironically undermined: Erhart's escape from the 'stuffy air' of the parental home to what he claims will be the 'great, glorious, living happiness' of life in the arms of Mrs. Wilton; Maja's escape from the 'cold damp cage' of her existence with Rubek for the 'free and unafraid' life, the sensual satisfactions, which Ulfheim can bring her; Foldal, finding exquisite joy in his daughter's abandonment of him, and wholly content in those circumstances to be 'run over' by life; and Borghejm who, despite the self-evident fulfilment which his road-building brings, still cannot think of life as anything other than 'a kind of game'.

The genuinely resonant things in these plays belong to a wholly different register: the complex harmonies of guilt and remorse; the profound capacities for self-deception; the dubious therapies indulged in by tormented and obsessed minds. What these plays are concerned to examine is the existential competence of those who would achieve, create, command, initiate—but whose careers merely betray their fatal lack of competence. In Eric Bentley's striking phrase, these are characters who reveal not unexpected depths but unexpected shallows; they contrive obligations which constitute a call upon their time, their energy, their attention, but which in reality are only designed to permit them to follow their own selfish inclination, or to escape from a course of action which they find distasteful, or for which they feel inadequate.

The conventions of irony require the dramatist to signal with greater or lesser clarity the disparity between things as they seem, and things as they really are. The clearer the signal, the broader the irony, and with that the greater the degree of confidence felt by the spectator that an ironic interpretation is admissible. Ibsen's method in these plays is to move closer and closer to the other end of this spectrum: to withhold the more obvious signals, and instead—so imperceptibly, sometimes, as to induce a seriously anxious uncertainty—do no more than drop veiled hints, start vague suspicions that perhaps things are not altogether as they are said by the characters to be.

Borkman, Rubek, and Allmers are all positioned on this ironic scale, but at different points of it; they represent, in this order, a descending series of explicitness. In Borkman, the disparity between the imagined and the real is comparatively emphatic; and when the pathetic swindler and ex-gaolbird characterizes himself as one of the élite, a superman, a Napoleon of industry, the jangled discords of self-delusion loudly invade his protestations. Rubek's progressive betrayal of his ineffectuality is more muted, sadder, in a way more honest. He has, it seems, achieved *one* masterpiece, though he is dubious even about claiming that; since then he has achieved nothing of note, no real 'poems' as he calls them, either in his life or his art—nothing but a few commercially successful but cynically conceived portraits. His life has been emptied of significance; and, as Irene remarks with the percipience of the damned, he too is really 'dead'. Allmers requires a receptive ear rather more finely tuned to differences in pitch between what is said and what is 'meant', and alert to the essential hollowness behind the utterance. When Borkman poses, he strikes a visible Napoleonic pose as he bids his callers enter; when Allmers 'poses', it is only by the slightest of exaggerations, the barest of over-emphases, the faintest falsity of phrase or gesture or reaction that the betrayal manifests itself. The discomfiture which criticism has often shown when confronted by these late plays might well in part trace its origins to this. Where the irony is so finely and accurately metered—in essence a kind of dramatic titration—where the trembling point of balance between the truth of what is said and the truth of what *is* is so audaciously maintained that simple certainty is impossible, it is not surprising that criticism in consequence has found it difficult to adopt a confident stance.

Applying this delicate technique to the task of communicating through drama something of the nature of life's deficiencies and imperfections, Ibsen at once set himself a problem of extreme delicacy and also at the same time exposed himself to immense risk. Put crudely, the problem was this: if, on the one hand, the concern of the plays was to be in large measure with what was flawed, deficient, inauthentic in life, with its discordant notes, its disharmonies, its moments of false tone; and if, on the other hand, his self-imposed technical brief was to reduce the element of overt irony at moments almost to vanishing point, in the belief that thereby unobtrusive irony achieves its most devastating effect; how then—if these two objectives are to be simultaneously realized—does one ensure that the flawed elements are acknowledged as a deliberate part of the dramatist's design and not merely the residual elements of the dramatist's incompetence? If a character's behaviour is designed to be unconvincing, spurious, 'theatrical', how does one prevent the transfer of the audience's censure from the fictive character to the dramatic composition itself, or the labelling as a structural weakness of something which in reality is a virtuoso achievement? It is doubtful whether any other dramatist has exposed himself to this risk so deliberately as Ibsen does in these plays. The natural and defensive inclination of any dramatist is to announce his ironic intent with the minimum necessary explicitness that will insure the work against misinterpretation; Ibsen, by contrast, reduced the ironic gap between what *is* and what *seems* to the point where the irony is left exquisitely poised. The consequence for criticism has been that too often those imperfections deliberately introduced into the plays as part of their controlled realization have been taken as simple ineptitude, by which (to take but one example) the final moments of *Little Eyolf* are taken not as a penetratingly observed and resolved portrait of a falsely sentimental man but only as a passage itself inherently marred by false sentimentality.

Deeply embedded in these late plays is also a large and irreducible measure of self-reproach. The bitterest term of abuse which Irene can find for Rubek is 'poet'. A poet is doubly culpable: not only does he (in common with all artists) mercilessly exploit the human situation for his artistic ends, taking young human life and 'ripping the soul out of it'; but also, when finally the enormity of his conduct is borne in on him, he offers merely *poetic* expiation, makes the stirrings of his conscience into the very stuff of art, and by condemning his created *alter ego* to an infinity of guilt and remorse, thinks thereby to win exoneration for himself. 'Why poet?' Rubek asks in astonishment at this mode of rebuke. 'Because you are soft and spineless and full of excuses for everything you've ever done or thought,' Irene replies. 'You killed my soul—then you go and model yourself as a figure of regret and remorse and penitence . . . and you think you've settled your account.'

As early as 1880, in phrases which have been much quoted since, Ibsen claimed that

> at *digte*—det er at holde
> dommedag over sig selv

—'to write is to pass judgement upon oneself'. *When We Dead Awaken*, Ibsen's 'epilogue', in setting out to pass judgement on the very act of passing judgement, in condemning those poetic acts of self-condemnation, pronounces upon the author a meta-judgement of extreme severity.

LITTLE EYOLF
[*Lille Eyolf*]

PLAY IN THREE ACTS
(1894)

CHARACTERS

ALFRED ALLMERS, land owner, man of letters, occasional teacher

MRS. RITA ALLMERS, his wife

EYOLF, their son, aged 9

MISS ASTA ALLMERS, Alfred's younger half-sister

BORGHEJM, an engineer

THE RAT WIFE

The action takes place on Allmers' estate out by a fjord, some miles from the town

ACT ONE

*An elegant and richly appointed garden room, well furnished with
many flowers and plants. At the rear, glass doors stand open to a
verandah, with a distant view over the fjord. Wooded hillsides in
the distance. A door in each of the side walls—the one on the right
is a double-door, upstage. Downstage, right, a sofa with loose
cushions and rugs. Chairs and a small table by the corner of the
sofa. Downstage, left, a somewhat larger table with armchairs
round it. On the table stands an open suitcase. It is early on a warm
and sunny summer's morning.*

*MRS. RITA ALLMERS stands at the table, facing left, unpacking
the suitcase. She is a good-looking woman, blond, fairly tall and
shapely, of about 30, dressed in a light morning gown.*

*After a few moments, MISS ASTA ALLMERS enters through the
door, right, dressed in light-brown summer clothes, with a hat, jacket,
and parasol. Under her arm she has a large, locked briefcase. She is
slim, of average height, with dark hair and deep, serious eyes. She
is 25 years old.*

ASTA [*in the doorway*]. Good morning, Rita my dear!

RITA [*turns her head and nods*]. Why, it's you, Asta! You're early to
have come from town! All that way out here!

ASTA [*puts her things on a chair by the door*]. Yes, I felt so restless. I felt I
had to come out and see little Eyolf today. And see you too. [*She
puts the briefcase on the table by the sofa.*] So I caught the steamer.

RITA [*smiles at her*]. And on board you just happened to meet one or
other of your friends? Entirely by chance, I mean.

ASTA [*calmly*]. No, in fact I saw nobody I knew. [*Sees the suitcase.*] But,
Rita, what's that?

RITA [*continues unpacking*]. Alfred's suitcase. Don't you recognize it?

ASTA [*happily, goes across*]. What! Is Alfred home!

RITA. Yes, would you believe it! He came quite unexpectedly by the
night train.

ASTA. Ah, so that's why I felt like that! That's what brought me out here! And he hadn't written first? Not even a postcard?

RITA. Not a word.

ASTA. No telegram either?

RITA. In fact, yes—about an hour before he arrived himself. Short and very much to the point. [*Laughs.*] Just like him, isn't it, Asta?

ASTA. Yes, it is. He always keeps things very much to himself.

RITA. That made it all the nicer to have him back again.

ASTA. Yes, I can believe that.

RITA. A whole fortnight before I was expecting him!

ASTA. And he's well? Not depressed?

RITA [*shuts the suitcase and smiles at her*]. When he came in through that door, he looked an absolutely changed man.

ASTA. But a bit tired, I imagine?

RITA. Tired? Yes, I'm sure he was. Dog tired. He'd covered most of the way on foot, the poor man.

ASTA. And all that mountain air must have been rather much for him.

RITA. I don't really think so. I haven't once heard him cough.

ASTA. There you are, you see! What a good thing after all that the doctor persuaded him to go on that walking tour.

RITA. Yes, I suppose so, now that it's over. . . . But I've had a terrible time, believe me, Asta. I didn't want to talk about it. And you so rarely came out to see me. . . .

ASTA. Yes, I wasn't very good about that. But. . . .

RITA. Ah, well . . . you had your school work there in town. [*Smiles.*] And our road builder . . . he's been away too, hasn't he?

ASTA. Oh, stop it, Rita!

RITA. All right! Let's leave our road builder, then. . . . But how I missed Alfred, Asta! The place was so empty! So desolate! Just as if somebody in the house had died. . . !

ASTA. But, heavens above ... it wasn't more than six or seven weeks. ...

RITA. Yes, but you have to remember Alfred had never been away from me before. Not even for a day. Never in all the ten years. ...

ASTA. But that's why I think this year it really was time he got away a bit. He should have gone off walking in the mountains every summer. He should really.

RITA [*half smiling*]. Ah, it's easy for you to talk, Asta. If I were as ... sensible as you, I'd have let him loose before now—perhaps. But I didn't feel I could, Asta! I imagined I'd never get him back again. Don't you understand?

ASTA. No. But that's probably because I've nobody to lose.

RITA [*with a teasing smile*]. Haven't you really anybody ... ?

ASTA. Not that *I* know of. [*Changing the subject.*] But tell me, Rita ... where is Alfred? Asleep perhaps?

RITA. Far from it! He was up as early this morning as ever.

ASTA. Then he can't have been as tired as all that.

RITA. Yes, he was last night. When he arrived. But he's had Eyolf in with him now for over an hour.

ASTA. The poor little lad! Is he now going to be made to sit all day at his books again?

RITA [*shrugs her shoulders*]. You know that's the way Alfred wants it.

ASTA. Yes, but I think you ought to stop it, Rita.

RITA [*somewhat impatiently*]. I can't really get mixed up in that, you know. Alfred understands these things much better than I do. ... And what else do you want Eyolf to do? *He* can't run around playing ... like other children.

ASTA [*firmly*]. I shall speak to Alfred about it.

RITA. Yes, my dear, do that. Well now, what have we here ...

[ALFRED ALLMERS, *dressed in a summer suit, enters through the door, left, leading* EYOLF *by the hand. He is a slim, slightly built man of about 36 or 37 years old, with gentle eyes and thinning brown hair and* beard. *The expression on his face is serious, pensive.* EYOLF *wears a suit looking rather like a uniform, with gold braid and lion-embossed buttons. He is lame, and walks with the aid of a crutch under his left arm. His leg is paralysed. He is undersized and frail-looking, but he has beautiful and intelligent eyes.*]

ALLMERS [*lets go of* EYOLF, *and walks happily with outstretched arms over to* Asta]. Asta! My dearest Asta! Fancy you being out here! Fancy seeing you so soon!

ASTA. I felt I had to. . . . Welcome home!

ALLMERS [*clasping her hands*]. Thank you, thank you!

RITA. Doesn't he look splendid!

ASTA [*staring fixedly at him*]. Marvellous. Absolutely marvellous. Those eyes—so bright. You must have done a lot of writing on your trip. [*With a glad cry.*] Perhaps you've even finished the whole book, Alfred?

ALLMERS [*shrugs his shoulders*]. The book. . . ? Oh, *that* . . .

ASTA. I felt sure things would come easily if only you could get away.

ALLMERS. I thought that too. But . . . it wasn't quite like that. In fact, I haven't written a line of the book.

ASTA. Not written. . . !

RITA. Aha! So that explains all that unused paper in your case.

ASTA. But my dear Alfred, what have you been doing all this time?

ALLMERS [*smiles*]. Walking and thinking . . . thinking . . . thinking.

RITA [*putting her arm round his shoulders*]. Thinking a little of those who were waiting at home?

ALLMERS. Of course, as you might imagine. A great deal. Every single day.

RITA [*lets go of him*]. Well, so that's all right then.

ASTA. But you've not written anything of your book? Yet you look so happy and contented? You don't usually. Not when work isn't going well, I mean.

ALLMERS. You're right. But, you know, that was just me being stupid. What is best in one goes into thinking. What gets down on paper doesn't count for much.

ASTA [*with a cry*]. Doesn't count for much!

RITA [*laughs*]. Have you gone mad, Alfred!

EYOLF [*looks up at him trustingly*]. But it does, Father. What *you* write counts for a lot.

ALLMERS [*smiles and strokes his hair*]. Of course it does . . . if *you* say so. But believe me . . . somebody will follow me and do it so much better.

EYOLF. Who can that be? Tell me!

ALLMERS. Give things time. He will come and make himself known.

EYOLF. And what will you do then?

ALLMERS [*earnestly*]. Then I'll go back to the mountains . . .

RITA. Shame on you, Alfred!

ALLMERS. . . . . Back to the high peaks and the wasteland.

EYOLF. Father! Don't you think I'll soon be well enough to go along with you?

ALLMERS [*sadly*]. Yes, perhaps, my boy.

EYOLF. I think it would be so marvellous if I could also come climbing in the mountains.

ASTA [*changing the subject*]. How nice and smart you're looking today, Eyolf!

EYOLF. I am, aren't I, Aunt Asta!

ASTA. You certainly are. And you've got your new outfit on to show your father, eh?

EYOLF. Yes, I asked Mother to let me. I wanted Father to see me in it.

ALLMERS [*in a low voice to* RITA]. You shouldn't have let him have a suit like that.

RITA [*quietly*]. But he went on and on about it. Begged me. Gave me no peace.

EYOLF. And something else, Father . . . Mr. Borghejm has bought me a bow. And he's shown me how to shoot with it.

ALLMERS. There now, Eyolf . . . that's just the thing for you.

EYOLF. And when he comes again next time, I'm going to ask him to teach me how to swim.

ALLMERS. To swim! Why do you want to do that?

EYOLF. Because all the boys down on the beach can swim. I'm the only one who can't.

ALLMERS [*moved, puts his arm round* EYOLF]. You can learn anything you want. Anything at all you want.

EYOLF. Do you know what I want most, Father.

ALLMERS. What? Tell me.

EYOLF. Most of all I'd like to be a soldier.

ALLMERS. Oh, Eyolf! So many other things are better than that.

EYOLF. But when I'm big, I must be a soldier. You know that.

ALLMERS [*wrings his hands*]. Yes, yes . . . we'll see.

ASTA [*sits down at the table, left*]. Eyolf! Come over here and I'll tell you something.

EYOLF [*goes across*]. What is it, Aunt Asta?

ASTA. What do you think, Eyolf . . . I've seen the Rat Wife.

EYOLF. What! Seen the Rat Wife! You're joking!

ASTA. No, it's true. I saw her yesterday.

EYOLF. Where did you see her?

ASTA. I saw her on the road outside the town.

ALLMERS. I also saw her, up country.

RITA [*seated on the sofa*]. So perhaps we'll see her too, Eyolf.

EYOLF. It's funny she's called the Rat Wife, isn't it?

ASTA. People call her that because she goes round everywhere getting rid of the rats.

ALLMERS. Her real name is said to be Wolf, I believe. Miss Wolf.

EYOLF. Wolf? Perhaps there's some special meaning in that.

ALLMERS [*patting his head*]. What sort of meaning, Eyolf?

EYOLF [*thoughtfully*]. There *might* be some truth after all in the story that she turns into a werewolf by night. Do you think she does, Father?

ALLMERS. No, I don't think so. . . . Perhaps you should go and play down in the garden a little now.

EYOLF. Should I not take some books with me?

ALLMERS. No, no books from now on. Run along down to the beach and play with the other boys.

EYOLF [*embarrassed*]. No, Father, I don't want to go and play with the boys today.

ALLMERS. Why not?

EYOLF. Because I've got these clothes on.

ALLMERS [*frowning*]. You mean they make fun of . . . of your nice clothes?

EYOLF [*hesitantly*]. No, they wouldn't dare. Because I'd hit them.

ALLMERS. Then why?

EYOLF. Because they say such horrid things. They say I can never be a soldier.

ALLMERS [*with suppressed anger*]. Why do you suppose they say that?

EYOLF. I think they must be envious. You see, Father, they're so poor they have to go barefoot.

ALLMERS [*in a low, choking voice*]. Oh, Rita . . . how all this gnaws at my heart!

RITA [*soothingly, as she gets up*]. There, there!

ALLMERS [*grimly*]. Those boys will learn one day who is the leader down there.

ASTA [*listening*]. Somebody's knocking.

EYOLF. It will be Borghejm!

RITA. Come in!

> [*The* RAT WIFE *comes softly and silently in through the door on the right. She is a little, thin, wizened creature, old and grey-haired, with sharp penetrating eyes. She is dressed in an old-fashioned flowered dress with a black hood and cape. She is carrying a large red umbrella, and a black bag hangs by a string from her arm.*]

EYOLF [*in a low voice, clutching* ASTA's *skirt*]. Aunt Asta! This must be her!

RAT WIFE [*curtsies at the door*]. Begging your most humble pardon, ladies and gentlemen . . . but have you anything gnawing in this house?

ALLMERS. Have we . . . ? No, I don't think so.

RAT WIFE. Because if you had, I'd be glad to help you get rid of it.

RITA. Yes, yes, we understand. But we don't have anything of that kind.

RAT WIFE. How very unfortunate. Because I'm now doing my rounds. And nobody knows when I'll be this way again. Ah, I'm so tired!

ALLMERS [*points to a chair*]. Yes, you look it.

RAT WIFE. I suppose really you shouldn't tire of doing them a kindness, poor little things—hated and persecuted as they are. But it does take its toll of your strength.

RITA. Perhaps you'll sit down and rest a little?

RAT WIFE. Many many thanks. [*Sits on a chair between the door and the sofa.*] I've been out on business all night.

ALLMERS. Have you?

RAT WIFE. Yes, over on the islands. [*Chuckles.*] Believe it or not, the people there sent for me. They didn't much like doing it. But there wasn't any other way. They just had to bite the sour apple, and like it. [*Looks at* EYOLF *and nods.*] Sour apple, young man. Sour apple.

EYOLF [*involuntarily, somewhat hesitantly*]. Why did they have to . . . ?

RAT WIFE. What?

EYOLF. Bite it?

RAT WIFE. Why, because they couldn't feed themselves any longer. Because of the rats, you see, young man. And all the little baby rats.

RITA. Ugh! Those poor people! Had they *so* many?

RAT WIFE. Swarming with them. Teeming with them. [*Smiles with quiet satisfaction.*] In the beds, creeping and crawling all night long. Falling into the milk churns. Over the floors, scratching and scraping in all the corners.

EYOLF [*softly, to* ASTA]. I'm never going there, Aunt Asta.

RAT WIFE. Then *I* arrived—I and one other. And we took them all away with us. The sweet little creatures! Between us we put paid to them all.

EYOLF [*with a shriek*]. Father . . . look! Look!

RITA. In God's name, Eyolf, what is it?

ALLMERS. What's going on?

EYOLF [*pointing*]. There something wriggling in her bag!

RITA [*moves left, screams*]. Ugh! Get rid of her, Alfred!

RAT WIFE [*laughs*]. Dear sweet lady, please don't be frightened of a harmless little thing like this.

ALLMERS. But what *is* it?

RAT WIFE. Only Mopseman. [*Undoing the bag.*]. Up you come out of the dark, my bonnie one.

[*A small dog with a broad black nose pokes its head out of the bag.*]

RAT WIFE [*nods and beckons to* EYOLF]. Come along, don't be frightened, my little wounded soldier! He won't bite! Come along! Come along!

EYOLF [*clinging to* ASTA]. No, I daren't.

RAT WIFE. Doesn't the young gentleman think he has a lovely, gentle face?

EYOLF [*amazed, points*]. That thing!

RAT WIFE. Yes, hasn't he?

EYOLF [*in an undertone, staring at the dog*]. I think he has the most horrible face I've ever seen.

RAT WIFE [*closing the bag*]. Ah, you'll learn. You'll learn in time.

EYOLF [*involuntarily drawn, goes across and lightly strokes the bag*]. And yet he's lovely . . . lovely.

RAT WIFE [*solicitously*]. But now he's so tired and weary, poor thing. So dreadfully tired. [*Looks at* ALLMERS.] It does tell on you, sir, that kind of game, believe me.

ALLMERS. What game are you talking about?

RAT WIFE. 'Follow my leader.'

ALLMERS. Ah! And the dog goes and leads on the rats, I take it?

RAT WIFE [*nods*]. Mopseman and I. We work together. It goes so smoothly. To watch it, at least. I tie a string to his collar. Then I lead him three times round the house, and play on my pipe. And when they hear *that*, they can't help themselves: up they come from the cellars, down they come from the attics, out they come from their holes—darling little creatures, all of them.

EYOLF. Then he bites them all till they are dead?

RAT WIFE. Not at all! We make our way down to the boat, he and I. And they follow us. The big grown-up rats as well as the little baby rats.

EYOLF [*tense*]. And then what . . . ? Tell me!

RAT WIFE. Then we pull away from the shore. I work the oar and play on my pipe. And Mopseman swims along behind. [*With flashing eyes.*] And all the little creepie-crawlies follow us out further and further into deep water. They can't help themselves!

EYOLF. Why can't they?

RAT WIFE. Because really they don't want to do it. Because really they are horribly afraid of the water—and that's just the reason that compels them to go.

EYOLF. So they drown?

RAT WIFE. Every single one. [*In a lower voice.*] Then it's all as nice and quiet and dark as they had ever wished for, dear little things. Down there they sleep a long sleep, a sweet sleep—they who are hated and persecuted of men. [*Gets up.*] Ah, in my earlier days I had no need of any Mopseman. I was sufficient attraction myself. On my own.

EYOLF. And you attracted—what?

RAT WIFE. People. One in particular.

EYOLF [*tense*]. Tell me who that was.

RAT WIFE [*laughs*]. It was my own dearest love, you little heart-breaker!

EYOLF. Where's he now?

RAT WIFE [*brutally*]. Down among all the rats. [*Gently again.*] But now I must get back to business again. Always on the go. [*To* RITA.] Have you really no work for me today? If you had, I could deal with it at once.

RITA. No, thank you. I don't think there's any need.

RAT WIFE. Ah well, sweet lady, you never know! But if ever you should come across anything here nibbling and gnawing... or creeping and crawling... just make sure you send for me and Mopseman. Farewell! A thousand times farewell.

[*She goes out through the door, right.*]

EYOLF [*in quiet triumph to* ASTA]. So now I too have seen the Rat Wife!

[RITA *goes out on to the verandah and fans herself with a handkerchief. Shortly afterwards* EYOLF *slips out unnoticed through the door, right.*]

ALLMERS [*picks up the briefcase from the table by the sofa*]. Is this your briefcase, Asta?

ASTA. Yes. I've got some of those old letters in it.

ALLMERS. Ah, the family letters...

ASTA. You asked me to go through them for you while you were away, remember?

ALLMERS [*pats her head*]. And you really found time to do *that*?

ASTA. Oh, yes. I did it partly out here and partly back home in town.

ALLMERS. Thank you, my dear. . . . Anything special in them?

ASTA [*casually*]. Oh . . . one always finds things of interest in old papers like these, you know. [*Quieter and more serious.*] Those in the briefcase are my mother's letters.

ALLMERS. You yourself must keep them, of course.

ASTA [*with an effort*]. No. I want you to look through them too, Alfred. Some time . . . in the years to come. I haven't the key of the briefcase with me today.

ALLMERS. No point, my dear Asta. I shan't ever read your mother's letters.

ASTA [*looks at him fixedly*]. Then sometime . . . some quiet evening . . . I'll tell you something of what's in them.

ALLMERS. Yes, do that instead. But you keep your mother's letters. You haven't many things to remind you of her.

[*He hands the briefcase to* ASTA. *She takes it and places it on the chair under her overcoat.* RITA *comes back into the room.*]

RITA. Ugh! Horrible old woman! Somehow she seems to have brought a smell of death into the house.

ALLMERS. Yes, she was rather horrible.

RITA. I felt quite ill while she was in the room.

ALLMERS. At the same time I can understand something of that compelling power of attraction she talked about. The solitude up among the mountain peaks and on the great desolate open spaces has something of the same power.

ASTA [*looks closely at him*]. What has happened to you, Alfred?

ALLMERS [*smiles*]. To me?

ASTA. Yes. There's something. Almost like a transformation. Rita has noticed it, too.

RITA. Yes, I saw it as soon as you arrived. But that's good, surely? Isn't it, Alfred?

ALLMERS. It ought to be good. And certainly it must be turned to good account.

RITA [*bursts out*]. Something happened to you when you were away. Don't deny it! I can see by looking at you!

ALLMERS [*shakes his head*]. Absolutely nothing happened . . . outwardly. But . . .

RITA [*tense*]. But . . . ?

ALLMERS. Inwardly I have indeed undergone something of a transformation.

RITA. Oh God!

ALLMERS [*pats her hand reassuringly*]. Only for the best, Rita dear. Rest assured.

RITA [*sits on the sofa*]. Now you must tell us about it. Everything!

ALLMERS [*turns to* ASTA]. Yes, let's all sit down. And I'll try to tell you. As best I can.

[*He sits on the sofa by the side of* RITA. ASTA *moves a chair forward and sits near him. Short pause.*]

RITA [*looks at him expectantly*]. Well?

ALLMERS [*staring straight ahead*]. When I look back over my life . . . over what was fated to be . . . these past ten or eleven years, it seems almost like a fairy-tale, or a dream. Don't you think so too, Asta?

ASTA. Yes, in many ways I do.

ALLMERS [*continues*]. When I think, Asta, what we once were—two poor penniless orphans . . .

RITA [*impatiently*]. Yes, but that was long ago.

ALLMERS [*pays no heed to her*]. And now I sit here, well placed and prosperous. Have been able to follow my calling. To work and to study . . . just as I pleased. [*Stretches out his hand.*] And all this great and inconceivable good fortune . . . we owe to you, my dearest Rita.

RITA [*half in jest, half ill-tempered, smacks his hand*]. Let's not have any more nonsense.

ALLMERS. I mention it merely as a kind of introduction . . .

RITA. Oh, spare us the introduction!

E1

ALLMERS. Rita, you mustn't think it was the doctor's advice that drove me up into the mountains.

ASTA. Wasn't it, Alfred?

RITA. What was it, then?

ALLMERS. It was because I could no longer find peace at my writing desk.

RITA. No peace! But, my dear, who was disturbing you?

ALLMERS [*shakes his head*]. Nobody . . . from without. But I had the feeling I was in fact misusing . . . well, no . . . neglecting my best talents. That I was wasting my time.

ASTA [*her eyes wide*]. Sitting writing your book?

ALLMERS [*nods*]. My talents surely are not limited to *that*. Surely there must be something else I am able to do.

RITA. So *that* was what you sat there worrying about?

ALLMERS. Yes, mostly.

RITA. And that's why you became so discontented with yourself as time went on. And with us, as well. Oh yes, you were, Alfred.

ALLMERS [*stares straight ahead*]. There I sat bent over my desk, writing, day after day. And sometimes half the night. Writing away at that great thick book on 'Human Responsibility'. Hm!

ASTA [*places her hand on his arm*]. But, my dear . . . that book will be your life's work.

RITA. You've said so yourself often enough.

ALLMERS. That's what I thought. Ever since I was a very young man. [*With a warm expression in his eyes.*] Then, my dear Rita, you provided me with the chance of embarking upon it . . .

RITA. Nonsense!

ALLMERS [*smiles at her*]. . . . you with your 'gold and your green forests' . . .

RITA [*half laughing, half annoyed*]. If you start all that nonsense again, I'll hit you.

ASTA [*looks anxiously at him*]. But the book, Alfred?

ALLMERS. That became more and more remote. And thoughts of a higher duty began more and more to exert a claim on me.

RITA [*seizes his hand, her eyes shining*]. Alfred!

ALLMERS. Thoughts of Eyolf, Rita my dear.

RITA [*disappointed, lets go his hand*]. Ah . . . Eyolf.

ALLMERS. Deeper and deeper these thoughts of poor little Eyolf have taken root in my mind. After that tragic fall from the table. . . . And especially when we knew for certain he would never be cured . . .

RITA [*urgently*]. But you do everything you can for him, Alfred!

ALLMERS. As a schoolmaster, yes. But not as a father. And from now on it is a father to Eyolf that I want to be.

RITA [*looks at him and shakes her head*]. I don't think I understand you.

ALLMERS. What I mean is I shall do everything in my power to soften for him—as far as is humanly possible—the blows of the inevitable.

RITA. But Alfred, I don't think Eyolf feels it all that deeply, thank God.

ASTA [*emotionally*]. Yes, Rita, he does.

ALLMERS. Yes, you may be sure he feels it deeply.

RITA [*impatiently*]. But, my dear Alfred, what more can you do for him?

ALLMERS. I want to bring light to bear on all the rich potential now dawning in his young mind. I want to encourage growth in all the budding ambitions he holds within himself—so that they put forth blossom and bring forth fruit. [*With increasing fervour, rises.*] I want to do more than that! I want to help him to achieve a harmonious relationship between what he desires and what lies within his reach. That is not how he approaches things now. All he longs for are things which must remain forever beyond his reach. I want to create within him a sense of happiness.

[*He paces up and down the room a few times.* ASTA *and* RITA *follow him with their eyes.*]

RITA. You should take a more relaxed view of these things, Alfred!

ALLMERS [*stops at the table, left, and looks at them*]. Eyolf shall take up my life's work. If he so wishes. Or he can choose something which is entirely his own. Perhaps that would be best. . . . In any case, I shall leave my own work where it is.

RITA [*rises*]. But, my dearest Alfred . . . can't you work both for yourself and for Eyolf?

ALLMERS. No, I can't. Impossible! I cannot divide myself in this. So I shall make way. Eyolf shall achieve the consummation of the family line. And my new life's work shall be that of bringing him to that consummation.

ASTA [*has risen, goes over to him*]. This has cost you a terribly hard battle, Alfred.

ALLMERS. Yes, it has. Here at home I would never have come to terms with myself. Never have brought myself to the point of renunciation. Never here at home.

RITA. Was that why you went off this summer?

ALLMERS [*with shining eyes*]. Yes. And then I climbed up into the infinite solitude. Saw the sun rise over the mountain peaks. Felt myself nearer the stars. Almost as though I understood them, belonged with them. Then I was able to do it.

ASTA [*looks sadly at him*]. Will you never write any more of your book on 'Human Responsibility'?

ALLMERS. No, never, Asta. I told you I cannot split myself between two tasks. But I shall carry through the concept of human responsibility —in my life.

RITA [*with a smile*]. Do you really think you'll be able to hold fast to such high ideals here at home?

ALLMERS [*takes her hand*]. In company with you I can. [*Holds out his other hand.*] And in company with you, too, Asta.

RITA [*withdraws her hand*]. With two people. So you *can* in fact divide yourself.

ALLMERS. But my dearest Rita . . . !

[RITA *moves away from him and takes up her position by the French windows. There is a quick, light knock on the door, right.* BORGHEJM *steps briskly in. He is a young man of about thirty; bright and cheerful expression; erect stance.*]

BORGHEJM. Good morning, good morning, Mrs. Allmers! [*Stops joyfully as he catches sight of* ALLMERS.] Well, what's this I see! Home again already, Mr. Allmers?

ALLMERS [*shakes his hand*]. Yes. I came last night.

RITA [*gaily*]. He didn't have permission to stay away longer, Mr. Borghejm.

ALLMERS. That's not true, Rita . . .

RITA [*approaching*]. Of course it's true. His leave had expired.

BORGHEJM. You keep a tight rein on your husband, Mrs. Allmers?

RITA. I insist on my rights. Anyway, everything has to end sometime.

BORGHEJM. Oh, not everything—I hope. Good morning, Miss Allmers!

ASTA [*avoiding his eyes*]. Good morning.

RITA [*looks at* BORGHEJM]. Not everything, did you say?

BORGHEJM. Yes, I firmly believe there is at least one thing in this world that has no end.

RITA. You are doubtless thinking of love . . . and similar things.

BORGHEJM [*warmly*]. I am thinking of anything which is delightful!

RITA. And which never ends. Yes, let's think of that. And hope for it, all of us.

ALLMERS [*goes over to them*]. I suppose you'll soon be finished building the road out here?

BORGHEJM. I'm already finished. Finished yesterday. It's lasted a pretty long time. But, thank heaven, *that* had an end to it.

RITA. And that's why you're on top of the world?

BORGHEJM. Yes, it is.

RITA. Well, I must say . . . !

BORGHEJM. What, Mrs. Allmers?

RITA. That's not altogether nice of you, Mr. Borghejm.

BORGHEJM. Oh? Why not?

RITA. Because after this you'll not be coming out very often to these parts.

BORGHEJM. That's true. I didn't think of that.

RITA. Surely you'll be able to manage an occasional visit to us out here.

BORGHEJM. No, I'm afraid that won't be possible for me. Not for a long time.

ALLMERS. Oh? Why not?

BORGHEJM. Because I've now got a big new job I must start on at once.

ALLMERS. No, have you? [*Presses his hand.*]

RITA. Congratulations, Mr. Borghejm!

BORGHEJM. Sssh! Actually I'm not supposed to talk about it yet! But I can't keep it to myself! It's an enormous piece of road-building . . . up in the North. There are mountains to cross . . . and quite incredible difficulties to overcome. [*Exclaims.*] Ah, what a marvellous life . . . and how fortunate I am to be a builder of roads!

RITA [*smiles and looks teasingly at him*]. Is it just this road-building that brings you out here today in such high spirits?

BORGHEJM. No, not just that. So many bright and promising prospects seem to be opening up for me.

RITA [*as before*]. And possibly beyond lies something even more delightful.

BORGHEJM [*glances at* ASTA]. Who knows? Once luck does run your way, it tends to come like a spring torrent. [*Turns to* ASTA.] Miss Asta, should we take a little stroll together? As we usually do?

ASTA [*quickly*]. No. No, thank you. Not now. Not today.

BORGHEJM. Oh, please come! Just a short walk. I feel I've so many things to talk to you about before I leave.

RITA. Another one of those things that can't be talked about yet, perhaps?

BORGHEJM. It all depends whether . . .

RITA. Well, you can always try whispering it. [*In a low voice.*] Asta, do go with him.

ASTA. But my dear Rita . . .

BORGHEJM [*pleading*]. Miss Asta . . . remember this is to be our parting walk . . . the last for a long long time.

ASTA [*takes her hat and parasol*]. Very well. Let's take a little walk down in the garden.

BORGHEJM. Thank you, thank you.

ALLMERS. Keep an eye open for little Eyolf while you're there.

BORGHEJM. Yes, Eyolf! That's right! Where is Eyolf today? I've brought something for him.

ALLMERS. He's off playing somewhere down there.

BORGHEJM. Really? So now he's taken to playing? He usually just sits inside reading.

ALLMERS. That's going to stop. Now he's going to be a real open-air lad.

BORGHEJM. That's right! Out into the fresh air with him, poor boy! Dear God, what better thing is there to do in this glorious world than play. I feel all life is a kind of game. Come, Miss Asta.

[BORGHEJM *and* ASTA *go out on to the verandah and down through the garden.*]

ALLMERS [*stands watching them*]. Rita, do you suppose there is anything between those two?

RITA. I don't know what to say. I used to think so before. But lately I simply haven't been able to understand Asta. She's become absolutely incomprehensible.

ALLMERS. Has she? While I've been away?

RITA. Yes, in the last few weeks, I'd say.

ALLMERS. And you don't think she's interested in him any longer?

RITA. Not seriously. Not totally. Not unreservedly. I don't think so. [*Looks searchingly at him.*] Would you be against it if she were?

ALLMERS. Not really against it! But it would undoubtedly be a worrying thought. . . .

RITA. Worrying?

ALLMERS. Remember I am responsible for Asta. For her happiness.

RITA. What! Responsible! Asta is a grown woman. She knows well enough how to make up her own mind, I should have thought.

ALLMERS. Let us hope so, Rita.

RITA. I myself see nothing wrong in Borghejm.

ALLMERS. No, my dear. Nor do I. Quite the reverse. All the same . . .

RITA [*persisting*]. I'd be very happy to see a match between Asta and him.

ALLMERS [*displeased*]. Why do you want that?

RITA [*with increasing agitation*]. Because then she'd have to go away with him, far far away! Then she couldn't keep coming out here as she does now.

ALLMERS [*stares at her in astonishment*]. What! You mean you want to be rid of Asta!

RITA. Yes, Alfred! Yes!

ALLMERS. But why in the world . . . ?

RITA [*throws her arms passionately around his neck*]. Then at last I'd have you all to myself! Except that . . . No, not even then! Not completely to myself! [*Bursts out sobbing.*] Oh, Alfred, Alfred . . . I cannot let you go.

ALLMERS [*gently frees himself*]. But my dearest Rita—do be reasonable!

RITA. I don't care a damn about being reasonable! All I care about is you! Nothing in the whole wide world but you! [*Again throws herself round his neck.*] You! you! you!

ALLMERS. Let go! let go! You're choking me!

RITA [*lets him go*]. God, if only I could! [*Looks at him with flashing eyes.*] Oh, if only you knew how I've hated you . . . !

ALLMERS. Hated me . . . !

RITA. Yes. When you sat there in your room alone. Poring over your work. Long . . . long into the night. [*Plaintively.*] So long, and so late, Alfred. Oh, how I hated that work of yours!

ALLMERS. But now that's all over and done with.

RITA [*laughs cuttingly*]. Oh, yes! Only now you are caught up by something worse.

ALLMERS [*outraged*]. Worse! You call our child 'something worse'?

RITA [*vehemently*]. Yes, I do. As far as it affects our relationship, I do. Because, on top of everything else, the child . . . the child is also a living being. [*With rising passion.*] But I won't stand for it, Alfred! I won't stand for it, I tell you!

ALLMERS [*looks steadily at her, then speaks quietly*]. Sometimes you almost frighten me, Rita.

RITA [*darkly*]. I often frighten myself. For that reason you mustn't rouse the evil in me.

ALLMERS. But in God's name . . . do I do that?

RITA. Yes, you do. When you break the sacred ties that bind us.

ALLMERS [*earnestly*]. Think what you are saying, Rita. It's your own child we are talking about . . . our only child.

RITA. The child is only half mine. [*Again bursts out.*] But *you* shall be all mine! Mine alone! I have a right to demand it!

ALLMERS [*shrugs his shoulders*]. My dear Rita, it's no use demanding. Everything has to be freely given.

RITA [*looks at him tensely*]. And perhaps from now on you can't do that?

ALLMERS. No, I can't. I must divide myself between Eyolf and you.

RITA. And if Eyolf had never been born? What then?

ALLMERS [*evasively*]. That would have been a different matter. Then I'd have had only you to love.

RITA [*in a low trembling voice*]. Then I could wish I'd never borne him.

ALLMERS [*starts up*]. Rita! You don't know what you are saying!

RITA [*shaking with emotion*]. I gave birth to him in unspeakable pain. But I endured it all gladly and joyfully for your sake.

ALLMERS [*warmly*]. Yes, yes. I know that.

RITA [*firmly*]. But that's past and done with. I want to *live*. Together with you. Wholly with you. I can't go on just being Eyolf's mother. And only that. Nothing else. I won't, I tell you! I can't! I want to be everything to you! To you, Alfred!

ALLMERS. But you *are*, Rita. Through our child . . .

RITA. Oh . . . these nauseating, warmed-up phrases! That's all they are! No, that's nothing for me. Motherhood for me was in *having* the child. But I'm not made to go on *being* mother to it. You must take me as I am, Alfred.

ALLMERS. Yet you were always so very fond of Eyolf before.

RITA. I felt so sorry for him. Because you just left him to drift. Just made him read and learn his lessons. You hardly ever saw him.

ALLMERS [*nods slowly*]. No, I was blind. The hour had not yet struck . . .

RITA [*looks at him*]. But now it has?

ALLMERS. Yes, finally. Now I see that my highest duty in this life is to be a true father to Eyolf.

RITA. And *me*? What will you be to me?

ALLMERS [*mildly*]. I shall go on loving you. With quiet devotion.

[*He tries to take her by the hands.*]

RITA [*avoids him*]. I'm not interested in your quiet devotion. I want you! All of you! You alone! The way I had you in those first glorious, throbbing days. [*Vehemently and hard.*] Nobody's going to fob me off with scraps and left-overs, Alfred!

ALLMERS [*gently*]. I think we could surely find enough happiness here to satisfy all three of us, Rita.

RITA [*scornfully*]. Then you are easily satisfied. [*Sits at the table, left.*] Now listen.

ALLMERS [*goes closer*]. Well? What is it?

RITA [*looks up at him with a dull glow in her eyes*]. When I got your telegram last night . . .

ALLMERS. Yes? What?

RITA. . . . I dressed in white . . .

ALLMERS. Yes. I saw you were wearing white when I arrived.

RITA. I'd let down my hair . . .

ALLMERS. Your long fragrant hair . . .

RITA. . . . so that it hung about my neck and shoulders . . .

ALLMERS. I saw. I saw. How lovely you were, Rita!

RITA. There were rose-red shades on both the lamps. We were alone, we two. The only ones awake in the whole house. And there was champagne on the table.

ALLMERS. I didn't drink any.

RITA [*looks bitterly at him*]. How true. [*With a sharp laugh.*] 'Champagne was yours, but you touched it not'—as the poet says.

[*She gets up from the armchair, goes as though tired to the sofa and half sits, half lies on it.*]

ALLMERS [*walks over and stands in front of her*]. I was so full of serious thoughts. I was determined to talk to you about our future life, Rita. And first and foremost about Eyolf.

RITA [*smiles*]. Which you did, my dear.

ALLMERS. No. I didn't get that far. Because you began to undress.

RITA. While you went on talking about Eyolf. Don't you remember? You asked me how little Eyolf's tummy was.

ALLMERS [*looks reproachfully at her*]. Rita!

RITA. And then you lay down in your bed. And fell fast asleep.

ALLMERS [*shakes his head*]. Rita! Rita!

RITA [*lies down full length and looks up at him*]. Alfred?

ALLMERS. Yes?

RITA. 'Champagne was yours, but you touched it not.'

ALLMERS [*almost hard*]. No. I didn't touch it.

[*He moves away from her and stands by the french window.* RITA *lies for some moments motionless, her eyes closed.*]

RITA [*suddenly jumps up*]. But one thing I will tell you, Alfred!

ALLMERS [*turns in the doorway*]. Well?

RITA. Don't be too sure of yourself.

ALLMERS. Sure of myself?

RITA. No. Don't take things for granted. Don't be too confident that you have me.

ALLMERS [*approaches*]. What do you mean by that?

RITA [*with trembling lips*]. I have never been unfaithful to you, Alfred—not even in thought. Never for a moment.

ALLMERS. I know that, Rita. I know you too well . . .

RITA [*with flashing eyes*]. But if you spurn me . . . !

ALLMERS. Spurn! I don't understand what you are getting at!

RITA. You don't know what ideas I might get if . . .

ALLMERS. If?

RITA. If I saw any sign that you no longer cared about me. No longer loved me as you did before.

ALLMERS. But my dearest Rita! People change with the years. And some time or other that's bound to happen to us, too, in our life together. As it does to everybody else.

RITA. Not to me! Ever! And I don't want to hear of any change in you either. I couldn't bear that, Alfred. I want to keep you all to myself.

ALLMERS [*looks troubled at her*]. You have a terribly jealous mind . . .

RITA. I can't make myself different from what I am. [*Threateningly.*] If you parcel yourself out between me and anybody else . . .

ALLMERS. Well?

RITA. I'll be revenged on you, Alfred!

ALLMERS. Revenge? How?

RITA. I don't know. . . . Yes, I do know!

ALLMERS. Well?

RITA. I'll go and throw myself away . . .

ALLMERS. Throw yourself away!

RITA. Yes, that's what I'll do. I'll throw myself into the arms . . . of the first man that comes along.

ALLMERS [*looks warmly at her and shakes his head*]. You'll never do that . . . my proud, honest, loyal Rita.

RITA [*puts her arms round his neck*]. Oh, you don't know what might become of me . . . if you didn't want me any more.

ALLMERS. Not want you, Rita? How can you say such a thing!

RITA [*half laughing, lets him go*]. I might set out my nets to catch this road-builder man of ours.

ALLMERS [*relieved*]. Ah, thank God, you are joking.

RITA. Not at all. Why not him just as much as the next man?

ALLMERS. Because he seems pretty well caught up already.

RITA. So much the better! Then I'd be taking him from somebody else. That's exactly the same as Eyolf has done to me.

ALLMERS. You say our little Eyolf has done *that*?

RITA [*pointing her finger*]. You see! You see! You've only got to mention Eyolf's name and you go all soft and your voice trembles. [*Threateningly, clenching her fists.*] Oh, I am almost tempted to wish . . . Well!

ALLMERS [*looks anxiously at her*]. To wish what, Rita?

RITA [*vehemently, moves away from him*]. No, no, no . . . I won't tell you! Never!

ALLMERS [*goes closer to her*]. Rita! I implore you . . . for your sake and mine . . . do not let yourself be tempted to anything evil.

[BORGHEJM *and* ASTA *come up from the garden. Both are visibly controlling their feelings. They look serious and upset.* ASTA *remains standing outside on the verandah.* BORGHEJM *comes into the room.*]

BORGHEJM. Ah well! Miss Asta and I have taken our last walk together.

RITA [*looks at him in surprise*]. Oh! And that's not to be followed by any longer journey?

BORGHEJM. Yes. For me.

RITA. For you alone?

BORGHEJM. Yes, for me alone.

RITA [*glancing darkly at* ALLMERS]. You hear that, Alfred? [*Turns to* BORGHEJM.] I'll wager it's the evil eye that's done this thing to you.

BORGHEJM [*looks at her*]. Evil eye?

RITA [*nods*]. Yes. Evil eye.

BORGHEJM. Do you believe in evil eyes, Mrs. Allmers?

RITA. Yes, I'm now beginning to believe in evil eyes. Particularly in children's evil eyes.

ALLMERS [*agitated, whispers*]. Rita, how can you . . . !

RITA [*half aloud*]. It is you, Alfred . . . you are making me evil and horrid.

[*Distant confused shouts and cries are heard from down by the water.*]

BORGHEJM [*goes to the french window*]. What's that noise . . . ?

ASTA [*in the opening*]. Look at all those people running down to the jetty!

ALLMERS. What can it be? [*Looks out for a moment.*] Those guttersnipes up to some game, I dare say.

BORGHEJM [*shouts down over the railings*]. Hi, you lads down there! What's going on?

[*Indistinct answers are heard, with several people talking at once.*]

RITA. What are they saying?

BORGHEJM. They say a child has been drowned.

ALLMERS. A child drowned?

ASTA [*uneasily*]. A little boy, they say.

ALLMERS. Oh, they can all swim.

RITA [*cries out in fear*]. Where's Eyolf gone?

ALLMERS. Be calm. Be calm. Eyolf is playing in the garden.

ASTA. No, he wasn't in the garden.

RITA [*with raised arms*]. As long as it isn't him!

BORGHEJM [*listens, and shouts down*]. Whose child is it, do you say?

[*Indistinct voices are heard.* BORGHEJM *and* ASTA *utter a suppressed cry and rush down through the garden.*]

ALLMERS [*in anguish*]. It isn't Eyolf. It isn't Eyolf, Rita.

RITA [*on the verandah, listening*]. Hush! Be quiet! Let me hear what they are saying! [RITA *rushes with a piercing shriek into the room.*]

ALLMERS [*follows her*]. What did they say?

RITA [*sinks down by the armchair, left*]. They said: 'The crutch is floating.'

ALLMERS [*almost stunned*]. No! no! no!

RITA [*hoarsely*]. Eyolf! Eyolf! They must save him!

ALLMERS [*half distraught*]. It *must* be possible! So dear a life! So dear a life!

[*He rushes down through the garden.*]

ACT TWO

A little narrow dene in the forest on ALLMERS' *land, down by the shore. Tall old trees, left, overhang the spot. Down the slope in the background rushes a stream which loses itself among the rocks on the edge of the wood. A path twists alongside the stream. A few scattered trees stand on the right, through which can be glimpsed the fjord. In the foreground can be seen the corner of a boathouse, with a boat drawn up. Under the old trees on the left stands a table with a bench and some chairs, hammered together from birch branches. It is a heavy, damp day with driving mist.*

ALFRED ALLMERS, *dressed as before, sits on the bench, propping his arms on the table. His hat lies in front of him. He stares out over the water, motionless, lost in thought.*

Shortly afterwards ASTA ALLMERS *comes down the path. She is carrying an open umbrella.*

ASTA [*goes quietly and cautiously up to him*]. You shouldn't be sitting down here in this grey weather, Alfred.

[ALLMERS *nods slowly without replying.*]

ASTA [*closes her umbrella*]. I've walked such a long way looking for you.

ALLMERS [*expressionlessly*]. Thank you.

ASTA [*moves a chair and sits down near him*]. Have you been sitting here long? The whole time?

ALLMERS [*at first does not answer; after a while he speaks*]. I can't understand it. It seems so absolutely impossible . . . all this.

ASTA [*puts her hand comfortingly on his arm*]. Poor Alfred.

ALLMERS [*stares at her*]. Is it really true, Asta? Or have I gone mad? Or am I just dreaming? Oh, if only it were a dream! How lovely if I were now to wake up!

ASTA. Oh, if only I could in fact wake you.

ALLMERS [*looks out over the water*]. How pitiless the fjord looks today. Lying there so heavy and sluggish. Leaden grey ... with a glint of yellow ... reflecting the rain clouds.

ASTA [*imploringly*]. Oh Alfred, don't sit here staring at the fjord!

ALLMERS [*does not listen to her*]. On the surface, yes. But in the depths ... *there* the undercurrent is strong.

ASTA [*fearfully*]. For God's sake don't think about the depths!

ALLMERS [*looks at her gently*]. You think he's lying just off here, don't you? But he isn't, Asta. You mustn't think that. Remember how strong the outgoing current is here. Right out to sea.

ASTA [*throws herself sobbing over the table, her hands over her face*]. Oh, God! Oh, God!

ALLMERS [*heavily*]. So by now little Eyolf has been carried far, far away from us.

ASTA [*looks up at him pleadingly*]. Oh, Alfred, please don't say things like that!

ALLMERS. Work it out for yourself—you are good at figures. . . . In twenty-eight ... twenty-nine hours ... Let me see ... ! Let me see ... !

ASTA [*screams and puts her hands over her ears*]. Alfred ... !

ALLMERS [*forces his fist hard against the table*]. But can you see any meaning in this?

ASTA [*looks at him*]. In what?

ALLMERS. In what's been done to me and Rita.

ASTA. The meaning in it?

ALLMERS [*impatiently*]. Yes, the meaning, I said. There must be some meaning in it. Life, existence, providence—surely they can't be so utterly meaningless.

ASTA. Oh, Alfred, who can speak with certainty about these things?

ALLMERS [*laughs bitterly*]. No, of course not. You are probably right. Perhaps the whole thing is just haphazard. An aimless drifting, like some wrecked and rudderless ship. That could well be it. It seems very much like that, at least.

F1

ASTA [*thoughtfully*]. What if it only seems . . . ?

ALLMERS [*vehemently*]. So? Perhaps *you* can find me some explanation? *I* cannot. [*Gentler.*] There is Eyolf on the very threshold of a new and fuller sense of life. There are endless possibilities open to him. Rich possibilities, maybe. Was about to fill my existence with pride and joy. Then all it needs is for some crazy old woman to come along . . . and produce a dog in a sack . . .

ASTA. But we don't really know how it all happened.

ALLMERS. Yes, we do. The boys saw her row out over the fjord. They saw Eyolf standing alone on the furthest point of the jetty. Saw him staring after her . . . and sway as if giddy. [*His voice trembles.*] It was then he fell . . . and disappeared.

ASTA. I know. And yet . . .

ALLMERS. She drew him down into the deep. That's certain.

ASTA. But, my dear, why should she?

ALLMERS. Exactly. Why should she? It can't be retribution that's behind it. There's nothing to atone for, I mean. Eyolf never did her any harm. Never called her names. Never threw stones at the dog. He had never set eyes on either her or the dog until yesterday. So it can't be retribution. The whole thing is so senseless. So absolutely meaningless, Asta. And yet the world order seems to require it.

ASTA. Have you spoken to Rita about these things?

ALLMERS [*shakes his head*]. I feel I am better talking to you about them. [*Draws a heavy breath.*] As indeed about everything else.

[ASTA *takes some sewing things and a small packet wrapped in paper out of her pocket.* ALLMERS *sits absentmindedly looking on.*]

ALLMERS. What have you got there, Asta?

ASTA [*takes his hat*]. Some black crape.

ALLMERS. What good will that do?

ASTA. Rita asked me to do it. May I?

ALLMERS. Oh yes, if you like. [*She sews the crape on the hat. He sits watching her.*] Where is Rita?

ASTA. Walking in the garden, I think. Borghejm is with her.

ALLMERS [*somewhat surprised*]. Oh? Is Borghejm out here again today?

ASTA. Yes. He came out by the midday train.

ALLMERS. I wouldn't have expected that.

ASTA [*sewing*]. He was very fond of Eyolf.

ALLMERS. Borghejm is a loyal soul, Asta.

ASTA [*warmly*]. Yes, he is loyal. That's very true.

ALLMERS [*looks closely at her*]. You are fond of him.

ASTA. Yes, I am.

ALLMERS. Yet you can't make up your mind to . . . ?

ASTA [*interrupting*]. Please, Alfred, don't talk about it.

ALLMERS. Won't you just tell me why . . . ?

ASTA. No, no! I beg you, please don't ask me. I find it very painful.—
There now, the hat's ready.

ALLMERS. Thank you.

ASTA. And now the left sleeve.

ALLMERS. Must that also have crape?

ASTA. Yes, it all belongs.

ALLMERS. As you will.

[*She moves nearer to him and begins to sew.*]

ASTA. Keep your arm still. So I don't prick you.

ALLMERS [*half smiles*]. This is like the old days.

ASTA. Yes, isn't it?

ALLMERS. When you were a little girl you used to sit like this and mend
my clothes.

ASTA. As best I could, yes.

ALLMERS. The first thing you sewed for me . . . was also some black
crape.

ASTA. Oh?

ALLMERS. On my student cap. When father died.

ASTA. Did I do that? I don't remember.

ALLMERS. You were still very little.

ASTA. Yes, I was little.

ALLMERS. Then, two years later . . . when we lost your mother . . . you sewed me a big black armband.

ASTA. Yes, I thought it was only right.

ALLMERS [*pats her hand*]. Of course it was right, Asta. Then when we two were left alone in the world . . . Are you finished already?

ASTA. Yes. [*Gathers her sewing things together.*] Yet really it turned out to be a happy time, Alfred. The two of us alone.

ALLMERS. Yes, it did. Hard work though it was.

ASTA. *You* worked hard.

ALLMERS [*more animated*]. You worked hard too, in your way . . . my dear, loyal . . . Eyolf.

ASTA. Don't remind me of all that silly business about the name.

ALLMERS. If you had been a boy, you would have been called Eyolf.

ASTA. Yes—if. Then when you became a student . . . [*Smiles involuntarily.*] Imagine your being so childish.

ALLMERS. Me childish?

ASTA. I think you were, now I look back. You were ashamed of not having any brother. Only a sister.

ALLMERS. No, it was you. *You* were ashamed.

ASTA. Perhaps I was, a little. And I also felt somehow sorry for you. . . .

ALLMERS. Yes, you must have. You looked out the old clothes I'd worn as a boy. . . .

ASTA. All your Sunday best. You remember that blue blouse and those knee breeches?

ALLMERS [*his eyes rest on her*]. How well I remember you when you put them on and walked about in them.

ASTA. But I only did it at home when we were alone together.

ALLMERS. How seriously, how solemnly we took ourselves. And I always called you Eyolf.

ASTA. Alfred, you haven't told anything of this to Rita, have you?

ALLMERS. Yes, I think I did tell her about it once.

ASTA. Oh, Alfred, how could you!

ALLMERS. Well ... doesn't one normally tell one's wife everything— or pretty nearly.

ASTA. I suppose one does.

ALLMERS [*as though waking up, clasps his forehead and jumps up*]. How can I sit here and ...

ASTA [*rises, looks anxiously at him*]. What is it?

ALLMERS. He almost escaped me. Completely escaped me.

ASTA. Eyolf!

ALLMERS. I sat here living in my memories. And he wasn't there.

ASTA. Yes he was, Alfred. Little Eyolf was behind everything.

ALLMERS. He was not. He slipped out of my mind. Out of my thoughts. Not for a moment did I see him while we sat together talking. Forgot him completely all that time.

ASTA. But you must have some respite from your grief.

ALLMERS. No, no, that's just what I must not have. I have no right. No warrant. ... And no heart for it, either. [*Walks agitatedly across, right.*] My place is out there, where he lies drifting in the deep water!

ASTA [*goes after him and holds him back*]. Alfred, Alfred! Don't go near the fjord!

ALLMERS. I must go out to him! Let me go, Asta! I want the boat.

ASTA [*in terror*]. Don't go near the fjord, I say!

ALLMERS [*yields*]. No, I won't. Just leave me alone.

ASTA [*leads him back to the table*]. You must let your mind rest, Alfred. Come here and sit down.

ALLMERS [*goes to sit on the bench*]. Very well. As you will.

ASTA. No, don't sit there.

ALLMERS. Yes. Please let me.

ASTA. No, don't! You'll just sit looking out over . . . [*Urges him on to a chair with his back to the right.*] There. That's better. [*She sits on the bench herself.*] Now let's talk a bit more.

› ALLMERS [*breathes audibly*]. It was good to have the pain of grief stilled for a moment.

ASTA. You must do that, Alfred.

ALLMERS. But don't you think of me as being terribly weak-willed— that I *can* do it?

ASTA. Oh, no! It's impossible for the mind to go circling endlessly round the one thing.

ALLMERS. Certainly, it's impossible for me. Before you came down, I sat here torturing myself with this crushing, gnawing grief. . . .

ASTA. Yes?

ALLMERS. Then would you believe it, Asta . . . ? Then . . .

ASTA. Well?

ALLMERS. In the middle of my torment I suddenly found myself trying to guess what we'd have for dinner today.

ASTA [*soothingly*]. Anything that brings respite . . .

ALLMERS. You know . . . I felt it did bring a kind of respite. [*Holds out his hand to her across the table.*] How good it is I have you, Asta. It makes me very happy. Happy, happy . . . in the midst of grief.

ASTA [*looks earnestly at him*]. Above all you should be happy that you have Rita.

ALLMERS. Yes, of course. That doesn't need saying. But Rita is not a blood relation. It's not like having a sister.

ASTA [*tense*]. You believe that, Alfred?

ALLMERS. Yes. *Our* family is different. [*Half in jest.*] We've always had our names beginning with a vowel. Remember how we often used to talk about it? And our relations . . . are all equally poor. And we all have the same eyes.

ASTA. Do you think I have, too?

ALLMERS. No, *you* take after your mother. You don't resemble the rest of us. Not even Father. And yet . . .

ASTA. And yet . . . ?

ALLMERS. I do believe that our life together has stamped each of us with the other's image. Our minds, I mean.

ASTA [*deeply moved*]. No, you can't say that, Alfred. I, and I alone, have taken from you. I owe everything to you . . . everything of any value.

ALLMERS [*shakes his head*]. You owe me nothing, Asta. On the contrary . . .

ASTA. I owe you everything! You must be able to see that! No sacrifice was too great for you. . . .

ALLMERS [*interrupts*]. Sacrifice! Don't talk nonsense. . . . I have simply loved you, Asta. Ever since you were a little child. [*After a short pause.*] Besides, I always felt I had to make amends for all the wrongs you had suffered.

ASTA [*astonished*]. Wrongs? From you?

ALLMERS. Not exactly from me. But . . .

ASTA [*tense*]. But . . .

ALLMERS. From Father.

ASTA [*half rises from the bench*]. Father! [*Sits down again.*] What do you mean by that, Alfred?

ALLMERS. Father was never very kind to you.

ASTA [*vehemently*]. You mustn't say that!

ALLMERS. It's true. He did not love you. Not as he should have done.

ASTA [*evasively*]. Perhaps not as much as he loved you. But that was natural.

ALLMERS [*persists*]. He was often very hard to your mother, too. At least in later years.

ASTA [*in a low voice*]. Mother was so very much younger than he was. You have to remember that.

ALLMERS. Don't you think they were suited to each other?

ASTA. Perhaps not.

ALLMERS. And yet . . . Father was always gentle and warm-hearted to other people . . . so kind to everybody. . . .

ASTA [*quietly*]. But neither was Mother always what she should have been.

ALLMERS. Your mother!

ASTA. Perhaps not always.

ALLMERS. To Father, you mean?

ASTA. Yes.

ALLMERS. I never noticed anything.

ASTA [*fighting her tears, gets up*]. Oh, Alfred dear . . . let the departed rest in peace.

[*She crosses, right.*]

ALLMERS [*gets up*]. Yes, let them rest. [*Wrings his hands.*] But the dead give us no peace, Asta. Neither by night nor by day.

ASTA [*looks sympathetically at him*]. Things will become easier with time, Alfred.

ALLMERS [*looks helplessly at her*]. You believe that, too? But how I am to survive these first terrible days . . . [*Vehemently.*] I don't understand.

ASTA [*pleadingly, puts her hands on his shoulders*]. Go to Rita, I beg you.

ALLMERS [*vehemently, pulling himself away*]. No, no! Don't talk to me about that! I can't, you see. [*Calmer.*] Let me stay here with you.

ASTA. Very well. I won't leave you.

ALLMERS [*seizes her hand and holds it fast*]. Thank you! [*He looks out for a while over the fjord.*] Where is my little Eyolf now? [*Smiles sadly at her.*] Can you tell me that—you, my big, wise Eyolf? [*Shakes his head.*] Nobody in the whole wide world can tell me that. I know only the one terrible truth: that I no longer have him.

ASTA [*looks up, left, and withdraws her hand*]. Here they come.

[RITA ALLMERS *and* BORGHEJM *come walking down the path. She is dressed in dark clothes, with a black veil over her face. He has an umbrella under his arm.*]

ALLMERS [*goes over to meet her*]. How are you, Rita?

RITA [*walks past him*]. Don't ask me.

ALLMERS. What are you doing here?

RITA. Looking for you. What are you doing?

ALLMERS. Nothing. Asta came down to join me.

RITA. But what about before Asta came? You've been away from me the whole morning.

ALLMERS. I've been sitting here looking out over the water.

RITA. Uh . . . how can you!

ALLMERS [*impatiently*]. I prefer to be alone now.

RITA [*walks about restlessly*]. Just sitting! Always at the same spot!

ALLMERS. There is absolutely nothing else for me to do.

RITA. I can't bear it anywhere. Least of all here . . . where the fjord comes right in.

ALLMERS. It's precisely because the fjord is so close.

RITA [*to* BORGHEJM]. Don't you think he should come up with the rest of us?

BORGHEJM [*to* ALLMERS]. I think it would be better for you.

ALLMERS. No, no. Let me stay where I am.

RITA. Then I'll stay with you, Alfred.

ALLMERS. As you please.—You stay too, Asta.

ASTA [*whispers to* BORGHEJM]. Let us leave them alone!

BORGHEJM [*with an understanding glance*]. Miss Allmers, shall we take a little walk . . . along the shore? For the very last time?

ASTA [*takes her umbrella*]. Yes, let's walk. Come.

> [ASTA *and* BORGHEJM *go out together behind the boathouse.* ALLMERS *walks about for a little; then he sits down on a rock under the trees in the foreground, left.*]

RITA [*approaches and stands in front of him, her hands clasped low in front of her*]. Alfred, can you bring yourself to believe . . . that we have lost Eyolf?

ALLMERS [*with a look of sadness*]. We shall have to get used to the thought.

RITA. I cannot. I cannot. That dreadful sight—it will remain with me as long as I live.

ALLMERS [*looks up*]. What sight? What did you see?

RITA. I didn't see it myself. I only heard about it. Oh!

ALLMERS. You'd better tell me.

RITA. I got Borghejm to come down with me to the jetty . . .

ALLMERS. What did you want there?

RITA. To question the boys about what happened.

ALLMERS. We know.

RITA. We found out more.

ALLMERS. Well?

RITA. It isn't true that he disappeared at once.

ALLMERS. Is that what they say now?

RITA. Yes. They say they saw him lying on the bottom. Deep down in the clear water.

ALLMERS [*bitterly*]. And they didn't save him?

RITA. I suppose they couldn't.

ALLMERS. They can swim. All of them. Did they say anything about how he was lying when they saw him?

RITA. Yes. They said he was lying on his back. With his eyes wide open.

ALLMERS. His eyes open. But quite still?

RITA. Yes, quite still. Then something came and took him out to sea. They called it the undercurrent.

ALLMERS [*nods slowly*]. And that was the last they saw of him?

RITA [*sobbing*]. Yes.

ALLMERS [*in a dull voice*]. And no one will ever . . . ever see him again.

RITA [*moaning*]. Night and day I shall see him lying there.

ALLMERS. With those big open eyes.

RITA [*shudders*]. With those big open eyes, yes. I can see them! I can see them so clearly!

ALLMERS [*slowly rises and looks quietly and threateningly at her*]. Were they evil, those eyes, Rita?

RITA [*turns pale*]. Evil?

ALLMERS [*goes close up to her*]. Were they evil eyes staring up from the depths?

RITA [*shrinks back*]. Alfred!

ALLMERS [*follows her*]. Answer me! Were the child's eyes evil?

RITA [*screams*]. Alfred! Alfred!

ALLMERS. Now we've got things . . . the way you wanted, Rita.

RITA. I? What did I want?

ALLMERS. Eyolf out of the way.

RITA. Never in my life did I want that! I didn't want him to stand between us, yes . . . but . . .

ALLMERS. Well . . . he won't do that any more.

RITA [*in a low voice, to herself*]. Now perhaps more than ever. [*Shudders.*] Oh, that dreadful sight!

ALLMERS [*nods*]. The evil eye of the child, yes.

RITA [*shrinks back, fearfully*]. Let me be, Alfred! You frighten me! I've never seen you like this before.

ALLMERS [*gives her a cold hard look*]. Grief brings pain and evil.

RITA [*frightened but still defiant*]. I feel the same.

[ALLMERS *crosses to the right and looks out over the fjord.* RITA *sits down at the table. Short pause.*]

ALLMERS [*turns his head towards her*]. You never really loved him. Not whole-heartedly. Never!

RITA [*cold and controlled*]. Eyolf would never whole-heartedly give himself to me.

ALLMERS. Because you wouldn't have it.

RITA. Yes, I would. I would so dearly. But somebody stood between us. Right from the beginning.

ALLMERS [*turns round*]. You mean *I* stood between you?

RITA. No. Not in the beginning.

ALLMERS [*goes closer*]. Who then?

RITA. His aunt.

ALLMERS. Asta?

RITA. Yes. Asta stood barring my way.

ALLMERS. You believe that, Rita?

RITA. Yes. Asta—she possessed him. Right from the time it happened . . . the accident.

ALLMERS. If she did, she did it from love.

RITA [*vehemently*]. Exactly. And I won't stand sharing with anyone! Not in love!

ALLMERS. We two should have shared him . . . in love.

RITA [*looks at him in scorn*]. We? You didn't ever really love him either, you know.

ALLMERS [*looks at her in astonishment*]. *I* never loved him!

RITA. No, you didn't. In the first place you were completely taken up by your book . . . on responsibility.

ALLMERS [*with emphasis*]. Yes, I was. But then I deliberately gave it up . . . for Eyolf's sake.

RITA. Not because you loved him.

ALLMERS. Why else then?

RITA. Because you were consumed by a lack of faith in yourself. Because you had begun to have doubts about this great mission you were giving your life to.

ALLMERS [*searchingly*]. Could you see the signs of this in me?

RITA. Oh, yes . . . gradually. Then you needed to find something new to give you satisfaction. . . . Clearly I wasn't enough any longer.

ALLMERS. Such is the law of change, Rita.

RITA. And this is why you wanted to make a child prodigy out of poor little Eyolf.

ALLMERS. I didn't. I wanted to make him happy. That's all.

RITA. But not because you loved him. Look inside yourself! [*With some embarrassment.*] And examine carefully all those things lying under . . . and behind . . . the surface.

ALLMERS [*avoids her eyes*]. You are avoiding something.

RITA. You too.

ALLMERS [*looks thoughtfully at her*]. If what you think is right, our own child never really belonged to us.

RITA. No. There was no real love.

ALLMERS. Yet here we are bitterly mourning his death.

RITA [*bitterly*]. Yes. Curious, when you think about it. That here we are mourning a little stranger boy.

ALLMERS [*bursts out*]. You mustn't call him a stranger!

RITA [*sadly shakes her head*]. We never won his love, Alfred. I didn't. Nor did you.

ALLMERS [*wringing his hands*]. And now it's too late! Too late!

RITA. It's so desolate . . . everything.

ALLMERS [*with sudden vehemence*]. You are the guilty one in this!

RITA [*rising*]. I?

ALLMERS. Yes, you. You are to blame for his being . . . the way he was. You are to blame for his not being able to save himself in the water.

RITA [*defensively*]. Alfred . . . you mustn't blame *me* for that!

ALLMERS [*more and more out of control*]. I do! I do! It was you who left that little baby on the table unattended.

RITA. He was lying so comfortably on the cushions. Sleeping so soundly. And you had promised to keep an eye on him.

ALLMERS. Yes, I had. [*Lowers his voice.*] Then you came . . . and tempted me to come to you.

RITA [*looks at him defiantly*]. Why don't you say you forgot all about the child, and everything else.

ALLMERS [*with suppressed fury*]. Yes, that's right. [*Lowers his voice.*] I forgot the child . . . in your arms.

RITA [*agitated*]. Alfred! Alfred! That's disgusting of you!

ALLMERS [*in a low voice, raising his fist to her*]. In that moment you condemned little Eyolf to death.

RITA [*wildly*]. You too! You too! In that case!

ALLMERS. Very well. Bring me to account, if you will. We are both guilty. So there was retribution in Eyolf's death, after all.

RITA. Retribution?

ALLMERS [*more controlled*]. Yes. A judgement on you and me. Now we have our deserts. Secret and cowardly feelings of remorse held us back from him while he was alive. We could not bear to look at the thing . . . he dragged himself about on. . . .

RITA [*quietly*]. The crutch.

ALLMERS. Exactly. And what we are now calling our grief, our loss, is merely the gnawing of our consciences. Nothing more.

RITA [*stares at him helplessly*]. I feel this can only lead us to despair . . . to madness, even. We can never make good what we have done.

ALLMERS [*in quieter mood*]. I dreamed of Eyolf last night. I thought I saw him coming up from the jetty! He could run, like other boys. As if nothing had happened to him. Absolutely nothing. This crushing reality was only a dream, I thought. Oh, how I thanked and praised . . . [*Stops.*] Hm. . . .

RITA [*looks at him*]. Whom?

ALLMERS [*evasively*]. Whom?

RITA. Yes. Whom did you thank and praise?

ALLMERS [*dismissively*]. I told you, I just lay there dreaming . . .

RITA. Somebody you don't yourself believe in?

ALLMERS. Just that something came over me. I told you, I was asleep. . . .

RITA [*reproachfully*]. You shouldn't have turned me into an unbeliever, Alfred.

ALLMERS. Would it have been right of me to let you go through life with a lot of empty illusions?

RITA. It would have been better for me. I'd have had somewhere to turn for comfort. Now I don't know where I am.

ALLMERS [*looks at her sharply*]. If you now had a choice . . . ? If you could follow Eyolf to where he is now . . . ?

RITA. Yes? What?

ALLMERS. . . . In absolute assurance that you would find him again . . . know him again . . . understand him . . . ?

RITA. Yes? Yes? What then?

ALLMERS. Would you be willing to take the leap to join him? Be willing to leave all this behind? Renounce all earthly life? Would you, Rita?

RITA [*in a low voice*]. Now? At this moment?

ALLMERS. Yes, now. Today. Within the hour. Answer me. Would you?

RITA [*hesitantly*]. Oh, I don't know, Alfred. . . . No. I think I'd want to remain here with you for a while.

ALLMERS. For my sake?

RITA. Yes. Only for your sake.

ALLMERS. And afterwards? Would you? Answer me.

RITA. Oh, what am I to say? You know I couldn't leave you. Never! Never!

ALLMERS. But suppose I were to join Eyolf? And you had absolute assurance that you would meet both him and me there. Would you come over to join us?

RITA. I should want to. So very much! Very much! But . . .

ALLMERS. Well?

RITA [*moans softly*]. I couldn't do it. I don't think. No, I absolutely couldn't. Not for all the glory of heaven.

ALLMERS. Neither could I.

RITA. No, Alfred! You couldn't either, could you!

ALLMERS. No. This earthly life is where we—the living—belong.

RITA. Yes. Here is the kind of happiness we understand.

ALLMERS [*gloomily*]. Oh, happiness . . . happiness.

RITA. You mean happiness . . . is something we shall never find again? [*Looks questioningly at him.*] But supposing . . . ? No, I daren't say it! Daren't even think it.

ALLMERS. Say it. Say it, Rita.

RITA [*hesitantly*]. Couldn't we try to . . . ? Might it not be possible to forget him?

ALLMERS. Forget Eyolf.

RITA. Forget our remorse. Forget our guilt, I mean.

ALLMERS. Would you wish that?

RITA. Yes. If it could be done. [*Bursts out.*] I can't bear things as they are much longer! Oh, can't we think of something that would let us forget!

ALLMERS [*shakes his head*]. What could that be?

RITA. Couldn't we try going away? Far away.

ALLMERS. Away from home? You know you can never thrive anywhere else but here.

RITA. Well, then, have lots of people here. Entertain a lot. Throw ourselves into something which might deaden and dull . . .

ALLMERS. That life is not for me. No, I'd rather try to take up my work again.

RITA [*caustically*]. Your work? Which has so often stood like a wall between us?

ALLMERS [*slowly, looking fixedly at her*]. There must always be a wall between us from now on.

RITA. Why must there . . . ?

ALLMERS. Who knows whether a child's eyes, opened wide, will not watch us night and day.

RITA [*in a low voice, shuddering*]. Alfred . . . it's too terrible to think!

ALLMERS. Our love has been a consuming fire. Now it must be extinguished. . . .

RITA [*faces him*]. Extinguished!

ALLMERS [*in a hard voice*]. It *is* extinguished . . . in one of us.

RITA [*as though turned to stone*]. You dare say that to me!

ALLMERS [*gentler*]. It is dead, Rita. And yet, in my feelings for you now— feelings born of a sense of shared guilt and remorse—I seem to glimpse a kind of resurrection. . . .

RITA [*violently*]. Oh, what do I care about resurrection!

ALLMERS. Rita!

G1

RITA. I am a creature of flesh and blood! I'm not one of your impassive kind that walk about with fish's blood in their veins. [*Wrings her hands.*] Why should I be shut away for life . . . a prisoner of guilt and remorse. Shut up with a man who is no longer mine, mine, mine!

ALLMERS. It would have to end like that some time, Rita.

RITA. End like that! When the beginning was that deep love we had for each other.

ALLMERS. My love for you was not at first very deep.

RITA. What did you feel at first.

ALLMERS. Terror.

RITA. That I can understand. So how did I win you in the end?

ALLMERS [*subdued*]. You were so devastatingly lovely, Rita.

RITA [*looks questioningly at him*]. Is that all? Answer me, Alfred! Was that the only thing?

ALLMERS [*with an effort*]. No. There was something else as well.

RITA [*agitatedly*]. I can guess what it was! It was 'the gold and the green forests', as you called them. Isn't that right, Alfred?

ALLMERS. Yes.

RITA [*looks utterly reproachfully at him*]. How could you! How could you!

ALLMERS. I had Asta to think of.

RITA [*vehemently*]. Asta, yes! [*Bitterly.*] So it was Asta who brought us together.

ALLMERS. She knew nothing. Even today she doesn't suspect.

RITA [*with a gesture of repudiation*]. Nevertheless it was Asta. [*Smiles and gives a scornful glance.*] No. It was little Eyolf. Little Eyolf, Alfred!

ALLMERS. Eyolf?

RITA. You used to call her Eyolf, didn't you? I think you once told me that . . . in an intimate moment. [*Comes nearer.*] You remember that 'devastatingly lovely' moment, Alfred?

ALLMERS [*shrinks back in terror*]. I remember nothing! I don't want to remember!

RITA [*follows him*]. It was the moment . . . your second little Eyolf became a cripple.

ALLMERS [*supports himself against the table; dully*]. Retribution.

RITA [*menacingly*]. Yes. Retribution.

[ASTA *and* BORGHEJM *return past the boathouse. She carries some water-lilies in her hand.*]

RITA [*controlled*]. Well, Asta . . . have you and Mr. Borghejm had a nice long talk together?

ASTA. Oh, yes . . . more or less.

[*She puts her umbrella down and puts the flowers on a chair.*]

BORGHEJM. Miss Allmers has been rather silent during our walk.

RITA. Has she? Well, Alfred and I have said enough to each other . . .

ASTA [*looks tensely at them both*]. Yes?

RITA. . . . To last us for life. [*Changing the subject.*] Come now, let's all go up to the house. We need company from now on. Alfred and I cannot manage alone.

ALLMERS. You two go on ahead. [*Turns.*] But I must have a word with you first, Asta.

RITA [*looks at him*]. Oh? Very well, you come with me, Mr. Borghejm.

[RITA *and* BORGHEJM *go out along the forest path.*]

ASTA [*anxiously*]. Alfred, what's happening?

ALLMERS [*gloomily*]. I can't bear it here any longer.

ASTA. Here? You mean with Rita?

ALLMERS. Yes. Rita and I cannot go on living together.

ASTA [*shakes his arm*]. Alfred, you mustn't say such terrible things.

ALLMERS. What I say is true. All we do is bring pain and evil to each other.

ASTA [*painfully moved*]. Oh, I'd never . . . never have imagined anything like this!

ALLMERS. I hadn't realized it until today.

ASTA. And now you want to . . . What is it you really want, Alfred?

ALLMERS. I want to get away from it all. Far away from everything.

ASTA. To be quite alone?

ALLMERS [*nods*]. Yes, as before.

ASTA. But you are not made for living alone.

ALLMERS. Yes, I am. At least I was once.

ASTA. Once before, yes. But then you had me with you.

ALLMERS [*tries to take her hand*]. Yes. And it's you, Asta, I want to come home to again.

ASTA [*moves away*]. To me! No, no, Alfred! That's quite impossible.

ALLMERS [*looks at her gloomily*]. I suppose Borghejm is the obstacle?

ASTA [*eagerly*]. No, no, he isn't! You are wrong!

ALLMERS. Good. Then I'll come to you, my dear, dear sister. I must come back to you. Home to you so that I can be cleansed and purified from living with . . .

ASTA [*disturbed*]. Alfred . . . this is a sin against Rita!

ALLMERS. Yes, I have sinned against her. But not in this. Oh, think back, Asta! Think how we used to live together? Wasn't it like one long high day and holiday from beginning to end?

ASTA. Yes, it was, Alfred. But you can never live that over again.

ALLMERS [*bitterly*]. You mean marriage has spoilt me irretrievably?

ASTA [*calmly*]. No. That's not what I mean.

ALLMERS. So why don't we live our past life over again.

ASTA [*firmly*]. We cannot do that, Alfred.

ALLMERS. Yes we can. Because the love between brother and sister . . .

ASTA [*tense*]. Well?

ALLMERS. That is one relationship which is not subject to the law of change.

ASTA [*in a low trembling voice*]. But what if that relationship happens not to be . . .

ALLMERS. Not . . . ?

ASTA. Not to be *our* relationship?

ALLMERS [*looks at her in amazement*]. Not ours? My dear Asta, what do you mean?

ASTA. It is best I tell you straight, Alfred.

ALLMERS. Yes, yes, tell me!

ASTA. Mother's letters . . . Those in the briefcase . . .

ALLMERS. Yes?

ASTA. You must read them . . . after I've left.

ALLMERS. Why must I?

ASTA [*fighting with herself*]. Then you'll see that . . .

ALLMERS. Well?

ASTA. . . . That I have no right . . . to bear your father's name.

ALLMERS [*reels back*]. Asta! What are you saying!

ASTA. Read the letters. Then you'll see. And understand. And perhaps forgive . . . Mother, too.

ALLMERS [*clasps his head*]. I can't comprehend it. Can't credit it. Asta! You are saying you are not . . .

ASTA. You are not my brother, Alfred.

ALLMERS [*quickly, half defiantly, looks at her*]. But what change does that make to our relationship? None at all.

ASTA [*shakes her head*]. It changes everything, Alfred. Our relationship is not that of brother and sister.

ALLMERS. Maybe not. But is equally sacred. Will always be sacred.

ASTA. Remember . . . it is subject to the law of change . . . as you said a moment ago.

ALLMERS [*looks searchingly at her*]. By that you mean . . . ?

ASTA [*quietly, with emotion*]. Not another word ... my dear, dear Alfred. [*She picks up the flowers from the chair.*] You see these water-lilies?

ALLMERS [*nods slowly*]. They are the kind that grow up to the surface ... from deep down below.

ASTA. I gathered them from the lake. Where it flows out into the fjord. [*Holds them out.*] Would you like them, Alfred?

ALLMERS [*takes them*]. Thanks!

ASTA [*with tears in her eyes*]. They are like a final greeting to you ... from little Eyolf.

ALLMERS [*looks at her*]. From Eyolf out there? Or from you?

ASTA [*quietly*]. From us both. [*She picks up her umbrella*]. Come now. Let's join Rita.

[*She goes up the path.*]

ALLMERS [*takes his hat from the table, and whispers sadly*]. Asta. Eyolf, Little Eyolf. ... !

[*He follows her up the path.*]

ACT THREE

A shrub-covered rise in ALLMERS' *garden. In the background a sheer drop, with railings at the edge, and steps leading down, left. Distant views over the fjord which lies far below. By the railings stands a flagpole, with ropes but no flag. In the foreground, right, is a summerhouse, covered with creeper and wild vine. Outside it stands a bench. It is late on a summer evening, with a clear sky. It is beginning to grow dark.*

ASTA *is sitting on the bench with her hands in her lap. She is wearing outdoor clothes and hat; her parasol is by her side, and she has a small travelling bag slung by a strap over her shoulder.*

BORGHEJM *comes into view in the background, left. He also has a travelling bag slung over his shoulder. Over his arm he carries a rolled-up flag.*

BORGHEJM [*catches sight of* ASTA]. Ah, so this is where you are.

ASTA. I'm sitting taking a last look out over the fjord.

BORGHEJM. Good thing I thought of looking up here too, then.

ASTA. Have you been looking for me?

BORGHEJM. Yes, I have. I wanted to say goodbye to you—goodbye for the time being. Not for good, I hope.

ASTA [*with a faint smile*]. You are persistent.

BORGHEJM. A road-builder has to be.

ASTA. Did you see anything of Alfred? Or Rita?

BORGHEJM. Yes, I saw them both.

ASTA. Together?

BORGHEJM. No. They are keeping to themselves.

ASTA. What are you going to do with the flag?

BORGHEJM. Mrs. Allmers asked me to come up and hoist it.

ASTA. Fly a flag—now?

BORGHEJM. At half-mast. She said it was to hang there night and day.

ASTA [*sighs*]. Poor Rita. And poor Alfred.

BORGHEJM [*busy with the flag*]. Have you the heart to leave them? I ask because I see you are dressed for a journey.

ASTA [*in a low voice*]. I must go.

BORGHEJM. Well, if you *must*, you . . .

ASTA. And you are leaving tonight, too.

BORGHEJM. I must go, too. I'm taking the train. Are you?

ASTA. No. I'm catching the steamer.

BORGHEJM [*glances at her*]. Different ways, then?

ASTA. Yes.

[*She sits watching as he hoists the flag to half-mast. When he is finished, he walks over to her.*]

BORGHEJM. Miss Asta . . . I can't tell you how grieved I am at little Eyolf's death.

ASTA [*looks up at him*]. Yes, I'm sure you are.

BORGHEJM. I find it very painful. Grieving doesn't come easily to me.

ASTA [*turns her eyes towards the flag*]. It will all pass over in time. All these sorrows.

BORGHEJM. All? You think so?

ASTA. Like a rain shower. As soon as you are well away from here . . .

BORGHEJM. It will have to be pretty far away.

ASTA. And you'll also have that big new road to work on.

BORGHEJM. But nobody to help me in it.

ASTA. Oh yes. Of course you will.

BORGHEJM [*shakes his head*]. Nobody. Nobody to share in the joy of it. It's the joy of it that matters most.

ASTA. Not all the toil and trouble?

BORGHEJM. Puh! You can pretty well always cope with that alone.

ASTA. But joy . . . is something that must be shared, you think?

BORGHEJM. Yes. Otherwise what pleasure would there be in being glad?

ASTA. Perhaps there's something in that.

BORGHEJM. Of course it's possible to feel inwardly happy for a while. But it cannot last. Real happiness takes two people.

ASTA. Always two? Never more? Never several people?

BORGHEJM. Ah . . . that would be something different. Miss Asta . . . couldn't you bring yourself to share the joy and happiness of life . . . and its toil and trouble . . . with one person, one person alone?

ASTA. I have tried it—once.

BORGHEJM. Have you?

ASTA. Yes. All those years when my brother . . . when Alfred and I lived together.

BORGHEJM. Ah yes, with your brother. That's something rather different. I think that might be called peace rather than happiness.

ASTA. Whatever it was, it was lovely.

BORGHEJM. You see! Already you think even that was lovely. But suppose . . . he hadn't been your brother!

ASTA [*begins to rise, but then remains sitting*]. In that case we'd never have lived together. For I was a child at the time. And he very little more.

BORGHEJM [*after a moment*]. Were they so lovely . . . those years?

ASTA. Oh, they were. Believe me.

BORGHEJM. And during that time you knew real happiness, real joy?

ASTA. Oh yes, so many times. Incredibly.

BORGHEJM. Tell me about them, Miss Asta.

ASTA. They were only little things, in the main.

BORGHEJM. Such as . . . ? Well?

ASTA. Such as the time Alfred passed his exams. And he'd done well. And when, as time went by, he got a job at this or that school. Or when he sat writing his thesis. And read it out to me. And then he got it printed in a periodical.

BORGHEJM. Yes, I can see it must have been a lovely peaceful life. A brother and sister sharing their happiness. [*Shakes his head.*] I can't understand how your brother came to let you go, Asta!

ASTA [*controlling her emotion*]. Alfred got married.

BORGHEJM. Didn't that make things difficult for you?

ASTA. Yes, to begin with. I thought it meant I'd completely lost him.

BORGHEJM. Fortunately you hadn't.

ASTA. No.

BORGHEJM. All the same—how could he? Marry, I mean. When he might have kept you all to himself!

ASTA [*staring vacantly*]. I suppose he was subject to the law of change.

BORGHEJM. The law of change?

ASTA. That's what Alfred calls it.

BORGHEJM. Pah! A stupid law that must be! I don't believe in it for a moment.

ASTA [*gets up*]. You might come to believe in it with time.

BORGHEJM. Never! [*Urgently.*] But listen to me, Miss Asta! Be sensible . . . for once. I mean, in this respect . . .

ASTA [*interrupts*]. Oh, please! Let's not start on *that* again!

BORGHEJM [*continues*]. Yes, Asta. I can't let you go as easily as that. Your brother has things now the way he always wanted them. Living quite contentedly without you. Not really missing you. And now *this* . . . this thing that immediately changes your whole position out here. . . .

ASTA [*starts*]. What do you mean?

BORGHEJM. The death of this child. What else?

ASTA [*composing herself*]. Little Eyolf . . . gone. Yes.

BORGHEJM. So what more is there for you to do here? There's no longer any poor little boy for you to look after. No duties . . . no obligations of any kind. . . .

ASTA. Oh, Mr. Borghejm, I beg you! Please don't try to force me!

BORGHEJM. I will. I'd be mad not to try desperate measures. One of these days I'll be leaving town. Might not even see you there. Might not see you again for many many years. And who knows what might happen in the meantime?

ASTA [*smiles seriously*]. Are you afraid of the law of change after all?

BORGHEJM. No, not at all. [*Laughs bitterly.*] There isn't even anything to change. Not in you, I mean. I can see you don't care very much about me.

ASTA. You know very well I do.

BORGHEJM. But not nearly enough. Not as I would like. [*More vehemently.*] Dear God, Asta . . . Miss Asta . . . can't you see the mistake you are making! It's incredible! Beyond today and tomorrow a whole lifetime of happiness may be lying waiting for us. Are we just going to let it lie there! Isn't that something we are going to regret, Asta?

ASTA [*quietly*]. I don't know. All I know is we must leave all such bright prospects lying there.

BORGHEJM [*controls himself, looks at her*]. So I am to build my roads alone?

ASTA [*warmly*]. Oh, if only I could be there with you! Help you in times of trouble. Share the joy of it with you . . .

BORGHEJM. Would you . . . if you could?

ASTA. Yes. I would.

BORGHEJM. But you can't?

ASTA [*looks down*]. Would you be content with one half of me?

BORGHEJM. No. I must have all of you.

ASTA [*looks at him and says softly*]. Then I cannot.

BORGHEJM. Goodbye then, Miss Asta.

[*He is about to go.* ALLMERS *climbs the rise in the background, left.* BORGHEJM *pauses.*]

ALLMERS [*still by the steps, points across and says in a low voice*]. Is Rita over there in the summerhouse?

BORGHEJM. No. There's nobody here but Miss Asta.

[ALLMERS *comes forward.*]

ASTA [*goes toward him*]. Shall I go down and look for her? Get her to come up here, perhaps?

ALLMERS [*with a dismissive gesture*]. No, no, no ... leave it. [*To* BORGHEJM.] Was it you who hoisted the flag?

BORGHEJM. Yes. Your wife asked me to. That's why I came up here.

ALLMERS. And tonight you are leaving?

BORGHEJM. Yes. Tonight. I really am leaving.

ALLMERS [*with a glance at* ASTA]. And assured yourself of a good travelling companion, I take it?

BORGHEJM [*shakes his head*]. I am travelling alone.

ALLMERS [*starts*]. Alone!

BORGHEJM. Quite alone.

ALLMERS [*abstractedly*]. Oh?

BORGHEJM. And will also remain alone.

ALLMERS. There is something terrifying about being alone. It makes my blood run cold when ...

ASTA. But, Alfred, you are not alone!

ALLMERS. There's something terrifying about that, too, Asta.

ASTA [*anxiously*]. You mustn't speak like that! Mustn't think like that!

ALLMERS [*does not listen to her*]. But if you are not going with ... If you have no ties ... why won't you stay out here with me ... and Rita?

ASTA [*uneasily*]. No, I can't do that. I must go back to town now.

ALLMERS. But only to town, Asta! You hear!

ASTA. Yes.

ALLMERS. Promise me you'll come out here again soon.

ASTA [*quickly*]. No, no. I can't promise it will be soon.

ALLMERS. Very well. As you wish. Then we'll meet in town.

ASTA [*pleadingly*]. But, Alfred, you must stay here with Rita now.

ALLMERS [*does not reply, turns to* BORGHEJM]. Perhaps it's for the best that you should be travelling unaccompanied.

BORGHEJM [*shortly*]. How can you say that!

ALLMERS. You never know whom you may not meet later. On the journey.

ASTA [*involuntarily*]. Alfred!

ALLMERS. The right travelling companion. When it's too late. Too late.

ASTA [*quietly, trembling*]. Alfred! Alfred!

BORGHEJM [*looks from one to the other*]. What does that mean? I don't understand. . . .

[RITA *comes up the slope in the background, left.*]

RITA [*plaintively*]. Please don't everybody leave me!

ASTA [*goes to meet her*]. You said you wanted to be alone . . .

RITA. Yes, but I daren't be. It's getting so horribly dark. I seem to see great wide-open eyes staring at me!

ASTA [*gently, sympathetically*]. What if they are, Rita? You shouldn't be afraid of those eyes.

RITA. How can you say that! Not afraid!

ALLMERS [*urgently*]. Asta, I beg you. Implore you. Stay here . . . with Rita!

RITA. Yes! And with Alfred, too! Please do, Asta!

ASTA [*fighting with herself*]. Oh! I would so very much like to . . .

RITA. Then do! Alfred and I cannot endure our grief, our loss, alone.

ALLMERS [*gloomily*]. Rather call it our gnawing torment.

RITA. Call it what you will—we cannot bear it alone. Oh, Asta, I do beg and implore you! Stay here and help us! Be what Eyolf was to us . . .

ASTA [*shrinks*]. Eyolf!

RITA. Shouldn't she do that, Alfred?

ALLMERS. If she can, and will.

RITA. You used to call her your little Eyolf once. [*Seizes her hand.*] From now on you shall be *our* Eyolf, Asta! Eyolf, as you were before.

ALLMERS [*concealing his emotion*]. Stay. And share your life with us, Asta. With Rita. With me. With me—your brother!

ASTA [*firmly, withdraws her hand*]. No. I cannot [*Turns.*] Borghejm, what time does the steamer leave?

BORGHEJM. Any minute now.

ASTA. Then I must get aboard. Will you come with me?

BORGHEJM [*with a subdued cry of joy*]. Will I . . . ! Yes, yes, yes!

ASTA. Come, then.

RITA [*slowly*]. Ah, that's how it is. In that case, you cannot stay here with us.

ASTA [*throws her arms round her neck*]. Thank you, Rita. For everything. [*Goes across to* ALLMERS *and grasps his hand.*] Goodbye, Alfred! And farewell!

ALLMERS [*quiet and tense*]. What is this, Asta? This looks like running away.

ASTA [*in quiet fear*]. Yes, Alfred—it *is* running away.

ALLMERS. Running away—from *me*?

ASTA [*whispers*]. From you—and from myself.

ALLMERS [*shrinks back*]. Ah!

[ASTA *hurries away, to the back.* BORGHEJM *waves his hat and follows her.* RITA *leans against the entrance to the summerhouse.* ALLMERS, *greatly agitated, goes to the railings and stands there, staring down. Pause.*]

ALLMERS [*turns and says with forced composure*]. Here's the steamer. Look, Rita.

RITA. I dare not look at it.

ALLMERS. Dare not?

RITA. No. Because it has a red eye. And a green one, too. Great glowing eyes.

ALLMERS. You know they are only the ship's lamps.

RITA. From now on they are eyes. For me they are. Staring out of the dark. And into the dark, too.

ALLMERS. Now it's coming in to tie up.

RITA. Where is it tying up tonight?

ALLMERS [*comes closer*]. At the jetty, as usual, my dear. . . .

RITA [*draws herself up*]. How *can* it tie up there!

ALLMERS. It must.

RITA. But it was there that Eyolf. . . . How can those people tie up there?

ALLMERS. Life is pitiless, Rita.

RITA. People are heartless. They pay no regard. Either to the living or to the dead.

ALLMERS. You are right. Life goes on, just as if nothing had happened.

RITA [*stares vacantly ahead*]. Nothing *has* happened. Not to other people. Only to you and me.

ALLMERS [*with quickening pain*]. Yes, Rita. What use was it your ever having borne him—with all that pain and suffering. For now he is gone—leaving no trace.

RITA. Only the crutch was saved.

ALLMERS [*vehemently*]. Be quiet! I don't want to hear that word!

RITA [*plaintively*]. Oh, I can't bear the thought that we no longer have him.

ALLMERS [*cold and bitter*]. You could do without him easily enough while he was there. Often the greater part of the day would go without your even seeing him.

RITA. Because I knew I could see him any time I wanted.

ALLMERS. Yes. That's the way we wasted our few brief years with little Eyolf.

RITA [*listens in fear*]. Listen, Alfred! That ringing! Again!

ALLMERS [*looks out over the fjord*]. It's the ship's bell. It's about to leave.

RITA. It's not that bell I mean. It's been ringing in my ears all day. Now it's ringing again!

ALLMERS [*goes to her*]. You are mistaken, Rita.

RITA. No. I can hear it so clearly. It sounds like a death knell. Slowly. Slowly. And always the same words.

ALLMERS. Words? What words?

RITA [*nods in rhythm*]. 'The crutch—is—float—ing. The—crutch—is— float—ing.' Surely you can hear it?

ALLMERS [*shakes his head*]. I hear nothing. There *is* nothing.

RITA. Say what you like. I can hear it so clearly.

ALLMERS [*looks over the railings*]. Now they are aboard, Rita. The ship is now on its way to town.

RITA. Can you really not hear it? 'The—crutch—is—float—ing, the— crutch— . . .'

ALLMERS [*comes closer*]. You mustn't stand here listening to something that doesn't exist. I am saying that Asta and Borghejm are now aboard. Already on their way. Asta is gone.

RITA [*looks at him timidly*]. Does that mean you'll soon be gone, too, Alfred?

ALLMERS [*quickly*]. What do you mean?

RITA. That you'll be following your sister.

ALLMERS. Has Asta said something?

RITA. No. But you said yourself that it was for Asta's sake . . . we came together.

ALLMERS. Yes, but you yourself bound me to you. By our life together.

RITA. Ah, but in your eyes I am not . . . not so 'devastatingly beautiful' any longer.

ALLMERS. Perhaps the law of change might nevertheless hold us together.

RITA [*nods slowly*]. A change *is* taking place in me. I can feel the pain of it.

ALLMERS. Pain?

RITA. Yes. Almost like giving birth.

ALLMERS. That's what it is. Or a resurrection. A transition to a higher life.

RITA [*stares dispiritedly ahead*]. Yes . . . and with it the loss of all life's happiness.

ALLMERS. In that loss is our gain.

RITA [*vehemently*]. Empty phrases! In God's name, we are still human. Creatures of the earth.

ALLMERS. But with some kinship to sea and sky, too, Rita.

RITA. You perhaps. Not I.

ALLMERS. Yes you have. More than you realize.

RITA [*takes a step nearer*]. Tell me, Alfred, couldn't you think of taking up your work again?

ALLMERS. That work you hated.

RITA. I am more amenable now. I am willing to share you with your book.

ALLMERS. Why?

RITA. Just to keep you here with me. Near me.

ALLMERS. Oh, I can be of little help to you, Rita.

RITA. But perhaps I could help you.

HI

ALLMERS. With the work, you mean?

RITA. No. With living.

ALLMERS [*shakes his head*]. I don't think I have any life left to live.

RITA. Then to *bear* life.

ALLMERS [*gloomily, almost to himself*]. I think it would be best for us both if we parted.

RITA [*looks questioningly at him*]. Where would you go? Perhaps to Asta? Despite all?

ALLMERS. No. Never to Asta. Not after this.

RITA. Where, then?

ALLMERS. Up to the solitude.

RITA. Up in the mountains? Is that what you mean?

ALLMERS. Yes.

RITA. But these are only day-dreams, Alfred! You could never live up there.

ALLMERS. Yet I feel myself drawn there.

RITA. Why? Tell me!

ALLMERS. Sit down. I want to tell you something.

RITA. Something that happened to you up there?

ALLMERS. Yes.

RITA. Something you kept from Asta and me.

ALLMERS. Yes.

RITA. How you do keep things to yourself. You shouldn't.

ALLMERS. Sit there, and I'll tell you about it.

RITA. Yes. Tell me.

[*She sits down on the bench by the summerhouse.*]

ALLMERS. I was alone up there. Right in among the high mountains. Then I came to a large desolate lake. This lake I had to get across. But I couldn't. There was no boat, and nobody about.

RITA. And then?

ALLMERS. So I struck off on my own up a side valley. Up there I thought I'd be able to make my way over the heights and between the peaks, and so down again on the other side of the lake.

RITA. And you lost your way, Alfred!

ALLMERS. Yes. I got my bearings wrong. There were no paths or tracks. I walked all that day. And the whole of the next night, too. In the end I thought I'd never find my way back to the land of the living.

RITA. Not back to us? I'm sure that's where your thoughts were.

ALLMERS. No, they weren't.

RITA. They weren't?

ALLMERS. No. It was very strange. Both you and Eyolf seemed to become utterly remote. Asta too.

RITA. So what did you think about?

ALLMERS. I didn't think. I clambered along the precipitous cliffs ... and enjoyed the peace and serenity that comes from the nearness of death.

RITA [*jumps up*]. Oh, don't use such words about this dreadful thing.

ALLMERS. That was how I felt. Absolutely no fear. I felt that Death and I walked side by side like two good travelling companions. It all seemed so reasonable ... so obvious at the time. People in my family don't usually live till they are old. . . .

RITA. Oh, please stop talking about these things, Alfred! You did come through all right, after all.

ALLMERS. Yes. Suddenly I was there. On the other side of the lake.

RITA. That was a night of terror for you, Alfred. But now it's all over, you won't admit it.

ALLMERS. That night brought me to a decision. I then turned round and came straight home. To Eyolf.

RITA [*quietly*]. Too late.

ALLMERS. Yes. And when that . . . travelling companion came and took him . . . it was then I felt utter loathing. For him. For the whole thing. For all this life—a life which, even so, we dare not quit. So completely earthbound are we, Rita, you and I.

RITA [*with some sign of joy*]. Yes, it's true! You feel that too. [*Comes closer.*] Oh, let us simply live our lives together—as long as we can.

ALLMERS [*shrugs his shoulders*]. Live? With nothing to fill one's life. It's all empty and barren, whichever way I look.

RITA [*fearfully*]. Oh, Alfred, sooner or later you will leave me! I feel it. I can see it in your face! You will leave me!

ALLMERS. With that travelling companion, you mean?

RITA. No. I mean something worse. Of your own free will you will leave me. Because you believe it's only here, with me, that you have nothing to live for. Answer me! Isn't that what you think.

ALLMERS [*looks fixedly at her*]. And if I do?

[*The sound of voices raised in anger can be heard far below.* ALLMERS *goes to the railings.*]

RITA. What is it? [*Breaks out.*] Ah, I know! They've found him.

ALLMERS. He will never be found.

RITA. What is it then?

ALLMERS [*comes forward*]. Just fighting and quarrelling. As usual.

RITA. Down by the waterfront.

ALLMERS. Yes. All that front ought to be cleared. The men have come home. Drunk, as they usually are. Beating the children. Listen to those boys yelling! And the women screaming for help. . . .

RITA. Shouldn't we get somebody to go down and help them?

ALLMERS [*hard and angry*]. Help them! When they did nothing to help Eyolf! Let them perish . . . the way they let Eyolf perish!

RITA. You mustn't talk like that, Alfred! Or even think like that!

ALLMERS. How can I think otherwise! All those old shacks ought to be pulled down.

RITA. Then what would all those poor people do?

ALLMERS. They can go somewhere else.

RITA. And the children?

ALLMERS. It doesn't much matter where they finish up.

RITA [*quietly, reproachfully*]. You are forcing yourself to be hard, Alfred.

ALLMERS [*vehemently*]. I've a right to be hard from now on! A duty!

RITA. A duty?

ALLMERS. My duty towards Eyolf. He must not lie unavenged. Make it quick, Rita! That's what I say. Think it over. Have the whole place razed to the ground—when I am gone.

RITA [*looks long at him*]. When you are gone?

ALLMERS. Then at least you'll have something to occupy your time. That you must have.

RITA [*firmly and decisively*]. You are right. I must. But can you guess what I'm going to do? When you've gone?

ALLMERS. No. What?

RITA [*slowly and deliberately*]. The moment you are gone, I shall go down to the waterfront and bring all those poor deprived children up to this house. All those uncouth boys . . .

ALLMERS. What will you do with them here?

RITA. I'm going to look after them.

ALLMERS. You what?

RITA. Yes, I am. The day you leave they'll all move in here—as if they were mine.

ALLMERS [*agitated*]. In our little Eyolf's place?

RITA. Yes, in little Eyolf's place. They shall live in Eyolf's room. Read his books. Play with his toys. Take turns at sitting in his place at table.

ALLMERS. But this is sheer madness! I can think of nobody—nobody at all—less suited to that kind of thing than you.

RITA. Then I shall have to rise to it. Teach myself to do it. Instruct myself. Train myself.

ALLMERS. If you are really serious about what you've just said, there certainly has been a change in you.

RITA. There has, Alfred. You have seen to that. You created a great emptiness within me. And I must try to fill it with something. Something perhaps resembling love.

ALLMERS [*stands for a moment in thought looking at her*]. In fact we haven't done much for those poor people down there.

RITA. We've done nothing for them.

ALLMERS. Hardly even given them a thought.

RITA. Never a sympathetic thought.

ALLMERS. We—with all 'our gold and our green forests'.

RITA. How tight-fisted we've been. And hard-hearted.

ALLMERS [*nods*]. Perhaps it wasn't altogether unreasonable that they wouldn't risk their lives to save little Eyolf.

RITA [*quietly*]. Ask yourself, Alfred. Are you quite certain . . . we would have risked our own?

ALLMERS [*uneasily*]. Rita! You don't doubt *that*!

RITA. Ah, we are but earthbound creatures, Alfred.

ALLMERS. What actually are you thinking of doing for all those neglected children?

RITA. I suppose in the first place to try to ease some of their hardship and better their chances in life.

ALLMERS. If you can do that, Eyolf will not have been born in vain.

RITA. Or been taken from us in vain.

ALLMERS [*looks intently at her*]. Just be clear about *one* thing, Rita. It is not love that leads you to do this.

RITA. No, it isn't. Not yet, anyway.

ALLMERS. So what is it?

RITA [*half evasively*]. You have often talked to Asta about human responsibility. . . .

ALLMERS. About the book you hated.

RITA. The book I still hate. But I sat and listened to you talking. And now I want to try and take things on from there myself. In *my* way.

ALLMERS [*shakes his head*]. Not for the sake of that unfinished book. . . .

RITA. No. I have another reason.

ALLMERS. What?

RITA [*quietly, with a sad smile*]. I want to win the approval of those big staring eyes.

ALLMERS [*struck, fastens his gaze on her*]. Perhaps I could join you? And help you, Rita?

RITA. Would you?

ALLMERS. Yes, if I thought I could.

RITA [*hesitantly*]. That would mean your staying here.

ALLMERS [*quietly*]. Let us try and make it work.

RITA [*scarcely audible*]. Let us do that, Alfred.

[*Both fall silent. Then* ALLMERS *goes over to the flagpole and hoists the flag to the top.* RITA *stands by the summerhouse quietly watching him.*]

ALLMERS [*comes over again*]. We have a strenuous working day ahead of us, Rita.

RITA. You will see. A Sunday calm will come over us now and then.

ALLMERS [*quietly, moved*]. Then we may perhaps sense the presence of spirits.

RITA [*whispers*]. Spirits?

ALLMERS [*as before*]. Yes. Perhaps they may visit us—those we have lost.

RITA [*nods slowly*]. Our little Eyolf. And your big Eyolf too.

ALLMERS [*staring straight ahead*]. Perhaps now and then, on life's way, we might catch a glimpse of them.

RITA. Where shall we look, Alfred?

ALLMERS [*gazes at her*]. Upwards.

RITA [*nods in agreement*]. Yes. Upwards.

ALLMERS. Up . . . towards the mountains. Towards the stars. Towards the vast silence.

RITA [*holds out her hand to him*]. Thank you.

FIRST COMPLETE DRAFT OF

LITTLE EYOLF

The manuscript that forms the basis of the following translation is described in Appendix I, 2, B1 (p. 311). It is not in every case easy to determine with any certainty which of the alterations to the MS. were made at the time of original composition, and which at a later revisionary stage. Nevertheless, an attempt has been made in the following version to reconstruct as far as possible the formulations that belonged to the earliest and unrevised stage of the draft. It must also be recognized that Ibsen may have made certain of the revisions which figure on the early pages of the MS. before turning to the work of drafting the later pages. As Appendix I makes clear, this version of the play is lacking its first folio, i.e. its title page, list of characters, and opening moments of dialogue. For changes in the names of the characters, see p. 314.

Yes, but that can only be good for him, surely.

RITA. You really believe that?

MRS. SKJOLDHEJM. I neither believe nor disbelieve. Hakon obviously understands such things best himself.

[HAKON SKJOLDHEJM *leading little* ALFRED *by the hand comes in through the door, left. He is a slim, slight figure, with a serious expression on his face. Thinning dark hair and beard.* ALFRED *is small, delicate and looks somewhat frail.*]

HAKON SKJOLDHEJM. Well, you out here, Rita?

RITA. Yes, I felt I had to. . . . Welcome home!

SKJOLDHEJM. Thank you.

MRS. SKJOLDHEJM. Doesn't he look splendid!

RITA. Marvellous. Absolutely marvellous. So lively about the eyes. You must have done a lot of writing on your trip. Perhaps the whole book is finished, Hakon?

SKJOLDHEJM. The book . . .?

RITA. I felt sure things would run easily if only you got away.

SKJOLDHEJM. In fact I haven't written a line of the book.

RITA. You haven't . . .!

MRS. SKJOLDHEJM. Aha! So that explains all the unused paper lying here in your case.

RITA. But, good Lord, what were you doing for those two months?

SKJOLDHEJM [*smiles*]. Only thinking, thinking, thinking.

MRS. SKJOLDHEJM [*putting her arm round his shoulder*]. Thinking a little of those who were waiting at home?

SKJOLDHEJM. Of course, as you might imagine. A great deal.

MRS. SKJOLDHEJM. Ah, how nice of you.

RITA. But not written anything of your book? Yet you look so happy ⟨and contented *crossed out*⟩. And so content with yourself. You don't usually. Not when work isn't going well, I mean.

SKJOLDHEJM. You're right. Because I was so stupid before, Rita. All that is best in one goes into thinking. What gets down on paper doesn't count for much.

RITA. Doesn't count for much!

MRS. SKJOLDHEJM. Oh, but Hakon . . . !

ALFRED. But it does, Father. What *you* write counts for a lot.

SKJOLDHEJM [*smiling, strokes his hair*]. Of course it does . . . if *you* say so. But believe me . . . somebody will come after me who will do it so much better.

ALFRED. Who can that be? Tell me!

SKJOLDHEJM. Give things time. He will surely come and make himself known. But next summer when I go to the mountains again, you shall come along with me, Alfred.

ALFRED. Shall I?

MRS. SKJOLDHEJM. Oh, shame, Hakon. Are you thinking of leaving me again!

RITA [*to* ALFRED]. Wouldn't you like to go along too, lad.

ALFRED [*dubiously*]. Oh yes—that I would. If it isn't very dangerous . . .

SKJOLDHEJM. Dangerous? How do you mean?

ALFRED. Well, might I not easily fall and dash myself to pieces?

SKJOLDHEJM [*decisively*]. The boy shall and must come with me into the mountains.

RITA. Then you must ask your father if you can learn to shoot, and hunt, and swim . . . and things like that. Wouldn't you like to do that, Alfred?

ALFRED. Yes, I would very much. Because as long as I'm just a little careful, then . . .

SKJOLDHEJM. Yes, you must certainly be that. But now you can run down into the garden and enjoy yourself.

ALFRED. Shall I not take some books with me?

SKJOLDHEJM. No, no. No books.

ALFRED. Then I'll just go down and amuse myself . . . [*He makes to go out on to the verandah, but stops and goes back.*] Oh, no . . . I daren't!

SKJOLDHEJM. Why daren't you?

ALFRED. Because Aunt Ellen is coming down there!

SKJOLDHEJM. Are *you* so afraid of her, too?

MRS. SKJOLDHEJM. What can she want here?

ALFRED. Father, do you think it's true that she's a werewolf by night?

SKJOLDHEJM. Oh, not at all. What gives you that idea?

ALFRED. Because I could well imagine it.

SKJOLDHEJM. She's gone through a lot. And she's become a bit peculiar. That's what it is.

[MISS VARG *comes up the steps to the verandah. She is old and grey-haired. Has sharp penetrating eyes. A little, thin, wizened creature. Mottled, old-fashioned dress. A black hood and black cape. She is carrying a large red umbrella and on her arm is a black bag.*]

MISS VARG. Good-day! Good-day, everybody! It is a long time since I set foot in here.

MRS. SKJOLDHEJM. Yes, it is a long time. Won't you sit down and rest a little?

MISS VARG. Yes, I will. Thanks. [*She sits down on a chair by the sofa.*] Because I've been out on my affairs. And I must go out again. And that takes toll of your strength.

SKJOLDHEJM. So you have been out this morning . . . ?

MISS VARG. Yes, over on Green Island. [*Laughs to herself.*] The people sent for me yesterday evening. They didn't much like doing it. But in the end they had to bite the sour apple. . . . [*Looks at* ALFRED *and nods.*] Sour apple, my lad. Sour apple.

ALFRED [*involuntarily, somewhat hesitantly*]. Why did they have to . . . ?

MISS VARG. What?

ALFRED. Bite it?

MISS VARG. Why, because they couldn't provide for themselves any more.

[ALFRED *looks uncertainly and questioningly up at his father.*]

SKJOLDHEJM. Why couldn't they provide for themselves?

MISS VARG. Because of rats and mice, you see.

ALFRED. Rats and . . . !

MRS. SKJOLDHEJM. Ugh! Those poor people. . . . Had they *so* many?

MISS VARG [*laughs*]. Swarming with them. Teeming with them. Outside and in. In the beds, creeping and crawling all night long. Falling into the milk churns. Over the floors scratching in all the corners. But then *I* arrived.

ALFRED. To think that anyone dared go there . . . !

MISS VARG. I dared. And then I took them away with me . . . every one of them. The sweet little creatures! I put paid to them all.

ALFRED [*with a shriek*]. Father . . . look! Look!

SKJOLDHEJM. In God's name, Alfred!

ALFRED. There's something wriggling in her bag!

MRS. SKJOLDHEJM [*shrieks*]. Ugh!

MISS VARG [*laughs*]. Oh, don't be frightened of such a little thing.

SKJOLDHEJM. Yes, but what is it?

MISS VARG [*undoes the bag*]. Only Mopseman. Come on out, my friend.

[*A small dog with a broad black nose pokes its head out of the bag.*]

MISS VARG [*to* ALFRED]. Just come a little nearer. He won't bite. Come, come!

ALFRED. No, I daren't.

MISS VARG [*strokes the dog*]. Doesn't the young gentleman think Mopseman has a nice friendly face?

ALFRED. That thing!

MISS VARG. Yes, hasn't he.

ALFRED [*in an undertone*]. I think he has the most horrible face I've ever seen.

MISS VARG [*closing the bag*]. Ah, you'll learn. You'll learn in time.

ALFRED [*lightly and involuntarily strokes the bag*]. And yet he's lovely . . . lovely.

MISS VARG [*solicitously*]. But now he's so tired, so dreadfully tired, poor thing. It does tell on you . . . *that* kind of work.

SKJOLDHEJM. What kind of work?

MISS VARG. Enticement.

SKJOLDHEJM. Is it the dog that entices the rats, perhaps?

MISS VARG. Mopseman and I. I tie a string to his collar. Then I lead him three times round the house. Then they have to come out of their hidey-holes. All of them. Whether they want to or not.

ALFRED. And then he bites them?

MISS VARG. Not at all! We make our way down to the boat, he and I. And then they follow us.

ALFRED [*tense*]. And then what . . . ?

MISS VARG. Then I sit in the back of the boat. And Trond pulls away from the shore. And Mopseman swims along behind. And I hold him by the string. And all the rats and all the mice, they follow us. They can't help themselves.

ALFRED. Why can't they?

MISS VARG. Because really they don't want to do it.

ALFRED. Do they drown?

MISS VARG. Every single one. [*She rises.*] Ah, in earlier days I had no need of any Mopseman. I was sufficient attraction myself. In a different way.

ALFRED. And you attracted—what?

MISS VARG. People. One most of all. One in particular.

ALFRED [*tense*]. Tell me who that was.

MISS VARG [*laughs*]. It was my own dearest sweetheart.

ALFRED. Why did you attract him?

MISS VARG. Because he had gone and left me. Far, far away across the briny sea. But I drew him . . . drew him home to me again. I almost had him. But then I lost my grip. He was gone . . . for all time.

ALFRED. And where is he now?

MISS VARG. Down among all the rats. . . . But now I must get back to business again. Have you any work for me here. I can deal with it at once.

MRS. SKJOLDHEJM. No, thank you, Miss Varg. I don't think there's any need.

MISS VARG. Ah well, you never know. . . . If there should be anything, just send for Aunt Ellen. [*Laughs.*] Isn't it strange that everybody calls me Aunt Ellen. Despite the fact that I haven't any living relative—either in heaven or on earth. Farewell! Many times farewell!

[*She goes out by the door, right. Shortly afterwards,* ALFRED *slips out cautiously and unnoticed into the garden.*]

RITA. Today she was quite uncanny.

MRS. SKJOLDHEJM. I think she's always that.

SKJOLDHEJM. I can understand something of that compelling power of attraction she talked about. Nature up among the glaciers and on the great desolate open spaces has something of the same power.

RITA [*looks closely at him*]. It's almost as if there had been a transformation in you, Hakon.

MRS. SKJOLDHEJM. Yes. You think so too?

SKJOLDHEJM. Something *has* occurred to transform me. It has happened within me. For as far as outward events are concerned, I have experienced absolutely nothing during my trip.

MRS. SKJOLDHEJM [*sits down on the sofa*]. You must tell us about this thing.

SKJOLDHEJM. Yes, let's sit down. . . . Then I'll try.

[*He sits on the sofa beside his wife.* RITA *sits on a chair by the table.*]

SKJOLDHEJM [*after a short pause*]. My trip actually made me feel very happy and relieved. But there was also an element of sadness from which I cannot free myself.

MRS. SKJOLDHEJM. That could well be because you didn't get any work done. . . .

SKJOLDHEJM [*smiles rather sadly*]. Yes, you know me. You know that up to now I have tended to take things that way.

MRS. SKJOLDHEJM [*smiles*]. Very cross and annoyed. In a very bad humour when on occasion things didn't go well with your writing.

SKJOLDHEJM. But now, you see, Andrea my dear . . . I have got over being affected by such things.

MRS. SKJOLDHEJM. On your holiday in the mountains?

SKJOLDHEJM. Yes, up there in the great solitude . . . Oh, I have also been a happy man until now, of course. But I have lived my life far too much at my writing desk. Without worries, without cares of any kind. A life of plenty on every hand. . . . [*Holds out his hands to them.*] And also you two to flatter and spoil me.

RITA. All we did was understand you, Hakon.

MRS. SKJOLDHEJM. Believed in you. And tried to be companions to you.

SKJOLDHEJM. When I now look back. . . . Book after book I have sent out into the world. I believe they were well written. And they were also well received. And now was to come my main work. The one about spiritual ⟨*later altered to* mental⟩ philosophy.[1]

MRS. SKJOLDHEJM. Yes, but that will come. That will come, Hakon. Now that you are back in your own home again. . . .

SKJOLDHEJM. It never will, my dear. It never shall.

MRS. SKJOLDHEJM. Good Lord, why not?

SKJOLDHEJM. Because it has one basic deficiency.

RITA. Basic deficiency? But can't you make that good?

SKJOLDHEJM. No, it is beyond making good, Rita.

MRS. SKJOLDHEJM. But now that you have discovered it . . .

RITA. But what kind of basic deficiency can this be?

SKJOLDHEJM. I have not included renunciation.

MRS. SKJOLDHEJM. Renunciation?

SKJOLDHEJM. Yes, renunciation. Self-denial. Willingness to sacrifice. Joy of sacrifice. Something which ought to be the central nucleus of one's way of life.

RITA. Well then, incorporate it all now.

SKJOLDHEJM [*shakes his head*]. That shall not go into any book. This is something I have learnt to see . . . it must be absorbed into my own way of life.

MRS. SKJOLDHEJM. How do you mean?

[1] In Norwegian: 'åndelige livslære' altered to 'sjælelige livslære'.

SKJOLDHEJM. You see. . . . Every single family line—which has any breeding, you understand—has its series of rising generations. It climbs from father to son, until it reaches the highest point the family line is capable of. Then it begins to go down again.

RITA. You will reach the highest point, Hakon.

SKJOLDHEJM. It has been the biggest mistake of my life to go on believing that.

MRS. SKJOLDHEJM. Don't you believe that any more!

SKJOLDHEJM. No, now I know it isn't so. I have usurped a kingly throne. Now I abdicate it. Yield pride of place. . . .

MRS. SKJOLDHEJM. To whom are you yielding pride of place?

SKJOLDHEJM. To the rightful one.

MRS. SKJOLDHEJM. Yes, but who? Who in God's name is the rightful one?

SKJOLDHEJM. It is Alfred ⟨*Added later, in brackets:* Ejvind⟩.

RITA. Alfred! ⟨*Added later, in brackets:* Ejvind⟩.

MRS. SKJOLDHEJM ⟨*added later, in brackets:* MRS. ALMER⟩. Alfred! ⟨*later crossed out and replaced by:* Ejvind⟩ You believe that!

SKJOLDHEJM ⟨*added later, in brackets:* ALMER⟩. I see it. He will be the topmost crown of the Skjoldhejm family line.

MRS. ALMER. You believe this, Alfred? ⟨*sic*⟩.

ALLMER ⟨*sic*⟩. I believe confidently in this. I will apply all my powers to it. I'll be a teacher to him. . . .

MRS. ALLMER. But why make life so sour for yourself? We don't need to.

ALLMER. I don't want to stuff him with book learning. It is the very art of life I want to try to make him comprehend. Make the art of life part of his nature.

MRS. ALLMER. But, my dear, what is this 'art of life'? I don't think living is any kind of art.

ALLMER. You don't think so?

MRS. ALLMER. No, it's the most straightforward thing in the world . . . this matter of living. When one has enough to live on, as we have. And when one can therefore live exactly as one wishes. And one needn't do anything other than what one considers right and proper.

ALLMER. Ah, you have an easy and happy mind, Andrea.

MRS. ALLMER. That is something you should also cultivate.

ALLMER. I shall achieve it by fulfilling my duty.

MRS. ALLMER. What duty?

ALLMER. My highest duty. That of getting Ejvind's personality to achieve its highest, fullest flowering in all matters.

MRS. ALLMER. You consider that to be your highest duty?

ALLMER. For a father there can be none higher.

MRS. ALLMER. Nor for a mother either?

ALLMER. No, that's obvious. When I say 'I', that's merely a manifestation, a residue, of my old self-love. Such things are not so easily removed root and branch. Of course I mean 'we'. We two together, Andrea.

MRS. ALLMER. No, my dearest Alfred, I can't really go along entirely with you in this.

ALLMER. Not devote our existence to realizing the best in our child! As far as we can.

MRS. ALLMER. Oh, you speak about existence. Existence—that is life. A feeling of happiness, I think it might be called.

ALLMER [*earnestly, almost sternly*]. I know of no more sincere form of happiness than that of seeing Ejvind growing under my hands.

MRS. ALLMER. But earlier you gave only very casual attention to him.

ALLMER. I'm afraid you are right there. I was much too much taken up by myself and by . . .

MRS. ALLMER. . . . And by . . . ?

ALLMER. . . . by all these unhealthy, mistaken and baseless notions that I myself had some special thing to achieve in the world. Something overwhelmingly important and imperative. A matter for one's own private calculations.

MRS. ALLMER. Is this all that's occupied you? Occupied your life, Alfred?

ALLMER. Yes.

MRS. ALLMER. Absolutely nothing else?

ALLMER. Nothing worth mentioning, as far as I know.

MRS. ALLMER. And no-*body* . . . nobody *else*, either?

ALLMER. Nobody else? What do you mean? Who might that be?

MRS. ALLMER. It might just be me.

ALLMER. Oh, yes. You. But my dearest Andrea, that is self-evident. . . .

MRS. ALLMER. No, no, no. Don't talk to me about things that are self-evident. I want it to be so because I am me. And because you are you.

ALLMER. But my dearest Andrea, that's only how things are on one's honeymoon. . . .

MRS. ALLMER. And that's just how they must continue to be.

ALLMER. Now, listen. . . . You know, we must start being reasonable some time.

MRS. ALLMER. Never in this world will you get me to be reasonable. Not in this matter. This business of being reasonable . . . it is merely a pretext . . . when somebody no longer cares about somebody else.

ALLMER. No, but listen to me. . . .

MRS. ALLMER. I want to tell you something, Alfred . . . I will never consent to give up my place—the first place in your mind. Not even for my own little boy.

RITA. Alfred must always have somebody he can take care of. He has always been like that. Towards me, too. From the very first moment I can remember.

[*There is a quick light knock on the door, right.* BORGHEJM *steps briskly in. He is a young man of about 30. Bright and cheerful expression. Erect stance. Brown curly hair and beard.*]

BORGHEJM. Good morning, Mrs. Allmer? [*Stops joyfully as he catches sight of* ALLMER.] Well, what's this I see! Home again already, Dr. Allmer.

ALLMER. Yes. I came last night.

MRS. ALLMER [*gaily*]. He didn't have permission to stay away longer, Mr. Borghejm. His leave had expired.

BORGHEJM. So you keep a tight rein on him, Mrs. Allmer?

MRS. ALLMER. I insist on my rights. Anyway, everything has to end sometime.

BORGHEJM. Oh, not everything—I hope. Good morning, Miss Rita.

RITA. Good morning.

BORGHEJM. Yes, I build firmly on the view that there is at least one thing in this world that has no end.

MRS. ALLMER. You are doubtless thinking of love and similar things.

BORGHEJM. Yes. I am thinking of anything which is delightful.

MRS. ALLMER. And which never ends. Yes, let us think of that. Hope for it.

ALLMER. I suppose you'll soon have finished this road project out here.

BORGHEJM. Yes, next week. It's lasted a pretty long time. But, thank heaven, *that* will have an end.

MRS. ALLMER. And that's why you are on top of the world?

BORGHEJM. Yes, it is.

MRS. ALLMER. Well, I must say . . .

BORGHEJM. What, Mrs. Allmer?

MRS. ALLMER. That's not altogether nice of you.

BORGHEJM. Oh? Why not?

MRS. ALLMER. Because after this you'll not be coming out very often to these parts.

BORGHEJM. That's true. I didn't think of that.

MRS. ALLMER. Surely you'll be able to manage an occasional visit.

BORGHEJM. No, I'm afraid that won't be possible. Not for a long time.

ALLMER. Oh? Why not?

BORGHEJM. Because I've got a big new job. Sssh! I'm not supposed to talk about it yet. But I can't keep it to myself.

ALLMER. No! Have you!

MRS. ALLMER. Congratulations!

BORGHEJM. It's up in the North. There are mountains to cross and quite incredible difficulties to overcome. Ah, what a splendid life—how marvellous it is to be a builder of roads!

MRS. ALLMER. Is that why you are in such high spirits today?

BORGHEJM. Because of all the bright and promising things I am brimming over with.

MRS. ALLMER. Is there still more?

BORGHEJM. Yes, there is! It is . . . No, I can't keep it to myself any longer. [*Turns to* RITA.] Shall we . . . ?

RITA [*quickly, in a low voice*]. No, no . . . ! Ah, you mean take a little walk down in the garden?

BORGHEJM. Walk . . . ? Yes, that's just what I meant.

RITA. Yes, I'd like to go with you.

ALLMER. Keep an eye open for Ejvind. He's down there playing.

BORGHEJM. Ah, so Ejvind has taken to playing now. He usually just sits reading.

ALLMER. That's going to stop. Now he's going to be a real open-air lad.

BORGHEJM. That's right! Out into the fresh air with him. Dear God, what better thing is there to do in this glorious world than play. I feel all life is a kind of game!

[*He and* RITA *go out on to the verandah and down through the garden.*]

ALLMER [*watching them*]. Is there something between those two?

MRS. ALLMER. I'm almost beginning to think so. Would you be against it if there were?

ALLMER. Not really against it. But I have a sort of responsibility for Rita. And it is always a matter of some concern when two people go and take on these ties.

MRS. ALLMER [*looks at him*]. You mean because in the long run it won't last?

ALLMER. One can never tell. Those who go and make the bond cannot know this themselves.

MRS. ALLMER. I myself see nothing wrong in Borghejm.

ALLMER. My dear—wrong? Who says that? But I'm so afraid that those two are not rightly endowed to change towards each other.

MRS. ALLMER. Change? Must they do that?

ALLMER. Or develop, then—if you prefer that. Mature. Grow. You must remember that in marriage new situations are formed. As it were, ⟨*the following 17 lines, which occupy the first side and a quarter of the second side of folio 10 of the MS. are then crossed out in pencil:* little by little you understand. New duties announce themselves. The children too demand their rights. Their rights do come first, Andrea.

MRS. ALLMER [*comes towards him, almost wild*]. Is that what you say! First. Is that what you say, Alfred!

ALLMER. Yes. That is how I have come to see things.

MRS. ALLMER. So you don't love me any more!

ALLMER. Andrea, how can you say a thing like that. Because you cannot possibly mean it!

MRS. ALLMER. Yes, I do. I have just about reached the point where I do mean it. You don't behave towards me as you did before. Not as you did in the first year.

ALLMER. You have never been dearer to me than you are now, Andrea.

MRS. ALLMER. But not in the same way. You have begun to divide yourself between me and your work. And that I won't stand. I want you all for myself. [*Throws her arms about his neck.*] Oh, Alfred, Alfred, I cannot let you go!⟩

ALLMER [*gently frees himself*]. But my dearest Andrea—do be reasonable.

MRS. ALLMER. I don't care a damn about being reasonable. All I care about is you. Nothing in the whole wide world but you. [*Again throws herself around his neck.*] You! you! you!

ALMER ⟨*sic*⟩. Let go! let go! You're choking me.

MRS. ALLMER. God, if only I could! [*Looks at him with flashing eyes.*] Oh, if only you knew how I've hated you . . .

ALLMER. Hated me!

MRS. ALLMER. Yes, when you sat there poring over your work long long into the night. So long, Alfred! Oh, how I hated that work of yours.

ALLMER. But now that's all over and done with.

MRS. ALLMER [*laughs cuttingly*]. Oh, yes. Only now you are caught up by something worse.

ALLMER. Worse! You call our child 'something worse'?

MRS. ALLMER. Yes, I do. Because the child is a living being.

ALLMER. Sometimes you almost frighten me, Andrea.

MRS. ALLMER. I am often afraid of ⟨you *crossed out*⟩ myself. For that reason you mustn't rouse the evil in me.

ALLMER. But in God's name . . . do I do that?

MRS. ALLMER. Yes, you do. When you break the sacred ties that bind us.

ALLMER. But it's your own child we are talking about.

MRS. ALLMER. The child is only half mine. It is yours and mine together. But *you* shall be all mine. Mine alone. I have a right to demand it.

ALLMER. My dear Andrea, it's no use demanding. Everything has to be freely given.

MRS. ALMER ⟨*sic*⟩. And you can't?

ALLMER. No. I must divide myself between you and the boy.

MRS. ALLMER. But what if the boy had never been born?

ALLMER. That is a different matter. Then I'd have had only you to love.

MRS. ALLMER [*in a low trembling voice*]. Then I could wish I had never borne him.

ALLMER. Andrea, you don't know what you are saying.

MRS. ALLMER. I gave birth to him in unspeakable pain. But I endured it gladly for your sake.

ALLMER. Yes, yes, I know that.

MRS. ALLMER. But that's past and done with. I want to *live*. With you. Wholly with you. I can't go on just being mother to Eyolf ⟨*sic*⟩. And only that. I won't, I tell you! I can't. I want to be everything to you! To you Alfred!

ALLMERS ⟨*sic*⟩. But you *are*. Through our child.

MRS. ALLMERS. Phrases. Nothing more. Motherhood for me was in having the child. But I'm not made to go on *being* mother to it. You must take me as I am, Alfred.

ALLMERS. But you were always so very fond of him before.

MRS. ALLMERS. Yes, I felt so sorry for him. Because you just left him to drift. Hardly ever saw him.

ALLMERS. No, the hour had not yet struck . . .

MRS. ALLMERS. But now it has?

ALLMERS. Yes, finally. Now I see that my highest duty in this life is to be a father to Eyolf.

MRS. ALLMERS. And *me*?

ALLMERS. I shall go on loving you in quiet devotion.

[*He tries to take her by the hands.*]

MRS. ALLMERS [*avoids him*]. I'm not interested in your quiet devotion! I want you! All of you! You alone! The way I had you in those first days. Nobody's going to fob me off with scraps and left-overs, Alfred.

ALLMERS. I think we could surely find enough happiness here to satisfy all three of us.

MRS. ALLMERS. Then you are easily satisfied. Now listen.

ALLMERS. Well?

MRS. ALMERS ⟨*sic*⟩ [*sits down at the table*]. When I got your telegram last night . . .

ALLMERS. Yes?

MRS. ALLMERS. I dressed in white . . .

ALLMERS. Yes, I saw you were wearing white.

MRS. ALLMERS. I'd let down my hair . . .

ALLMERS. Your long, fragrant hair . . .

MRS. ALLMERS. . . . So that it hung about my neck and shoulders . . .

ALLMERS. I saw. I saw. How lovely you were, Andrea!

MRS. ALLMERS. All the candles were lit. We were alone, we two. The only ones awake in the whole house. And there was champagne on the table.

ALLMERS. I didn't drink any.

MRS. ALLMERS. How true. [*With a sharp laugh.*] 'Champagne was yours, but you touched it not'—as the poet says.

[*She gets up, walks across and lies down on the sofa.*]

ALLMERS [*goes closer to her*]. I was so full of serious thoughts. I was determined to talk to you about our future life, Andrea. And first and foremost about the child.

MRS. ALLMERS. Which you did.

ALLMERS. No. I didn't get that far. Because you began to undress.

MRS. ALLMERS. While you went on talking about the child. Don't you remember? You asked me how Eyolf's tummy was.

ALLMERS [*looks reproachfully at her*]. Andrea!

MRS. ALLMERS. Then you lay down and fell fast asleep.

ALLMERS [*shakes his head*]. Andrea! Andrea!

MRS. ALLMERS [*lies looking up at him*]. Alfred?

ALLMERS. Yes?

MRS. ALLMERS. 'Champagne was yours, but you touched it not.'

ALLMERS [*almost hard*]. No. I didn't touch it.

[*He moves away from her and stands by the French window.* MRS. ALLMERS *lies for some moments motionless, her eyes closed.*]

MRS. ALLMERS [*suddenly jumps up*]. But one thing I will tell you, Alfred!

ALLMERS [*turns in the doorway*]. Well?

MRS. ALLMERS. Don't be too sure of yourself . . .

ALLMERS. Sure of myself?

MRS. ALLMERS. No, don't take things for granted. Don't be too confident that you have me. . . .

ALLMERS [*approaches*]. What do you mean by that?

MRS. ALLMERS. I have never been unfaithful to you, even in thought. Never for a moment.

ALLMERS. I know that. I know you too well . . .

MRS. ALLMERS. You don't know what ideas I might get if . . .

ALLMERS. If . . . ?

MRS. ALLMERS. If I saw any sign that you no longer cared about me. No longer loved me as you did before.

ALLMERS. But, heavens above, Andrea . . . some time the natural change must happen to us too. As it does to everybody else.

MRS. ALLMERS. Not to me! Ever! And I don't want to hear of any change in you either. I couldn't bear that. I want to keep you all to myself. Just as you were when we won each other.

ALLMERS. You have a jealous nature. Previously you were jealous of my work. Now you are jealous of Eyolf.

MRS. ALLMERS. I cannot be different from what I am. If you parcel yourself out between us . . .

ALLMERS. Well?

MRS. ALLMERS. I'll be revenged on you, Alfred!

ALLMERS. Revenged? How?

MRS. ALLMERS. I don't know. . . . Yes, I do know!

ALLMERS. Well?

MRS. ALMERS ⟨*sic*⟩. I'll go and throw myself away. . . .

ALLMER ⟨*sic*⟩. Throw yourself away?

MRS. ALMERS ⟨*sic*⟩. Yes, that's what I'll do. I'll throw myself into the arms . . . of the first man that comes along.

ALLMERS. You'll never do that . . . my proud, honest, loyal Andrea!

MRS. ALLMERS [*puts her arms round his neck*]. Oh, you don't know what might become of me . . . if you didn't want me any more.

ALLMERS. Want you any more! How can you say such a thing!

MRS. ALLMERS [*half laughing*]. I might set out my nets to catch . . . this engineer man.

ALLMERS. Ah, thank God, you are joking.

MRS. ALLMERS. Not at all. Why not him just as much as the next man?

ALLMERS. Because he seems pretty well caught up already.

MRS. ALLMERS. So much the better. Then I'd be taking him from somebody else. That's exactly the same as Eyolf has done to me and you.

ALLMERS. You say our little Eyolf has done that.

MRS. ALLMERS. You see! You see! You've only got to mention his name and you go all soft and your voice trembles. Oh, I am almost tempted to wish . . . Well!

ALLMERS [*looks anxiously at her*]. To wish what, Andrea . . .?

MRS. ALLMERS [*vehemently*]. No, no, no . . . I won't tell you! Never!

ALMERS ⟨*sic*⟩ [*goes closer to her*]. Andrea! I implore you . . . for your sake and mine . . . do not let yourself be tempted to anything evil.

[*Engineer* BORGHEJM *and* RITA *come up from the garden.*]

BORGHEJM. Well then! ⟨*The following 4 lines are crossed out in pencil on the MS.:* Hurrah! Now I am allowed to say it!

MRS. ALLMERS. Surely there is scarcely any need of that, dear Mr. Borghejm.

BORGHEJM. Oh? Isn't there? Could you in fact see from our faces?

MRS. ALLMERS. Yes, pretty well.⟩

BORGHEJM. Yes, now she has surrendered. To me . . . unconditionally. Has no more misgivings . . .

MRS. ALLMERS. Had she before?

BORGHEJM. Yes. Wasn't altogether free of them.

ALLMERS. May this bring you happiness, Rita dear.

RITA [*kisses his hand*]. Thanks for everything . . . everything you have been to me.

ALLMERS. Rita! My little Rita!

BORGHEJM. And now she will go along together with me. To our work together. There'll be plenty of mountain passes to conquer. And precipitous drops that could well make one's head reel.

ALLMERS. And as long as you hold together in understanding . . . things will be all right.

MRS. ALLMERS. And don't let any evil eyes stare him away from you, Rita.

RITA. Evil eyes?

BORGHEJM. Do you believe in evil eyes, Mrs. Allmers?

MRS. ALLMERS. Yes, I have begun to believe in evil children's eyes.

ALLMERS. Andrea, how can you . . . !

MRS. ALLMERS. It is you, Alfred . . . you are making me evil and horrid.

[*Distant cries are heard from down by the water.*]

BORGHEJM [*goes to the french window*]. What's that noise . . . ?

RITA [*similarly goes across*]. Look at all those people running down to the jetty!

ALLMERS. What can it be?

BORGHEJM [*shouts, out on the verandah*]. Hi, you men down there! What's going on?

[*An answer is indistinctly heard.*]

ALLMERS. What does he say?

BORGHEJM. He says a child has been drowned.

ALLMERS. A child drowned!

RITA. A little boy, they say.

MRS. ALLMERS [*cries out in fear*]. Where's Eyolf gone?

ALLMERS. Be calm, Be calm. Eyolf is playing in the garden.

RITA. No, he wasn't in the garden . . .

MRS. ALLMERS [*wringing her hands*]. As long as it isn't *him*!

BORGHEJM [*shouts down*]. Who is it, do you say? [*Indistinct voices are heard.* BORGHEJM *and* RITA *utter a cry.*]

BORGHEJM. Oh, my God . . .

ALLMER ⟨*sic*⟩. It can't ever be Eyolf.

BORGHEJM [*rushes out*]. Yes, they say it is . . .

[*He and* RITA *rush out.*]

MRS. ALLMERS. Eyolf, Eyolf! Oh, but they must save him!

ALLMERS [*half distraught*]. It *must* be possible! So dear a life! So dear a life!

[*He rushes down through the garden.*]

⟨*dated*⟩ 10.7.94

ACT TWO

A little clearing in ALLMERS' *forests down by the shore. Mostly conifers but with some birches among them. A bench, a round table and a couple of chairs, all made of tree trunks and branches still with the bark on, are positioned right. A few large boulders lie on the edge of the shore and in the water. It is about midday on a brilliantly sunny day. The fjord stretches out calm as a mirror.*

ALFRED ALLMERS, *dressed in his grey summer suit but with a crape band round his sleeve, is sitting on the bench resting his arms on the table. On one of the chairs lies his grey felt hat, also bound with crape. He sits quietly for some time staring out over the water, lost in thought. Then* MISS ANDREA ⟨*sic*⟩ ALLMERS, *in full mourning, comes down a little forest slope, left, and goes quietly over to him.*

MISS ANDREA. Are you sitting down here, Alfred?

[ALLMERS *nods slowly without replying.* ANDREA *moves his hat on to the table and sits down on the chair.*]

ANDREA. I've walked such a long way looking for you. Have you been sitting here all the time?

ALLMERS [*does not answer; after a while he speaks*]. No, I can't understand it.

ANDREA. Poor Alfred.

ALLMERS. Is it really true, Andrea? Or have I gone mad? Or am I just dreaming? Oh, if only it were a dream! How lovely if I were now to wake up . . . !

ANDREA. Oh, if only I could in fact wake you!

ALLMERS [*looks out over the water*]. Look how dead calm the fjord is . . . on the surface . . .

ANDREA. Oh Alfred, don't sit here staring at the fjord. . . .

ALLMERS. . . . but deep down the undercurrent is strong . . .

ANDREA. Oh, for God's sake don't think about the depths!

ALLMERS [*looks at her gently*]. You think he's lying just off here, don't you? But he isn't, Andrea. You mustn't think that. Remember how strong the outgoing current is here.

ANDREA [*throws herself sobbing over the table, her hands over her face*]. Oh, God! Oh, God!

ALLMERS [*heavily*]. So by now little Eyolf has been carried far far away from us.

ANDREA [*looks entreatingly at him*]. Oh, please don't say things like that!

ALLMERS. You can work it out for yourself. In twenty-eight hours . . . ? Let me see! Let me see!

ANDREA [*screams*]. Alfred . . . !

ALLMERS [*forces his fist hard against the table*]. But can you see any meaning in this?

ANDREA. In what?

ALLMERS. In what's been done to Rita and me.

ANDREA. The meaning in it?

ALLMERS. Yes. For there must be some meaning in it. Life, existence, providence surely can't be so utterly meaningless.

ANDREA. Oh, Alfred, who can speak with certainty about these things?

ALLMERS [*bitterly, scornfully*]. No. You are probably right. Perhaps the whole thing is just haphazard. An aimless drifting, like some wrecked and rudderless ship. That could well be it. It seems very much like that, at least.

ANDREA. What if it only seems . . . ?

ALLMERS. So? Perhaps you can find me some explanation? I cannot. There is Eyolf on the very threshold of conscious life. Great possibilities open to him. Was about to fill my existence with pride and joy. Then all it needs is for some crazy old woman to come along. And show him a dog in a sack . . .

ANDREA. But it isn't at all clear that that's how it happened.

ALLMERS. Yes it is. I am certain of it. It must have happened like that. The people down there—they'll tell you that Mistress Warg rowed out. She sat at the back of the boat. And the dog swam behind on a string. . . .

ANDREA. Yes, yes. And yet . . . all the same . . .

ALLMERS. And there are some people who saw Eyolf standing on the steamer jetty. A short time after, he was gone. Nobody has seen anything of him since.

ANDREA. Yes, that's what they say, but . . .

ALLMERS. She lured him, Andrea. There is no doubt about it.

ANDREA. But, my dear, why should she do that?

ALLMERS. Exactly. Why should she . . . ? Eyolf surely never did her any harm. Never called her names. Never threw stones at the dog. He'd never seen it until yesterday. That sort of thing wouldn't have been like Eyolf. So meaningless. So absolutely meaningless. And yet the world order seems to require it.

ANDREA. Have you spoken to Rita about this?

ALLMERS. I feel I am better talking to you about it.

ANDREA. Alfred, you should talk to Rita, too.

ALLMERS. I will. Both to you and to her. . . . But soon now you'll be leaving us.

ANDREA. We two will not be separated by that.

ALLMERS. No, I don't think I could imagine that.

ANDREA. We two will remain close to each other no matter how far away I go.

ALLMERS. But it will be lonely for Rita and me. When *you* have left us too.

ANDREA. I think Rita would rather have it that way.

ALLMERS [*looks at her*]. She would rather . . . ?

ANDREA. Rather have you to herself alone.

ALLMERS. You have noticed that?

ANDREA. Yes. Now and again.

ALLMERS. But I don't think it has to do with you, Andrea.

ANDREA. No, perhaps not so ⟨*omitted* much⟩ me as others.

ALLMERS. For she knows what we two have meant for each other all our days.

ANDREA. Oh, Alfred—say rather what you have meant for me. You have meant everything to me. No sacrifice has been too great for you.

ALLMERS. Come now—sacrifice. Oh, I have loved you ever since you were a little child. And I felt I had so many wrongs to make amends for.

ANDREA. Wrongs. You?

ALLMERS. Not exactly from me. But . . .

ANDREA. But . . . ?

ALLMERS. From Father.

ANDREA [*starts up*]. Father? What do you mean by that, Alfred!

ALLMERS. Father wasn't very kind to you.

ANDREA. You mustn't say that!

ALLMERS. It's true. And he was often very hard to your mother, too. At least in later years.

ANDREA. ⟨Don't speak any more about these things, Alfred, I beg you! You *crossed out*⟩ [*Quietly*.] Mother was not always what she should have been.

ALLMERS. Your mother?

ANDREA. Perhaps not always.

ALLMERS. To Father, you mean?

ANDREA. Yes.

ALLMERS. I never noticed anything.

ANDREA. You were for the most part away from home at that time. I am thinking mostly of those years when you were at university.

ALLMERS. Yes, but my dearest Andrea . . . I was often at home on a visit.

ANDREA. All the same . . .

ALLMERS. You've never referred to these things before now. I believed the blame must all have been on Father's side. If indeed there *was* any blame.

ANDREA. Oh, surely the blame never lies entirely on one side . . .

ALMERS ⟨*sic*⟩. You may be right, But just tell me . . .

ANDREA. Oh, I do beg you, Alfred . . . don't say any more about these things. [*Looks into the forest, right*.] Here come Rita and Berghejm ⟨*sic*⟩.

ALLMERS. Shall we go to meet them?

ANDREA. I'm sure they've seen us. They are coming here.

ALLMERS. How long have you been in love with Berghejm?

ANDREA [*looks quickly at him*]. Been in love with him?

ALLMERS. Yes?

ANDREA. I've only known him a short time.

ALLMERS. And now you are going off with him. So far, so far. I had never imagined we two would be parted.

ANDREA. Nor I.

ALLMERS [*staring vacantly*]. Where is Eyolf now? Can anybody tell me that? Nobody in the whole wide world. All I know is that I no longer have him. And soon I won't have you any longer, Andrea. Nobody, nobody, whom ⟨you *crossed out*⟩ I have any kinship with.

ANDREA. You have Rita.

ALLMERS. I have no kinship with Rita. It isn't like having a sister . . .

ANDREA [*tense*]. You say that Alfred?

ALLMERS. Yes. The Allmers family is a thing on its own. We've always had vowels for the initial letter of our names. And we've always had the same eyes.

ANDREA. Me too, you think?

ALLMERS. No, that's true. Actually, you haven't. You don't resemble Father. You are more akin to your mother. All the same . . .

ANDREA. All the same . . .

ALLMERS. Our life together, I do believe, has left its mark on us both . . . formed each of us in the other's image. Inwardly in our minds and outwardly.

ANDREA. Is that how you feel, Alfred?

ALLMERS. Yes. Exactly like that.

ANDREA. Then you compel me to tell you . . .

ALLMERS. What? What? Tell me!

ANDREA [*looks out, right*]. Later. They are coming now.

[MRS. RITA ALLMERS *and Engineer* BORGHEJM *appear through the trees.*]

ALLMERS [*goes over to meet her*]. How are you, Rita?

MRS. ALLMERS. Don't ask me.

ALLMERS. What are you doing here?

MRS. ALLMERS. Just looking for you. What are you doing down here?

ALLMERS. Nothing. Andrea came down to join me.

MRS. ALLMERS. But what about before Andrea came? You've been away from me the whole morning.

ALLMERS. I've been sitting here looking out over the water.

MRS. ALLMERS. Uh . . . how can you! And alone too!

ALLMERS. I prefer to be alone now.

MRS. ALLMERS. Just sitting. Always at the same spot.

ALLMERS. There is absolutely nothing else for me to do.

MRS. ALLMERS. I can't bear it anywhere. There is something in me that keeps driving me restlessly on. Don't you think he should come with the rest of us, Mr. Borghejm.

BORGHEJM [*to* ALLMERS]. I think it would be better for you.

ALLMERS. No, no. Let me stay where I am.

MRS. ALLMERS. Then I'll stay with you, Alfred.

ALLMERS. Yes, do that.

BORGHEJM [*to* ANDREA]. Andrea, shall we go for a little walk down the road in the meantime?

ANDREA. With pleasure.

[*She and* BORGHEJM *go off along the shore, left.* ALLMERS *walks about a little; then he sits down on the bench, left.* RITA *goes over to him.*]

MRS. ALLMERS. Can you bear the thought that we have lost him, Alfred!

ALLMERS. We shall have to get accustomed to that thought.

MRS. ALLMERS. I cannot. I cannot. But is it then so certain that he is gone—for ever?

ALLMERS. People saw him lying on the bottom. Then the current came and took him.

MRS. ALLMERS. Yes, yes, I know that. But that isn't what I mean.

ALLMERS. What then?

MRS. ALLMERS. It seems to me he is still as much as ever about me. More, a thousand times more than before.

ALLMERS [*bitterly*]. Now you think so?

MRS. ALLMERS. Yes, yes. But that doesn't suffice. I must see him. Hear him. Touch him . . .

ALLMERS. Previously you could nicely do without him. . . . For half a day at a time. . . .

MRS. ALLMERS. Yes, for then I knew that at all events I had him.]

K1

ALLMERS [*gloomily*]. Now we no longer have him. You have got what you wanted. . . .

MRS. ALLMERS. What did I want?

ALLMERS [*looks sternly at her*]. That little Eyolf was not there.

MRS. ALLMERS. That little Eyolf no longer stood between us two. That was what I wanted!

ALLMERS. Well, he doesn't any longer, poor boy.

MRS. ALMERS ⟨*sic*⟩ [*looks at him*]. Perhaps now more than ever.

ALLMERS. You never loved him really and truly.

MRS. ALLMERS. Eyolf would never really and truly let me care for him.

ALLMERS. Because you wouldn't do it.

MRS. ALLMERS. Yes, I would. I certainly would. But somebody stood between us. Right from the start.

ALLMERS. Me, you mean?

MRS. ALLMERS. Oh, no. Not from the start.

ALLMERS. Who then?

MRS. ALLMERS. Andrea.

ALLMERS. Andrea? You think so, Rita?

MRS. ALLMERS. Yes. Andrea possessed him right from the time when he was quite small.

ALLMERS. If she did, she did it from love.

MRS. ALLMERS. Exactly. I can't bear sharing with others. Not in love.

ALLMERS. We two should have shared him between us in love.

MRS. ALLMERS. We? Actually you have never had any real love for the child.

ALLMERS [*looks at her astonished*]. I haven't. . . ! How can you say . . . how can you believe such a thing!

MRS. ALLMERS. No, you haven't. Previously you were entirely taken up by your work.

ALLMERS. Yes. And this I have sacrificed for Eyolf's sake. . . .

MRS. ALLMERS. Yes, but not because you loved him.

ALLMERS. Why then? Tell me what you mean!

MRS. ALLMERS. You were beginning to be consumed by doubts in yourself. All that happy confidence, all that hope that you had some great task to perform —this began to desert you. I saw it clearly enough.

ALLMERS. Oh yes, you may be right. All the same . . .

MRS. ALLMERS. Then you went away on your trip. Up among the great, free mountain wastes. And this doubtless elevated your mind. . . .

ALLMERS. It has. It has. You may be sure of that, Andrea!

MRS. ALLMERS. But has not elevated it to love. . . .

ALLMERS [*eagerly*]. It was up there in the grandeur and the solitude that I gave up my place in life for the sake of little Eyolf.

MRS. ALLMERS. But why, why did you give it up?

ALLMERS. Why . . . ?

MRS. ALLMERS. Because you needed to find something new to give you satisfaction. Andrea had often spoken to you about Eyolf's great abilities, about all the potential he was supposed to have . . . and things like that . . .

ALLMERS. Yes, she paid him the most attention. But you mean that was why . . . ?

MRS. ALLMERS. You wanted to make a child prodigy out of him, Alfred. Because he was *your* child. But you never really loved him. Never really genuinely cared for him for his own sake.

ALLMERS. You think so?

MRS. ALLMERS. Yes. If I had known that you sincerely cared for him, I might have found it in me to share you with him. Although . . . no, perhaps not, after all.

ALLMERS [*looks thoughtfully at her*]. But if that is so, Rita, then we two have never actually possessed our own child.

MRS. ALLMERS. No, not in complete love.

ALLMERS. And here we are now grieving bitterly for him.

MRS. ALLMERS. Yes, isn't it a curious thought. Grieving here like this for a little stranger boy.

ALLMERS [*in pain*]. You musn't call him a stranger!

MRS. ALLMERS. We never won his love, Alfred. I didn't. Nor did you.

ALLMERS [*wringing his hands*]. And now it's too late! Too late!

MRS. ALLMERS. And so desolate. So utterly hopeless. Everything.

ALLMERS [*with quiet emotion*]. I dreamt of him last night. I thought I saw him standing down in the garden. I became so happy. So rich. He hadn't departed from us. We had him. This terrible reality was thus only a dream. Oh, how I thanked and praised . . .

MRS. ALLMERS. Whom?

ALLMERS. Whom?

MRS. ALLMERS. Yes. Whom did you thank and praise?

ALLMERS. I just lay there dreaming, Rita.

MRS. ALLMERS. Somebody you don't yourself believe in.

ALLMERS. It was just that something came over me. For it was in my sleep, I tell you. . . .

MRS. ALLMERS. You shouldn't have turned me into an unbeliever.

ALLMERS. Would it have been right of me to let you go through life with a lot of empty illusions?

MRS. ALLMERS. It would have been better for me. Now I'd have had somewhere to turn for comfort. Now I don't know where I am.

ALLMERS. If you now had a choice. If you could follow Eyolf where he is now . . .

MRS. ALMERS ⟨*sic*⟩. Yes? What?

ALLMERS. If you had absolute assurance that you would meet him again, recognize him . . .

MRS. ALLMERS. Yes? Yes? What then?

ALLMERS. Would you be willing to take the leap? Be willing to leave all this behind. All the loss and the grief? Would you?

MRS. ALLMERS [*somewhat hesitantly*]. Now? Immediately?

ALLMERS. Yes, now. Today. Answer me. Would you?

MRS. ALLMERS [*in a low voice*]. Oh, I don't know, Alfred. . . . No. I think I'd want to remain here with you for a while.

ALLMERS. For my sake?

MRS. ALLMERS. Yes, only for your sake!

ALLMERS. But afterwards? Would you then . . . ?

MRS. ALLMERS. Oh, what am I to say? You know I couldn't leave you. Never! Never!

ALLMERS. But suppose I were to join Eyolf? And you had absolute assurance that you would meet him and me there. Would you come over to join us?

MRS. ALLMERS [*almost screaming*]. I should want to. So very much! Very much! But . . .

ALLMERS. But? Well?

MRS. ALLMERS [*moans softly*]. I couldn't do it. Couldn't do it?

ALLMERS. Not even if I went this very moment?

MRS. ALLMERS. No, no! Not for all the glory of heaven!

ALLMERS. Neither could I.

MRS. ALLMERS. No . . . you couldn't either, could you!

ALLMERS. For here is where we have our home . . . For the present.

MRS. ALLMERS. Yes, for here is happiness.

ALLMERS. Happiness?

MRS. ALLMERS. Yes, we *must* find happiness again. Without happiness I cannot live.

ALLMERS. Where will we find it now?

MRS. ALLMERS [*shakes her head*]. No, no, no . . . you are right. We'll never find it . . . whilst all we do is grieve over little Eyolf. [*Looks questioningly at him.*] But . . . ?

ALLMERS. But . . . ?

MRS. ALLMERS [*quickly, as if in terror*]. No, no, I daren't say it! Daren't even think it!

ALLMERS. Say it! Say it, Rita!

MRS. ALLMERS [*hesitantly*]. Couldn't we try to . . . ? Might it not be possible to forget him?

ALLMERS. Forget Eyolf!

MRS. ALLMERS. Forget our grief for him, I mean.

ALLMERS. Would you wish that?

MRS. ALLMERS. Yes. If it could be done. [*Bursts out.*] I can't bear things as they are much longer!

ALLMERS. But the memory, Rita. That we will never escape. And memory is a gnawing thing.

MRS. ALLMERS. The memory of little Eyolf will soften with time. Oh, don't you believe that, Alfred?

ALLMERS. It could happen . . . some time, perhaps. But the sense of loss—that will never be dulled.

MRS. ALLMERS [*looking into space*]. Ah, *there* we have it. The sense of loss . . . loss. Every day, every hour . . . it will announce itself in even the smallest things.

ALLMERS. Even just the empty place at table. Even that his jacket is not hanging in its place in the hall. . . .

MRS. ALLMERS. And happiness does not grow within a sense of loss. Neither you nor I are capable of bearing that, Alfred. We must try to think of something that would let us forget.

ALLMERS. What might that be?

MRS. ALLMERS. Couldn't we try going away? Far away.

ALLMERS. Away from home? You know you never really thrive anywhere else but here.

MRS. ALLMERS. Well then, have lots of people here? Entertain a lot. Find something which might deaden and dull . . .

ALLMERS. That life is not for me. You know that. I simply couldn't bear it. No, I'd rather try to take up my work again.

MRS. ALLMERS. Your work? Which has stood like a wall between us!

ALLMERS. It hasn't, Rita. There you are mistaken.

MRS. ALLMERS. No, I am not. But I will not consent to share you. I want you wholly and completely as you were before. You shall give me that love again, unadulterated . . . I *want* it, do you hear.

ALLMERS. That love was an intoxication. And it is dead in me.

MRS. ALLMERS. How can you say that!

ALLMERS. It is dead. And yet in my feelings for you now there is resurrection. . . .

MRS. ALLMERS. Oh, what do I care about resurrection. . . .

ALLMERS. Rita!

MRS. ALLMERS. I am a creature of flesh and blood. I haven't got fish blood in my veins. Why should I be shut away for life! A prisoner of grief and loss.

ALLMERS [*looks thoughtfully at her*]. Can this really be called grief and loss? What we now feel?

MRS. ALLMERS. What else?

ALLMERS. Despair.

ALLMERS. Yes ... despair. I think that is the right name for it.

MRS. ALLMERS [*looks anxiously and questioningly at him*]. Why should we ... !

ALLMERS. Don't you see the reason for that?

MRS. ALLMERS. No. Yes. No. Say it!

ALLMERS. You say it first.

MRS. ALLMERS. No, you must ...

ALLMERS. Actually, the thing most in our way was little Eyolf ...

MRS. ALLMERS. Oh, Alfred ... how can you ... !

ALLMERS. You have never been a real mother to him. And I never really a proper father.

MRS. ALLMERS. What else?

ALLMERS. It sounds so shabby when I say it.

MRS. ALLMERS. I don't understand you, Alfred.

ALLMERS. But it isn't shabby. I don't think it can be called that.

MRS. ALLMERS. No, no ... but what in the world ... ?

ALLMERS. You were rich and I was poor, Rita.

MRS. ALLMERS [*taking a step towards him*]. I don't believe that!

ALLMERS. That's how it was, nevertheless.

MRS. ALLMERS. That is shabby!

ALLMERS. I had a sister to provide for. Remember that.

MRS. ALLMERS. So it was for her sake, then ... !

ALLMERS. We were alone in the world, she and I. I worked for her as long as I was able. Was on the point of collapsing under it all ...

MRS. ALLMERS. That you can stand there and admit all this now!

ALLMERS. I felt I had to free you from these painful self-recriminations. Now I think you know the reason why you could never really love little Eyolf.

MRS. ALLMERS. Oh, but I did love him too!

ALLMERS. You always looked at him as though some inexplicable mystery lay behind it all.

MRS. ALLMERS. You interpreted wrongly. I was always in fear and trembling in case he was going to take you from me. [*Bursts out wildly.*] And now you yourself say that you were never really mine.

ALLMERS. I was! I took you and held you so dearly when Eyolf was born.

MRS. ALLMERS [*scornfully*]. Oh, yes . . . indeed! Because he belonged to the family line didn't he! The child . . . and the sister! That is something special. . . . Ah, how I hate . . . how I hate her!

[ANDREA *and* BORGHEJM *come along the path by the shore.*]

ALLMERS. Yes, we are still here, Andrea.

ANDREA. And had a good talk together. We don't want to disturb you.

MRS. ALLMERS. No, let us all go, all four of us. We need company from now on. Alfred and I cannot manage alone.

ALLMERS. Yes, do go, the rest of you. But I must talk to you, Andrea!

MRS. ALLMERS. Oh? Very well, come along, Mr. Borghejm.

[MRS. ALLMERS *and* BORGHEJM *go up the path through the trees, right.*]

ANDREA. Is there something you want of me, Alfred?

ALLMERS. Yes, there is something I want to ask you.

ANDREA. Well?

ALLMERS. Tell me, is there anything between you and Borghejm?

ANDREA. Oh, I don't know what to answer.

ALLMERS. How do you mean? Don't you know.

ANDREA. I have no right to answer.

ALLMERS. We two must stay together.

ANDREA. We are together.

ALLMERS. Not here. I don't think my home is here any longer.

ANDREA. Alfred!

ALLMERS. Rita and I cannot return the same love.

ANDREA. Oh, don't say that!

ALLMERS. Yes, yes. I see it now. And that is why I turn to you.

ANDREA. In this I cannot help you.

ALLMERS. Yes, you can. You alone. It is a sister I need. . . .

ANDREA [*half whispering*]. A sister!

ALLMERS. A sister's love. Something pure. Something sacred. I feel I am becoming evil here.

ANDREA. Alfred! Alfred!

ALLMERS. Ever since you were a little child we have held together. We two alone. At that time you needed me. And I did what I could for you.

ANDREA. All that I am I owe to you.

ALLMERS. Not particularly to me. Much more to our beautiful and sacred life together.

ANDREA. Every fibre of my mind has taken shape from you. By you. Through you.

ALLMERS. No, no. It was achieved by that quiet ineffable mystery. . . .

ANDREA. Which, Alfred?

ALLMERS. The mystery of a brother's and sister's love. That mysterious drawing power of sister to brother and brother to sister.

ANDREA. You felt it in *that* way?

ALLMERS. Always. And you too. You too, Andrea. I am convinced.

ANDREA. And now? What do you want to do now?

ALLMERS. I want the two of us to turn to each other again. . . .

ANDREA [*tremblingly*]. The two of us.

ALLMERS. Previously you needed me. Now I need you. Don't let anyone come between us. Promise me you will continue to be a sister to me.

ANDREA. I cannot, Alfred.

ALLMERS. You cannot!

ANDREA. No, not any more. Not as you now are. I can no longer be like a sister to you.

ALLMERS. And why can't you?

ANDREA. Because I *am* none.

ALLMERS. What does that mean!

ANDREA. That I have no right to bear the name of Allmers.

ALLMERS. Andrea!

ANDREA. I have long known it. Now you know it too. And now we must part.

ALLMERS. No right to bear . . . Tell me! Explain to me . . . !

ANDREA. Not another word! That's how it is.

ALLMERS [*heavily*]. Oh, how unspeakably poor I am, then.

ANDREA. You could be so rich . . . so rich, Alfred.

ALLMERS. I? I rich?

ANDREA. Yes, you. For you have Rita, and you have the gold of both grief and loss.

[*She goes up the forest path, right.*]

ALLMERS [*to himself*]. No sister. . . . And little Eyolf driven by the fjord currents.

[*He walks slowly up the path.*]

⟨*dated*⟩ 24.7.94

ACT THREE

A rise in ALLMERS' *garden. In the background a sheer drop, with railings at the edge. Distant views over the fjord. Flag at half-mast by the railings. A summerhouse, right. It is late on a summer evening.*

 MISS ASTA ⟨sic⟩ ALLMERS *is sitting on a bench, left, and seems to be waiting for somebody. Her hands in her lap. Shortly afterwards, Engineer* BORGHEJM *comes up the slope in the background.*

BORGHEJM. So I've found you at last!

ASTA. I have been sitting here waiting. . . .

BORGHEJM. Surely not for me?

ASTA. Yes. I have been waiting for you.

BORGHEJM [*approaching*]. Then I may approach?

ASTA. Yes, indeed you may.

BORGHEJM. And talk to you—once more?

ASTA. Yes. Or first . . . let me talk to you.

BORGHEJM [*stands in front of her*]. Well?

ASTA. Are you leaving this evening?

BORGHEJM. I am leaving tonight. With the steamer. I must.

ASTA. Yes, yes. I imagine you must. But I want you to understand something, Borghejm.

BORGHEJM. Gladly.

ASTA. Oh, if only one could divide oneself up. Be in two places at one time.

BORGHEJM [*with suppressed passion*]. If you could . . . what would you do?

ASTA. I would leave with you. . . .

BORGHEJM. You would leave . . . !

ASTA. With you. Tonight, with the steamer.

BORGHEJM. You'd do that! Despite everything ... !

ASTA. But I *cannot* divide myself! Cannot let my brother go.

BORGHEJM. No. That you've said to me twice before already, Asta.

ASTA. And least of all now that he no longer has little Eyolf. Think of what he has been to me all my life. ...

BORGHEJM. Yes, I understand all that, Asta. You consider it your duty ...

ASTA. Oh, no. That's not why. Not because it's my duty. ...

BORGHEJM. But ... ?

ASTA. Because I care for him as ... well, as I think only a sister can care for a brother.

BORGHEJM. And that goes deepest, you think?

ASTA. I do rather think that. Because it is the purest—the most sacred.

BORGHEJM. What do you say of a mother's love for her child?

ASTA. I haven't had much experience of that.

BORGHEJM. And a father's?

ASTA. I know nothing of that. Do you?

BORGHEJM. Yes. Both of a mother's and a father's. And I think it's that which has given me such an easy, happy cast of mind. Well now ... ?

ASTA. Now?

BORGHEJM. Now I shall build my roads alone.

ASTA. Oh, if only I could come with you. Help you. ...

BORGHEJM. Would you, if you could?

ASTA. Yes I would.

BORGHEJM. But you can't.

ASTA. Would you be content with having half of me, Borghejm?

BORGHEJM. No. I must have you wholly and completely.

ASTA. Then I can't.

[ALFRED ALLMER ⟨sic⟩ *comes up from below on to the rise.*]

ALLMERS [*stops and looks at them*]. Aha! Both of you here, eh?

BORGHEJM. You know I am leaving tonight.

ALLMERS. Yes. And what then? Are you leaving on your own?

BORGHEJM. Yes, I am. And will remain alone . . . after this.

ALLMERS. Alone. There is something terrible about being alone.

ASTA. Oh, but Alfred, you are not that!

ALLMERS. Am I not! When I no longer have the child. And no sister either.

ASTA [*fearfully*]. Alfred, Alfred, you mustn't . . . !

BORGHEJM. How can you say that? Didn't you hear—your sister is not leaving with me.

ALLMERS. It's all the same. Oh, Asta, I no longer have you. Not the way I had you before.

BORGHEJM [*looks at them in astonishment*]. But I don't understand. . . .

ASTA. Oh, but you do, Alfred. Believe me . . . for you I will always be the same as I was.

ALLMERS. But not I.

ASTA [*shrinks back*]. Ah . . . ?

ALLMERS. Never bind yourself, Borghejm! The time might come when you will regret it. But then it is too late.

BORGHEJM. Never in this world could I come to regret anything here.

ALLMERS. Oh, it is quite incredible how a person can change.

ASTA. Two people might well change together. And then they might become completely one.

ALLMERS. Don't build on that, Asta. That would indeed be happiness for life.

[MRS. RITA ALLMERS *comes up the hill.*]

RITA. Are you also up here, Alfred?

[*She turns to go again.*]

ALLMERS. No, stay, Rita. What did you want?

RITA. Just to walk and walk. I can't find peace of mind anywhere.

ALLMERS. Nor I.

RITA. Also the fact that we cannot walk together.

ASTA. Oh, but can you not? Try it.

RITA. That seems to me so completely impossible now. After this we must each go our own ways.

ALLMERS. I cannot bear the loneliness . . .

RITA. I see that. I know that. Feel it. Asta, you must never leave him.

ASTA. I!

BORGHEJM. Never!

RITA. No, he must have somebody to cling to.

ASTA. What about you, Rita!

RITA. Not any longer. Something stands between.

ALLMERS. That must go—if we are to live.

RITA. It will never go. You thrive in the shade. And ⬤ must have sunshine. Stay with us, Asta.

ALLMERS. Is that your wish!

RITA. Yes, for your sake. Stay with him. And if I stand in the way, I will give way.

ALLMERS. You shall never give way.

RITA. I have given way once before. Given way to my own child. Surely that must be right.

ALLMERS. But . . . Rita!

RITA. You shall be our child, Asta. We will take you in Eyolf's place. For we must have a child who can bring us together.

ASTA [*looks at him*]. What do you say, Alfred?

ALLMERS [*uncertainly*]. I . . . ?

RITA. You must! You must! Something calm, warm, passionless is what you need. A child or a sister.

ALLMERS [*with a glance at* ASTA]. Ah, a sister.

ASTA. Do you want me to stay here, Alfred?

ALLMERS. No, you shall leave.

RITA. You won't be allowed to.

ASTA. I will and must leave. This very evening.

RITA. Where will you go.

ASTA. First only into town. But after that . . .

BORGHEJM. After that . . . ?

ASTA. Far, far away from here. [*Looks at* BORGHEJM *and holds out her hand to him.*] I'm going with you.

BORGHEJM [*beaming with joy*]. You will!

ASTA. Tomorrow you shall learn everything. Then you can choose.

BORGHEJM. Oh, nothing matters to me but having you, Asta!

RITA. Ah, so it's like that . . . !

ASTA. Farewell, Rita. [*Puts her arms round her neck.*] And thank you for being so good to me. [*Holds out her hand.*] Farewell, Alfred.

ALLMERS [*going with open arms towards her*]. Asta . . .

ASTA [*shrinks back*]. Farewell, farewell. [*To* BORGHEJM.] Come, come. Now we must hurry.

[BORGHEJM *shakes hands silently with* ALLMERS *and* RITA *and follows* ASTA *down the slope.*]

ALLMERS [*stands by the railings looking out over the fjord*]. There comes the steamer. Soon they will be gone.

RITA. And we two alone.

ALLMERS. So be it.

RITA. Can we?

ALLMERS. We must.

RITA. Yes, for Asta's sake.

ALLMERS [*looks across at her*]. For Asta's . . . What do you mean?

RITA. She couldn't stay here. She too wanted to be all things to you. Same as me.

ALLMERS. For her own sake she had no cause to leave. But . . .

RITA. But . . . ?

ALLMERS. For mine, there was.

RITA. Alfred! You could think . . . desire . . . something criminal! Never in the world!

ALLMERS [*shakes his head*]. No, nothing criminal. But there is a secret in the family. . . .

RITA. In your family?

ALLMERS. Yes. Asta and I are free of any relationship.

RITA. And you have kept this from me?

ALLMERS. I only learnt of it today.

RITA. From her?

ALLMERS. Yes.

RITA. And so she leaves.

ALLMERS. Yes. So she leaves.

RITA. And you did not ask her to stay . . . ?

ALLMERS. It was best for all of us that Asta should leave.

RITA. How could you do it, Alfred. I'd never have been able to do a thing like that. Oh, but it's just like I say . . . fish's blood. . . . No, no, I don't mean it. It is the great and pure side of you which has won the victory!

ALLMERS. Oh, victory is still a long way off.

RITA. Then let us help each other.

ALLMERS. To find happiness again?

RITA. Not the happiness we have lost. That we'll never find again. But . . .

ALLMERS. But . . . ?

RITA. Oh, I don't know, Alfred. But there must be something to put in its place.

ALLMERS. Something to counterbalance the loss of happiness, you mean?

RITA. Not something to balance happiness. But something which might make life livable. ·

ALLMERS. And you want to live life by hook or by crook? At any price?

RITA. Yes, Alfred . . . I really do. In spite of all. In spite of all.

ALLMERS [*after a brief silence*]. Rita . . . I wrote a few brief lines of verse this afternoon.

RITA. Could you do that?

ALLMERS. Yes, today I could. Would you like to hear them?

RITA. Yes, I would very much. Is it something about me?

ALLMERS. About you too. [*Sits on the bench.*] Come and sit down, and then you can listen.

[*She sits down on a chair by the table directly facing him. He takes a paper out of his breast-pocket.*]

ALLMERS [*reads*].
They sat there, those two, in so snug a house
in autumn and in winter days.
Then the house burnt. All lies in ruins.
Those two must rake in the ashes.

For down in the ashes a jewel is hidden,
a jewel that can never burn.
And if they search in faith, it could perhaps happen
That it is found by him or her.

But even if this fire-scarred pair ever do find
That precious fire-proof jewel—
She will never find her burnt peace—
He never his burnt happiness.

[*He looks questioningly at* RITA.]

Did you understand that, Rita?

RITA [*rising*]. Yes. And I also understood that you didn't write those lines about me.

ALLMERS. Who else . . . ?

RITA. You wrote them about yourself and Asta.

ALLMERS. About little Eyolf in the first place. . . .

RITA. Oh, not at all about little Eyolf who is lying deep deep down out there.

ALLMERS. Rita, Rita, how can you . . .

RITA. You wrote them about the other one. About her whom you called little Eyolf when she was a child.

ALLMERS. Both to the big one and to the little one. And to you also, Rita. I had to find expression for something I cannot bear any longer in silence.

RITA. Would it help you to be free of me?

ALLMERS. No.

RITA. But neither can we live together as man and wife.

Lı

ALLMERS. No.

RITA. For little Eyolf might perhaps be watching. Who knows? And he must not see us living in happiness without him.

ALLMERS. We couldn't do that either, Rita. However much we wanted.

RITA. No, we couldn't. [*Stops.*] But if we could bring him to life again, Alfred!

ALLMERS. How do you mean?

RITA. If we could make him live within us, I mean.

ALLMERS. But he is living within us. In grief, and in a sense of loss and . . . and in remorse too.

RITA. Oh, grief, loss, remorse—that isn't life. That is nothing for Eyolf and his child's mind. We must think of something that can fill him with quiet pleasure.

ALLMERS [*shakes his head with a heavy smile*]. As if he could see what we might set about doing here!

RITA. Perhaps he can in fact see—in his own way. We must live and act as though he were behind us. Looking at us. Seeing everything and understanding everything. All our actions and all our thoughts.

ALLMERS [*wringing his hands*]. Oh, if only he had been able to live with us. Live his own life. Now it is as if he had never existed. What was he meant to do in this world, when he never got . . .

RITA. Nevertheless he did not live in vain.

ALLMERS. Empty phrases, my dear. [*Pointing over the railings.*] Listen to them down there. All those screaming, bawling youngsters. All those who let him go to his end. And who didn't help him.

RITA. They will also go to their ends, Alfred. Meet their end in those unhappy homes.

ALLMERS. Perhaps you are right.

RITA. And we stand up here on our hill and look down on it all. And give them no help.

ALLMERS. We . . . ?

RITA. We could help them if we wanted to. But we don't.

ALLMERS [*staring vacantly*]. That would be little Eyolf's revenge. To repay death with life.

RITA. Then he would not have lived in vain.

ALLMERS. And would not have died in vain, either.

RITA. If that is what you will—we'll do it, Alfred. Stand by each other like two loyal friends.

ALLMERS. Little Eyolf shall continue to live through us.

[*He walks over to the flagpole and hoists the flag right up to the masthead.*]

RITA. No symbols of death any more. That's a relief, Alfred. Oh, what a relief.

ALLMERS. Thank you for rousing me to do that.

RITA. Thank little Eyolf.

ALLMERS. Yes, him first.—In deeds.

RITA. If only one does not demand happiness . . . at any price . . . it seems to me surely possible for life to be lived.

ALLMERS. Eyolf's memory shall teach us how to live life.

RITA. Yes, yes, Alfred. And he himself will live in that.

RITA ⟨*sic*⟩. Yes, he will live with us. No more will we seek him down in the deep, dark, muddy currents.

ALLMERS. He is not down there. He is up here, unseen, on earth with us. Taking part in daily life. Helping us to take care of insecure, changing human destinies.

RITA. And if from time to time a hushed Sunday calm comes over our minds . . .

ALLMERS. What then, Rita?

RITA. Don't you think it might be a visit from the departed?

ALLMERS. Who knows. We will look for those who are departed. Perhaps we may catch a glimpse of them.

RITA. Little Eyolf. And big Eyolf. Where shall we look, Alfred?

ALLMERS. Upwards.

RITA [*nods in agreement*]. Yes, upwards!

ALLMERS. Upwards . . . towards the stars. And towards the vast silence.

RITA [*holds out her hand to him*]. Thank you.

⟨*dated*⟩ 7.8.94.

JOHN GABRIEL BORKMAN
[*John Gabriel Borkman*]

PLAY IN FOUR ACTS

(1896)

CHARACTERS

JOHN GABRIEL BORKMAN, onetime banker

MRS. GUNHILD BORKMAN, his wife

ERHART BORKMAN, their son, a student

MISS ELLA RENTHEIM, Mrs. Borkman's twin sister

MRS. FANNY WILTON

VILHELM FOLDAL, part-time clerk in a Government office

FRIDA FOLDAL, his daughter

MRS. BORKMAN'S MAID

The action takes place one winter evening in the Rentheim family residence on the outskirts of the capital

ACT ONE

MRS. BORKMAN's *sitting-room, furnished in old-fashioned, faded splendour. At the back, an open sliding door gives on to a garden room, with windows and a glass door. Through them is a view to the garden, with flurrying snow in the half-light. On the side wall, right, a door leads from the hall. Further downstage is a large, old-fashioned iron stove, where a fire is burning. On the left, further back, a single smaller door. Forward of it, on the same side, a window hung with heavy curtains. Between the window and the door, a sofa covered in horsehair; in front of it, a table with a cloth over it. On the table a lighted lamp with a shade. By the stove a high-backed armchair.*

MRS. GUNHILD BORKMAN *is sitting on the sofa with her crochet-work. She is an elderly lady of coldly dignified appearance; she holds herself stiffly, and her expression is impassive. Her abundant hair is heavily streaked with grey. Delicate transparent hands. She wears a heavy dark silk dress which once was elegant but is now somewhat worn and shabby. A woollen shawl over her shoulders.*

She sits for some moments erect and motionless at her crochet-work. Then outside there is the sound of bells from a passing sleigh.

MRS. BORKMAN [*listens; her eyes light up with pleasure, and involuntarily she whispers*]. Erhart! At last!

[*She gets up and looks out through the curtains. Looks disappointed, and sits down to her work again on the sofa. A moment or two later, the* MAID *comes in from the hall with a visiting card on a small tray.*]

MRS. BORKMAN [*quickly*]. Has Mr. Erhart come?

MAID. No, madam. But there's a lady outside. . . .

MRS. BORKMAN [*puts down her crochet-work*]. Oh, that will be Mrs. Wilton. . . .

MAID [*approaches*]. No, this lady is a stranger. . . .

MRS. BORKMAN [*picks up the card*]. Let me see. . . . [*Reads it, rises quickly and looks fixedly at the* MAID.] Are you sure this is meant for me?

MAID. Yes, I understood it was for you, madam.

MRS. BORKMAN. Did she ask to speak to Mrs. Borkman?

MAID. Yes, she did.

MRS. BORKMAN [*curtly and decisively*]. Very well. Tell her I am at home.

> [*The* MAID *opens the door for the caller and goes out.* MISS ELLA RENTHEIM *comes into the room. She resembles her sister in appearance; but her face is marked by suffering rather than by hardness. It still retains some of the great and characterful beauty of her younger days. Her abundant hair is gathered back in natural waves off her forehead; it is silver-white. She is dressed in black velvet, with hat and fur-lined coat of the same material.*
>   *The two sisters stand in silence for a moment looking searchingly at each other. Each is evidently waiting for the other to speak first.*]

ELLA RENTHEIM [*who has remained standing near the door*]. You look somewhat surprised to see me, Gunhild.

MRS. BORKMAN [*stands rigid and unmoving between the sofa and the table, with her finger-tips pressing on the cloth*]. Haven't you made a mistake? The bailiff lives in the side wing, you know.

ELLA RENTHEIM. It's not the bailiff I want to see today.

MRS. BORKMAN. Is it me you want?

ELLA RENTHEIM. Yes. I want a word with you.

MRS. BORKMAN [*walks forward*]. Very well. Sit down.

ELLA RENTHEIM. Thank you. I can just as well stand.

MRS. BORKMAN. As you wish. At least loosen your coat.

ELLA RENTHEIM [*unbuttoning her coat*]. Yes, it's very hot in here. . . .

MRS. BORKMAN. I am always cold.

ELLA RENTHEIM [*stands for a moment looking at her, her arms resting on the back of the armchair*]. Well, Gunhild. It's nearly eight years now since we last saw each other.

MRS. BORKMAN [*coldly*]. Since we spoke, at least.

ELLA RENTHEIM. More correctly, since we spoke, yes. . . . You must have seen me on occasion . . . when I paid my yearly visit to the bailiff.

MRS. BORKMAN. Once or twice, I believe.

ELLA RENTHEIM. I've also caught a few glimpses of you, too. There, at the window.

MRS. BORKMAN. Behind the curtains, it must have been. You have sharp eyes. [*Hard and incisively.*] But the last time we *spoke* . . . was here in this room. . . .

ELLA RENTHEIM [*with a dismissive gesture*]. Yes, yes, Gunhild, I know that!

MRS. BORKMAN. The week before he . . . before he was let out.

ELLA RENTHEIM [*walks upstage*]. Oh, let us not start on that!

MRS. BORKMAN [*firmly, in a low voice*]. It was the week before he . . . he was set free.

ELLA RENTHEIM [*walks downstage*]. Yes, yes, yes! I'm not likely to forget. But it is too terrible to think about. Even for a moment. . . . Oh!

MRS. BORKMAN [*gloomily*]. Yet one's thoughts forever keep returning to it! [*Vehemently, striking her hands together.*] I can't understand it! Ever! I can't understand how a thing like this . . . this terrible thing . . . .could happen to one family. To *our* family. A distinguished family like ours! That *we* should be singled out!

ELLA RENTHEIM. Oh, Gunhild . . . many many more families than ours suffered.

MRS. BORKMAN. All right. But I'm not greatly concerned about those others. All it meant for them was losing a bit of money . . . or a few bonds. But for us . . . ! For me! And for Erhart! Only a child at the time! [*With increasing agitation.*] The shame that we two suffered . . . innocent as we were. The disgrace! The terrible, hateful disgrace! As well as complete and utter ruin!

ELLA RENTHEIM [*cautiously*]. Tell me, Gunhild. How is he taking it?

MRS. BORKMAN. Erhart, you mean?

ELLA RENTHEIM. No—he. How is he taking it?

MRS. BORKMAN [*scornfully*]. Do you think I enquire about *that*?

ELLA RENTHEIM. Enquire? You don't have to enquire . . .

MRS. BORKMAN [*looks at her in astonishment*]. You don't imagine I ever consort with him? Ever meet him? Ever see him even?

ELLA RENTHEIM. Not even see him!

MRS. BORKMAN [*as before*]. A man who had to serve five years in gaol! [*Buries her face in her hands.*] The crushing shame! [*Flares up.*] And think what the name John Gabriel Borkman once meant! No, no, no! I never want to see him again! Ever!

ELLA RENTHEIM [*regards her for a moment*]. You are hard, Gunhild.

MRS. BORKMAN. Towards him, yes.

ELLA RENTHEIM. He *is* your husband.

MRS. BORKMAN. Did he not tell the court it was I who had led him to ruin? That I spent too much money . . . ?

ELLA RENTHEIM [*cautiously*]. But wasn't there some truth in that?

MRS. BORKMAN. But he was the one who wanted it like that! Everything had to be so absurdly lavishly done. . . .

ELLA RENTHEIM. I know. But that's just why you might have held back. Yet you didn't.

MRS. BORKMAN. Did I know it wasn't his own money he gave me to throw around? And which he threw around too—ten times more than I did!

ELLA RENTHEIM [*quietly*]. Well, I suppose that went with his position. A lot of it, at least.

MRS. BORKMAN [*scornfully*]. Yes, always the talk was of having 'to create an impression'. Oh, he created his impression all right! Drove round in his coach-and-four as though he were a king. Had people bowing and scraping to him as if he were a king. [*Laughs.*] And they called him by his Christian names—all over the country—just as if he *was* the King. 'John Gabriel.' 'John Gabriel.' Everybody knew what a great man 'John Gabriel' was!

ELLA RENTHEIM [*warmly and emphatically*]. He *was* a great man then, Gunhild.

MRS. BORKMAN. Yes, so it appeared. But he never said one word to me about the real state of his affairs. Never gave any hint as to where he took the money from.

ELLA RENTHEIM. No . . . but none of the others had any idea, either.

MRS. BORKMAN. The others are neither here nor there. But to *me* it was his duty to tell the truth. And he never did. He simply lied to me . . . lied incessantly. . . .

ELLA RENTHEIM [*interrupting*]. Surely not, Gunhild! Concealed things, perhaps. But he didn't lie.

MRS. BORKMAN. Well, call it what you will. It's the same thing in the end. . . . For it all collapsed. Everything. And all the glory was over.

ELLA RENTHEIM [*to herself*]. Yes, everything collapsed . . . for him . . . and for others.

MRS. BORKMAN [*drawing herself up, defiantly*]. But I tell you, Ella . . . I haven't given up! I shall win restitution yet. Take that from me!

ELLA RENTHEIM [*tense*]. Restitution? What do you mean?

MRS. BORKMAN. Restitution of name, of honour, of fortune. Restitution for the whole of my ruined life! That's what I mean! And I have somebody already standing by, I'll have you know. Somebody who will wipe the record clean of every stain left by that man.

ELLA RENTHEIM. Gunhild! Gunhild!

MRS. BORKMAN [*with rising passion*]. He will be the avenger! The man who will put right the wrong his father did me.

ELLA RENTHEIM. You mean Erhart.

MRS. BORKMAN. Yes, Erhart . . . my boy! He'll find a way to restore the family, the house, the name. All that *can* be restored. And more besides, perhaps.

ELLA RENTHEIM. And how do you expect this to happen?

MRS. BORKMAN. It will happen some way. Quite how I don't know. All I know is that happen it must, and happen it *will*. [*Looks searchingly at her.*] Come now, Ella—haven't you also had this same thing in mind ever since he was a child?

ELLA RENTHEIM. No. I can't say I have.

MRS. BORKMAN. No? Then why did you take him and look after him when the disaster struck?

ELLA RENTHEIM. Because at the time you couldn't, Gunhild.

MRS. BORKMAN. No ... I couldn't. And his father—he was legally exempt ... sitting there behind bars ... in good keeping. ...

ELLA RENTHEIM [*indignant*]. How can you say a thing like that!

MRS. BORKMAN [*with a venomous look*]. And what made *you* so ready to bring up the child of this ... of this John Gabriel? Just as though the child were your own. Taking him away from me ... home to you. And keeping him there, year after year, till he was nearly grown up. [*Looks suspiciously at her.*] Why did you hold on to him?

ELLA RENTHEIM. I came to love him dearly.

MRS. BORKMAN. More than I? His mother?

ELLA RENTHEIM [*evasively*]. That I don't know. And Erhart was of course rather weakly as a child. ...

MRS. BORKMAN. Erhart—weakly!

ELLA RENTHEIM. Yes, I thought so ... at the time, anyway. And the air over on the west coast is so much milder than here, as you know.

MRS. BORKMAN [*smiles bitterly*]. Hm ... is it, now? [*Breaking off.*] Yes, really you've done a lot for Erhart, haven't you? [*Changes her tone.*] Of course, you could afford it. [*Smiles.*] You were lucky, Ella. You managed to make quite sure all *your* money was saved.

ELLA RENTHEIM [*offended*]. Not because of anything *I* did, let me tell you. It wasn't until a long time afterwards I discovered that the securities in my name at the bank had escaped ...

MRS. BORKMAN. Well, I don't understand these things. All I can say is you were lucky. [*Looks searchingly at her.*] But when you took it upon yourself to bring up Erhart for me ...? What was your motive in doing that?

ELLA RENTHEIM [*looks at her*]. My motive?

MRS. BORKMAN. Yes, you must have had some motive. What was he meant to become? What did you want to make of him, I mean?

ELLA RENTHEIM [*slowly*]. I wanted to give Erhart every chance of finding happiness in life.

MRS. BORKMAN [*snorting*]. Pah! People in our position have better things to do than think about happiness.

ELLA RENTHEIM. Such as what?

MRS. BORKMAN [*looks steadily and earnestly at her*]. Erhart's first duty is to shine so brilliantly that people no longer see the shadow his father cast over me . . . and over my son.

ELLA RENTHEIM [*searchingly*]. Tell me, Gunhild . . . is this the aim Erhart *himself* demands of life?

MRS. BORKMAN [*taken aback*]. Yes, I should very much hope so!

ELLA RENTHEIM. Or isn't it rather one that *you* are demanding of him?

MRS. BORKMAN [*curtly*]. Erhart and I always have the same aims.

ELLA RENTHEIM [*sadly and slowly*]. You are very sure of your son, Gunhild.

MRS. BORKMAN [*with concealed triumph*]. Yes, thank God, I am. Take that as certain!

ELLA RENTHEIM. Then I think you must be quite happy, all in all. Despite these other things.

MRS. BORKMAN. Yes, I am. Up to a point. Yet not a moment passes . . . but what this other thing comes sweeping over me like a blizzard.

ELLA RENTHEIM [*with a change of tone*]. Tell me . . . There is no point in delaying it. What I wanted to see you about . . .

MRS. BORKMAN. Yes?

ELLA RENTHEIM. . . . Something I felt I had to discuss with you. . . . Tell me, Erhart isn't living out here with . . . with the two of you, is he?

MRS. BORKMAN [*hard*]. Erhart *cannot* live out here with me. He has to live in town. . . .

ELLA RENTHEIM. Yes, he wrote and told me so.

MRS. BORKMAN. He has to, for the sake of his studies. But he looks in to see me every evening.

ELLA RENTHEIM. Well, perhaps I might be allowed to see him? May I talk to him? Now?

MRS. BORKMAN. He's not here yet. I'm expecting him any minute.

ELLA RENTHEIM. He must have come, Gunhild. I can hear his footsteps upstairs.

MRS. BORKMAN [*with a fleeting glance*]. Up in the great room?

ELLA RENTHEIM. Yes. I've heard him up there, walking about, ever since I arrived.

MRS. BORKMAN [*turns her eyes away*]. That isn't him, Ella.

ELLA RENTHEIM [*startled*]. Not Erhart? [*Beginning to suspect.*] Who is it then?

MRS. BORKMAN. Him.

ELLA RENTHEIM [*quietly, with suppressed pain*]. Borkman? John Gabriel Borkman?

MRS. BORKMAN. Up and down like that he goes. Backwards and forwards. From morning till night. Day in and day out.

ELLA RENTHEIM. I had in fact heard something of this.

MRS. BORKMAN. I dare say. I imagine people find plenty to say about us.

ELLA RENTHEIM. Erhart touched on it in his letters. That his father kept himself to himself . . . up there. And you to yourself down here.

MRS. BORKMAN. Yes. That's how it's been with us, Ella. Ever since they let him out, and sent him home to me. All these eight long years.

ELLA RENTHEIM. I could never believe it was true. That it could be possible . . . !

MRS. BORKMAN [*nods*]. It is true. And can never be otherwise.

ELLA RENTHEIM [*looks at her*]. This must be a terrible existence, Gunhild.

MRS. BORKMAN. Worse than terrible. I can't bear it much longer.

ELLA RENTHEIM. I can understand that.

MRS. BORKMAN. Constantly hearing his footsteps up there. From early morning till late at night. You can hear every sound down here.

ELLA RENTHEIM. Yes, it does resound here.

MRS. BORKMAN. Many a time I feel as though I had a sick wolf pacing his cage up there in the great room. Right above my head. [*Listens and whispers.*] Listen, Ella! Listen! Backwards and forwards, backwards and forwards goes the wolf.

ELLA RENTHEIM [*cautiously*]. Couldn't something be done about it, Gunhild?

MRS. BORKMAN [*with a repudiating gesture*]. He has never made any move.

ELLA RENTHEIM. Couldn't you make the first move, then?

MRS. BORKMAN [*angrily*]. I? After all that he's done to me! No, thank you! Let the wolf keep to his prowling up there.

ELLA RENTHEIM. It's too hot for me in here. I will take my things off after all.

MRS. BORKMAN. I did ask you earlier. . . .

[ELLA RENTHEIM *takes off her hat and coat and places them on a chair beside the hall door.*]

ELLA RENTHEIM. Don't you ever run across him outside the house?

MRS. BORKMAN [*laughs bitterly*]. At parties, you mean?

ELLA RENTHEIM. I mean when he takes a breath of fresh air. When he takes a walk in the woods, or . . .

MRS. BORKMAN. He never goes out.

ELLA RENTHEIM. Not even in the dark?

MRS. BORKMAN. Never.

ELLA RENTHEIM [*with emotion*]. He can't bring himself to?

MRS. BORKMAN. I suppose not. He still has his cape and his felt hat hanging in the hall cupboard. . . .

ELLA RENTHEIM [*to herself*]. The cupboard we used to hide in when we were little. . . .

M1

MRS. BORKMAN [*nods*]. Occasionally ... in the late evening ... I've sometimes heard him come down ... as though he was on his way out. But then, halfway down the stairs, he stops ... and turns back. And then he goes back to his room.

ELLA RENTHEIM [*quietly*]. Don't any of his old friends drop in to see him?

MRS. BORKMAN. He hasn't any old friends.

ELLA RENTHEIM. He used to have a lot—at one time.

MRS. BORKMAN. Ha! He managed very nicely to get rid of them. He became a somewhat expensive friend—did John Gabriel.

ELLA RENTHEIM. Oh, I imagine you are right there, Gunhild.

MRS. BORKMAN [*vehemently*]. Though I must say I think it's mean and petty and contemptible of them to attach all that importance to the paltry amounts they might have lost through him. It was only money they lost, after all. Nothing more.

ELLA RENTHEIM [*not answering*]. So he lives up there all alone. Quite by himself.

MRS. BORKMAN. Yes, he does indeed. They tell me an old clerk looks in to see him from time to time.

ELLA RENTHEIM. That'll be a man called Foldal. They knew each other when they were young.

MRS. BORKMAN. Yes, I believe they did. I don't really know anything about him. He didn't move in our circles—in the days when we *had* a circle. ...

ELLA RENTHEIM. But he comes now to see Borkman?

MRS. BORKMAN. Yes, he doesn't have to be particularly choosey. But of course even he only comes after dark.

ELLA RENTHEIM. This Foldal ... he was also one of those who lost his money when the bank failed.

MRS. BORKMAN [*indifferently*]. Yes, I seem to remember he did lose some money. Nothing of any consequence.

ELLA RENTHEIM [*with slight emphasis*]. Only everything he possessed.

MRS. BORKMAN [*smiling*]. But good Lord ... what he possessed was scarcely anything. Not worth mentioning.

ELLA RENTHEIM. Nor was it mentioned ... by Foldal ... at the trial.

MRS. BORKMAN. Anyway, let me tell you that Erhart has amply repaid what little he lost.

ELLA RENTHEIM. Erhart! How did Erhart manage that?

MRS. BORKMAN. He's taken an interest in Foldal's youngest daughter. He's given her some coaching ... so she'll be able to make something of herself, and earn her own living. See! That's a good deal more than her father could ever have done for her.

ELLA RENTHEIM. Her father isn't all that well off, I imagine.

MRS. BORKMAN. And Erhart's arranged for her to study music. She's now quite good—good enough to come and play for ... him up there.

ELLA RENTHEIM. So he is still fond of music?

MRS. BORKMAN. Yes, he must be. He has the piano you sent out here ... when he was expected out.

ELLA RENTHEIM. And she plays it for him?

MRS. BORKMAN. Yes, now and again. In the evenings. Erhart arranged that, too.

ELLA RENTHEIM. But, poor girl, she doesn't have to come all the way out here, then back again to town, does she?

MRS. BORKMAN. No, there's no need for that. Erhart has arranged for her to stay with a lady who lives near. A Mrs. Wilton. ...

ELLA RENTHEIM [*attentively*]. Mrs. Wilton!

MRS. BORKMAN. A very rich woman. You don't know her.

ELLA RENTHEIM. I've heard the name. Mrs. Fanny Wilton, I believe.

MRS. BORKMAN. That's right.

ELLA RENTHEIM. Erhart has written about her a number of times. Does she live out here now?

MRS. BORKMAN. Yes, she's rented a villa here. She moved out of town some time ago.

ELLA RENTHEIM [*a little hesitantly*]. They say she's divorced from her husband.

MRS. BORKMAN. Her husband died some years ago, I believe.

ELLA RENTHEIM. Yes, but they were divorced. He divorced her.

MRS. BORKMAN. He left her. The fault was not hers.

ELLA RENTHEIM. You know her well, Gunhild?

MRS. BORKMAN. Pretty well. She lives quite near. She looks in to see me occasionally.

ELLA RENTHEIM. And you like her?

MRS. BORKMAN. She's unusually intelligent. Remarkably shrewd in her judgement.

ELLA RENTHEIM. In her judgement of people, you mean?

MRS. BORKMAN. Especially of people. She's made a particular study of Erhart . . . a really deep study . . . deep into his mind. Naturally she idolizes him . . . as one might expect.

ELLA RENTHEIM [*a little slyly*]. So perhaps she knows Erhart even better than she knows you?

MRS. BORKMAN. Yes, Erhart used to see her quite often in town. Before she moved out here.

ELLA RENTHEIM [*unguardedly*]. Yet for all that she still moved out of town?

MRS. BORKMAN [*startled, looks sharply at her*]. For all that? What do you mean?

ELLA RENTHEIM [*evasively*]. Well . . . er . . . I mean . . .

MRS. BORKMAN. You said that in such a strange way. You did mean something, Ella!

ELLA RENTHEIM [*looking her straight in the eyes*]. Yes, I did. I did mean something.

MRS. BORKMAN. Then tell me.

ELLA RENTHEIM. First let me say that I think I too have a certain claim on Erhart. Perhaps you don't agree?

MRS. BORKMAN [*looks round the room*]. Doubtless. After all the money you have spent on him. . . .

ELLA RENTHEIM. Not for that reason, Gunhild. But because I love him. . . .

MRS. BORKMAN [*smiles scornfully*]. Love *my* son? You? Can you? In spite of everything?

ELLA RENTHEIM. Yes, I can. In spite of everything. And I do. I do love Erhart. As dearly as I can love anyone . . . now. At my age.

MRS. BORKMAN. All right, all right. But . . .

ELLA RENTHEIM. That's why I get worried as soon as I see anything threatening him.

MRS. BORKMAN. Threatening Erhart? What threatens him? Or who threatens him?

ELLA RENTHEIM. In the first place—you. In your own way.

MRS. BORKMAN [*vehemently*]. *I!*

ELLA RENTHEIM. And then this Mrs. Wilton. She worries me.

MRS. BORKMAN [*looks at her for a moment, speechless*]. You can think that of Erhart! Of my own son! He who has this great mission to complete!

ELLA RENTHEIM [*carelessly*]. Mission!

MRS. BORKMAN [*indignantly*]. How dare you say that so scornfully!

ELLA RENTHEIM. Do you think any young man of Erhart's age . . . sound in body and mind . . . is going to go off and sacrifice himself on some 'mission'!

MRS. BORKMAN [*firmly and emphatically*]. Erhart will! I know. I am certain.

ELLA RENTHEIM [*shakes her head*]. You don't know it, Gunhild. Nor do you believe it.

MRS. BORKMAN. Don't believe it!

ELLA RENTHEIM. It's only something you dream of. Because if you hadn't that to cling to, you know you would be in utter despair.

MRS. BORKMAN. Yes, indeed I would be in despair. [*Vehemently.*] Perhaps you would prefer it that way, Ella!

ELLA RENTHEIM [*with head erect*]. Yes, I would—if you can't win free except by making Erhart suffer.

MRS. BORKMAN [*threateningly*]. You want to come between us! Between mother and son! You!

ELLA RENTHEIM. I want to free him from your power ... your tyranny ... your domination.

MRS. BORKMAN [*triumphantly*]. You can't do that any longer. You had him in your clutches ... right until he was fifteen. But now I've won him back, you see!

ELLA RENTHEIM. Then I will win him back from you again! [*In a hoarse whisper.*] We two have fought over a man before, Gunhild!

MRS. BORKMAN [*looks at her in triumph*]. Yes, and I won.

ELLA RENTHEIM [*smiles scornfully*]. And you still think that victory was worth winning?

MRS. BORKMAN [*darkly*]. No. God knows you are right.

ELLA RENTHEIM. You'll gain nothing this time, either.

MRS. BORKMAN. Nothing gained in keeping a mother's power over Erhart!

ELLA RENTHEIM. No. Because it's only the *power* you want.

MRS. BORKMAN. What about you!

ELLA RENTHEIM [*warmly*]. I want his affection ... his soul ... his loving heart!

MRS. BORKMAN [*bursting out*]. That you will never have again!

ELLA RENTHEIM [*looks at her*]. You've already seen to that?

MRS. BORKMAN [*smiles*]. Yes, I have allowed myself that liberty. Could you not tell that from his letters?

ELLA RENTHEIM [*nods slowly*]. Yes, I could clearly see you at work in his letters of late.

MRS. BORKMAN [*provokingly*]. I made good use of these eight years he's been under my eye, you see.

ELLA RENTHEIM [*controlling herself*]. What have you told Erhart about me? Can you tell me?

MRS. BORKMAN. Oh yes. That's easily done.

ELLA RENTHEIM. Then do it!

MRS. BORKMAN. I simply told him the truth.

ELLA RENTHEIM. Well?

MRS. BORKMAN. I have constantly impressed on him please to remember that it is you we have to thank for being able to live as we do. For being able to live at all, indeed.

ELLA RENTHEIM. Is that all?

MRS. BORKMAN. Oh, that rankles, you know. I feel that myself.

ELLA RENTHEIM. But that's no more than what Erhart knew already.

MRS. BORKMAN. When he first came home, he used to think you'd done it all out of the goodness of your heart. [*Looks maliciously at her.*] He doesn't any longer, Ella.

ELLA RENTHEIM. What does he believe now?

MRS. BORKMAN. He believes the truth. I asked him how he explained the fact that Aunt Ella never came to visit us. . . .

ELLA RENTHEIM [*interrupting*]. He knew that already!

MRS. BORKMAN. He knows better now. You'd made him believe it was to spare my feelings . . . and his, upstairs.

ELLA RENTHEIM. It was.

MRS. BORKMAN. He now doesn't believe a word of it.

ELLA RENTHEIM. What have you got him to believe about me now?

MRS. BORKMAN. He believes what is the truth. That you are ashamed of us, despise us. Or don't you? Didn't you once consider trying to take him away from me altogether? Think, Ella. You remember.

ELLA RENTHEIM. That was when the scandal was at its height. When the case was before the court. I've given up any idea of that now.

MRS. BORKMAN. In any case it wouldn't get you anywhere. For what would then become of his mission? No, thank you. It's me Erhart needs, not you. As far as you are concerned, he might as well be dead! And you to him!

ELLA RENTHEIM [*coldly and firmly*]. We'll see. Now I shall stay here.

MRS. BORKMAN [*stares at her*]. Here in this house?

ELLA RENTHEIM. Yes, here.

MRS. BORKMAN. Here—with us? For the night?

ELLA RENTHEIM. I shall stay here for the rest of my days, if need be.

MRS. BORKMAN [*collecting herself*]. Yes, yes, Ella—of course, the house is yours.

ELLA RENTHEIM. Oh, Gunhild. . . .

MRS. BORKMAN. The whole lot is yours. The chair I am sitting on is yours. The bed I toss and turn in belongs to you. The very food we eat is by courtesy of you.

ELLA RENTHEIM. That can't be arranged any other way. Borkman can't have any property of his own. Somebody would come and take it straight away.

MRS. BORKMAN. Yes, I know. We have to put up with living on your grace and charity.

ELLA RENTHEIM [*coldly*]. If you must see it in that light, I can't prevent you, Gunhild.

MRS. BORKMAN. No, you can't. When do you want us to move out?

ELLA RENTHEIM [*looks at her*]. Move out?

MRS. BORKMAN [*agitatedly*]. Yes. You don't for a moment imagine I would live under the same roof as you! I'd rather go to the workhouse, or tramp the roads!

ELLA RENTHEIM. Good. Then let me take Erhart with me. . . .

MRS. BORKMAN. Erhart! My own son! My child!

ELLA RENTHEIM. If you do, I'll leave for home at once.

MRS. BORKMAN [*reflects for a moment; then speaks firmly*]. Erhart himself shall choose between us.

ELLA RENTHEIM [*looks dubiously and uncertainly at her*]. He choose? Dare you, Gunhild?

MRS. BORKMAN [*with a hard laugh*]. Dare? Let my boy choose between his mother and you! Certainly I dare!

ELLA RENTHEIM [*listening*]. Is that someone coming? I thought I heard . . .

MRS. BORKMAN. It must be Erhart. . . .

[*There is a brisk knock on the door from the hall, which is then opened at once. MRS. WILTON, in evening dress and coat, enters. Behind her the MAID, who has not had time to announce her, stands looking confused. The door is left standing half-open. MRS. WILTON is a shapely and strikingly beautiful woman in her thirties; generous, smiling red lips; sparkling eyes; rich, dark hair.*]

MRS. WILTON. Good evening, my dear Mrs. Borkman!

MRS. BORKMAN [*somewhat drily*]. Good evening. [*To the MAID, pointing to the garden room.*] Fetch the lamp out of there and light it.

[*The MAID takes the lamp and goes out.*]

MRS. WILTON [*sees ELLA RENTHEIM*]. Oh, forgive me . . . you have visitor.

MRS. BORKMAN. Only my sister paying a visit. . . .

[ERHART BORKMAN *pushes wide the half-open door and comes rushing in. He is a young man with bright cheerful eyes. Elegantly dressed. The beginnings of a moustache.*]

ERHART BORKMAN [*radiant with joy, stands in the doorway*]. What's this! Aunt Ella here! [*Across to her and seizes her hand.*] Aunt! aunt! Is it possible! You here?

ELLA RENTHEIM [*throws her arms round his neck*]. Erhart! My dear, dear boy! How tall you've grown! Oh, how good it is to see you again!

MRS. BORKMAN [*sharply*]. What does this mean, Erhart? Were you hiding out in the hall?

MRS. WILTON [*quickly*]. Erhart . . . Mr. Borkman arrived with me.

MRS. BORKMAN [*looks him up and down*]. Indeed, Erhart. So your first call isn't at your mother's?

ERHART. I just had to look in at Mrs. Wilton's for a moment . . . to collect little Frida.

MRS. BORKMAN. Is this Miss Foldal also with you?

MRS. WILTON. Yes, we left her in the hall.

ERHART [*speaking through the open door*]. Just go on upstairs, Frida.

[*Pause.* ELLA RENTHEIM *observes* ERHART. *He seems embarrassed and rather impatient. His face has a strained, cold expression. The* MAID *brings the lighted lamp into the room and goes out again, closing the door behind her.*]

MRS. BORKMAN [*with forced politeness*]. Well, Mrs. Wilton . . . if you would care to join us for the evening, won't you please. . . .

MRS. WILTON. Thank you very much, dear Mrs. Borkman, but I really can't. We have another engagement. We are on our way down to the Hinkels.

MRS. BORKMAN [*looking at her*]. 'We'? Whom do you mean by 'we'?

MRS. WILTON [*laughing*]. Actually, I should only say 'I'. But I was instructed by the ladies of the house to bring Mr. Borkman along with me if I happened to run into him.

MRS. BORKMAN. Which you did, I see.

MRS. WILTON. Happily, yes. Since he was kind enough to look in on me . . . on little Frida's account.

MRS. BORKMAN [*drily*]. Erhart, I wasn't aware that you knew this family—the Hinkels.

ERHART [*irritably*]. Actually, I don't know them. [*Adds somewhat impatiently.*] You know better than anyone, Mother, which people I know and don't know.

MRS. WILTON. Puh! You are not a stranger for long in *that* house! They are easy, friendly, hospitable people. Lots of young ladies.

MRS. BORKMAN [*with emphasis*]. If I know my son, that's hardly the company for him, Mrs. Wilton.

MRS. WILTON. Good heavens, dear Mrs. Borkman, he's young too, isn't he!

MRS. BORKMAN. Yes, he is young, fortunately. Otherwise there'd be little excuse.

ERHART [*concealing his impatience*]. Yes, yes, Mother ... I obviously can't go to the Hinkels this evening. Naturally I'll stay here with you and Aunt Ella.

MRS. BORKMAN. I knew you would, Erhart dear.

ELLA RENTHEIM. No, Erhart ... I won't have you putting it off for my sake. ...

ERHART. Nonsense, Aunt dear! I wouldn't hear of it. [*Looks uncertainly at* MRS. WILTON.] But how shall we put things straight? Will it be all right? You've already accepted on my behalf.

MRS. WILTON [*gaily*]. Rubbish! Why shouldn't it be all right? When I get there—all alone and abandoned in that brilliantly gay company—I shall simply convey regrets ... on your behalf.

ERHART [*hesitatingly*]. Well, if you really do think it's all right. ...

MRS. WILTON [*lightly sweeping the matter aside*]. Many's the time I answer both 'yes' and 'no' ... on my own behalf. You can't go and leave your aunt the moment she arrives! Shame on you, Monsieur Erhart ... is that the way for a son to behave?

MRS. BORKMAN [*annoyed*]. A son?

MRS. WILTON. Well—*foster*-son, then, Mrs. Borkman.

MRS. BORKMAN. That's more like it.

MRS. WILTON. Oh, I think a good foster-mother often deserves more thanks than one's real mother.

MRS. BORKMAN. Has that been your experience?

MRS. WILTON. Bless you ... I scarcely knew my mother. But if I'd had a good foster-mother, I might not have become as ... as badly behaved as people say I am. [*Turns to* ERHART.] Now, you just stay at home like a good boy with Mummy and Auntie and have a nice cup of tea. [*To the ladies.*] Good-bye, good-bye, Mrs. Borkman! Good-bye, Miss Rentheim!

[*The ladies take their leave of each other in silence. She goes towards the door.*]

ERHART [*follows her*]. Shouldn't I see you some of the way. . . ?

MRS. WILTON [*in the doorway, with a dismissive gesture*]. Not one step. I am used to finding my way alone. [*Stands in the doorway, looks at him and nods.*] But beware now, Master Borkman—I am warning you!

ERHART. Why should I beware?

MRS. WILTON [*gaily*]. Because as I go down the road—all alone and abandoned, as I said before—I shall try to cast a spell over you.

ERHART [*laughs*]. Oh, that! You want to try your hand at *that* again.

MRS. WILTON [*half seriously*]. So watch out. As I walk down the road I shall say to myself—summoning together all my will-power, I shall say: 'Mr. Erhart Borkman, pick up your hat!'

MRS. BORKMAN. And you think then he'll pick it up?

MRS. WILTON [*laughs*]. Bless you, yes. He'll snatch up his hat at once. And then I'll say: 'Put on your overcoat, Erhart Borkman! And your galoshes. Don't forget your galoshes! And follow me! Good boy! Good boy!'

ERHART [*with forced gaiety*]. Rely on me.

MRS. WILTON [*with raised forefinger*]. Good boy! Good boy!. . . Goodnight!

[*She laughs, nods to the ladies and shuts the door behind her.*]

MRS. BORKMAN. Does she really go in for that kind of magic?

ERHART. Not at all. How could you believe that? It's only in fun. [*Breaks off.*] But don't let us talk about Mrs. Wilton now. [*He urges* ELLA RENTHEIM *to sit in the easy chair by the stove; then he stands looking at her.*] To think you've made that long journey, Aunt Ella! And in winter!

ELLA RENTHEIM. In the end I had to, Erhart.

ERHART. Oh? Why?

ELLA RENTHEIM. I had to come in to talk to the doctors.

ERHART. Well, that's good!

ELLA RENTHEIM [*smiles*]. You think that's good?

ERHART. That you finally decided, I mean.

MRS. BORKMAN [*on the sofa, coldly*]. Are you ill, Ella?

ELLA RENTHEIM [*looks hard at her*]. You know very well I'm ill.

MRS. BORKMAN. I know of course you haven't been very well for years. . . .

ERHART. When I was staying with you, I often told you you ought to see a doctor.

ELLA RENTHEIM. Where I live, there's nobody I have any real confidence in. Besides, it didn't feel so bad in those days.

ERHART. Is it worse now, Aunt Ella?

ELLA RENTHEIM. Yes, my boy. It is rather worse now.

ERHART. But it's not dangerous?

ELLA RENTHEIM. Depends how you look at it.

ERHART [*eagerly*]. You know what, Aunt Ella? You shouldn't go back home too soon.

ELLA RENTHEIM. No, I don't think I will.

ERHART. You must stay here in town. Here you have all the best doctors to choose from.

ELLA RENTHEIM. That was in my mind when I left home.

ERHART. So now you must find a really nice place to stay . . . some comfortable and quiet little hotel.

ELLA RENTHEIM. I booked in this morning at the old place I used to stay at.

ERHART. Well, you'll be nice and comfortable there.

ELLA RENTHEIM. But I shan't be staying there after all.

ERHART. Oh? Why not?

ELLA RENTHEIM. I changed my mind when I came out here.

ERHART [*surprised*]. You changed your mind . . . ?

MRS. BORKMAN [*crocheting, without looking up*]. Your aunt wants to live here, in her own house, Erhart.

ERHART [*looks from one to the other*]. Here! With us! With *us*! Is this true, Aunt Ella?

ELLA RENTHEIM. Yes. I've made up my mind.

MRS. BORKMAN [*as before*]. You know of course that everything here belongs to your aunt.

ELLA RENTHEIM. So I'll be staying out here, Erhart. To begin with. For the time being. I shall look after myself. Over there in the bailiff's wing.

ERHART. That's a good idea. You always kept some rooms there ready for occupation. [*Suddenly animated.*] Well now, Aunt Ella—aren't you very tired after your journey?

ELLA RENTHEIM. I am rather.

ERHART. Then I think you ought to have a really early night.

ELLA RENTHEIM [*looks at him, smilingly*]. I think I will.

ERHART [*eagerly*]. Then we could have a nice long talk tomorrow . . . or some other day. About all sorts of things. You and Mother and I. That would be much the best thing, wouldn't it, Aunt Ella?

MRS. BORKMAN [*rising from the sofa, bursts out*]. Erhart, I can see you want to leave me!

ERHART [*startled*]. What do you mean?

MRS. BORKMAN. You want to go on to the Hinkels!

ERHART [*involuntarily*]. Oh, that. [*Composes himself.*] Do you think I ought to sit here keeping Aunt Ella up half the night? When she's ill? Remember that, Mother.

MRS. BORKMAN. Erhart! You want to go to the Hinkels!

ERHART [*impatiently*]. Good Lord, Mother! I don't really see how I can get out of it. What do you say, Aunt Ella?

ELLA RENTHEIM. You must decide for yourself, Erhart.

MRS. BORKMAN [*goes across to her, threateningly*]. You want to part him from me!

ELLA RENTHEIM [*rises*]. If only I could, Gunhild!

[*Music is heard from above.*]

ERHART [*twisting as though in pain*]. Oh, I can't stand this any longer! [*Looks about him.*] Where's my hat? [*To* ELLA.] Do you recognize that music up there?

ELLA RENTHEIM. No. What is it?

ERHART. *Danse macabre.* The dance of death. Don't you recognize the dance of death, Aunt Ella?

ELLA RENTHEIM [*smiles sadly*]. Not yet, Erhart.

ERHART [*to* MRS. BORKMAN]. Mother . . . I beg you . . . please let me go.

MRS. BORKMAN [*looks hard at him*]. Leave your mother? Is that what you want?

ERHART. I'll be back . . . perhaps tomorrow!

MRS. BORKMAN [*with deep passion*]. You want to leave me! Want to be with strangers! With . . . with . . . no, I don't want to think about it.

ERHART. There are bright lights down there. And young, happy faces. And music, mother!

MRS. BORKMAN [*pointing up at the ceiling*]. There is music up there too, Erhart.

ERHART. Yes, that music . . . is just what is driving me out of the house.

ELLA RENTHEIM. Do you grudge your father his chance to forget things for a while?

ERHART. No, I don't. He's welcome to it a thousand times over. Just as long as I don't have to listen to it, too.

MRS. BORKMAN [*looks admonishingly at him*]. Be strong, Erhart! Be strong, my son! And never forget your great mission!

ERHART. Oh, Mother . . . please don't start on that! I wasn't made to be a missionary. Goodnight, dear Aunt Ella! Goodnight, Mother!

[*He hurries out through the hall.*]

MRS. BORKMAN [*after a brief silence*]. You've got him back very quickly, Ella, haven't you?

ELLA RENTHEIM. I wish I could believe that.

MRS. BORKMAN. But you won't keep him long. You'll see.

ELLA RENTHEIM. Away from you, you mean?

MRS. BORKMAN. Away from me or—away from *her*.

ELLA RENTHEIM. I'd rather she had him than you.

MRS. BORKMAN [*nods slowly*]. That I understand. I say the same. Rather she than you.

ELLA RENTHEIM. Whatever it might mean in the end for him?

MRS. BORKMAN. I don't think that greatly matters.

ELLA RENTHEIM [*putting her coat over her arm*]. For the first time in our lives we twin sisters agree. Goodnight, Gunhild!

[*She goes out through the hall. The music from above gains in volume.*]

MRS. BORKMAN [*stands still for a moment, starts, then shudders and whispers involuntarily*]. The wolf howls again. The sick wolf. [*She pauses a moment, then throws herself on the floor, writhing in pain and whispering in grief.*] Erhart! Erhart! Be loyal to me! Come home and help your mother! I can't bear this life any longer!

ACT TWO

*What was formerly the great hall of the Rentheim residence, on the
first floor. The walls are covered with old tapestries, portraying
hunting scenes, shepherds and shepherdesses, all in faded colours.
On the left, folding doors; forward of that, a piano. In the left-hand
corner of the rear wall, a tapestry-covered door without surround.
In the middle of the wall, right, a large carved oak desk covered
with books and papers. Forward of this, on the same side, a sofa
with table and chairs. The furniture is restricted to a severely Empire
style. Lighted lamps stand on the desk and on the tables.*

*JOHN GABRIEL BORKMAN stands with his hands behind his back
by the piano, listening to FRIDA FOLDAL sitting there playing the last
few bars of* Danse macabre.

*BORKMAN is of medium height, a well-built, powerful-looking
man in his sixties. Distinguished appearance, with a firmly-cut
profile, sharp eyes and grey-white curling hair and beard. He is
dressed in a rather old-fashioned black suit, with a white cravat.
FRIDA FOLDAL is a pretty, pale girl of fifteen, with a somewhat
tired and strained expression. She is inexpensively dressed in light
colours.*

The music ends. Silence.

BORKMAN. Can you guess where I first heard music like this?

FRIDA [*looks up at him*]. No, Mr. Borkman.

BORKMAN. Down in the mines.

FRIDA [*uncomprehendingly*]. Really? Down in the mines?

BORKMAN. As you know, I am a miner's son. Perhaps you didn't know
that?

FRIDA. No, Mr. Borkman.

BORKMAN. A miner's son. And sometimes my father took me down
into the mines. Down there the metal ore sings.

FRIDA. Sings? Really?

N1

BORKMAN. When it is broken free. The hammer-blows that loosen it . . . are the strokes of the midnight bell which set it free. And that is why the metal sings . . . for joy . . . after its fashion.

FRIDA. Why does it do that, Mr. Borkman?

BORKMAN. It wants to come up into the light of day and serve mankind.

[*He walks up and down the floor of the room, always with his hands behind his back.*]

FRIDA [*sits waiting for some time, then glances at her watch and gets up*]. If you'll excuse me, Mr. Borkman . . . I'm afraid I must go now.

BORKMAN [*stands in front of her*]. Are you going already?

FRIDA [*puts her music in her music case*]. Yes, I really must. [*Clearly embarrassed.*] I have an engagement to play somewhere else this evening.

BORKMAN. At a party?

FRIDA. Yes.

BORKMAN. And you have to perform for the guests?

FRIDA [*bites her lip*]. I have to play for them to dance to.

BORKMAN. Only to dance to.

FRIDA. Yes. There is to be dancing after supper.

BORKMAN [*stands and looks at her*]. Do you like playing for dancing? In various houses?

FRIDA [*putting on her outdoor things*]. Yes, when I can get an engagement. I manage to earn a little money that way.

BORKMAN [*quizzically*]. Is that what you think about as you sit there playing while they dance?

FRIDA. No. I generally find myself thinking it's pretty hard I can't join in the dancing myself.

BORKMAN [*nods*]. I thought as much. [*Walks restlessly about the room.*] Yes, yes, yes. . . . Not to be able to join in oneself—that's the hardest thing of all. [*Stops.*] But one thing outweighs that in your case, Frida.

FRIDA [*looks questioningly at him*]. What's that, Mr. Borkman?

BORKMAN. The fact that you have ten times more music in you than all the dancers put together.

FRIDA [*smiles deprecatingly*]. Oh, I'm not so sure of that.

BORKMAN [*raising an admonitory finger*]. Never be so foolish as to doubt yourself!

FRIDA. But what if nobody else knows it?

BORKMAN. As long as you know it yourself, that is enough. Where are you playing this evening?

FRIDA. Over at the Hinkels.

BORKMAN [*looks sharply at her*]. Did you say Hinkel? The lawyer?

FRIDA. Yes.

BORKMAN [*with a cutting smile*]. Parties in that man's house? People accept invitations from *him*?

FRIDA. Yes, lots of people go, from what Mrs. Wilton says.

BORKMAN [*vehemently*]. But what kind of people? Can you tell me that?

FRIDA [*nervously*]. Well, I don't really know. Oh yes . . . I do know young Mr. Borkman will be there this evening.

BORKMAN [*starts*]. Erhart! My son?

FRIDA. Yes, he'll be there.

BORKMAN. How do you know that?

FRIDA. He said so himself. An hour ago.

BORKMAN. Is he out here today?

FRIDA. Yes, he's been at Mrs. Wilton's the whole afternoon.

BORKMAN [*searchingly*]. Do you know whether he called in here as well? Whether he came and talked to anybody downstairs, I mean?

FRIDA. Yes, he looked in briefly on Mrs. Borkman.

BORKMAN [*bitterly*]. Aha . . . I might have known.

FRIDA. But there was another lady in with her, I think—a stranger.

BORKMAN. Ah. Was there? Ah well, people do call on her now and then, I suppose.

FRIDA. If I see young Mr. Borkman later, shall I tell him to come up and see you too?

BORKMAN [*gruffly*]. You'll say nothing of the kind! I'm having none of that, thank you very much. Anybody who wants to see me, can. I don't ask people.

FRIDA. Very well, I'll say nothing. Goodnight, Mr. Borkman.

BORKMAN [*pacing about, growling*]. Goodnight.

FRIDA. Do you mind if I run down the back stairs? It's quicker.

BORKMAN. Heavens, girl . . . take whatever stairs you like. Goodnight to you.

FRIDA. Goodnight, Mr. Borkman.

> [*She goes out through the little tapestry-covered door at the back, left.*
> BORKMAN *walks pensively over to the piano to close it, but then leaves it. Looks round at all the emptiness, then begins to pace the floor from the corner near the piano to the corner at the back, right—restlessly and uneasily back and forth, unceasingly. Finally, he walks across to his desk, listens at the folding doors, quickly picks up a hand-mirror, looks at himself in it and straightens his cravat.*
> *There is a knock at the door.* BORKMAN *hears it, glances quickly across, but says nothing. A moment later, there is another knock, this time louder.*]

BORKMAN [*standing at his desk, his left hand resting on the desk top, and his right hand thrust into the breast of his coat*]. Come in!

> [VILHELM FOLDAL *cautiously enters the room. He is a bent, worn-looking man, with mild blue eyes and long thin grey hair hanging down over his coat collar. He has a portfolio under his arm, a soft felt hat in his hand, and large horn-rimmed spectacles which he pushes up over his forehead.*]

BORKMAN [*changes stance, and looks at the newcomer with an expression partly of disappointment, partly pleasure*]. Oh! It's only you.

FOLDAL. Good evening, John Gabriel. Yes, it's me.

BORKMAN [*with a severe look*]. It strikes me you are rather late.

FOLDAL. Well, it's a fair way, you know. Especially if you do it all on foot.

BORKMAN. But why do you always walk, Vilhelm? The tram goes quite close to you.

FOLDAL. It's healthier to walk. And it saves a few pence. Well, has Frida been out to play for you lately?

BORKMAN. She's just this moment gone. Didn't you meet her outside?

FOLDAL. No. I haven't seen her for a long time. Not since she went to live out at this Mrs. Wilton's.

BORKMAN [*sits on the sofa and waves towards a chair*]. Have a seat, Vilhelm.

FOLDAL [*sits on the edge of the chair*]. Thank you. [*Looks gloomily at him.*] You wouldn't believe how lonely I've felt since Frida left home.

BORKMAN. Nonsense. You've still got plenty left.

FOLDAL. Yes, God knows I have. Five of them. But Frida was the only one who understood me a little. [*Sadly shakes his head.*] None of the others understands me at all.

BORKMAN [*darkly, staring vacantly ahead and drumming his fingers on the desk*]. Ah, that's it. That is the curse we chosen individuals have to bear. The masses, the common herd . . . they don't understand us, Vilhelm.

FOLDAL [*resignedly*]. I can get by well enough without being understood. A bit of patience, and some day it will come. [*With a tear-choked voice.*] There are bitterer things than that.

BORKMAN [*vehemently*]. There is nothing more bitter than that.

FOLDAL. Yes, there is, John Gabriel. I've had a domestic row, just before I came out.

BORKMAN. Oh? What about?

FOLDAL [*bursting out*]. My family—they despise me.

BORKMAN [*indignantly*]. Despise . . . !

FOLDAL [*wiping his eyes*]. I've known it long enough. But today it all came out.

BORKMAN [*is silent for a moment*]. You made a bad choice when you married, didn't you?

FOLDAL. Didn't really have much choice. Besides, when you are getting on in years, you are quite glad to get married. Especially in the reduced circumstances I was in, having been brought so low. . . .

BORKMAN [*springs up in anger*]. Is that meant as a stricture on me? An accusation . . . ?

FOLDAL [*fearfully*]. Please, for God's sake, John Gabriel . . . !

BORKMAN. Yes it is! You are thinking of the bank disaster . . . !

FOLDAL [*soothingly*]. But I don't blame you for that! God forbid . . . !

BORKMAN [*growling, sits down again*]. Well, that's all right then.

FOLDAL. Anyway, you mustn't think it's my wife I'm complaining about. She hasn't much education, poor thing, that's true. But she's not a bad soul. No, it's the children. . . .

BORKMAN. I might have known.

FOLDAL. The children—they are more educated, you see. And consequently they expect more from life.

BORKMAN [*looks sympathetically at him*]. And that's why your children despise you, Vilhelm?

FOLDAL [*shrugs his shoulders*]. I haven't made much of a career. That one has to admit. . . .

BORKMAN [*moves his chair nearer and places his hand on* FOLDAL's *arm*]. Don't they know that you wrote a tragedy when you were young?

FOLDAL. Yes, of course they do. But it doesn't seem to impress them particularly.

BORKMAN. They just don't understand. Your tragedy is good. I believe that absolutely.

FOLDAL [*brightening up*]. Yes, there *are* a number of good things in it, don't you think so, John Gabriel? Oh God, if only I could succeed in getting it put on . . . [*Opens the portfolio and begins eagerly to leaf through the pages.*] Look here now! I want to show you where I've made a change. . . .

BORKMAN. You've got it with you?

FOLDAL. Yes, I brought it along. It's so long since I read it to you. And I thought it might pass the time if you were to listen to an act or two. . . .

BORKMAN [*rises, with a dismissive gesture*]. No, no, let's keep it for another time.

FOLDAL. Very well. As you will.

[BORKMAN *paces up and down.* FOLDAL *puts the manuscript back again.*]

BORKMAN [*stops in front of him*]. You were right in what you said just now—you haven't made much of a career. But this I promise you, Vilhelm, that when the hour of restitution strikes for me. . . .

FOLDAL [*begins to rise*]. Oh, please. . . .

BORKMAN [*waves his hand*]. No, don't get up. [*With rising excitement.*] When the hour of my restitution strikes. . . . When they realize they cannot do without me. . . . When they make their way up to me in this room . . . and on their bended knees implore me to take over the reins of the bank again . . . ! This new bank they have established . . . but are incapable of running. . . . [*Positions himself beside the desk as before, and strikes his breast.*] Here I shall stand and receive them! And throughout the land men will talk of the conditions John Gabriel Borkman is laying down before he . . . [*Stops abruptly and stares at* FOLDAL.] You are looking very dubious! Perhaps you think they won't come? Don't you see they *must* come . . . *must* come some time? Don't you believe that?

FOLDAL. Yes, yes! God knows I do, John Gabriel.

BORKMAN [*sits down again on the sofa*]. I believe it absolutely. I'm utterly convinced . . . that they'll come. If I weren't, I'd have put a bullet through my head long ago.

FOLDAL [*anxiously*]. No, no, for heaven's sake . . .

BORKMAN [*triumphantly*]. But they will come! They will come! You'll see! I expect them any day, any hour. You see how I hold myself in readiness to receive them.

FOLDAL [*sighs*]. If only they would come soon.

BORKMAN [*restlessly*]. Yes, Vilhelm. Time goes by. The years go by. Life . . . no, I daren't think of it. [*Looks at him.*] Do you know how I sometimes feel?

FOLDAL. How?

BORKMAN. I feel like a Napoleon who has been maimed in his first battle.

FOLDAL [*places his hand on his portfolio*]. I know the feeling.

BORKMAN. On a smaller scale, of course.

FOLDAL [*quietly*]. My little world of poetry means a great deal to me, John Gabriel.

BORKMAN [*vehemently*]. Yes, but in *my* case . . . I could have made millions! All those mines I could have controlled! The enormous mineral deposits! The water power! The quarries! The trade links . . . the shipping lines in every part of the globe! All this I would have created . . . created alone.

FOLDAL. Yes, I know. There was nothing you wouldn't have taken on.

BORKMAN [*clenching his hands*]. And here I have to sit like a wounded eagle watching the others getting in ahead of me . . . and robbing me of it, piece by piece!

FOLDAL. It's happening to me too.

BORKMAN [*paying no attention to him*]. When I think . . . how close I was to my goal. If only I'd had another eight days to make certain dispositions. Every deposit would have been covered. All the securities I had so boldly used would have been back in place. Gigantic companies were within a hairsbreadth of being established. Nobody would have lost a penny.

FOLDAL. Dear me, yes . . . how nearly there you were.

BORKMAN [*with choked fury*]. And then came treachery! Just when things were reaching a climax. [*Looks at him.*] Do you know what I consider the most infamous crime a man can commit?

FOLDAL. No, tell me.

BORKMAN. Not murder. Not robbery or burglary. Not even perjury. For these are things which people do to those they hate, or care nothing about.

FOLDAL. So what is it, John Gabriel?

BORKMAN [*with emphasis*]. The most infamous of all crimes is to betray the trust of a friend.

FOLDAL [*somewhat dubiously*]. Yes, but listen. . . .

BORKMAN [*flaring up*]. I know what you are going to say! I can see by your face. But you are wrong. Everybody who had money in the bank would have got it all back. Every penny of it. . . . No, Vilhelm! The most infamous crime a man can commit is to misuse his friend's letters . . . to publish for all the world to read things which were confided to him and him alone, like a whisper in a dark, empty, locked room. The man who can stoop to such means is rotten through and through with the most poisonous evil. But such a friend was mine. And he it was who broke me.

FOLDAL. I think I know whom you mean.

BORKMAN. There was no aspect of my affairs I ever felt I couldn't reveal to him. And then, when the moment came, he turned against me those weapons I had myself placed in his hands.

FOLDAL. I've never been able to understand why he . . . Of course there were lots of rumours at the time.

BORKMAN. What rumours? Tell me. I know nothing. Because I went straight into . . . into isolation. What did the rumours say, Vilhelm?

FOLDAL. People said you would have been made a Cabinet Minister.

BORKMAN. I was offered that. But I turned it down.

FOLDAL. So you weren't in his way there?

BORKMAN. No. That wasn't why he betrayed me.

FOLDAL. Then really I can't understand . . .

BORKMAN. I might as well tell you, Vilhelm.

FOLDAL. Well?

BORKMAN. There was a woman in it.

FOLDAL. A woman? But, John Gabriel . . .

BORKMAN [*interrupting*]. Yes, yes. . . . It's a stupid story. Let's say no more about it. . . . In the end, neither of us became a Cabinet Minister.

FOLDAL. But he rose to the top.

BORKMAN. And I sank to the bottom.

FOLDAL. A terrible tragedy . . .

BORKMAN [*nods to him*]. Nearly as terrible as *yours*, when I think about it.

FOLDAL [*innocently*]. Yes, just as terrible.

BORKMAN [*laughs quietly*]. But looked at from another side, it's really also a sort of comedy.

FOLDAL. A comedy?

BORKMAN. Yes, the way it seems to be shaping. Listen. . . .

FOLDAL. What?

BORKMAN. You didn't meet Frida as you arrived.

FOLDAL. No.

BORKMAN. While we two sit here, she is down there playing the piano for the guests of the man who betrayed and ruined me.

FOLDAL. I had no idea.

BORKMAN. Yes, She just picked up her music and went straight on from me to . . . that house.

FOLDAL [*apologetically*]. Yes, yes, poor child. . . .

BORKMAN. And can you guess for whom—among others—she'll be playing?

FOLDAL. Well?

BORKMAN. For my son.

FOLDAL. What!

BORKMAN. Yes, Vilhelm, what do you think of that? My son is among the dancers there tonight. Didn't I say it was a comedy?

FOLDAL. Yes, but he doesn't know . . .

BORKMAN. What doesn't he know . . . ?

FOLDAL. He doesn't know how he . . . this man . . .

BORKMAN. Speak his name, if you wish. I can bear it now.

FOLDAL. I am sure your son knows nothing of what happened, John Gabriel.

BORKMAN [*gloomily, sitting and striking the table*]. He knows, Vilhelm. As surely as I am sitting here.

FOLDAL. But in that case, could you ever imagine him going there?

BORKMAN [*shakes his head*]. I don't suppose my son sees things with my eyes. I swear he's on the side of my enemies. He probably thinks like the rest of them—that Hinkel damn well only did his duty as a lawyer when he went ahead and betrayed me.

FOLDAL. But, my dear fellow, who would have put things to him in that light?

BORKMAN. Who? Have you forgotten who brought him up? First his aunt—from the age of six or seven. And after that—his mother!

FOLDAL. I think you are being unjust to them.

BORKMAN [*flaring up*]. I'm never unjust to anybody. They've both of them gone and poisoned his mind against me.

FOLDAL [*meekly*]. Yes, yes, I dare say they have.

BORKMAN [*angrily*]. Oh, women! How they distort and corrupt our lives! Tamper with our destinies! Rob us of our victories!

FOLDAL. Not all women!

BORKMAN. Oh? Name me a single one who is worth anything!

FOLDAL. That's very true. None of the few I know are worth very much.

BORKMAN [*snorts scornfully*]. So what's the use of that—that such women do exist somewhere? When you don't know any?

FOLDAL [*warmly*]. Yes, John Gabriel, it does matter. It is a noble and uplifting thought that somewhere out in the wide wide world, far away perhaps, there is to be found the true woman.

BORKMAN [*shifting about impatiently on the sofa*]. Oh, enough of this poetic drivel!

FOLDAL [*looks at him, deeply hurt*]. You call my most sacred belief poetic drivel?

BORKMAN [*hard*]. Yes, I do! That's what's stopped you from ever getting on. If only you would give up all business, I could still get you on your feet again . . . help you to get ahead.

FOLDAL [*inwardly boiling*]. Oh, you couldn't do that!

BORKMAN. I can, once I am returned to power.

FOLDAL. The prospects of that are pretty remote.

BORKMAN [*vehemently*]. Maybe you think that day will never come? Answer me!

FOLDAL. I don't know what to say.

BORKMAN [*rises, cold and dignified, and points to the door*]. Then I have no further use for you.

FOLDAL [*rises from his chair*]. No use . . . !

BORKMAN. If you do not believe that my destiny will change. . . .

FOLDAL. How can I, when it's against all reason . . . ! You would require formal restitution . . .

BORKMAN. Go on! Go on!

FOLDAL. It's true I never took my examinations, but I've studied enough to know . . .

BORKMAN [*quickly*]. You think it's impossible?

FOLDAL. There's no precedent for it.

BORKMAN. Only ordinary people need precedents.

FOLDAL. The law doesn't recognize such distinctions.

BORKMAN [*with deliberate harshness*]. You are no poet, Vilhelm.

FOLDAL [*involuntarily clasping his hands*]. You seriously mean that?

BORKMAN [*dismissively, without answering*]. We are simply wasting each other's time. It would be best if you didn't come again.

FOLDAL. So you want me to go?

BORKMAN [*without looking at him*]. I have no further use for you.

FOLDAL [*meekly taking his portfolio*]. No, no. That could well be.

BORKMAN. So all this time you've lied to me.

FOLDAL [*shakes his head*]. Never lied, John Gabriel.

BORKMAN. Have you not sat there feeding my hopes and beliefs and confidence with lies?

FOLDAL. They weren't lies as long as *you* believed in *my* calling. As long as you believed in me, I believed in you.

BORKMAN. Then it's just been mutual deception. And perhaps self-deception too—on both sides.

FOLDAL. But isn't that what friendship really is, John Gabriel?

BORKMAN [*with a bitter smile*]. Yes. To deceive . . . that's what friendship is. You are right. I have had this experience once before.

FOLDAL [*looks unseeingly ahead*]. So you tell me I'm no poet! How could you be so callous.

BORKMAN [*in a gentler tone*]. Well, I'm no real expert in these matters.

FOLDAL. Perhaps you are—more than you think.

BORKMAN. Am I?

FOLDAL [*softly*]. Yes. You see, there are moments . . . when I too have my doubts. A horrible feeling . . . of having wasted my whole life on an illusion.

BORKMAN. To doubt yourself is to walk with faltering feet.

FOLDAL. That's why it was such a comfort for me to come here and lean on you. You believed. [*Picks up his hat.*] But now you are like a stranger to me.

BORKMAN. And you to me.

FOLDAL. Goodnight, John Gabriel.

BORKMAN. Goodnight, Vilhelm.

[FOLDAL *goes out, left.* BORKMAN *stands for a moment staring at the closed door. He makes a move as though to call* FOLDAL *back, but changes his mind and begins to pace the floor with his hands behind his back. Then he stops at the table beside the sofa and puts out the lamp. The room becomes half dark. A moment later there is a knock on the tapestry-lined door at the back, left.*]

BORKMAN [*standing by the table, startled, turns and asks in a loud voice*]. Who's that knocking? [*No answer; there is another knock.* BORKMAN *remains standing where he is.*] Who is it? Come in!

[ELLA RENTHEIM, *a lighted candle in her hand, appears in the doorway. She is wearing her black dress, as before, with her coat thrown loosely over her shoulders.*]

BORKMAN [*stares at her*]. Who are you? What do you want with me?

ELLA RENTHEIM [*closes the door and approaches*]. It's me, Borkman.

[*She sets the candle on the piano, and remains standing there.*]

BORKMAN [*stands thunderstruck staring at her, then whispers*]. Is it . . . is it Ella? Is it Ella Rentheim?

ELLA RENTHEIM. Yes. It is 'your' Ella . . . as you used to call me. Once. Many, many years ago.

BORKMAN [*as before*]. Yes, Ella, it is you . . . I see it now.

ELLA RENTHEIM. You recognize me?

BORKMAN. Yes, now I begin to . . .

ELLA RENTHEIM. The years have taken a hard toll of me, Borkman. Don't you think so.

BORKMAN [*reluctantly*]. You have changed somewhat. At first sight I . . .

ELLA RENTHEIM. No longer those dark curls, falling over my shoulders. Remember how you used to love to twist them round your fingers?

BORKMAN [*quickly*]. That's it! I see now. You have changed your hair style.

ELLA RENTHEIM [*with a sad smile*]. Exactly. It's the hair style that does it.

BORKMAN [*changing the subject*]. I had no idea you were in this part of the country.

ELLA RENTHEIM. I've only just come.

BORKMAN. Why have you come here . . . now, in winter?

ELLA RENTHEIM. I'll tell you.

BORKMAN. Something you want from me?

ELLA RENTHEIM. You, among others. But if we are to talk about these things, I must begin a long time back.

BORKMAN. You must be tired.

ELLA RENTHEIM. Yes, I am tired.

BORKMAN. Won't you sit down? There, on the sofa.

ELLA RENTHEIM. Thank you. I need to sit down.

[*She walks across, right, and sits down in the corner of the sofa.* BORKMAN *stands by the table, his hands behind his back, and looks at her. Short silence.*]

ELLA RENTHEIM. It's an unbelievably long time since we last met, face to face, Borkman.

BORKMAN [*darkly*]. A long long time. Since when many terrible things have happened.

ELLA RENTHEIM. A whole lifetime. A wasted lifetime.

BORKMAN [*looks sharply at her*]. Wasted!

ELLA RENTHEIM. Yes, wasted. For both of us.

BORKMAN [*in a cold, businessman's tone*]. I do not regard my life as wasted—yet.

ELLA RENTHEIM. But what about mine?

BORKMAN. You've only yourself to blame, Ella.

ELLA RENTHEIM [*with a start*]. You can say that!

BORKMAN. You could quite well have been happy without me.

ELLA RENTHEIM. You think so?

BORKMAN. If only you'd wanted to.

ELLA RENTHEIM [*bitterly*]. Oh, yes. I know well enough somebody else was prepared to have me. . . .

BORKMAN. But you rejected him.

ELLA RENTHEIM. Yes, I did.

BORKMAN. Time after time you rejected him. Year after year . . .

ELLA RENTHEIM [*scornfully*]. . . . Year after year I rejected happiness, I suppose you mean?

BORKMAN. You could have been just as happy with him. Then I'd have been saved.

ELLA RENTHEIM. You?

BORKMAN. Yes. Then you would have saved me, Ella.

ELLA RENTHEIM. How do you mean?

BORKMAN. He thought I was behind all those rejections . . . those end-less refusals. So he took his revenge. It was just too easy—he had all my confidential, indiscreet letters in his possession. He made use of them—and that was the end of me . . . for the time being. You see, all that is your fault, Ella!

ELLA RENTHEIM. Is that so, Borkman. . . ! So when it comes to the point, it seems *I* am the one who has to make it up to *you*.

BORKMAN. Depends how you look at it. I know how much I have to thank you for. You made it your business to acquire the whole estate, the entire property, at the auction. Put the house completely at my . . . and your sister's . . . disposal. You took Erhart . . . looked after him in every way. . . .

ELLA RENTHEIM. For as long as I was allowed to.

BORKMAN. Allowed by your sister, yes. I never got mixed up in these domestic matters. As I was saying—I know what sacrifices you have made for me and for your sister. But at least you *could* do it, Ella. And you must remember it was I who made that possible for you.

ELLA RENTHEIM [*indignantly*]. There you are greatly mistaken, Borkman! It was my deep love and devotion for Erhart—and for you, too—that impelled me to do what I did.

BORKMAN. My dear, let us not bring emotion into it. I mean of course that when you acted as you did, it was I who gave you the means to do it.

ELLA RENTHEIM [*smiles*]. Ah yes . . . the means, the means . . .

BORKMAN [*flaring up*]. Yes, exactly! The means! As the last decisive battle approached . . . when I could spare neither family nor friends . . . when I had to take, and did take, those millions that had been trusted to me . . . I spared everything that was yours, every-thing you possessed . . . though I could have taken and used it all, in the same way I had used everything else!

ELLA RENTHEIM [*coldly and calmly*]. That is perfectly true, Borkman.

BORKMAN. It is. And that is why, when they came and took me away, they found everything of yours in the strongroom of the bank, untouched.

ELLA RENTHEIM [*looking across at him*]. I've often thought about that— why in fact you spared everything belonging to me? And only that?

BORKMAN. Why?

ELLA RENTHEIM. Yes, why? Tell me.

BORKMAN [*harshly and scathingly*]. Perhaps you think it was to have something to fall back on . . . if things went wrong?

ELLA RENTHEIM. Oh, no! In those days you never thought of that.

BORKMAN. No, never! I was so absolutely certain of victory.

ELLA RENTHEIM. So why was it then . . . ?

BORKMAN [*shrugs his shoulders*]. Dear God, Ella . . . it isn't easy to remember one's motives twenty years afterwards. All I remember is that when I used to turn over in my mind, quietly and alone, all those great schemes that were to be put into operation, I felt almost like some explorer of the skies. In those sleepless nights I felt I was filling some giant balloon with which to sail across unknown perilous seas.

ELLA RENTHEIM [*smiles*]. You, who never had any doubts about victory?

BORKMAN [*impatiently*]. That's how people *are*, Ella. Doubting yet believing in one and the same thing. [*Stares vacantly ahead.*] And I suppose that's why I didn't want you and yours in the balloon with me.

O1

ELLA RENTHEIM [*tensely*]. Why? I ask you. Tell me why?

BORKMAN [*without looking at her*]. One doesn't take what one holds most precious on a journey like that.

ELLA RENTHEIM. But you *had* the most precious thing aboard with you. Your whole future life. . . .

BORKMAN. Life is not always the most precious thing.

ELLA RENTHEIM [*breathlessly*]. Was that how you felt then?

BORKMAN. I fancy it was.

ELLA RENTHEIM. That *I* was what you held most precious?

BORKMAN. Yes, I have an idea . . . it was something like that.

ELLA RENTHEIM. But by then, years had passed since you had broken faith with me . . . and married somebody else!

BORKMAN. Broken faith, you say? You know very well it was higher motives . . . well, other motives, then . . . that forced my hand. Without *his* support I couldn't get anywhere.

ELLA RENTHEIM [*controlling herself*]. So you broke faith from . . . higher motives.

BORKMAN. I could do nothing without his help. And the price he put on his help was *you*.

ELLA RENTHEIM. And you paid the price. In full. No haggling.

BORKMAN. Had no choice. I had to conquer or be conquered.

ELLA RENTHEIM [*in a trembling voice, looking at him*]. Is what you say true: that I was then the most precious thing in the world to you?

BORKMAN. Both then and afterwards. Long, long afterwards.

ELLA RENTHEIM. Yet you made me part of your cheap bargain, all the same. Traded your love with another man. Sold my love for . . . a bank directorship!

BORKMAN [*darkly, bowed*]. I was forced by necessity, Ella.

ELLA RENTHEIM [*gets up from the sofa, trembling with passion*]. You criminal!

BORKMAN [*starts, but controls himself*]. I have heard that word before.

ELLA RENTHEIM. Oh, don't think I'm referring to your crimes against the law of the land! What it was you did with all those bonds and sureties—do you think I care? If only I could have stood at your side when the crash came. . . .

BORKMAN [*tense*]. What, Ella?

ELLA RENTHEIM. I'd have borne it all so gladly with you, believe me. The shame, the ruin . . . everything I'd have helped you to bear. . . .

BORKMAN. Would you? Could you?

ELLA RENTHEIM. I could have—and would have—done it. Because at that time I didn't know about your truly monstrous crime. . . .

BORKMAN. Which crime? What are you talking about?

ELLA RENTHEIM. I'm talking about that crime for which there is no forgiveness.

BORKMAN [*stares at her*]. You must be out of your mind.

ELLA RENTHEIM [*approaches closer*]. You are a murderer! You have committed the great mortal sin!

BORKMAN [*retreats towards the piano*]. You are mad, Ella!

ELLA RENTHEIM. You have killed love in me. [*Goes closer to him.*] Do you understand what that means? The Bible speaks of a mysterious sin for which there is no forgiveness. I have never understood before what that could be. Now I do understand. The great sin for which there is no forgiveness is to murder love in a human soul.

BORKMAN. And you tell me that's what I've done?

ELLA RENTHEIM. Yes, you have. I have never really understood what happened to me until this evening. That you broke faith with me and turned instead to Gunhild—this I took as simple straightforward inconstancy on your part. Helped on by some heartless scheming on hers. I think I even despised you a little—in spite of everything. But I see it all now! You broke faith with the woman you *loved*! Me, me, me! The thing you held most precious in all the world— and you were prepared to dispose of it in the interest of profit-making. You are guilty of double murder. The murder of your own soul and of mine!

BORKMAN [*cold and controlled*]. How clearly I recognize your passionate and unbridled nature in all this, Ella. No doubt it is natural for you to see things the way you do. You are a woman. It would therefore seem that you simply ignore everything else. Nothing else in the whole wide world matters to you.

ELLA RENTHEIM. You are right. It doesn't.

BORKMAN. Only the promptings of your own heart. . . .

ELLA RENTHEIM. That alone! You are right.

BORKMAN. But you must remember that I am a man. As a woman, you were the most precious thing in the world to me. But in the last resort, one woman can always be replaced by another. . . .

ELLA RENTHEIM [*looks at him with a smile*]. Was that your experience after you had married Gunhild?

BORKMAN. No. But my ambitions in life helped me to bear that too. I wanted to gain command of all the sources of power in this land. Earth, mountain, forest, and sea—I wanted control of all their resources. I wanted to build myself an empire, and thereby create prosperity for thousands and thousands of others.

ELLA RENTHEIM [*lost in memories*]. I know. All those evenings we spent talking about your plans. . . .

BORKMAN. Yes, I could talk to you, Ella.

ELLA RENTHEIM. I used to make jokes about your plans. Used to ask if you meant to wake 'all the slumbering spirits of gold'.

BORKMAN [*nods*]. I remember that phrase. [*Slowly.*] 'All the slumbering spirits of gold.'

ELLA RENTHEIM. But you didn't take it as a joke. You said: 'Yes, yes, Ella, that's exactly what I want to do.'

BORKMAN. It was, too. I only needed to get my foot in the stirrup . . . and that depended on this one man. He could get me appointed in control of the bank, and would do so . . . provided I for my part . . .

ELLA RENTHEIM. Exactly! Provided you for your part renounced the woman you loved . . . and who loved you beyond measure in return.

BORKMAN. I knew of his consuming passion for you. I knew he would accept no other terms. . . .

ELLA RENTHEIM. So you struck the bargain.

BORKMAN [*vehemently*]. Yes, I did, Ella! Don't you see, I simply could not control this desire for power. So I struck the bargain. I had to. And he helped me towards the top—halfway to those beckoning heights I had made up my mind to reach. And I climbed and climbed. Year after year I climbed. . . .

ELLA RENTHEIM. And I was as though obliterated from your life.

BORKMAN. Then in the end he threw me back again into the abyss. Because of you, Ella.

ELLA RENTHEIM [*after a short, thoughtful silence*]. Borkman—don't you feel there's been a kind of curse on our relationship?

BORKMAN [*looks at her*]. A curse?

ELLA RENTHEIM. Yes. Don't you feel that?

BORKMAN [*uneasily*]. Yes, I do. But why should . . . ? [*Bursts out.*] Oh, Ella . . . I no longer know who is right—you or I!

ELLA RENTHEIM. It is you who have sinned. You have killed all human happiness in me.

BORKMAN [*fearfully*]. Don't say that, Ella!

ELLA RENTHEIM. All my happiness as a woman, at least. From the moment your image began to fade within me, I have lived my life as though under an eclipse. Over the years it has become more and more difficult—and in the end quite impossible—for me to love any living thing: human, animal or plant. Save only one . . .

BORKMAN. One? Who?

ELLA RENTHEIM. Erhart, of course.

BORKMAN. Erhart?

ELLA RENTHEIM. Erhart . . . your son, Borkman.

BORKMAN. Has he really meant so much to you?

ELLA RENTHEIM. Why do you think I had him to live with me? And kept him as long as I could? Why?

BORKMAN. I thought it was out of pity. Like all the other things.

ELLA RENTHEIM [*inwardly agitated*]. Pity, you say! Ha! I have never felt pity for anyone—not since you broke faith with me. I simply couldn't. If a poor starving child came into my kitchen, frozen and crying and asking for something to eat, I got the kitchen maid to see to it. I never felt any urge to pick up the child, to warm it at my own hearth, to sit and enjoy watching it eating its fill. And I was never like that when I was young—I clearly remember! It's *you* who have created this emptiness, this barrenness within me—and all around me, too!

BORKMAN. Except for Erhart.

ELLA RENTHEIM. Yes. Except for *your* son. But for all other living things. You have cheated me of a mother's joy and happiness—and of a mother's sorrows and tears, too. And that was perhaps my cruellest loss.

BORKMAN. Really, Ella?

ELLA RENTHEIM. Who knows? A mother's sorrows and tears were perhaps what would have served me best. [*With deeper emotion.*] But I couldn't resign myself to the loss at the time. That's why I took Erhart. Won his love. Won all his childish confidence . . . until . . . Oh!

BORKMAN. Until what?

ELLA RENTHEIM. Until his mother—his mother in the physical sense, I mean—took him away from me again.

BORKMAN. He had to leave you, anyway. To come and live in town.

ELLA RENTHEIM [*wringing her hands*]. Yes, but I cannot bear the loneliness! The emptiness! The loss of your son's loving heart!

BORKMAN [*with an evil glint in his eye*]. Hm! I don't think you've lost that Ella. Hearts are not so easily lost and won . . . in that room downstairs.

ELLA RENTHEIM. I have lost him. And she has won him back. Or somebody else has. That's pretty obvious from the letters he writes me occasionally.

BORKMAN. Have you come here to take him back home with you?

ELLA RENTHEIM. Yes, if in fact it can be done.

BORKMAN. Certainly it can, if you've set your mind to it. You have the first and greatest claim on him.

ELLA RENTHEIM. Claim! claim! What do claims count for here? If it isn't from his own free choice, I don't really have him at all. And that I *must* have! I must have my child's love, whole-heartedly, unshared!

BORKMAN. You must remember that Erhart is now in his twenties. You can't count on keeping his heart unshared—as you put it—for very long.

ELLA RENTHEIM [*with a sad smile*]. It needn't be so very long.

BORKMAN. Oh? I thought that whatever it is you want, you would want it to the end of your days.

ELLA RENTHEIM. I do. But that need not be for all that long.

BORKMAN [*startled*]. What do you mean by that?

ELLA RENTHEIM. You know that I haven't been well in recent years?

BORKMAN. Haven't you?

ELLA RENTHEIM. Didn't you know?

BORKMAN. No, I didn't actually. . . .

ELLA RENTHEIM [*looking at him in surprise*]. Didn't Erhart tell you?

BORKMAN. Can't for the moment remember.

ELLA RENTHEIM. Perhaps he hasn't spoken of me at all?

BORKMAN. Oh, I'm pretty sure he's mentioned you. The thing is I so seldom see him—scarcely ever. There is somebody downstairs who keeps him away from me. Well away, you understand.

ELLA RENTHEIM. Are you sure of that, Borkman?

BORKMAN. Absolutely sure. [*Changes his tone.*] So it seems you haven't been well, Ella?

ELLA RENTHEIM. That's so. Then this autumn things took a turn for the worse, and I've had to come to town to consult a specialist.

BORKMAN. And now you've seen him?

ELLA RENTHEIM. Yes. This morning.

BORKMAN. What does he say?

ELLA RENTHEIM. He confirmed what I have long suspected. . . .

BORKMAN. Well?

ELLA RENTHEIM [*evenly and calmly*]. I am suffering from an incurable disease, Borkman.

BORKMAN. You mustn't believe that, Ella.

ELLA RENTHEIM. A disease from which there is no salvation. The doctors know of no cure for it. They can only let it run its course. Can do nothing to check it. Perhaps ease the pain a little. And that is something, at least.

BORKMAN. But it might not be for a long time yet. Believe me. . . .

ELLA RENTHEIM. They tell me I might last the winter.

BORKMAN [*unthinkingly*]. Ah, well, the winter is long.

ELLA RENTHEIM [*quietly*]. Long enough for me, at any rate.

BORKMAN [*eagerly, changing the subject*]. But what on earth can have caused this disease? You've always led such a regular and healthy life. Whatever can have caused it?

ELLA RENTHEIM [*looks at him*]. The doctor wondered whether I'd perhaps at some time suffered any particular emotional stress.

BORKMAN [*flaring up*]. Emotional stress! Aha! I understand! You mean it's all *my* fault?

ELLA RENTHEIM [*with growing inner agitation*]. It's too late to go into all that now. But I must have my child again, my own dear heart again, before I go. Think how infinitely sad it is for me to know I shall be taking leave of all living things, of sun and light and air, without leaving behind me a single person who will think of me with affection and sadness, remember me the way a son remembers a mother he has lost.

BORKMAN [*after a short pause*]. Take him, Ella—if you can win him.

ELLA RENTHEIM [*animatedly*]. You give your consent? *Can* you?

BORKMAN [*darkly*]. Yes. Not that it's much of a sacrifice. He's not really mine to give.

ELLA RENTHEIM. Thank you! Thank you for that sacrifice, all the same! But I have one other thing to beg of you. Something that means much to me, Borkman.

BORKMAN. Tell me.

ELLA RENTHEIM. You may think it childish. Might not understand. . . .

BORKMAN. Tell me! Tell me!

ELLA RENTHEIM. When I'm gone . . . which will be soon . . . I shall leave a not inconsiderable fortune. . . .

BORKMAN. I imagine you will.

ELLA RENTHEIM. And I intend to leave it all to Erhart.

BORKMAN. Actually you don't have anybody closer.

ELLA RENTHEIM [*warmly*]. Indeed, I have nobody closer than he.

BORKMAN. Nobody in your own family. You are the last.

ELLA RENTHEIM [*nods slowly*]. Yes, exactly. When I die, the name of Rentheim dies too. I feel strangled by the very thought. To be obliterated from existence . . . even to the extent of one's name.

BORKMAN [*flaring up*]. Ah! Now I see what you are after.

ELLA RENTHEIM [*with passion*]. Don't let it happen. Let Erhart bear my name after me!

BORKMAN [*looking hard at her*]. I understand you. You want to free my son from having his father's name. Isn't that it?

ELLA RENTHEIM. No, never that! I would gladly and defiantly have borne your name with you. But when a mother is nearing her death. . . . A name is a closer bond than you think, Borkman.

BORKMAN [*coldly and proudly*]. Very well, Ella. I am man enough to bear my name alone.

ELLA RENTHEIM [*seizes and presses his hand*]. Thank you! thank you! That fully settles our account. Yes, yes, let us accept that. You have done all you could to make amends. And when I am dead, Erhart Rentheim will live on after me!

[*The tapestry-lined door is thrown open.* MRS. BORKMAN, *her large shawl over her head, stands in the doorway.*]

MRS. BORKMAN [*in extreme agitation*]. Never, never shall Erhart be called by that name.

ELLA RENTHEIM [*shrinking back*]. Gunhild!

BORKMAN [*harshly and threateningly*]. Nobody has permission to come up here!

MRS. BORKMAN [*takes a step into the room*]. I give myself permission.

BORKMAN [*going up to her*]. What do you want with me?

MRS. BORKMAN. I want to fight for you. Protect you against the forces of evil.

ELLA RENTHEIM. The most evil forces are to be found in *you*, Gunhild!

MRS. BORKMAN [*hard*]. Be that as it may. [*Threateningly, with arm upraised.*] But this I tell you: he shall bear his father's name! And raise it once more to a place of honour! And I alone shall be his mother! I alone! My son's heart shall be mine—mine, and no one else's.

[*She goes out through the tapestry-lined door and shuts it after her.*]

ELLA RENTHEIM [*shaken and upset*]. Borkman—Erhart will be destroyed by this climate of hate. You and Gunhild *must* reach an understanding. We must go down to her at once.

BORKMAN [*looks at her*]. We? You mean I should go, too?

ELLA RENTHEIM. Both you and I.

BORKMAN [*shakes his head*]. She is hard, Ella. Hard as the iron I once dreamed of quarrying from the rock.

ELLA RENTHEIM. Try. Try it now!

[BORKMAN *does not reply; he stands looking uncertainly at her.*]

ACT THREE

MRS. BORKMAN's *sitting-room. The lamp is still burning on the table by the sofa. In the garden room the lamp is out, and all is dark.*

MRS. BORKMAN, *her shawl over her head, comes in by the hall door in great agitation; she walks across to the window and draws the curtain slightly to one side; then she goes across and sits down beside the stove, but soon jumps up again, walks across to the bell-pull and rings. She stands by the sofa and waits for a moment. Nobody comes. Then she rings again, this time more urgently.*

Presently the MAID *comes in from the hall. She looks sleepy and annoyed, and appears to have dressed in great haste.*

MRS. BORKMAN [*impatiently*]. Where've you been, Malene? I've rung twice!

MAID. Yes, ma'am, I heard you.

MRS. BORKMAN. So why didn't you come?

MAID [*sullenly*]. I had to put some clothes on first, didn't I?

MRS. BORKMAN. Go now and get dressed properly. I want you to run down at once and fetch my son.

MAID [*looks at her in astonishment*]. You want me to fetch Mr. Erhart?

MRS. BORKMAN. Yes. Just tell him he's to come home at once. I want to speak to him.

MAID [*sulkily*]. Then I'd best go and wake the coachman across at the bailiff's.

MRS. BORKMAN. Why?

MAID. So he can harness the sledge. It's snowing something terrible out there.

MRS. BORKMAN. Oh, never mind that! Just run down there—quickly! It's only just round the corner.

MAID. But, ma'am, you don't call *that* just round the corner!

MRS. BORKMAN. Of course it is. You know where Mr. Hinkel's house is, don't you?

MAID [*tartly*]. Oh, so that's where he is tonight, is it?

MRS. BORKMAN [*starts*]. Yes. Where else would he be?

MAID [*smirking*]. I just thought he'd be where he usually is.

MRS. BORKMAN. Where's that?

MAID. At that Mrs. Wilton's, or whatever they call her.

MRS. BORKMAN. Mrs. Wilton's? But my son isn't in the habit of going *there* very often.

MAID [*mumbling*]. From what I hear, he's there every day.

MRS. BORKMAN. That's just gossip, Malene. Now go on down to Mr. Hinkel's and see you find him.

MAID [*tossing her head*]. All right! all right! I'm going!

[*She turns to go out through the hall. At that moment, the door opens and* ELLA RENTHEIM *and* BORKMAN *appear on the threshold.*]

MRS. BORKMAN [*staggers backwards*]. What's this!

MAID [*terrified, clasps her hands*]. Oh, Jesus!

MRS. BORKMAN [*whispers to the* MAID]. Tell him to come at once.

MAID [*in a low voice*]. Yes, ma'am.

[ELLA RENTHEIM *comes into the room, followed by* BORKMAN. *The* MAID *sidles behind them, out through the door which she closes behind her. There is a brief silence.*]

MRS. BORKMAN [*once more in control of herself, turns to* ELLA]. What does he want down here?

ELLA RENTHEIM. He wants to try to reach an understanding with you, Gunhild.

MRS. BORKMAN. He's never tried before.

ELLA RENTHEIM. He wants to tonight.

MRS. BORKMAN. The last time we faced each other . . . was in court. When I was summoned to give an explanation. . . .

BORKMAN [*approaching*]. I am the one who will do the explaining tonight.

MRS. BORKMAN [*looks at him*]. You!

BORKMAN. Not of the offence I committed. All the world knows of that.

MRS. BORKMAN [*with a bitter sigh*]. That is true. All the world knows that.

BORKMAN. But what they don't know is *why* I did it. Why I *had* to do it. People don't understand that I *had* to do it because I am as I am— because I am John Gabriel Borkman, and not somebody else. That's what I want to try to explain to you.

MRS. BORKMAN [*shakes her head*]. No use! Motives are no excuse. They don't acquit you.

BORKMAN. In your own eyes they can.

MRS. BORKMAN [*with a dismissive gesture*]. Oh, let's leave this! I've brooded enough on this murky business.

BORKMAN. So have I. Five endless years in a prison cell—on top of everything else—gave me good time for that. And the eight years I've spent in that room upstairs have given me even more. Time after time I've conducted a complete re-trial of the whole case—in my own mind. I have been my own prosecutor, my own defending counsel, my own judge. I think I can honestly say I have been more impartial than anybody else could possibly have been. I have paced that floor up there, turning every one of my actions inside out and upside down, scrutinizing them from every angle, as mercilessly and ruthlessly as ever any lawyer could. And the verdict I reach is always the same: that the only person I have committed any offence against—is myself.

MRS. BORKMAN. Not against me? Not against your son?

BORKMAN. I include you and him in it when I say 'myself'.

MRS. BORKMAN. And what about the hundreds of others—all those people you are supposed to have ruined?

BORKMAN [*vehemently*]. I had the power! And the indomitable sense of ambition! All those millions lay there, imprisoned, over the whole land, deep in the mountains, and called to me! Cried out to me for release! But nobody else heard it. Only me.

MRS. BORKMAN. Yes, and it branded the name of Borkman for ever.

BORKMAN. Do you think if others had had the power, they wouldn't have acted exactly as I did?

MRS. BORKMAN. Nobody, nobody would have done as you did.

BORKMAN. Perhaps not. But that would be because they didn't have my abilities. And if they *had* done it, it wouldn't have been done with the same purpose in view as mine. The course of action would have been quite different. . . . In short, I have acquitted myself.

ELLA RENTHEIM [*softly and appealingly*]. How can you say that so confidently, Borkman?

BORKMAN [*nods*]. Acquitted myself thus far. But then comes the really appalling accusation I have to make against myself.

MRS. BORKMAN. What is that?

BORKMAN. I've now gone and wasted eight precious years of my life up there! The day I was released I should have stepped straight out into reality—into the iron-hard, dreamless world of reality! I should have started at the bottom and swung my way up to the heights again—higher than ever before—despite everything that had happened in the meantime.

MRS. BORKMAN. Oh, that would have simply meant living the same life all over again, believe me.

BORKMAN [*shakes his head and looks sententiously at her*]. Nothing new ever happens. But what *has* happened doesn't repeat itself either. All change is in the eye of the beholder. A new vision transforms the old deed. [*Breaks off.*] But you wouldn't understand.

MRS. BORKMAN [*curtly*]. No, I don't understand.

BORKMAN. That's exactly my curse—I have never found a single living soul who understood me.

ELLA RENTHEIM [*looks at him*]. Never, Borkman?

BORKMAN. With one exception—perhaps. Long, long ago. In the days when I didn't think I needed understanding. Since then—nobody! Nobody alert enough to anticipate my needs . . . to rouse me to action . . . to sound a clarion call . . . to inspire me to renewed achievement. And nobody, either, to reassure me that I've done nothing that was beyond redemption.

MRS. BORKMAN [*laughs scornfully*]. So you still need reassurance about that!

BORKMAN [*with growing anger*]. When the whole world yelps in chorus that I am a beaten man, there are moments when I almost believe it myself. [*Raises his head.*] But then my sovereign spirit reasserts itself. And that acquits me!

MRS. BORKMAN [*looks hard at him*]. Why did you never come and ask me for what you call 'understanding'?

BORKMAN. Would it have been any use if I had?

MRS. BORKMAN [*waves her hand in repudiation*]. You have never loved anything outside yourself—that's the truth of the matter.

BORKMAN [*proudly*]. I have loved power. . . .

MRS. BORKMAN. Yes, power!

BORKMAN. The power to create human happiness all around me.

MRS. BORKMAN. Once you had the power to make me happy. Did you ever use it?

BORKMAN [*not looking at her*]. In a shipwreck . . . somebody's almost bound to go down.

MRS. BORKMAN. And your own son! Did you ever use your power . . . did you devote any part of your life . . . to making him happy?

BORKMAN. I do not know him.

MRS. BORKMAN. No, that is true. You do not even know him.

BORKMAN [*harshly*]. You—his mother—took care of that.

MRS. BORKMAN [*looks at him with an air of triumph*]. Oh, you don't know what else I've taken care of.

BORKMAN. You?

MRS. BORKMAN. Yes, I. I alone.

BORKMAN. Then tell me.

MRS. BORKMAN. I've taken care of your epitaph.

BORKMAN [*with a short, dry laugh*]. My epitaph? Aha! That makes it sound as though I were already dead.

MRS. BORKMAN [*with emphasis*]. You are.

BORKMAN [*slowly*]. Yes, perhaps you are right. [*Flares up.*] No, no! Not yet! I have been close ... so very close to death. But now I am revived. I am well again. Life still lies ahead. I can see it ... this new life ... bright and sparkling ... beckoning to me. And you shall see it too. You too.

MRS. BORKMAN [*raises her hand*]. Dream no more of life. Remain in peace where you lie!

ELLA RENTHEIM [*shocked*]. Gunhild! Gunhild! How can you. . . !

MRS. BORKMAN [*without listening to her*]. I shall erect a monument over your grave.

BORKMAN. A pillar of shame, I suppose?

MRS. BORKMAN [*increasingly agitated*]. Oh, no. It won't be any monument of stone or metal. And nobody is going to carve any scornful inscription on the monument I erect. I will plant, as it were, an impenetrable clump of trees and bushes about your tomb—a living hedge to obliterate all the dark shame of the past ... shrouding in eternal oblivion what once was John Gabriel Borkman.

BORKMAN [*hoarsely and cuttingly*]. And you will perform this labour of love?

MRS. BORKMAN. Not with my own hands. I haven't the strength. But I have an assistant, someone I have brought up to dedicate his life to this. He will live a life so clear and pure and bright it will obliterate all memory of your own pit-blackened existence.

BORKMAN [*darkly and threateningly*]. If you mean Erhart, say so!

MRS. BORKMAN [*looking him straight in the eye*]. Yes, Erhart. My son. Whom you now want to cast off—as atonement for your own misdeeds.

BORKMAN [*with a glance at* ELLA RENTHEIM]. As atonement for my greatest sin.

MRS. BORKMAN [*repudiatingly*]. That was only a sin against a stranger. Remember the sin against me! [*Looks triumphantly at them both.*] But he will not do as you ask! When I cry to him in my need, he will come! He wants to be with me! With me, and with nobody else. [*Suddenly listens and cries.*] I hear him coming. Here he is! Here he is! Erhart!

[ERHART BORKMAN *flings open the hall door and comes into the room. He is wearing an overcoat, and still has his hat on.*]

ERHART [*pale and anxious*]. Mother! What in God's name ... ! [*He sees* BORKMAN *standing in the doorway of the garden room, starts, and takes his hat off. He is silent for a moment, then asks.*] What do you want with me, Mother? What's happened?

MRS. BORKMAN [*holding out her arms towards him*]. I want to see you, Erhart. I want to have you with me—always!

ERHART [*stammering*]. Have me ... ? Always? What do you mean?

MRS. BORKMAN. I want you ... *want* you! Because somebody else wants to take you away from me!

ERHART [*recoiling a step*]. Ah ... so you know!

MRS. BORKMAN. Yes. Do you know too?

ERHART [*startled, looks at her*]. Do I know? Yes, of course, I know. ...

MRS. BORKMAN. Aha! So it's all arranged! Behind my back! Erhart! Erhart!

ERHART [*quickly*]. Mother, tell me what you know.

MRS. BORKMAN. I know everything. I know your aunt has come here to take you away from me.

ERHART. Aunt Ella!

ELLA RENTHEIM. Oh, please listen to me for a moment, Erhart!

MRS. BORKMAN [*continuing*]. She wants me to pass you over to her. She wants to take your mother's place, Erhart! From now on, she wants you to be *her* son, and not mine. She wants you to inherit everything from her. To renounce your own name and take hers instead!

ERHART. Aunt Ella, is this true?

ELLA RENTHEIM. Yes, it is true.

ERHART. I knew nothing of this. Why do you want me back?

ELLA RENTHEIM. Because I feel I am losing you here.

MRS. BORKMAN [*harshly*]. Losing him to *me*, yes! And that is as it should be.

ELLA RENTHEIM [*looks imploringly at him*]. Erhart, I can't afford to lose you. I have to tell you I am a lonely . . . dying woman.

ERHART. Dying . . . ?

ELLA RENTHEIM. Yes, dying. Won't you come and be with me at the end? Join with me. Be to me as though you were my own child. . . .

MRS. BORKMAN [*interrupting*]. And forsake your mother, and perhaps also your mission in life? Will you do that, Erhart?

ELLA RENTHEIM. Soon I will be no more. What is your answer, Erhart?

ERHART [*warmly, with emotion*]. Aunt Ella . . . you have been unbelievably good to me. With you, my childhood was as happy and carefree as ever any child could hope for . . .

MRS. BORKMAN. Erhart! Erhart!

ELLA RENTHEIM. Thank God you still think so!

ERHART. . . . But I cannot sacrifice myself to you now. I can't possibly throw up everything to try to be a son to you. . . .

MRS. BORKMAN [*triumphantly*]. I knew it! You won't get him! You won't get him, Ella!

ELLA RENTHEIM [*sadly*]. I see that. You have won him back.

MRS. BORKMAN. Yes, yes! He is mine and he'll stay mine. Erhart . . . it's true, isn't it. . . . ? We two still have some way to go together, haven't we?

ERHART [*battling with himself*]. Mother . . . I might as well tell you straight . . .

MRS. BORKMAN [*tense*]. Well?

ERHART. I fear it won't be long before we reach the parting of the ways, Mother.

MRS. BORKMAN [*stands as though thunderstruck*]. What do you mean by that?

ERHART [*plucking up courage*]. Good God, Mother! I'm young! I think I'd absolutely suffocate in the stuffy air of this place.

MRS. BORKMAN. Here? In my house?

ERHART. Yes, here in your house, Mother.

ELLA RENTHEIM. Then come with me, Erhart!

ERHART. Oh, Aunt Ella, it's not the slightest bit better in your house. It's different ... but no better. Not for me. There it's roses and lavender—but it's as stuffy as it is here.

MRS. BORKMAN [*shaken, but composes herself with an effort*]. Stuffy, you say! At your mother's!

ERHART [*with rising impatience*]. Yes, I don't know what else to call it. All this pampered attention ... this adulation ... or whatever it might be called. I can't stand it any longer.

MRS. BORKMAN [*looks earnestly at him*]. Have you forgotten what you have dedicated your life to, Erhart?

ERHART [*exploding*]. You mean what *you* have dedicated my life to! You, Mother, you have been my will. I've never been allowed to have a will of my own! But I can't bear this yoke any longer. I am young! Remember that, Mother! [*With a respectful and considerate glance at* BORKMAN.] I can't dedicate my life to making atonement for somebody else. No matter who that person may be.

MRS. BORKMAN [*seized with a growing fear*]. Who is it who has changed you so, Erhart?

ERHART [*startled*]. Who? Why not myself...?

MRS. BORKMAN. No, no, no! You are being dictated to by outside forces. This isn't your mother's influence. Nor your ... your foster-mother's, either.

ERHART [*with forced defiance*]. I now determine my own actions, Mother! And my will is my own!

BORKMAN [*advances towards* ERHART]. Then perhaps my moment has arrived at last.

ERHART [*distantly and with studied politeness*]. What do you mean by that, Father?

MRS. BORKMAN [*scornfully*]. Yes, I would like to ask the same.

BORKMAN [*continues undisturbed*]. Listen, Erhart . . . what about coming with your father, then? No man can find redemption for his failure in another man's achievements. That's nothing but an empty dream, a story you've been given to believe . . . down here in this stuffy room. Even if you were to lead a life like all the saints in the calendar put together—it wouldn't help me one iota.

ERHART [*with cautious respect*]. What you say is true.

BORKMAN. Yes, it is. Nor would it help very much if I let myself abjectly wither away doing penance. All these years I have tried to keep myself going on dreams and hopes. But I can't be content with that. And now I'm finished with dreams.

ERHART [*with a slight bow*]. So what do you mean to do, Father?

BORKMAN. Achieve my own redemption. Begin at the bottom again. It is only by his own present and his own future that a man can atone for his past. Through work . . . unrelenting work for all those things which in my youth I felt made life worthwhile . . . and which now seem a thousand times more valuable still. Erhart—will you join me and help me in this new life?

MRS. BORKMAN [*raises a warning hand*]. Don't do it, Erhart!

ELLA RENTHEIM [*warmly*]. Oh yes, *do* do it! Help him, Erhart!

MRS. BORKMAN. What kind of advice is this from *you*—a lonely, dying woman?

ELLA RENTHEIM. I don't care.

MRS. BORKMAN. Ah! So long as I am not the one to take him from you.

ELLA RENTHEIM. Exactly, Gunhild.

BORKMAN. Will you, Erhart?

ERHART [*in extreme anguish*]. Father . . . I can't now. It's completely impossible!

BORKMAN. Then what do you meant to do?

ERHART [*with fire*]. I am young! I too want to live! I want to live my own life!

ELLA RENTHEIM. And you won't sacrifice a few short months to brighten the end of a poor, ailing life?

ERHART. Aunt Ella, I *can't*—however much I might wish to.

ELLA RENTHEIM. Not even for one who loves you so dearly?

ERHART. As I live and breathe, Aunt Ella . . . I cannot.

MRS. BORKMAN [*looking sharply at him*]. And you no longer feel any ties to your mother?

ERHART. I shall always love you, Mother. But I can't just live for you alone. That's no life for me.

BORKMAN. Then come and join me! Life is work, Erhart! Come! We two will go out together into life and work!

ERHART [*passionately*]. But I don't *want* to work just yet! I'm young! I never realized it before. But now I feel it coursing through my veins. I don't want to work. I just want to live, live, live!

MRS. BORKMAN [*sensing the truth, cries out*]. Erhart—what *do* you want to live for?

ERHART [*his eyes glistening*]. For happiness, Mother!

MRS. BORKMAN. And where do you expect to find *that*?

ERHART. I've already found it!

MRS. BORKMAN [*shrieks*]. Erhart . . . !

[ERHART *walks quickly across and opens the hall door.*]

ERHART [*shouts*]. Fanny . . . you can come in now!

[MRS. WILTON, *in her outdoor things, appears in the doorway.*]

MRS. BORKMAN [*with raised hands*]. Mrs. Wilton . . . !

MRS. WILTON [*hesitantly, with an enquiring glance at* ERHART]. May I . . . ?

ERHART. Please come in. I have told them everything.

[MRS. WILTON *comes into the room.* ERHART *closes the door behind her. She bows respectfully to* BORKMAN, *who returns the greeting silently. Brief silence.*]

MRS. WILTON [*in a low but firm voice*]. So the word is out. I fear I must be thought of as having brought great unhappiness to this house.

MRS. BORKMAN [*slowly, looking fixedly at her*]. You have destroyed the little that remained of what I had to live for. [*Bursts out.*] But this . . . this is utterly impossible.

MRS. WILTON. I quite understand how impossible it must seem to you, Mrs. Borkman.

MRS. BORKMAN. Surely you can see yourself how impossible it is. Or is it . . . ?

MRS. WILTON. Should one rather say improbable. Nevertheless, it is so.

MRS. BORKMAN [*turning*]. Are you quite serious about this, Erhart?

ERHART. This means happiness for me, Mother . . . great, glorious, living happiness. I can't pretend otherwise.

MRS. BORKMAN [*to* MRS. WILTON, *wringing her hands*]. You have duped and seduced my unhappy son!

MRS. WILTON [*tossing her head proudly*]. I have not.

MRS. BORKMAN. You are not trying to deny it?

MRS. WILTON. Yes. I have neither duped him nor seduced him. Erhart came to me of his own free will. And of my own free will I met him halfway.

MRS. BORKMAN [*looking haughtily at her*]. Oh, yes. I'm quite ready to believe that.

MRS. WILTON [*controlled*]. Mrs. Borkman—there are some forces in human life you don't seem to know a great deal about.

MRS. BORKMAN. Which forces are they, if I may ask?

MRS. WILTON. Those forces which enjoin two people to bind their lives indissolubly together, regardless of all else.

MRS. BORKMAN [*smiles*]. I thought you *were* indissolubly bound—to somebody else.

MRS. WILTON [*shortly*]. He has left me.

MRS. BORKMAN. But people say he's still alive.

MRS. WILTON. As far as I am concerned, he is dead.

ERHART [*insistently*]. Yes, Mother. As far as Fanny is concerned, he is dead. And to me he means nothing.

MRS. BORKMAN [*looks severely at him*]. So you know all about ... this other man?

ERHART. Yes, Mother. I know the whole story!

MRS. BORKMAN. Yet you say it means nothing to you!

ERHART [*defiantly*]. All I can say to you is that I want to be happy! I'm young! I want to live, live, live!

MRS. BORKMAN. Yes, you are young, Erhart. Much too young for all this.

MRS. WILTON [*firmly and earnestly*]. You mustn't think I haven't said the same to him, Mrs. Borkman. I've told him everything about myself and my way of life. I've repeatedly reminded him that I'm a full seven years older than he is ...

ERHART [*interrupting*]. Oh, please, Fanny—I knew that all the time.

MRS. WILTON. But all ... to no avail.

MRS. BORKMAN. Oh? Really? So why didn't you simply send him packing? Shut your doors to him? That you might have done while there was still time!

MRS. WILTON [*looks at her and says in a low voice*]. I simply couldn't, Mrs. Borkman.

MRS. BORKMAN. Why couldn't you?

MRS. WILTON. Because my own happiness was involved, too.

MRS. BORKMAN [*scornfully*]. Oh ... happiness, happiness. ...

MRS. WILTON. Never in my life before have I known what happiness was. And I cannot turn it away now, just because it comes so late.

MRS. BORKMAN. And how long do you think this happiness will last?

ERHART [*interrupting*]. Whether it lasts or not—what does it matter?

MRS. BORKMAN [*in anger*]. Blind fool that you are! Can't you see where all this is leading?

ERHART. I don't want to look to the future. I don't want to look to *anything* very much. All I want is the chance to live my own life for once!

MRS. BORKMAN [*distressed*]. And you call that living, Erhart!

ERHART. Yes. Don't you see how lovely she is!

MRS. BORKMAN [*wringing her hands*]. And this new and crushing burden of shame is something else I shall have to bear!

BORKMAN [*at the rear, in a harsh and cutting voice*]. Ah, you are used to bearing that sort of thing, Gunhild!

ELLA RENTHEIM [*imploringly*]. Borkman!

ERHART [*similarly*]. Father!

MRS. BORKMAN. Every day here I'll have to endure the sight of my own son in the company of a . . .

ERHART [*interrupting harshly*]. I assure you, Mother, you won't see any such thing! I'm not staying here.

MRS. WILTON [*quickly and decisively*]. We are going away, Mrs. Borkman.

MRS. BORKMAN. You are leaving too. Together?

MRS. WILTON [*nods*]. Yes, I'm going South. Abroad. I am taking a young girl along. And Erhart is coming too.

MRS. BORKMAN. With you? And a young girl?

MRS. WILTON. Yes. It's little Frida Foldal whom I took into my house. I want her to get away and study music.

MRS. BORKMAN. So you are taking her with you?

MRS. WILTON. Yes, I can't very well let the child loose abroad on her own.

MRS. BORKMAN [*suppressing a smile*]. What do you say to this, Erhart?

ERHART [*shrugs his shoulders, somewhat embarrassed*]. Well, Mother, if that's the way Fanny wants it . . .

MRS. BORKMAN [*coldly*]. And when is the party leaving, if one may ask?

MRS. WILTON. We're leaving now. Tonight. My sleigh is standing out on the road—outside the Hinkels.

MRS. BORKMAN [*looks her up and down*]. Ah! So that's what the party was about!

MRS. WILTON [*smiles*]. Yes, the only guests were Erhart and me. And little Frida, of course.

MRS. BORKMAN. And where is she now?

MRS. WILTON. She's sitting in the sleigh waiting for us.

ERHART [*deeply embarrassed*]. Mother . . . you do understand . . . I wanted to spare you—and everybody—all this.

MRS. BORKMAN [*looks at him, greatly offended*]. You would have left without saying goodbye to me?

ERHART. Yes, I thought it was best that way. Best for both of us. Everything was arranged. All my things packed. But when you sent for me . . . [*He makes to stretch out his hands to her.*] Goodbye, Mother.

MRS. BORKMAN [*waves him away*]. Don't touch me!

ERHART [*gently*]. Is that your last word?

MRS. BORKMAN [*hard*]. Yes.

ERHART [*turns*]. Goodbye then, Aunt Ella.

ELLA RENTHEIM [*pressing his hands*]. Goodbye, Erhart! Live your life . . . and be happy . . . as happy as ever you can!

ERHART. Thank you, Aunt Ella. [*He bows to* BORKMAN.] Goodbye, Father. [*Whispers to* MRS. WILTON.] Let's get away from here—the sooner the better.

MRS. WILTON [*softly*]. Yes, let's.

MRS. BORKMAN [*with a malicious smile*]. Mrs. Wilton . . . do you think it's wise to take that young girl with you?

MRS. WILTON [*returns the smile, half ironically, half seriously*]. Men are so unreliable, Mrs. Borkman. And women too. When Erhart is finished with me . . . and I with him . . . then it'll be good for both of us, poor boy, if he has somebody else to fall back on.

MRS. BORKMAN. What about you?

MRS. WILTON. Oh, I can take care of myself, don't you worry. Goodbye all!

[*She nods and goes out through the hall door.* ERHART *stands for a moment, as though wavering; then he turns and follows her.*]

MRS. BORKMAN [*lowering her clasped hands*]. Childless!

BORKMAN [*as though waking to a decision*]. So out into the storm alone! My hat! My cape!

[*He rushes towards the door.*]

ELLA RENTHEIM [*in terror, stops him*]. John Gabriel, where are you going?

BORKMAN. Out into the storm of life, I said. Let me go, Ella!

ELLA RENTHEIM [*holds him firmly*]. No, no. I won't let you go! You are a sick man. I can see it in your face!

BORKMAN. Let me go, I say!

[*He tears himself free, and goes out into the hall.*]

ELLA RENTHEIM [*in the doorway*]. Help me to hold him back, Gunhild!

MRS. BORKMAN [*cold and hard, standing in the middle of the room*]. I will hold nobody back, nobody at all. Let them all leave me. Every single one. Let them go . . . as far as they please. [*Suddenly, with a piercing shriek.*] Erhart, don't go!

[*She rushes with outstretched arms towards the door.* ELLA RENTHEIM *stops her.*]

ACT FOUR

An open courtyard outside the main building, which is situated to the right. A corner of this projects out; it has the entrance door and a flight of low stone steps. In the background, quite close to the house, is a line of steep fir-clad slopes. Left is the edge of a wood, with scattered trees and undergrowth. It has stopped snowing, but the ground has a deep covering of freshly fallen snow. The branches of the trees are also heavy with snow. The night is dark, with driving clouds. Occasionally the pale moon is visible. The only light is that reflected dimly from the snow.

BORKMAN, MRS. BORKMAN, and ELLA RENTHEIM are standing outside on the steps. BORKMAN is leaning wearily against the wall of the house. He has an old-fashioned cape thrown over his shoulders, and is holding a soft grey felt hat in one hand and a thick knotted stick in the other. ELLA RENTHEIM is carrying her cape over her arm. MRS. BORKMAN's big shawl has slipped down over her shoulders, leaving her bare-headed.

ELLA RENTHEIM [*barring* MRS. BORKMAN's *path*]. Don't go after him, Gunhild!

MRS. BORKMAN [*in fear and agitation*]. Let me past! He mustn't leave me.

ELLA RENTHEIM. It's no use, I tell you! You'll never catch him.

MRS. BORKMAN. Let me go all the same, Ella! I'll call out to him as I go down the road. Surely he'll hear his mother's cries!

ELLA RENTHEIM. He *can't* hear you. He'll already be sitting inside the sleigh. . . .

MRS. BORKMAN. No, no! He can't be sitting in the sleigh yet.

ELLA RENTHEIM. Yes he is, you must believe me.

MRS. BORKMAN [*in despair*]. If he is, he must be sitting beside her . . . that woman!

BORKMAN [*laughs grimly*]. So he won't hear his mother's cries then, will he?

MRS. BORKMAN. No . . . he won't. [*Listens.*] Ssh! What's that?

ELLA RENTHEIM [*also listening*]. It sounds like bells. . . .

MRS. BORKMAN [*with a choked cry*]. It is *her* sleigh!

ELLA RENTHEIM. Perhaps it's someone else's.

MRS. BORKMAN. No, no, it is Mrs. Wilton's sleigh carriage. I know those silver bells. Listen! They are driving right past here . . . at the bottom of the hill!

ELLA RENTHEIM [*quickly*]. Gunhild, if you want to cry out to him, do it now! It's just possible he might . . . [*The bells sound quite close by, in the wood.*] Quickly, Gunhild! They are just below us!

MRS. BORKMAN [*stands a moment undecided, then stiffens and says coldly and severely*]. No. I will not cry out to him. Let Erhart Borkman drive past me. On, on . . . far away to what he calls life and happiness.

[*The sound dies away in the distance.*]

ELLA RENTHEIM [*after some time*]. Can't hear the bells any more.

MRS. BORKMAN. I thought they sounded like funeral bells.

BORKMAN [*with a dry suppressed laugh*]. Aha! But they are not ringing for me yet.

MRS. BORKMAN. But they are for me. And for him who has left me.

ELLA RENTHEIM [*nods thoughtfully*]. Who knows. Perhaps they ring in life and happiness for him, Gunhild.

MRS. BORKMAN [*flaring up, gives her a hard look*]. Did you say life and happiness?

ELLA RENTHEIM. For a little while, at least.

MRS. BORKMAN. Can you really wish him life and happiness—with her?

ELLA RENTHEIM [*warmly and sincerely*]. Yes I can, with all my heart and soul.

MRS. BORKMAN [*coldly*]. Then your capacity for love must be much greater than mine.

ELLA RENTHEIM [*with a far-away look*]. Perhaps it's the very *want* of love that sustains it.

MRS. BORKMAN [*fixes her eyes on her*]. In which case, mine will soon be as great as yours, Ella.

[*She turns and goes into the house.*]

ELLA RENTHEIM [*stands for a moment, looking with a troubled expression at* BORKMAN, *then lays her hand cautiously on his shoulder*]. John, come along in, too.

BORKMAN [*as though waking*]. I?

ELLA RENTHEIM. Yes. This biting cold is too much for you. I can see that, John. Come along in with me. Inside, where it's warm.

BORKMAN [*angrily*]. Back upstairs?

ELLA RENTHEIM. No, downstairs, in *her* room.

BORKMAN [*flaring up*]. Never again shall I set foot under that roof!

ELLA RENTHEIM. But where will you go? It's night-time, John, and late.

BORKMAN [*putting on his hat*]. First I'll go and see to all my buried treasures.

ELLA RENTHEIM [*looks anxiously at him*]. John . . . I don't understand you.

BORKMAN [*coughing and laughing*]. Oh, I don't mean hidden plunder. Don't be afraid of that, Ella. [*He stops and points.*] Look at that man! Who is it?

[VILHELM FOLDAL, *in an old jacket covered with snow, with hat-brim turned down and a big umbrella in his hand, enters in front of the corner of the house, stumbling laboriously through the snow. He is limping badly with his left foot.*]

BORKMAN. Vilhelm! Back here again! What do you want?

FOLDAL [*looks up*]. Good Heavens! What are you doing out here on the steps, John Gabriel? [*Bows.*] And Mrs. Borkman too, I see!

BORKMAN [*curtly*]. This is not my wife.

FOLDAL. Oh, I beg your pardon. You see, I've lost my glasses in the snow.—But normally you never set foot outside the door. . . .

BORKMAN [*gaily, recklessly*]. It's about time I got a bit of fresh air and exercise, you see. Nearly three years in detention; five years in a cell; eight years in that room upstairs. . . .

ELLA RENTHEIM [*concerned*]. Borkman . . . please!

FOLDAL. Ah yes! Ah yes!

BORKMAN. But tell me, what do you want me for?

FOLDAL [*still standing at the bottom of the steps*]. I wanted to come up and see you, John Gabriel. I felt I *had* to come up and see you in your room. Oh God . . . that room!

BORKMAN. You wanted to come and see me, even though I'd shown you the door?

FOLDAL. Dear God, I don't hold that against you.

BORKMAN. What have you done to your foot? You are limping.

FOLDAL. Would you believe it . . . I've been run over.

ELLA RENTHEIM. Run over!

FOLDAL. Yes, by a sleigh. . . .

BORKMAN. Aha!

FOLDAL. With two horses. They came rushing down the hill. I couldn't get out of the way quick enough, and . . .

ELLA RENTHEIM. And they ran you over?

FOLDAL. They drove straight at me, Mrs. . . . or Miss . . . Straight at me they drove, so I went head over heels in the snow and I lost my glasses and broke my umbrella. [*Rubs himself.*] And I hurt my foot, too.

BORKMAN [*laughs to himself*]. Do you know who was sitting in that sleigh, Vilhelm?

FOLDAL. No. How could I see? It was a closed sleigh, and the curtains were drawn. And the driver didn't stop for a moment as I lay there sprawling. But *that* doesn't matter either, because . . . [*Bursts out.*] Oh, I'm so incredibly happy!

BORKMAN. Happy?

FOLDAL. Well, I don't really know how to describe it. But I suppose 'happy' is as near as anything. Something quite extraordinary has happened! So I couldn't help it . . . I *had* to come up and share my happiness with you, John Gabriel.

BORKMAN [*gruffly*]. Go on then—share it!

ELLA RENTHEIM. But take your friend inside first, Borkman.

BORKMAN [*hard*]. I told you I will not enter that house again.

ELLA RENTHEIM. But you've just heard he's been run over!

BORKMAN. Oh, we all get run over ... some time in our lives. The thing then is to pick yourself up again. And pretend nothing's happened.

FOLDAL. That's very profound, John Gabriel. But I could nicely tell you about it out here. Wouldn't take long.

BORKMAN [*more gently*]. Yes, please, Vilhelm. Do me that service.

FOLDAL. Listen! When I got home this evening after seeing you, what do you think I should find but a letter. And can you guess who it was from?

BORKMAN. Your little Frida, perhaps?

FOLDAL. Exactly. Fancy you getting it first go! Yes, it was a long letter from Frida—fairly long, anyway. A servant brought it. And can you guess what was in the letter?

BORKMAN. Possibly a farewell to her parents?

FOLDAL. Precisely! You are remarkably good at guessing, John Gabriel! Yes, she writes to say that Mrs. Wilton has been taking a great interest in her, and now she wants to take Frida abroad with her to study music. And Mrs. Wilton has engaged a very able tutor who will go along with them and see to Frida's education. She is a little weak in some subjects, I'm afraid.

BORKMAN [*shaking with inward laughter*]. Of course, of course! I understand it all very well, Vilhelm.

FOLDAL [*continues eagerly*]. And what do you think? She knew nothing about it until tonight. At that party, you know ... er ... hm! Yet she still found time to write. Such a nice, warm, loving letter it is, too—let me tell you. Not a trace of contempt for her father anywhere. And how refined of her to say goodbye to us in writing— before leaving. [*Laughs.*] But, of course, she won't get away with that!

BORKMAN [*looks questioningly at him*]. How do you mean?

FOLDAL. She writes that they are leaving early tomorrow morning. Quite early.

BORKMAN. Tomorrow, eh? Is that what she says?

FOLDAL [*laughs and rubs his hands*]. So I shall be cunning! I'm now going straight up to Mrs. Wilton's. . . .

BORKMAN. Tonight?

FOLDAL. Heavens, it's not so very late. And if everything is shut, I'll ring. Just like that. I *must* see Frida before she leaves. Goodnight! goodnight!

[*He turns to go.*]

BORKMAN. My poor Vilhelm, listen to me. You can spare yourself that long walk.

FOLDAL. Ah, you are thinking of my foot. . . .

BORKMAN. Yes. And you won't get into Mrs. Wilton's house in any case.

FOLDAL. Yes I will. I just go on ringing the bell till somebody comes and opens up. I must see Frida.

ELLA RENTHEIM. Your daughter has already left, Mr. Foldal.

FOLDAL [*as though thunderstruck*]. Already left? Frida? Are you sure? Who told you?

BORKMAN. We have it from her tutor-to-be.

FOLDAL. Oh? Who is he?

BORKMAN. A student by the name of Erhart Borkman.

FOLDAL [*radiant with joy*]. Your son, John Gabriel. Is *he* going with them?

BORKMAN. Yes. He's the one who is going to help Mrs. Wilton educate your little Frida.

FOLDAL. God be praised! Then the child is in the best of hands. But is it really quite certain that they've left with her?

BORKMAN. They left in that sleigh which ran you down in the road.

FOLDAL [*claps his hands*]. My little Frida in that magnificent sleigh!

BORKMAN [*nods*]. Yes, yes, Vilhelm. Your daughter is not doing too badly. And Erhart Borkman too. Did you notice the silver bells?

FOLDAL. Oh, yes ... *Silver* bells, did you say? Were they silver bells? Real genuine silver?

BORKMAN. You may be sure they were. Everything was genuine. Both outside and ... and inside.

FOLDAL [*with quiet emotion*]. How strange are the workings of fate! There's my ... my modest talent for poetry been transformed into music in Frida. So after all's said and done I haven't been a poet for nothing. Now she's got the chance of going out into the great wide world which I once used to dream so passionately of seeing. Little Frida travelling in a grand sleigh. With silver bells on the harness ... !

BORKMAN. And running over her own father.

FOLDAL [*happily*]. Oh that! What does it matter to me ... so long as the child ... So I was too late after all. I'll go home now and comfort her mother who is sitting in the kitchen crying.

BORKMAN. Crying?

FOLDAL [*smiling*]. Yes, would you believe it. She was sitting there crying her heart out as I came away.

BORKMAN. And you are laughing, Vilhelm.

FOLDAL. I am, yes. But, poor thing, she doesn't know any better. Well, goodbye! It's good that the tram isn't far. Goodbye, goodbye, John Gabriel! Goodbye, Miss!

[*He waves and goes limping out the same way as he entered.*]

BORKMAN [*stands silently for a moment, staring vacantly*]. Goodbye, Vilhelm! It's not the first time in your life you have been run over, old friend.

ELLA RENTHEIM [*looks at him with suppressed anxiety*]. You are so pale, John, so pale. ...

BORKMAN. That comes from the prison air upstairs.

ELLA RENTHEIM. I have never seen you like this before.

Q1

BORKMAN. No. Because you've never seen an escaped convict before, have you?

ELLA RENTHEIM. Please come inside with me, John.

BORKMAN. It's no use trying to coax me. Haven't I told you. . . .

ELLA RENTHEIM. I beg and implore you. For your own sake. . . .

[*The* MAID *appears in the doorway at the top of the steps.*]

MAID. Excuse me, but Mrs. Borkman has told me to lock the front door now.

BORKMAN [*in a low voice, to* ELLA]. You hear that! They want to shut me in again.

ELLA RENTHEIM [*to the* MAID]. Mr. Borkman isn't feeling well. He wants a little fresh air first.

MAID. But Mrs. Borkman herself told me . . .

ELLA RENTHEIM. I shall lock the door. Just leave the key in the lock. . . .

MAID. Very well. I'll do that.

[*She goes into the house again.*]

BORKMAN [*stands silent for a moment, listening, then walks quickly down to the courtyard*]. Now I am outside the walls, Ella. They'll never take me again!

ELLA RENTHEIM [*goes down to him*]. But you are a free man in there too, John. You can come and go just as you please.

BORKMAN [*softly, as though in terror*]. Never under a roof again! How good it is to be out here in the night. If I went up to that room now . . . the walls and the ceiling would shrink and crush me . . . crush me like a fly. . . .

ELLA RENTHEIM. But where will you go?

BORKMAN. I will go on, and on, and on. To see if I can make my way to freedom and life and humanity again. Will you go with me, Ella?

ELLA RENTHEIM. I? Now?

BORKMAN. Yes, yes. At once!

ELLA RENTHEIM. But how far?

BORKMAN. As far as I can.

ELLA RENTHEIM. Oh, think what you're doing! A cold, wet winter night like this....

BORKMAN [*hoarsely*]. Aha! The lady is worried about her health, eh? Ah, yes ... it's not altogether robust, is it?

ELLA RENTHEIM. It's your health I'm worried about.

BORKMAN. Ha! ha! A dead man's health! You make me laugh, Ella!

[*He walks on.*]

ELLA RENTHEIM [*goes after him to hold him back*]. What did you say you were?

BORKMAN. A dead man, was what I said. Don't you remember Gunhild saying I ought to rest peacefully where I lay?

ELLA RENTHEIM [*resolved, throws her coat around her*]. I'm going with you, John.

BORKMAN. Yes, we two belong together, Ella. You and I. [*He walks on.*] Come.

[*They have gradually moved in among the trees, left. Little by little they are lost to sight. The house and the courtyard disappear. The landscape, with slopes and ridges, slowly changes and grows wilder and wilder.*]

ELLA RENTHEIM'S VOICE [*is heard within the forest, right*]. Where are we going, John. I don't know my way here.

BORKMAN'S VOICE [*higher up*]. Just follow my footprints in the snow!

ELLA RENTHEIM'S VOICE. But why do we have to climb so high?

BORKMAN'S VOICE [*closer*]. We must follow the winding path.

ELLA RENTHEIM [*still concealed*]. But I can't keep going much further.

BORKMAN [*at the edge of the forest, left*]. Come, come! We are not far from the look-out place. There used to be a bench there....

ELLA RENTHEIM [*comes into view among the trees*]. You remember that?

BORKMAN. There you can rest.

[*They have arrived at a small clearing high up in the forest. The mountain side rises steeply behind them. To the left, far below, the landscape stretches into the distance, with fjords and distant massed peaks. On the left of the clearing is a dead pine tree with a bench under it. The snow lies deep on the clearing.*

BORKMAN, *followed by* ELLA RENTHEIM, *enters from the right and wades with difficulty through the snow.*]

BORKMAN [*stops by the precipice, left*]. Come here, Ella! I want to show you something.

ELLA RENTHEIM [*by him*]. What do you want to show me, John?

BORKMAN [*pointing*]. See how open and free the land lies before us . . . far into the distance.

ELLA RENTHEIM. We often sat on that bench . . . and took even more distant views.

BORKMAN. It was a land of dreams we gazed out at.

ELLA RENTHEIM [*nods sadly*]. Yes, the dreamland of our lives. And now it is covered in snow. And the old tree is dead.

BORKMAN [*not listening to her*]. Can you see the smoke from the great steamships out on the fjord?

ELLA RENTHEIM. No.

BORKMAN. I can. They come and they go. They create a world-wide sense of community. They bring light and warmth to the hearts of men in many thousands of homes. That was what I dreamed of achieving.

ELLA RENTHEIM [*softly*]. And it remained a dream.

BORKMAN. Yes. It remained a dream. [*Listens.*] And listen! Down there by the river! The factories at work! *My* factories! Factories I would have created! Going full blast! It's the night shift. Day and night they work. Listen to them! The wheels spinning, the rollers turning . . . round and round. Can't you hear them, Ella?

ELLA RENTHEIM. No.

BORKMAN. I can hear them.

ELLA RENTHEIM [*fearfully*]. I think you are mistaken, John.

BORKMAN [*more and more excited*]. Yet all these . . . are merely the out-works around the kingdom, you know!

ELLA RENTHEIM. The kingdom? What kingdom . . . ?

BORKMAN. *My* kingdom, of course. The kingdom I was about to take possession of when . . . when I died.

ELLA RENTHEIM [*softly, shaken*]. Oh, John, John!

BORKMAN. And now it lies there—defenceless, leaderless, exposed to thieving and plundering and attack. Ella, you see those distant mountains there—ranging, soaring, towering. That is my vast, my infinite, my inexhaustible kingdom!

ELLA RENTHEIM. But it's an icy blast that blows from that kingdom, John.

BORKMAN. To me it is the breath of life. To me it comes like a greeting from loyal subject spirits. I sense their presence—those captive millions. I feel the veins of metal reaching out their twisting, sinuous, beckoning arms to me. Standing that night in the vaults of the bank, a lantern in my hand, I saw them as living shadows. You wanted to be freed. And I tried. But could not succeed. And the treasure sank back into the depths. [*With outstretched arms.*] But let me whisper this to you, here in the stillness of the night. I love you: you who lie in a trance of death in the darkness and the deep. I love you! You and your life-seeking treasures and all your bright retinue of power and glory. I love you, love you, love you.

ELLA RENTHEIM [*with quiet but growing agitation*]. Yes, your love is still down there, John. There where it's always been. But up here, in the light of day, there throbbed a warm and living human heart. Beating for you. You broke that heart. Worse . . . oh, ten times worse! You sold it for . . .

BORKMAN [*trembles, as a cold shudder seems to pass through him*]. For the kingdom . . . and the power . . . and the glory, you mean?

ELLA RENTHEIM. That is what I do mean. I have said it once before tonight. You murdered love in the woman who loved you. And whom you loved in return. In so far as you ever could love anyone. [*With uplifted arm.*] I therefore prophecy this, John Gabriel Borkman: you will never collect the price you demanded for this murder. You will never enter triumphant into your cold dark kingdom.

BORKMAN [*staggers to the bench and sits down heavily*]. I fear your prophecy is probably right, Ella.

ELLA RENTHEIM [*goes over to him*]. You must not *fear* it, John. It would be the best that could happen to you.

BORKMAN [*gives a cry and clutches his chest*]. Ah . . . ! [*Feebly.*] Now it's let me go.

ELLA RENTHEIM [*shaking him*]. What was it, John?

BORKMAN [*sinks back on the bench*]. A hand of ice clutched at my heart.

ELLA RENTHEIM. John! Was it a hand of ice you felt?

BORKMAN [*mumbling*]. No. Not a hand of ice. A hand of iron.

[*He slumps down on the bench.*]

ELLA RENTHEIM [*tears her coat off and places it over him*]. Stay there! Lie quietly! I shall go and bring help. [*She goes a few steps to the right, stops, goes back and feels his pulse and his face. Speaks softly but firmly.*] No. It is best so, John Borkman. Best for you.

[*She wraps the coat more tightly round him and sits down in the snow in front of the bench. Short silence.* MRS. BORKMAN, *in an overcoat, appears through the trees, right. In front of her goes the* MAID *carrying a lighted lantern.*]

MAID [*shining the light on the snow*]. Yes, yes, ma'am. Here are their footprints.

MRS. BORKMAN [*peering about*]. Yes, here they are! Over there on the bench. [*Shouts.*] Ella!

ELLA RENTHEIM [*rises*]. Are you looking for us?

MRS. BORKMAN [*hard*]. Yes, what else could I do?

ELLA RENTHEIM [*points*]. There he is, Gunhild.

MRS. BORKMAN. Asleep!

ELLA RENTHEIM [*nods*]. A long deep sleep, I fear.

MRS. BORKMAN [*bursts out*]. Ella! [*Controls herself and asks quietly.*] Was it . . . deliberate.

ELLA RENTHEIM. No.

MRS. BORKMAN [*relieved*]. Not by his own hand, then?

ELLA RENTHEIM. No. An icy hand of iron gripped his heart.

MRS. BORKMAN [*to the* MAID]. Fetch help. Get the people from the farm.

MAID. Very good, ma'am. [*Softly.*] God save us!

[*She goes out through the trees, right.*]

MRS. BORKMAN [*standing behind the bench*]. So the night air killed him . . .

ELLA RENTHEIM. So it seems.

MRS. BORKMAN. The strong man.

ELLA RENTHEIM [*coming in front of the bench*]. Don't you want to see him, Gunhild?

MRS. BORKMAN [*with a gesture of rejection*]. No, no, no. [*Lowers her voice.*] John Gabriel Borkman was a miner's son. He couldn't live in the fresh air.

ELLA RENTHEIM. It was more likely the cold that killed him.

MRS. BORKMAN [*shakes her head*]. The cold, you say? The cold . . . had killed him long ago.

ELLA RENTHEIM [*nods to her*]. And turned us into shadows.

MRS. BORKMAN. You are right.

ELLA RENTHEIM [*with a painful smile*]. One dead man and two shadows. That is what the cold has done.

MRS. BORKMAN. Yes, the coldness of the heart. . . . And we two can surely now join hands, Ella.

ELLA RENTHEIM. I think now we can.

MRS. BORKMAN. We twin sisters . . . over the man we both loved.

ELLA RENTHEIM. We two shadows . . . over the dead man.

[MRS. BORKMAN, *behind the bench, and* ELLA RENTHEIM, *in front of it, take each other's hands.*]

WHEN WE DEAD AWAKEN
[*Når vi døde vågner*]

A DRAMATIC EPILOGUE
IN THREE ACTS

(1899)

CHARACTERS

PROFESSOR ARNOLD RUBEK, sculptor

MRS. MAJA RUBEK, his wife

THE SUPERINTENDENT of the Spa

ULFHEIM, a landowner

A WOMAN TRAVELLER

A NUN

SERVANTS, TOURISTS, and CHILDREN

The first act takes place at a seaside resort. The second and third acts in the vicinity of a mountain sanatorium

ACT ONE

Outside the spa hotel, of which part of the main building can be seen, right. Open park-like space with a fountain, groups of tall old trees and shrubs. Left, a little pavilion, almost overgrown with ivy and wild vine. Outside stand a table and a chair. A view of the fjord in the background running out to sea, with promontories and small islets in the distance. It is a still, hot, summer's morning.

PROFESSOR RUBEK and his wife MAJA are sitting after lunch in basket chairs at a laid table on the lawn in front of the hotel. They are now drinking champagne and seltzer, and each is holding a newspaper. The PROFESSOR is an elderly distinguished-looking man, wearing a black velvet jacket but otherwise dressed in light summer clothes. MAJA RUBEK is quite youthful, with a vivacious face and bright roguish eyes, though she has a slightly weary air. She is elegantly dressed in travelling clothes.

MAJA [*sits for a while as though waiting for the PROFESSOR to say something, then lowers her newspaper and sighs*]. Aah . . . !

RUBEK [*looks up from his paper*]. Well, Maja? What is it?

MAJA. Listen to the stillness!

RUBEK [*smiles indulgently*]. You can hear it?

MAJA. Hear what?

RUBEK. The stillness?

MAJA. Of course I can.

RUBEK. Well, perhaps you are right, mein Kind. You can in fact hear stillness.

MAJA. Good God, of course you can. Particularly when it's as overwhelming as it is here. . . .

RUBEK. Here at the resort, you mean?

MAJA. I mean everywhere in this country. I grant you there was a fair amount of noise and bustle back there in the town. At the same time, I felt even the noise and bustle were in a sense . . . somehow dead.

RUBEK [*with searching look*]. Aren't you in any way glad to be back home again, Maja?

MAJA [*looks at him*]. Are *you* glad?

RUBEK [*evasively*]. Who, me . . . ?

MAJA. Yes. You've been away so much longer than I have. Are *you* really glad to be back home again?

RUBEK. Well, to be honest, not what you'd really call glad. . . .

MAJA [*animatedly*]. There, you see! I knew it!

RUBEK. Perhaps I've been away too long. I've completely lost touch with . . . things as they are here at home.

MAJA [*eagerly, moving her chair closer to him*]. There you see, Rubek! Let's be on our way again! As quickly as we can!

RUBEK [*somewhat impatiently*]. Yes, yes, Maja my dear! You know very well that's the intention.

MAJA. But why not now? Immediately? Think how happy and comfortable we could be down there in our nice new house. . . .

RUBEK [*smiles indulgently*]. Shouldn't one rather say 'our nice new home'?

MAJA [*curtly*]. I prefer to say 'house'. Let's keep it at that.

RUBEK [*looks long at her*]. What a strange person you are!

MAJA. Am I so strange?

RUBEK. I think so.

MAJA. But why? Because I don't particularly want to waste my time idling around up here. . . ?

RUBEK. Who was determined that we should come north this summer? Absolutely determined?

MAJA. I was, I suppose.

RUBEK. It certainly wasn't me.

MAJA. But, good Lord, who'd have imagined things would have changed so dreadfully! And in such a short time! Just think, it can't be more than about four years since I left this country. . . .

RUBEK. As a married woman.

MAJA. Married? What's that got to do with it?

RUBEK [*continues*]. . . . Since you became Frau Professor and acquired a fine home. . . . Forgive me, I suppose I ought to say a splendid house. And a villa on the Taunitzer See where everything's now so grand. . . . In fact, Maja, I'd say the whole thing's a bit *too* fine and splendid. And masses of space. No need for us always to be hanging over each other. . . .

MAJA [*indifferently*]. No, no. . . . No shortage of space in the house . . . and things like that. . . .

RUBEK. And the fact that you found yourself living a generally grander and more spacious life. Moving in more exclusive circles than you were used to at home.

MAJA [*looking at him*]. So you think I'm the one who's changed?

RUBEK. Actually I do, Maja.

MAJA. So it's just me? Not the people here?

RUBEK. Oh, they've changed too, probably. A little. And certainly not for the better, that I must say.

MAJA. Yes, that you may well say.

RUBEK [*changing the subject*]. Do you know the kind of feeling I get when I look around me at the lives people lead here?

MAJA. No. Tell me.

RUBEK. I am reminded of the night we travelled up in the train. . . .

MAJA. You sat sleeping in the compartment.

RUBEK. Not all the time. I noticed how silent it was at all the little stopping places . . . I *heard* the stillness . . . Like you, Maja . . .

MAJA. Hm! Like me.

RUBEK. . . . And then I knew we'd crossed the frontier. Then we really were back home. Because the train stopped at every little wayside halt, and stood silent—though nobody was waiting for it.

MAJA. Why did it stand so silently? When there was nobody there?

RUBEK. Don't know. Nobody got off, and nobody got on. The train would just stand there, silently, for what seemed like an eternity. And at every station I would hear a couple of railwaymen walking the platform—one of them with a lamp in his hand—talking to each other, softly, tonelessly, meaninglessly, far into the night.

MAJA. Yes, you are right. Always there's a couple of men walking up and down talking to each other . . .

RUBEK. . . . About nothing. [*Changing to a brisker manner.*] But wait till tomorrow, eh? Then our nice big steamer will have docked, and we'll go on board and sail right round the coast . . . far to the North . . . right up to the Arctic.

MAJA. But then you'll see nothing of the country, and nothing of the life of the people. And that was really what you wanted.

RUBEK [*curtly, irritably*]. I've seen more than enough.

MAJA. Do you think a cruise would be any better for you?

RUBEK. It's always a change.

MAJA. All right, as long as it does *you* some good. . . .

RUBEK. Me some good? There's nothing wrong with me, nothing whatsoever.

MAJA [*gets up and walks across to him*]. Yes there is, Rubek. You know there is, surely.

RUBEK. And what, my dearest Maja, might that be?

MAJA [*behind him, leaning over the back of his chair*]. You tell me. You've become so restless. You can't settle anywhere, either at home or abroad. You've been avoiding people of late.

RUBEK [*somewhat sarcastically*]. Indeed! You've noticed that!

MAJA. Nobody who knows you could help noticing it! I also think it's sad you've lost the desire to work.

RUBEK. Have I?

MAJA. So tireless you used to be once, working all hours of the day and night!

RUBEK [*gloomily*]. Once . . . yes!

MAJA. But as soon as you had finished your big masterpiece . . .

RUBEK [*nods pensively*]. 'The Day of Resurrection'.

MAJA. . . . the work that went all round the world . . . the work that made you famous . . .

RUBEK. Perhaps that was the tragedy, Maja.

MAJA. How?

RUBEK. When I had created this masterpiece of mine . . . [*With a violent gesture.*] . . . For 'The Day of Resurrection' *is* a masterpiece! Or was to begin with. No, still is! It must be . . . shall be a masterpiece!

MAJA [*looks wonderingly at him*]. Yes, Rubek. The whole world knows it is.

RUBEK [*curtly, repudiatingly*]. The whole world knows nothing! Understands nothing!

MAJA. Well, they seem to have *some* idea at least of . . .

RUBEK. Of something that simply isn't there! Yes! Something that was never in my mind. And it's this that people go into raptures over. [*Growls.*] It's simply not worth the trouble—slaving away like that for the sake of the masses, the mob, your 'whole world'.

MAJA. Do you think it's any better—is it even worthy of you—just to go on turning out the odd portrait bust every now and then?

RUBEK [*smiling slyly*]. The things I make aren't really portrait busts Maja.

MAJA. Good heavens, of course they are! These last two or three years— once you'd got that big group finished and out of the house. . . .

RUBEK. All the same, they are not straight *portraits*, I tell you.

MAJA. What are they, then?

RUBEK. There's something equivocal, something hidden within and behind these portraits. . . . Something secret that people cannot see. . . .

MAJA. Oh?

RI

RUBEK [*firmly*]. I alone can see it. And it amuses me intensely. Outwardly there's this 'striking likeness', as it's called . . . this thing that
people all gape at in astonishment . . . [*Lowers his voice.*] . . . But
really, at the deepest level, they are just a lot of decent honest
carthorses, of simple-minded donkeys, of lop-eared low-browed
dogs, of overfed heavy-jowled pigs . . . plus a few dull-eyed thick-
skulled bullnecks thrown in . . .

MAJA [*indifferently*]. . . . All the dear old barnyard.

RUBEK. Simply the dear old barnyard, Maja! All those animals that
man has corrupted in his own image. And which have corrupted
man in return. [*He empties his champagne glass and laughs.*] And these
double-dealing works of art are the things our good well-heeled
citizens come and commission from me. And pay for in good faith—
and pay handsomely for. Very nearly worth their weight in gold, as
they say.

MAJA [*fills his glass*]. Shame on you, Rubek! Drink, and be happy.

RUBEK [*wipes his brow repeatedly and leans back in his chair*]. I am happy,
Maja. Really happy. In a way. [*Is silent for a moment.*] Because after
all, there is a certain happiness in feeling free and independent of
everything. In having everything one could wish for. Material
things that is. Don't you agree with me, Maja?

MAJA. Yes, on the whole. It's very nice, I suppose. [*Looks at him.*] But
you remember what you promised me that day we came to an
agreement about . . . about that difficult business . . .

RUBEK [*nods*]. . . . Agreed that you and I should get married. That
wasn't too easy for you, Maja, was it?

MAJA [*continues undisturbed*]. . . . And that I was to go abroad with
you . . . and settle down out there permanently . . . and enjoy life.
Can you remember what you promised me then?

RUBEK [*shakes his head*]. No, honestly, I can't. Well, what did I promise
you?

MAJA. You said you'd take me up with you to the top of a high
mountain and show me all the glory of the world.

RUBEK [*starts*]. Did I actually promise *you* that, too?

MAJA [*looks at him*]. Me too? Who else?

RUBEK [*casually*]. All I mean is: did I promise to show you . . . ?

MAJA. . . . All the glory of the world. Yes, that's what you said. And all that glory was to be mine and yours, you said.

RUBEK. It's a kind of catchphrase I once used to use.

MAJA. Only a catchphrase?

RUBEK. Yes, from my schooldays. The sort of thing I said when I wanted to get the other children to come out and play with me in the forest or up in the mountains.

MAJA [*looks fixedly at him*]. Perhaps all you wanted was to get *me* to come out and play?

RUBEK [*making a joke of it*]. Well, it's been quite an enjoyable game, hasn't it, Maja?

MAJA [*coldly*]. I didn't go away with you just to play games.

RUBEK. No, no, I dare say you're right.

MAJA. Nor did you ever take me with you up any high mountain to show me . . .

RUBEK [*irritably*]. . . . All the glory of the world? No, I didn't. And let me tell you why. You aren't really made for mountain climbing, my little Maja.

MAJA [*tries to control herself*]. Yet you seemed to think so once.

RUBEK. Four or five years ago, yes. [*Stretches in his chair.*] Four or five years . . . is a long long time, Maja.

MAJA [*looks at him with a bitter expression*]. Has it seemed so terribly long to you, Rubek?

RUBEK. It's beginning to seem rather long now. [*Yawns.*] Now and then, that is.

MAJA [*crosses to her chair*]. I shan't bore you any longer.

[*She sits down in her chair, picks up the newspaper and glances through it. Silence from both sides.*]

RUBEK [*leans across on his elbows and looks quizzically at her*]. Offended, Frau Professor?

MAJA [*coldly, without looking up*]. No, not at all.

[*Visitors to the spa, mostly ladies, begin singly and in groups to walk through the park, entering right and going out left. Waiters carry refreshments out from the hotel and behind the pavilion. The* SUPERINTENDENT, *gloves and stick in hand, returns from his round of the park, greets the visitors respectfully and exchanges a few words with some of them.*]

SUPERINTENDENT [*walks across to* PROFESSOR RUBEK's *table and respectfully raises his hat*]. A very good morning, Mrs. Rubek! Good morning, Professor!

RUBEK. Good morning, good morning, Superintendent.

SUPERINTENDENT [*turning to* MAJA]. May I enquire whether madam has had a good night's rest?

MAJA. Thank you, yes. Excellent . . . for *my* part. I always sleep like a log.

SUPERINTENDENT. Delighted, delighted! The first night in a strange place can sometimes be rather trying. And the professor. . . ?

RUBEK. Oh, I myself have some difficulty in sleeping. Especially recently.

SUPERINTENDENT [*showing sympathy*]. Oh, I'm sorry. But a few weeks here at the spa . . . will soon put that right.

RUBEK [*looks up at him*]. Tell me, Superintendent . . . are any of your patients in the habit of bathing at night?

SUPERINTENDENT [*wonderingly*]. At night? No, I've never heard any mention of that.

RUBEK. You haven't?

SUPERINTENDENT. No, I know of nobody *so* ill as to be in need of that.

RUBEK. Well, is anybody in the habit of taking walks in the park at night?

SUPERINTENDENT [*smiles and shakes his head*]. No, Professor . . . that would be against the rules.

MAJA [*impatiently*]. For God's sake, Rubek, I told you this morning. You dreamt it.

RUBEK [*drily*]. Did I indeed? Thank you! [*Turns to the* SUPERINTENDENT.] Actually I got up during the night. I couldn't sleep. I wanted to see what the weather was like. . . .

SUPERINTENDENT [*attentively*]. Yes, Professor? And then . . . ?

RUBEK. I looked out of the window . . . and I saw a white figure in among the trees over there.

MAJA [*smiling at the* SUPERINTENDENT]. And my husband says that this figure was wearing a bathing wrap . . .

RUBEK. . . . Or something like it, I said. I couldn't distinguish it very clearly. But what I saw was something white.

SUPERINTENDENT. Most remarkable. Was it a man or a woman?

RUBEK. I felt pretty sure it was a woman. But behind it there was another figure. And it was quite dark. Like a shadow. . . .

SUPERINTENDENT [*attentive*]. A dark figure? Quite black, perhaps?

RUBEK. Yes, it looked like that to my eyes.

SUPERINTENDENT [*as realization dawns*]. Behind the white one? Close behind her. . . ?

RUBEK. Yes. A short distance. . . .

SUPERINTENDENT. Ah! Perhaps I have the explanation, Professor.

RUBEK. Well, what was it?

MAJA [*simultaneously*]. You mean my husband wasn't dreaming after all?

SUPERINTENDENT [*suddenly whispering, points towards the background, right*]. Hush! Look over there. . . ! Please keep your voices down for the present.

[*A slender* LADY, *dressed in fine creamy-white cashmere, enters from behind the corner of the hotel, followed by a* NUN *dressed in black with a silver cross hanging by a chain on her breast. She walks across the park towards the pavilion, left. Her face is pale, her features are stiff and immobile; her eyelids are lowered, and her eyes seem to stare unseeingly. Her dress is floorlength, and falls about her body in long regular folds. Over her head, neck, breast, shoulders and arms, she wears a large, white crêpe shawl. She holds her arms crossed over her breast. She holds this posture unwaveringly; she walks with stiff and measured steps. The* NUN's *bearing is equally deliberate; she seems to be in attendance. Her sharp brown eyes follow the* LADY *ceaselessly. Waiters with napkins over their arms appear at the hotel door and stare curiously at the two strangers, who pay no attention and, without looking round, go into the pavilion.*]

RUBEK [*has risen slowly and involuntarily from his chair and stares at the closed pavilion door*]. Who was that lady?

SUPERINTENDENT. A visitor who has rented that little pavilion.

RUBEK. A foreigner?

SUPERINTENDENT. Quite likely. Certainly they both arrived from abroad. A week ago. Never been here before.

RUBEK [*firmly, looking at him*]. It was her I saw in the park last night.

SUPERINTENDENT. It must have been. I thought that at once.

RUBEK. What is the name of this lady, Superintendent?

SUPERINTENDENT. She registered as Madame de Satow and companion. We don't know any more.

RUBEK [*ponders*]. Satow? Satow. . . ?

MAJA [*laughs scornfully*]. Do you know anybody of that name, Rubek? Eh?

RUBEK [*shakes his head*]. No, nobody. . . . Satow? It sounds Russian. Or Slav, at any rate. [*To the* SUPERINTENDENT.] What language does she speak?

SUPERINTENDENT. When the two ladies talk to each other, they speak a language I can't understand. Otherwise she speaks good native Norwegian.

RUBEK [*startled*]. Norwegian! Sure you're not mistaken?

SUPERINTENDENT. No, I couldn't mistake *that*.

RUBEK [*looks at him tensely*]. You've heard her yourself?

SUPERINTENDENT. Yes. I've talked to her myself. Several times. Only a few words, of course. She's not very communicative. But . . .

RUBEK. But it *was* Norwegian?

SUPERINTENDENT. Absolutely pure Norwegian. Perhaps with a slight Nordland intonation.

RUBEK [*stares absently and whispers*]. That too!

MAJA [*somewhat offended, and crossly*]. Perhaps this lady once modelled for you, Rubek? Think, now!

RUBEK [*looks sharply at her*]. Model?

MAJA [*smiles mockingly*]. Yes, in your younger days, I mean. Aren't you supposed to have had innumerable models? That's some time ago, of course.

RUBEK [*in the same tone of voice*]. No, my dear little Maja. Actually I have only ever had one model. Only one . . . for everything I have created.

SUPERINTENDENT [*who has turned and stood looking out to the left*]. I fear I must ask you to excuse me now. Here comes somebody I can't say it is an inordinate pleasure to run into. Especially in the company of ladies.

RUBEK [*also looks across*]. That sporting gentleman coming along over there? Who is he?

SUPERINTENDENT. That is Squire Ulfheim from . . .

RUBEK. Ah, Squire Ulfheim.

SUPERINTENDENT. The bear-hunting man, as they call him.

RUBEK. I know him.

SUPERINTENDENT. Indeed who doesn't?

RUBEK. Only slightly, though. Is he here as a patient . . . at long last?

SUPERINTENDENT. No, strangely enough . . . not yet. He just looks in here briefly once a year . . . on his way up to the hunting grounds. . . . Excuse me, please. . . .

[*He turns to go into the hotel.*]

ULFHEIM [*shouting from offstage*]. Wait a minute! Wait, God damn it! Why are you always running away from me?

SUPERINTENDENT [*stops*]. I am *not* running, Mr. Ulfheim.

[SQUIRE ULFHEIM *enters left, followed by a* SERVANT *leading a pair of dogs.* ULFHEIM *is in shooting costume, with top-boots and a felt hat with a feather in it. He is a tall, lean, sinewy man, with matted hair and beard; and loud-voiced. It is difficult to determine his age from his appearance, but he is no longer young.*]

ULFHEIM [*storms up to the* SUPERINTENDENT]. Is that the way to receive visitors, eh? Darting off with your tail between your legs . . . as if the Devil himself were at your heels!

SUPERINTENDENT [*calmly, ignoring the question*]. Have you arrived with the steamer, Mr. Ulfheim?

ULFHEIM [*growls*]. Haven't even seen your precious steamer. [*With his hands on his hips.*] Don't you know I always sail in my own yacht? [*To the* SERVANT.] Go and see to your fellow-creatures, Lars. But make sure they stay ravenous. Listen! Fresh meat-bones, but not too much meat on them! Raw with lots of warm blood. And put something in your own belly as well. [*Aims a kick at him.*] Now get to hell out of it!

[*The* SERVANT *goes out with the dogs behind the corner of the hotel.*]

SUPERINTENDENT. Wouldn't you like to take a seat in the restaurant, Mr. Ulfheim?

ULFHEIM. Among all those half-dead flies and half-dead people? No, thank you, my dear Superintendent.

SUPERINTENDENT. Well, every man to his taste.

ULFHEIM. But get the housekeeper to make the usual arrangements for me. See there's plenty of food. And lots of drink. . . ! You can tell her that I or Lars will come and play merry hell with her if she doesn't. . . .

SUPERINTENDENT. We know that from the last time. [*Turns.*] Can I pass your order to the waiter, Professor? Or something for Mrs. Rubek, perhaps?

RUBEK. No thank you. Nothing for me.

MAJA. Nor for me either.

[*The* SUPERINTENDENT *goes into the hotel.*]

ULFHEIM [*stares at them for a moment, then raises his hat*]. Well I'll be damned! Distinguished company indeed for a country bumpkin to come barging in on!

RUBEK [*looks up*]. What do you mean by that?

ULFHEIM [*more restrained and more politely*]. It's Professor Rubek himself, surely? The sculptor? Am I not right?

RUBEK [*nods*]. We have met socially once or twice. That autumn I was last home.

ULFHEIM. But that's many years ago. And you weren't as famous *then* as you seem to be now. In those days even a clod-hopping bear hunter dared come near you.

RUBEK [*smiles*]. I don't bite even now.

MAJA [*looks at* ULFHEIM *with interest*]. Do you really hunt bears?

ULFHEIM [*sits down at the neighbouring table, nearer the hotel*]. Bears for preference, ma'am. But I'm happy to take any kind of game that offers itself—eagles, wolves, women, elk, reindeer.... Anything that's got life and vigour and warm blood....

[*He drinks from his hip flask.*]

MAJA [*looks at him intently*]. But bears for preference?

ULFHEIM. For preference, yes. Because then you can use your knife if things get difficult. [*Smiling a little.*] We both work with hard materials, ma'am—your husband and I. He wrestles with blocks of marble, I suppose it'd be. And I wrestle with taut and quivering bear sinews. And both of us get on top of our material in the end. Make ourselves lord and master of it. We don't give up till we've got the upper hand, however hard it resists.

RUBEK [*to himself, thoughtfully*]. There's a lot of truth in what you say.

ULFHEIM. Because the marble has also got something to fight for, you know. It's dead, yet it'll resist with might and main being chiselled into life. Just like the bear when somebody comes along and prods it in its lair.

MAJA. Are you going up shooting in the forest?

ULFHEIM. I am making for high up in the mountains.—I don't suppose you've ever been in the high mountains, Mrs. Rubek?

MAJA. No, never.

ULFHEIM. Then you damn well see you get yourself up there this summer! You can come along with me. Both you and the professor.

MAJA. Thank you, but my husband is thinking this summer of going on a cruise.

RUBEK. Along the coast, in among the islands.

ULFHEIM. Pah! What the hell takes you into those damn stinking sewers? Imagine wallowing about in all that ditchwater! Dishwater, more like it.

MAJA. You hear that, Rubek?

ULFHEIM. Come up into the mountains with me instead. *There* it's clean and free from any taint of man. You can't imagine what that means to somebody like me. But as for a little woman like . . . [*He stops. The* NUN *comes out of the pavilion and goes into the hotel.* ULFHEIM *follows her with his eyes.*] Look at her there. The black crow! Where's the funeral?

RUBEK. I don't know that anybody . . .

ULFHEIM. Then somebody here must be at his last gasp. In some corner or other. People who are sick and feeble damn well ought to get on with it and get themselves buried . . . and the quicker the better.

MAJA. Have you ever been ill yourself, Mr. Ulfheim?

ULFHEIM. Never. Otherwise I wouldn't be sitting here. But some of my nearest and dearest—they have been ill, poor devils.

MAJA. And what did you do for them?

ULFHEIM. Shot them, of course.

RUBEK [*looks at him*]. Shot them?

MAJA [*pushes her chair back*]. Shot them dead?

ULFHEIM [*nods*]. I never miss, ma'am.

MAJA. But what makes you think you can go about shooting people?

ULFHEIM. I'm not talking about people. . . .

MAJA. You said your nearest and dearest. . . .

ULFHEIM. My dogs.

MAJA. Dogs! Your nearest and dearest!

ULFHEIM. None nearer! Decent, honest, faithful sporting friends of mine! If any one of them turns sick or feeble—bang! That takes care of him. Into the next world. [*The* NUN *comes out of the hotel with a tray of bread and milk which she places on the table outside the pavilion, which she then re-enters.* ULFHEIM *laughs scornfully.*] Is *that* supposed to be food for human consumption! Milk and water, and soft, squashy bread. Ah, you ought to see my friends here eat! Would you like to see them?

MAJA [*smiles across at* RUBEK *and gets up*]. Yes, I would.

ULFHEIM [*gets up too*]. There's a game woman for you! Come along with me then. Great enormous meatbones they gulp down whole. Then they'll bring the whole lot back, and gulp them down again. It's a real joy to watch them. Come, and I'll show you. And we'll talk a bit more about this trip up into the mountains. . . .

> [*He goes out round the corner of the hotel.* MAJA *follows him. Almost immediately afterwards, the* STRANGE LADY *comes out of the pavilion and sits down at the table. She lifts the glass of milk and is about to drink but stops and looks across at* RUBEK *with blank, expressionless eyes.* RUBEK *remains sitting at his table, and stares earnestly and unwaveringly at her. Finally he gets up, walks a few steps towards her, stops and speaks in a low voice.*]

RUBEK. I recognize you again, Irene.

IRENE [*tonelessly, putting down her glass*]. You've guessed, have you, Arnold?

RUBEK [*without answering the question*]. And you also recognize me, I see.

IRENE. In your case it's entirely different.

RUBEK. Why in my case?

IRENE. You are still alive.

RUBEK [*does not understand*]. Alive?

IRENE [*after a brief pause*]. Who was that other woman? The one you had with you . . . at the table there?

RUBEK [*somewhat hesitantly*]. That was . . . my wife.

IRENE [*nods slowly*]. Indeed. That's good, Arnold. In other words, nobody of any concern to me. . . .

RUBEK [*uncertainly*]. No, of course not. . . .

IRENE. Somebody you acquired after my own life was over.

RUBEK [*suddenly looks fixedly at her*]. After your . . . ? How do you mean, Irene?

IRENE [*does not answer the question*]. And the child? The child is well? Our child lives on after me. In honour and glory.

RUBEK [*smiles as at some distant memory*]. Our child? Yes, that's what we used to call it—then.

IRENE. During my lifetime.

RUBEK [*attempting to sound gay*]. Yes, Irene . . . 'our child' has indeed become famous the whole world over. I dare say you've read about it?

IRENE [*nods*]. And has also made its father famous. That was your dream.

RUBEK [*quietly, moved*]. I owe everything . . . everything to you, Irene. Thank you.

IRENE [*sits and ponders*]. If I'd done then what was right, Arnold . . .

RUBEK. What?

IRENE. I should have killed that child.

RUBEK. Killed it, you say!

IRENE [*whispering*]. Killed it . . . before I left you. Smashed it. Smashed it to pieces.

RUBEK [*shakes his head reproachfully*]. You couldn't have, Irene. Wouldn't have had the heart.

IRENE. No. I hadn't that kind of heart then.

RUBEK. But since then? Afterwards?

IRENE. Since then I've killed it countless times. By day and by night. Killed it in hatred, in vengeance, in torment.

RUBEK [*goes across to her table and asks gently*]. Irene . . . tell me after all these years. Why did you leave me at that time? Disappeared without trace . . . Nowhere to be found. . . .

IRENE [*slowly shakes her head*]. Oh, Arnold. . . . Why tell you now . . . now that I have passed over?

RUBEK. Was there someone else you had come to love?

IRENE. There was someone who had no use for my love. No use any longer for my life.

RUBEK [*evasively*]. Let us not talk any more about the past. . . .

IRENE. No, let us not talk of things beyond the grave. The other side of the grave from *me*.

RUBEK. Where have you been, Irene? None of my enquiries revealed anything about you.

IRENE. I went into the darkness . . . whilst the child stood transfigured in light.

RUBEK. Have you travelled much about the world?

IRENE. Yes. In many lands.

RUBEK [*looking at her with compassion*]. And what did you do with yourself, Irene?

IRENE [*turns her eyes upon him*]. Wait a moment. Let me think. . . . Yes, now I have it. I have posed on a revolving pedestal in variety halls. Posed as a naked statue in peep shows. Made a lot of money. I wasn't used to that with you, Arnold—you never had any. And I've also been with men—men I could drive quite mad. I wasn't used to that with you, either, Arnold. You kept better control of yourself.

RUBEK [*passing quickly over the matter*]. And you also got married, didn't you?

IRENE. Yes. To one of them.

RUBEK. Who is your husband?

IRENE. He was a South American. High diplomat. [*With a glassy smile.*] I drove him utterly mad. Mad . . . incurably mad . . . implacably mad. Believe me, it was quite amusing while it lasted. I could nicely have gone on laughing inwardly for ever—if only I'd *had* anything within me.

RUBEK. And where is he now?

IRENE. In some churchyard somewhere. With a tall imposing monument on top of him. And a lead bullet rattling in his skull.

RUBEK. Did he kill himself?

IRENE. Yes. He was kind enough to anticipate me.

RUBEK. Don't you grieve for him, Irene?

IRENE [*uncomprehendingly*]. Grieve for whom?

RUBEK. For Herr von Satow.

IRENE. He wasn't called Satow.

RUBEK. He wasn't?

IRENE. My second husband is called Satow. He is a Russian. . . .

RUBEK. And where is he?

IRENE. Far away in the Ural Mountains. Among all his gold mines.

RUBEK. He lives there?

IRENE [*shrugs her shoulders*]. Lives? Lives? In fact I've killed him. . . .

RUBEK [*startled*]. Killed . . . !

IRENE. Killed him with a fine, sharp dagger I always have in bed with me. . . .

RUBEK [*bursts out*]. I don't believe you, Irene!

IRENE [*smiles gently*]. Believe me truly, Arnold.

RUBEK [*looks at her with sympathy*]. Have you never had any children?

IRENE. Yes, I have had many children.

RUBEK. And where are those children now?

IRENE. I killed them.

RUBEK [*sternly*]. Now you are lying to me again!

IRENE. I killed them, I tell you. With murderous passion. As soon as they came into the world. Oh, long, long before that. One after the other.

RUBEK [*heavily and seriously*]. Something lies hidden behind everything you say.

IRENE. Can I help that? Every word I say to you is whispered into my ear.

RUBEK. I think I'm the only one who can sense the meaning.

IRENE. Surely you ought to be the only one.

RUBEK [*props his hands on the table and looks deep into her eyes*]. There are strings within you which have snapped.

IRENE [*gently*]. Surely that always happens when a young, warm-blooded woman dies.

RUBEK. Oh, Irene, put these wild ideas behind you ... ! Of course you're alive! Alive, alive!

IRENE [*rises slowly from her chair and says in a trembling voice*]. I was dead for many years. They came and bound me. Tied my arms behind my back.... Then they lowered me into a tomb with iron bars over the opening. And with padded walls ... so that nobody up above ground could hear the shrieks from the grave.... But now, I'm half beginning to rise from the dead.

[*She sits down again.*]

RUBEK [*after a pause*]. Do you hold me guilty of this?

IRENE. Yes.

RUBEK. Guilty of ... what you call your death.

IRENE. Guilty of making my death inevitable. [*Changing to a tone of indifference.*] Why don't you sit down, Arnold?

RUBEK. May I?

IRENE. Yes. You won't shiver, don't be afraid. I don't think I'm quite yet turned to ice.

RUBEK [*moves a chair and sits down at the table*]. Look, Irene. Now we two are sitting together just as in the old days.

IRENE. A little apart from each other. Also as in the old days.

RUBEK [*moves nearer*]. It *had* to be like that, at that time.

IRENE. Had to?

RUBEK [*firmly*]. There *had* to be a distance between us. . . .

IRENE. Had there, in fact, Arnold?

RUBEK [*persisting*]. Do you remember what you answered when I asked you if you'd follow me out into the wide wide world?

IRENE. I raised three fingers in the air and promised I'd follow you to the end of the world and the end of life. And that I would serve you in all things. . . .

RUBEK. As a model for my art . . .

IRENE. . . . Fully and freely naked. . . .

RUBEK [*moved*]. And serve me you did, Irene . . . joyfully, gladly, unreservedly.

IRENE. Yes, I served you with all the throbbing blood of my youth. . . .

RUBEK [*nods, with a grateful glance*]. As you rightly say.

IRENE. I fell at your feet and served you, Arnold! [*Raises her fist to him.*] But you . . . you . . . you . . . !

RUBEK [*defensively*]. But I never did you any wrong! Never, Irene!

IRENE. Yes, you did! You did wrong to my deepest inmost being. . . .

RUBEK [*falls back*]. I did . . . !

IRENE. Yes, you! I offered myself wholly and completely to your gaze. . . . [*Quieter.*] And never once did you touch me.

RUBEK. Irene, didn't you realize that many's the time I was nearly driven out of my mind by all your loveliness?

IRENE. And yet, if you *had* touched me, I think I'd have killed you on the spot. I always had a sharp needle by me. Hidden in my hair. . . . [*Passes her hand over her forehead.*] Yet . . . all the same . . . that you could . . .

RUBEK [*looks intently at her*]. I was an artist, Irene.

IRENE [*darkly*]. Exactly. Exactly.

RUBEK. Above all else an artist. And there I was sick with desire to create the great work of my life. [*Lost in recollection.*] It was to be called 'The Day of Resurrection'. It was to take the form of a young woman waking from the sleep of death. . . .

IRENE. Our child, yes.

RUBEK [*continuing*]. This waking girl was to be the world's noblest, purest, most perfect woman. Then I found *you*. I knew I could use you, wholly, entirely. And you agreed so readily, so gladly. You left your family and your home . . . to go with me.

IRENE. My going with you was my childhood's resurrection.

RUBEK. That, above all, was why I was able to use you. You, and nobody else. For me you became a sacred being, untouchable, a thing to worship in thought alone. I was still young then, Irene. I was obsessed with the idea that if I touched you, if I desired you sensually, my mind would be profaned and I would be unable to achieve what I was striving to create. And I still think there is some truth in that.

IRENE [*nods, with a hint of scorn*]. The work of art first . . . the human being second.

RUBEK. Judge that as you will. But I was completely in the power of my work. And felt so deliriously happy in it.

IRENE. And you were successful with your work, Arnold.

RUBEK. Thanks to you, bless you, I was successful with my work. I wanted to create my vision of how the pure woman would wake on Resurrection Day. Not wondering at things new and unfamiliar and unimagined, but filled with a holy joy at finding herself unchanged—a mortal woman—in those higher, freer, happier realms, after the long and dreamless sleep of death. [*Speaking softly.*] That is how I created her. Created her in *your* image, Irene.

IRENE [*places her hands flat on the table and leans back in her chair*]. Then you finished with me. . . .

RUBEK [*reproachfully*]. Irene!

IRENE. Had no further use for me. . . .

RUBEK. How can you say that!

S₁

IRENE. Began looking round for other ideals. . . .

RUBEK. I found none, none after you.

IRENE. And no other models, Arnold?

RUBEK. You were no model to me. You were the source of my creation.

IRENE [*is silent for a moment*]. What have you created since then? What poems in marble, I mean? Since the day I left you.

RUBEK. I have created nothing since that day. No poems. I've merely toyed at sculpture.

IRENE. And the woman you are now living with . . . ?

RUBEK [*interrupts with vehemence*]. Don't talk about her now! It is too painful.

IRENE. Where are you planning to go with her?

RUBEK [*wearily*]. I'm probably taking a long and tedious trip up north along the coast.

IRENE [*looks at him, smiles almost imperceptibly and whispers*]. Go high up into the mountains instead. As high as you can get. Higher, higher . . . ever higher, Arnold.

RUBEK [*tense and expectant*]. Are you going up there?

IRENE. Dare you meet me once more?

RUBEK [*uncertainly, struggling with himself*]. If only we could! Oh, if only we could!

IRENE. Why can't we do what we want? [*Looks at him and with clasped hands says in an imploring whisper.*] Come, come, Arnold! Oh, please come to me . . . !

[MAJA, *flushed with pleasure, appears round the corner of the hotel and hurries across to the table where they were sitting before.*]

MAJA [*still at the corner, without looking across*]. You can say what you like, Rubek, but. . . . [*Stops as she catches sight of* IRENE.] Oh, excuse me! I see you've made a new acquaintance.

RUBEK [*curtly*]. Renewed an old acquaintance. [*Gets up.*] What did you want me for?

MAJA. All I wanted to say to you was . . . that you can do as you please, but you are not getting me to come with you on that awful steamer.

RUBEK. Why not?

MAJA. Because I want to go up in the mountains and in the forests. That's what I want! [*Coaxingly.*] Oh, please let me, Rubek! I'll be so nice to you afterwards!

RUBEK. Who's put these ideas into your mind?

MAJA. *He* has. That awful bear-hunting man. You can't imagine all the incredible things he's been telling me about the mountains. And about the life up there! I'm pretty sure most of it is lies—he tells the most horrible, nasty, repulsive stories. Yet somehow it all sounds marvellously attractive. Please, do let me go with him. Just so I can see if all he says is true. May I, Rubek?

RUBEK. Please do, as far as I am concerned. Off you go up into the mountains . . . as high as you like, for as long as you like. I might follow the same path myself.

MAJA [*quickly*]. No, no, there's no need for you to come. Not on my account.

RUBEK. I *want* to go to the mountains. I've made up my mind.

MAJA. Oh, thank you, thank you! May I go and tell him straight away?

RUBEK. Go and tell your bear-hunting man anything you like.

MAJA. Oh, thank you, thank you! [*She tries to seize his hand, he avoids her.*] How nice and sweet you are today, Rubek!

[*She runs into the hotel. At that same moment, the door of the pavilion is slowly and noiselessly opened a short distance. The* NUN *stands in the door opening, observing them. Nobody sees her.*]

RUBEK [*determinedly, turns to* IRENE]. Shall we meet up there, then?

IRENE [*rises slowly*]. Certainly we shall meet. I've searched so long for you.

RUBEK. When did you begin searching for me, Irene?

IRENE [*with a bitter smile*]. From the moment I realized I'd given you something really rather precious. Something one should never part with.

RUBEK [*bows his head*]. Yes, that is painfully true. You gave me three . . . four years of your youth.

IRENE. Much, much more than that I gave you. Prodigal that I was.

RUBEK. Yes, you were prodigal, Irene. You gave me all your naked beauty. . . .

IRENE. To look at.

RUBEK. And glorify.

IRENE. Yes, for your own glorification. And for the child's.

RUBEK. For yours too, Irene.

IRENE. But the most precious gift you've forgotten.

RUBEK. The most precious . . . ? What gift was that?

IRENE. I gave you my young living soul. Then I was left standing there, all empty within. Soul-less. [*Looks fixedly at him.*] That's what I died of, Arnold.

[*The* NUN *opens the door wide, and stands aside for her. She goes into the pavilion.*]

RUBEK [*stands and watches her go, then whispers*]. Irene!

ACT TWO

A sanatorium up in the mountains. A vast expanse of bare treeless wasteland stretches away towards a long mountain lake. On the far side of the lake rises a range of mountain peaks, the snow in their crevasses tinged with blue. In the foreground, left, a stream divides and tumbles down a steep rocky face and flows smoothly away across the wasteland to the right. Shrubs, plants, and boulders line the course of the stream. In the foreground, right, is a hillock with a stone bench at the top. It is a summer evening, near to sunset.

Beyond the stream, some distance away, a group of small children sing and dance and play. Some are dressed in town clothes, others in folk costume. During the following scenes, merry laughter can be faintly heard.

PROFESSOR RUBEK *is sitting up on the bench with a plaid over his shoulders, looking down on the children at play.*

After a short while, MAJA *enters from among some bushes, left, centre, and looks out, shading her eyes with her hand. She is wearing a flat travelling bonnet, a short skirt hitched halfway up her legs, and heavy, laced, calf-length boots. In her hand she carries a long staff.*

MAJA [*at last catches sight of* RUBEK *and shouts*]. Hallo! [*She walks on, uses her staff to vault across the stream, and climbs up the hill. Breathes heavily.*] Oh, Rubek, I've been chasing everywhere, trying to find you.

RUBEK [*nods casually and asks*]. Have you come down from the sanatorium?

MAJA. Yes, I've only just got away from it—the fly-trap.

RUBEK [*glances at her*]. I noticed you weren't down to lunch.

MAJA. No, we had our lunch outside. In the open.

RUBEK. 'We'? Who's 'we'?

MAJA. That awful bear-hunting man and me, of course.

RUBEK. Oh, him!

MAJA. Yes. And tomorrow we're going out again. First thing.

RUBEK. Bears?

MAJA. Yes. Out killing bears.

RUBEK. Have you found any traces?

MAJA [*superior*]. I doubt if you'll find any bears as high up as this.

RUBEK. Where, then?

MAJA. Way down below. Down in the valleys. In thick, thick forest. Where your ordinary town-dweller can never hope to penetrate. . . .

RUBEK. And that's where you two are going tomorrow?

MAJA [*throwing herself down in the heather*]. Yes, that's what we've agreed. We might even set off this evening. As long as you've no objection?

RUBEK. I? Not in the least. . . .

MAJA [*quickly*]. Lars will be there too, of course. With the dogs.

RUBEK. Mr. Lars and his dogs don't greatly concern me. [*Changing the subject.*] Wouldn't you like to sit down here on the bench?

MAJA [*drowsily*]. No thank you. This soft heather is so lovely to lie in.

RUBEK. I can see you are tired.

MAJA [*yawns*]. I do believe I am beginning to be.

RUBEK. That only comes afterwards. When the excitement is over. . . .

MAJA [*sleepily*]. Yes. I'll try shutting my eyes. [*Short pause. Then suddenly, and impatiently.*] Oh, Rubek . . . how can you bear to sit here and listen to that children's noise! And watch all their antics!

RUBEK. There's a kind of harmony—almost like music—in their movements from time to time. In among all that awkwardness. It's pleasant to sit and wait for those few occasions when it happens.

MAJA [*laughs scornfully*]. Always the artist, aren't you.

RUBEK. And would be happy to stay that way.

MAJA [*rolls over and thereby turns her back on him*]. No trace of the artist about *him*.

RUBEK [*attentively*]. No trace of the artist about whom?

MAJA [*again sleepily*]. You know—him.

RUBEK. The bear-hunting man, you mean?

MAJA. Yes. Not a trace of the artist there. Not a trace!

RUBEK [*smiles*]. I'm sure you're absolutely right.

MAJA [*vehemently, without moving*]. What an ugly man he is! [*Plucks a sprig of heather and throws it away.*] So ugly, so ugly! Ugh!

RUBEK. Is that why you feel so safe going off with him . . . into the wilds?

MAJA [*shortly*]. I don't know. [*Turns to face him.*] You're ugly too, Rubek.

RUBEK. Have you only now discovered that?

MAJA. No, I noticed it long ago.

RUBEK [*shrugs his shoulders*]. One grows older. One grows older, Maja.

MAJA. That's not what I mean. But there's a kind of tiredness about your eyes, a resigned look . . . when you deign to glance my way . . . which you do occasionally.

RUBEK. So that's what you see, you think.

MAJA [*nods*]. Little by little your eyes have become evil. It's almost as though you were plotting something against me.

RUBEK. Oh? [*Friendly, but earnestly.*] Come and sit by me, Maja. And we'll have a little talk.

MAJA [*half rises*]. May I sit on your knee, then? Like the early days?

RUBEK. No, you mustn't do that. People can see us from the hotel. [*Moves along a little.*] But you can sit here on the bench . . . beside me.

MAJA. No, thank you. In that case I'd rather stay where I am, on the ground. I can hear quite nicely from here. [*Looks inquisitively at him.*] Well, what was it you wanted to talk about?

RUBEK [*begins slowly*]. What do you suppose was my real reason for agreeing that we should come on this holiday?

MAJA. Well . . . among other things you insisted that it would do *me* such a lot of good. But . . .

RUBEK. But?

MAJA. But I don't believe now for a moment that was the reason. . . .

RUBEK. What was it then, do you think?

MAJA. I think it was because of this woman, the pale one.

RUBEK. Frau von Satow. . . !

MAJA. Yes, the woman who keeps following us about. Yesterday evening she turned up here too.

RUBEK. But what on earth . . . !

MAJA. You knew her well, didn't you . . . very well. Long before you knew *me*.

RUBEK. I'd also forgotten her again . . . long before I knew you.

MAJA [*sits upright*]. Can you forget so easily, Rubek?

RUBEK [*curtly*]. Yes, extremely easily. [*Adds brusquely.*] When I *want* to.

MAJA. Even a woman who has been your model?

RUBEK [*dismissively*]. When I have no more use for her. . . .

MAJA. Somebody who has stripped naked for you?

RUBEK. Means nothing. Not for us artists. [*Changes his tone.*] And how— if I may ask—was I supposed to know she was going to be around these parts.

MAJA. You might have seen her name on a visitors list. In some newspaper.

RUBEK. But I'd no idea at all of the name she now goes by. I'd never even heard of Herr von Satow.

MAJA [*puts on a weary air*]. Oh, Lord, then I suppose you had some other reason for wanting to come here.

RUBEK [*gravely*]. Yes, Maja . . . there *was* another reason. Quite different. And that's what we two, sooner or later, will have to discuss.

MAJA [*suppressing her laughter*]. My God, how solemn you look.

RUBEK [*eyes her suspiciously*]. Perhaps slightly more solemn than is necessary.

MAJA. What do you mean?

RUBEK. And may be that's just as well for us both.

MAJA. You begin to make me curious, Rubek.

RUBEK. Only curious? Not a little worried?

MAJA [*shakes her head*]. Not a bit.

RUBEK. Good. Then listen. You said the other day down at the spa that you thought I'd become very nervy of late. . . .

MAJA. Yes, and so you have.

RUBEK. And what do you think the cause of *that* might be?

MAJA. How should I know? [*Quickly.*] Perhaps you are bored by always being with me.

RUBEK. *Always* . . . ? Why don't you say 'everlastingly'?

MAJA. Well . . . every day, at least. There we've been, just the two of us, living together for four or five years, and we've hardly been away from each other for an hour. Just the two of us—all on our own.

RUBEK [*interested*]. Yes. Well?

MAJA [*somewhat sadly*]. You are not much of a man for company, Rubek. You'd rather be on your own, thinking about your own affairs. And I can't really talk to you about things that concern you. All this art business and so on. . . . [*Gestures with her hand.*] God knows I don't care very much about it, either!

RUBEK. Yes, yes. That's why we mostly sit by the fire talking about *your* affairs.

MAJA. Good Lord—I've nothing much to talk about.

RUBEK. Perhaps they *are* trivial. But at least it's a way of passing the time, Maja.

MAJA. Yes, you're right. Time passes. It's passing you by, Rubek. . . . And that is what is making you so uneasy. . . !

RUBEK [*nods vehemently*]. And so restless! [*He twists about on the bench.*] I can't stand this miserable life much longer!

MAJA [*stands up, and pauses a moment looking at him*]. If you want to be rid of me, just say so.

RUBEK. What kind of talk is this? Be rid of you?

MAJA. Yes, if you want to finish with me, say so straight out. And I'll go at once.

RUBEK [*smiles almost imperceptibly*]. Is that meant as a threat, Maja?

MAJA. What I said cannot possibly be a threat to you.

RUBEK [*rises*]. You're right, of course. [*Adds, after a moment.*] You and I can't possibly go on living together like this. . . .

MAJA. Therefore . . . ?

RUBEK. No 'therefore' about it. [*Emphasizing his words.*] Just because we two can't go on living together *alone*, it doesn't mean that we have to divorce.

MAJA [*smiles scornfully*]. Just separate for a little while, you mean?

RUBEK [*shakes his head*]. That's not necessary, either.

MAJA. Well then? What do you want to do with me?

RUBEK [*somewhat uncertainly*]. I feel a deep . . . a tormenting need of having somebody near who is really close to me. . . .

MAJA [*interrupts him tensely*]. Am I not that, Rubek?

RUBEK [*with a gesture of repudiation*]. Not in that sense. I need to live with somebody who can fulfil me . . . make me complete . . . be as one with me in everything I do.

MAJA [*slowly*]. In big things like that, I doubt if I'd be any use to you.

RUBEK. No, you'd soon quietly give that up, Maja.

MAJA [*bursts out*]. By God, I wouldn't really want to be, either!

RUBEK. I know that only too well. . . . Nor was it really with that in mind that I married you.

MAJA [*observing him*]. I can see that you are thinking about somebody else.

RUBEK. Oh? I didn't know you were a mind-reader. Can you really see *that*?

MAJA. Yes, I can. I know you so well, Rubek! So well!

RUBEK. Then perhaps you can also see *who* it is I'm thinking of?

MAJA. Certainly I can.

RUBEK. Well? Be so good as to . . .

MAJA. You're thinking of that . . . that model you once used for . . . [*Suddenly changes her thread of thought.*] You know the people down in the hotel think she's mad?

RUBEK. Oh? And what do the people down in the hotel think about you and the bear-hunting man?

MAJA. That's nothing to do with it. [*Continues where she left off before.*] It was that pale woman you were thinking about.

RUBEK [*unabashed*]. Precisely. About her. When I no longer had any use for her . . . And when she left me, anyway . . . disappeared . . . just like that . . .

MAJA. You took me on as a kind of makeshift, perhaps?

RUBEK [*relentlessly*]. To be honest, Maja dear, it *was* something of the sort. For a year or eighteen months I'd been brooding away in solitude, putting the last and final touches to my work. 'The Day of Resurrection' went on exhibition all over the world, and brought me fame. And lots of other honours. [*Animatedly.*] But I no longer loved my own work. The public so nauseated and appalled me with their bouquets and their incense that I was almost driven to flee, deep deep into the forests. [*Looks at her.*] Well, you are a mind-reader. Can you guess what occurred to me then?

MAJA [*off-handedly*]. Yes, you got the idea of doing portrait busts of ladies and gentlemen.

RUBEK [*nods*]. On commission, yes. With animal faces behind the masks. That was something they got thrown in free as an extra. [*Smiles.*] But that wasn't exactly what I was meaning.

MAJA. What was it then?

RUBEK [*serious again*]. I'll tell you what it was. I began to think that all this business about the artist's mission and the artist's vocation was all so much empty, hollow, meaningless talk.

MAJA. What would you put in its place?

RUBEK. Life, Maja.

MAJA. Life?

RUBEK. Yes. Hasn't life in sunlight and beauty a value altogether different from toiling away to the end of your days in some cold damp cellar, wrestling with lumps of clay and blocks of stone?

MAJA [*with a little sigh*]. Yes, I've always thought that.

RUBEK. And hadn't I become rich enough to live in luxury and the lazy warmth of the sun? To build myself a villa on the Taunitzer See and a residence in town? And everything that went with it?

MAJA [*adopting the same tone*]. And for the final touch, you could afford to acquire me. And to let me share all your wealth.

RUBEK [*jestingly, as a distraction*]. Didn't I promise to take you with me up a high mountain and show you all the glory of the world?

MAJA [*with a sad expression*]. Perhaps you have taken me up a pretty high mountain, Rubek. But you haven't shown me all the glory of the world.

RUBEK [*with an irritated laugh*]. How impossible you are, Maja! Never satisfied! [*Bursts out vehemently.*] But do you know what it is that drives me absolutely to despair? Have you any idea?

MAJA [*quietly defiant*]. Yes. The fact that you went and took me—for life.

RUBEK. I wouldn't express it quite so heartlessly.

MAJA. But the thought is equally heartless, no doubt.

RUBEK. You have no real understanding of what it's like inside an artist's mind.

MAJA [*smiles and shakes her head*]. Good Lord, I don't even understand what it's like inside my own mind.

RUBEK [*continues imperturbably*]. I live at such a pace, Maja. We live like that, we artists. For my part, I've lived through a whole lifetime in these few years we've known each other. I've come to realize that to seek for happiness in idle pleasure is not for me. Life isn't like that for me and my kind. I must keep on producing . . . creating work after work . . . until my dying day. [*With an effort.*] That's why I can't get on with you any longer, Maja. Not with you alone.

MAJA [*calmly*]. Does that mean, in plain simple language, that you're tired of me?

RUBEK [*vehemently*]. That's just what it does mean! I'm tired—sick and tired and unendurably bored with living with you! Now you know. [*Controls himself.*] These are hard ugly words I'm using. I know that very well. And you are not to blame in all this . . . this I readily admit. It's my fault, and mine alone. I am going through another upheaval . . . [*Half to himself.*] . . . An awakening to the life that is really mine.

MAJA [*clasps her hands involuntarily*]. Then why in the world can't we just part?

RUBEK [*looks at her in astonishment*]. Would you want to?

MAJA [*shrugs her shoulders*]. Well . . . if there's nothing else. . . .

RUBEK [*eagerly*]. But there *is* something else. There's another way. . . .

MAJA [*raises her forefinger*]. Now you are thinking of that pale lady again!

RUBEK. Yes, to be honest, I can't stop thinking about her. Ever since I met her again. [*Moves a step nearer.*] Let me confess something, Maja.

MAJA. Well?

RUBEK [*strikes his chest*]. In here, Maja . . . in here I have a tiny casket, securely locked. And in that casket lie all my visions. But when she went away, vanished without trace, the casket snapped shut. She had the key . . . and she took it with her. . . . Poor little Maja, you had no key. So everything inside remains unused. And the years go by! And it's impossible for me to get at the treasure!

MAJA [*suppresses a sly smile*]. Then get her to unlock it for you. . . .

RUBEK [*uncomprehendingly*]. Maja. . . ?

MAJA. She's here, isn't she? And doubtless it's because of that casket she's come.

RUBEK. I've never spoken a single word to her about these matters!

MAJA [*looking at him innocently*]. But my dear Rubek . . . is it worth making all this fuss and bother about something that's so straightforward?

RUBEK. You think it's straightforward?

MAJA. I do indeed. Attach yourself to the one you need the most. [*Nods to him.*] I'll always find a place for myself somewhere.

RUBEK. Where?

MAJA [*carelessly, evasively*]. Well . . . I can simply move out to the villa if it becomes necessary. But it won't. In that great big town house of ours . . . surely it should be possible, with a bit of goodwill, to find room for three.

RUBEK [*uncertainly*]. Do you think that might work? In time?

MAJA [*lightly*]. Good Lord, if it doesn't work, it doesn't work. There's not much point in talking about it.

RUBEK. So what do we do then, Maja . . . if it doesn't work?

MAJA [*unconcerned*]. Then we simply go our separate ways. Complete break. I'll always find something new, somewhere. Something free! Free! Free! . . . Nothing to worry about *there*, Professor Rubek! [*Suddenly points, right.*] Look! There she is!

RUBEK [*turns*]. Where?

MAJA. Out there. Pacing along . . . like a marble statue. She's coming over here.

RUBEK [*stands staring, his hand shading his eyes*]. Doesn't she look like the Resurrection incarnate? [*To himself.*] How could I ever have moved her . . . Put her in the shade . . . Altered her . . . ? Fool, fool that I was!

MAJA. What does all *that* mean?

RUBEK [*evasively*]. Nothing. Nothing that *you* would understand.

[IRENE *comes from the right across the plateau. The playing children have already caught sight of her and have gone running to meet her. Now she is surrounded by the crowd of children; some of them appear happy and trusting, others are shy and fearful. She speaks quietly to them and indicates that they are to go down to the sanatorium; she herself wishes to rest a while by the stream. The children run off down the slope to the left.* IRENE *crosses to the rock face and allows the rivulets to run cool over her hands.*]

MAJA [*softly*]. Go down and talk to her, Rubek. Just the two of you.

RUBEK. And where will you go, meanwhile?

MAJA [*looks meaningfully at him*]. From now on I go my own way. [*She goes down the hillside and vaults across the stream with her stave. She stops beside* IRENE.] Professor Rubek is up there waiting for you, madam.

IRENE. What does he want?

MAJA. He wants you to help him with a casket of his that's somehow got locked.

IRENE. Can I help him with that?

MAJA. He thinks you are the only one who can.

IRENE. Then I'd better try.

MAJA. You had indeed, madam.

[*She goes down the path to the Sanatorium. Shortly afterwards* PROFESSOR RUBEK *makes his way down to* IRENE, *but keeps the stream between them.*]

IRENE [*after a short pause*]. She said that you've been waiting for me.

RUBEK. I've been waiting for you for years and years ... without knowing it.

IRENE. I couldn't come to you, Arnold. I was lying down there, sleeping. A long, deep, dream-filled sleep.

RUBEK. Ah, but now you have awakened, Irene!

IRENE [*shakes her head*]. My eyes are still full of sleep. Deep, heavy sleep.

RUBEK. The day will dawn and all will grow bright for the two of us. You'll see.

IRENE. Never believe that!

RUBEK [*urgently*]. I do believe it. I know it will! Now that I've found you again. . . .

IRENE. Risen.

RUBEK. Transfigured!

IRENE. Only risen, Arnold. But not transfigured.

[*He crosses to her on the stones below the waterfall.*]

RUBEK. Where have you been all day, Irene?

IRENE [*pointing*]. Far, far into that vast dead land. . . .

RUBEK [*trying to distract her*]. You don't have your . . . your friend with you today, I see.

IRENE [*smiles*]. My friend keeps a good eye on me, all the same.

RUBEK. Can she?

IRENE [*glancing round*]. Believe me, she can, she can. Wherever I am, wherever I go. Never loses sight of me. . . . [*Whispers.*] Until one fine and sunny morning I kill her.

RUBEK. Do you want to?

IRENE. Desperately. If only I could.

RUBEK. Why do you want to?

IRENE. Because she practises witchcraft. [*Confidentially.*] Do you know, Arnold . . . she's changed herself into my shadow!

RUBEK [*tries to calm her*]. Well, well . . . we all have to have a shadow.

IRENE. I am my own shadow. [*Bursts out.*] Don't you understand that!

RUBEK [*sadly*]. Yes, yes, Irene. . . . I understand.

[*He sits down on a stone by the stream. She stands behind him, leaning against the rock wall.*]

IRENE [*after a moment*]. Why do you sit there with your eyes turned away from me?

RUBEK [*softly, shaking his head*]. I dare not . . . dare not look at you.

IRENE. Why daren't you?

RUBEK. You have a shadow tormenting you. And I have my heavy conscience.

IRENE [*with a glad cry of liberation*]. At last!

RUBEK [*leaps up*]. Irene! What is it!

IRENE [*reassuringly*]. Be calm, be calm. [*She takes a deep breath and speaks as though relieved of some burden.*] See! They've let me go. For this occasion anyway. Now we can sit down and talk to each other as we used to before—in life.

RUBEK. If only we really could talk as we used to.

IRENE. Sit there where you were sitting before. Then I'll sit down here beside you. [*He sits down again. She sits on another stone close by him. A short silence.*] Now I have come back to you from a far distant country, Arnold.

RUBEK. From an endlessly long journey, certainly.

IRENE. Come home to my lord and master. . . .

RUBEK. To our home. Our own home, Irene.

IRENE. Have you waited for me every day?

RUBEK. How dared I wait?

IRENE [*with a sidelong look*]. No, I suppose you didn't dare. Because you understood nothing.

RUBEK. So, really, it wasn't on account of somebody else that you suddenly disappeared like that?

IRENE. Mightn't it just as easily have been on your account, Arnold?

RUBEK [*looks uncertainly at her*]. But I don't understand you. . . .

IRENE. After I had served you with my soul and body . . . and the sculpture was complete—our child, as you called it—I laid at your feet the dearest sacrifice I could make. I removed all trace of myself for ever.

RUBEK [*bows his head*]. And made of my life a desert.

T1

IRENE [*suddenly flares up*]. That's exactly what I wanted! Never were you to create anything again! Never! Not after you had created this child, our only child.

RUBEK. Was this your jealous mind?

IRENE [*coldly*]. Hatred rather, I think.

RUBEK. Hatred? Hatred of me!

IRENE [*again vehement*]. Yes, of you! Of the artist who calmly and casually took a warm living body, a young human life, and ripped the soul out of it—because you needed it to make a work of art.

RUBEK. How can *you* say that? You who gave yourself to my work with such vibrant desire, with such exalted passion. That work for which each morning we came together as for an act of worship.

IRENE [*coldly, as before*]. One thing I will tell you, Arnold.

RUBEK. Well?

IRENE. I never loved your art before I met you. Nor afterwards.

RUBEK. But . . . the artist, Irene?

IRENE. The artist I hate.

RUBEK. The artist in me, too?

IRENE. Above all in you. When I stripped myself naked and stood there before you, I hated you, Arnold. . . .

RUBEK [*vehemently*]. You did not, Irene! It's not true!

IRENE. I hated you because you could stand there so unmoved. . . .

RUBEK [*laughs*]. Unmoved? You think that?

IRENE. . . . Or so maddeningly in control of yourself, then! Because you were an artist, merely an artist . . . and not a man! [*Her voice becomes warm and intimate.*] But that statue in wet, living clay . . . *it* I loved. As out of that raw and shapeless mass gradually there emerged a living soul, a human child. That was *our* creation, *our* child. *Mine*, and *yours*.

RUBEK [*heavily*]. It was. In spirit and in truth.

IRENE. Don't you see, Arnold. . . . It's for our child's sake that I have undertaken this long pilgrimage.

RUBEK [*suddenly alert*]. For that marble image . . . ?

IRENE. Call it what you will. I call it our child.

RUBEK [*uneasily*]. And now you want to see it? Finished? In marble, which you always thought was so cold? [*Eagerly.*] Perhaps you don't know that it now stands in one of the world's great museums . . . far, far away?

IRENE. I have heard tales to that effect.

RUBEK. And you always loathed museums. You called them sepulchres. . . .

IRENE. I will make a pilgrimage to the place where my soul and my soul's child lie buried.

RUBEK [*fearfully and uneasily*]. You must never see that sculpture again. Do you hear, Irene! I implore you! Never, never again!

IRENE. Perhaps you think I would die a second time?

RUBEK [*wringing his hands*]. I don't know what to think. How was I to know that you would cling so inseparably to this image? You, who left me . . . before it was fully formed!

IRENE. It *was* fully formed! That was why I could leave you. Leave you alone.

RUBEK [*sits with his elbows on his knees, his head in his hands, his eyes covered*]. It wasn't *then* what it later became.

IRENE [*silently and swiftly draws a thin sharp knife from her bosom, and whispers hoarsely*]. Arnold . . . have you done harm to our child?

RUBEK [*evasively*]. Harm? I don't exactly know what you would call it.

IRENE [*breathlessly*]. Tell me, what have you done to the child?

RUBEK. If you'll sit down and listen calmly to what I have to say, I'll tell you.

IRENE [*puts the knife away*]. As calmly as ever a mother can who . . .

RUBEK [*interrupting*]. And you mustn't look at me whilst I'm talking.

IRENE [*moves across to a stone behind his back*]. I'll sit here behind you. Now tell me.

RUBEK [*takes his hands away from his eyes and stares ahead*]. When I found you, I knew at once how I was to use you in my work.

IRENE. The work you called 'The Day of Resurrection'. And which I call 'our child'.

RUBEK. I was young then. With no experience of life. My vision of Resurrection—the loveliest, most beautiful image I could think of—was of a pure young woman, untainted by the world, waking to light and glory, and having nothing ugly or unclean to rid herself of.

IRENE [*quickly*]. Yes . . . and that's how I now stand in the work.

RUBEK [*hesitantly*]. Not quite like that, Irene.

IRENE [*with mounting tension*]. Not quite. . . ? Do I not stand there as I stood before you?

RUBEK [*not answering her*]. In the years that followed, Irene, the world taught me many things. I began to conceive 'The Day of Resurrection' as something bigger, something . . . something more complex. That little round plinth on which your statue stood, erect and lonely . . . no longer provided space for all the other things I now wanted to say. . . .

IRENE [*reaches for the knife, then stops*]. What other things? Tell me!

RUBEK. Things I saw with my own eyes in the world around me. I had to bring them in. I had no choice, Irene. I extended the plinth . . . made it broad and spacious. And on it I created an area of cracked and heaving earth. And out of the cracks swarmed people, their faces animal beneath the skin. Women and men . . . as I knew them from life.

IRENE [*breathless and expectant*]. But at the centre of the throng stands the young and radiant woman? I do, don't I, Arnold?

RUBEK [*evasively*]. Not quite in the middle. I'm afraid I had to move the figure back a little. For the sake of the total effect, you understand. Otherwise it would have been much too dominant.

IRENE. But my face is still radiant with the light of joy?

RUBEK. Yes, it is, Irene. In a way, that is. A little subdued, perhaps. As was demanded by my changed conception.

IRENE [*rises silently*]. And this sculpture expresses life as you now see it, Arnold.

RUBEK. Yes, I suppose it does.

IRENE. And in this sculpture you've moved me . . . made a background figure of me . . . pale and indeterminate . . . one of a crowd.

[*She draws the knife.*]

RUBEK. Not a background figure. Let us at worst call it a middleground figure . . . or something like that.

IRENE [*whispers hoarsely*]. Now you have pronounced judgement upon yourself.

[*She moves to strike him with the knife.*]

RUBEK [*turns and looks up at her*]. Judgement?

IRENE [*quickly conceals the knife, and speaks in a choked voice*]. My entire soul . . . you and I . . . we, we, we and our child were in that lonely figure.

RUBEK [*eagerly, tears off his hat and mops the sweat from his brow*]. Yes, but listen now how I have placed myself in the group. In the foreground, beside a spring—as it might be here—sits a man weighed down with guilt. He cannot quite break free from the earth's crust. I call him remorse for a forfeit life. He sits there dipping his fingers in the rippling water—to wash them clean. He is racked and tormented by the thought that he will never, never succeed. Never in all eternity will he win free to achieve the life of the resurrection. He must remain forever captive in his hell.

IRENE [*hard and cold*]. Poet!

RUBEK. Why poet?

IRENE. Because you are soft and spineless and full of excuses for everything you've ever done or thought. You killed my soul—then you go and model yourself as a figure of regret and remorse and penitence . . . [*Smiles.*] . . . and you think you've settled your account.

RUBEK [*defiantly*]. I am an artist, Irene. And I'm not ashamed of those human frailties I may have. Don't you see, I was *born* to be an artist. And I'll never be anything other than an artist.

IRENE [*looks at him with a suppressed malevolent smile, and says gently*]. You are a poet, Arnold. [*Smooths his hair.*] You great big, middle-aged baby—can't you see that!

RUBEK [*displeased*]. Why do you keep calling me a poet?

IRENE [*with watchful eyes*]. Because there's something exonerating about that word, my friend. Forgiving all sins, and drawing a veil over all human frailty. [*Suddenly changing her tone.*] But I was a human being—then! I, too, had a life to live . . . and a human destiny to fulfil. All that I put aside . . . threw it all away in order to serve you. It was suicide. A mortal sin against myself. [*Whispering.*] And that sin I can never expiate. [*She sits down beside him by the stream, and watches him unobserved. Seemingly absentmindedly, she picks a few flowers from the bushes around them. She speaks, apparently in control of herself.*] I should have borne children. Many children. Real children. Not the kind that are preserved in tombs. That should have been my calling. I should never have served you—poet!

RUBEK [*lost in memories*]. But they were wonderful times, Irene. Marvellously wonderful times . . . when I look back. . . .

IRENE [*looks at him mildly*]. Can you remember a little word you used . . . when you were finished . . . finished with me and our child? [*Nodding.*] Can you remember that little word, Arnold?

RUBEK [*looks at her questioningly*]. Some little word I used which you still remember?

IRENE. Yes. Can't you remember it any longer?

RUBEK [*shakes his head*]. No, I can't really say I do. Not at the moment, anyway.

IRENE. You took both my hands and pressed them warmly. And I stood there, breathless, waiting. And then you said: 'My very sincere thanks to you, Irene. This', you said, 'has been for me a delightful episode.'

RUBEK [*looks doubtful*]. I said 'episode'? That's not a word I normally use.

IRENE. You said 'episode'.

RUBEK [*putting a bold face on it*]. All right. . . . in fact it *was* an episode.

IRENE [*curtly*]. At that word I left you.

RUBEK. You take everything so painfully to heart, Irene.

IRENE [*runs her hand over her forehead*]. You may be right. Let us banish all this gloom from our hearts. [*She plucks the petals from a mountain rose and throws them in the stream.*] Look, Arnold. Our birds, swimming.

RUBEK. What kind of birds?

IRENE. Can't you see? They're flamingoes. Rose-pink.

RUBEK. Flamingoes don't swim. They only wade.

IRENE. Then they're not flamingoes. They're gulls.

RUBEK. Yes, they could be gulls with red bills. [*He plucks broad green leaves and throws them in the stream.*] Now I'm sending my ships out after them.

IRENE. But there mustn't be any birdcatchers aboard.

RUBEK. No, there'll be no birdcatchers. [*Smiles at her.*] Can you remember the summer when we sat like this outside that little farmhouse on the Taunitzer See?

IRENE [*nods*]. On Saturday evenings, yes . . . when we'd finished our work for the week. . . .

RUBEK. . . . Travelled down by train. Stayed there over Sunday. . . .

IRENE [*with a hate-filled glance*]. An episode, Arnold.

RUBEK [*pretends not to hear*]. You made birds swim in the stream then, too. They were water-lilies. . . .

IRENE. They were white swans.

RUBEK. Yes, I meant swans. And I remember I fastened a big hairy leaf to one of the swans. It was a dock-leaf. . . .

IRENE. Which became Lohengrin's boat . . . drawn by the swan.

RUBEK. How you loved that game, Irene.

IRENE. We played it over and over again.

RUBEK. Every single Saturday, I think. All through the summer.

IRENE. You said I was the swan drawing *your* boat.

RUBEK. Did I say that? Yes, I might well have. [*Absorbed in the game.*] Just look how the gulls go swimming down the river.

IRENE [*laughs*]. And all your ships have run aground.

RUBEK [*puts more leaves in the stream*]. I have plenty of ships in hand. [*Follows the leaves with his eyes, then throws several more; a moment's pause.*] Irene . . . I bought that little farmhouse on the Taunitzer See.

IRENE. Bought it, have you? You often said you'd buy it if you could afford it.

RUBEK. Later I found I could nicely afford it. So I bought it.

IRENE [*glancing at him*]. Do you live out there now . . . in our old house?

RUBEK. No, I had it pulled down long ago. Then I built myself a big, fine, comfortable villa on the land . . . surrounded by parkland. That's where we generally . . . [*Stops and corrects himself.*] . . . where I generally go for the summer. . . .

IRENE [*controls herself*]. So you and . . . that woman live out there now?

RUBEK [*somewhat defiantly*]. Yes. When my wife and I aren't travelling . . . as we are this year.

IRENE [*looks unseeingly into space*]. Beautiful! Life on the Taunitzer See was beautiful!

RUBEK [*as though looking back within himself*]. And yet, Irene . . .

IRENE [*completes the thought*]. And yet we let that life and all its beauty slip through our fingers.

RUBEK [*softly, urgently*]. Are we too late with our regrets?

IRENE [*does not answer him, but sits silent for a moment; then she points away across the mountain waste*]. Look, Arnold. The sun is setting behind the mountains. Look over there, how the sun catches the heather, all red.

RUBEK [*looks across*]. It's a long time since I saw a sunset in the mountains.

IRENE. Or a sunrise?

RUBEK. I don't think I've ever seen a sunrise.

IRENE [*smiles as though lost in memory*]. I once saw a marvellously beautiful sunrise.

RUBEK. Did you? Where was that?

IRENE. High, high up on a soaring mountain peak. You lured me up there, and promised me I should see all the glory of the world, if only I . . .

> [*She stops abruptly.*]

RUBEK. If only you. . . ? Well?

IRENE. I did as you said. Followed you up to the heights. And there I fell on my knees . . . and worshipped you. And served you. [*Is silent for a moment; then speaks softly.*] Then I saw the sunrise.

RUBEK [*changing the subject*]. Wouldn't you like to come and live with us in the villa down there?

IRENE [*looking at him with a scornful smile*]. With you . . . and that other woman?

RUBEK [*urgently*]. With *me* . . . as in our creative days. Release everything that is locked up inside me. Couldn't you, Irene?

IRENE [*shakes her head*]. I no longer have the key to you, Arnold.

RUBEK. You *have* the key! You, and nobody but you! [*Begs and pleads.*] Help me . . . to live my life over again.

IRENE [*implacably, as before*]. Empty dreams! Dead, futile dreams! Our life together is beyond resurrecting.

RUBEK [*curtly, abruptly*]. Then let us go on playing our game!

IRENE. Our game . . . yes! Our game!

> [*They sit throwing leaves and petals into the stream, to float and sail. Over the slope, left, come* ULFHEIM *and* MAJA, *dressed for shooting. Behind them comes the* SERVANT *leading the dogs which he takes out to the right.*]

RUBEK [*catching sight of them*]. Look, there goes little Maja with the bear-hunting man.

IRENE. Your lady, yes.

RUBEK. Or that man's.

MAJA [*looks out across the mountain waste, sees the couple by the stream and shouts across*]. Good night, professor! Dream about me! I'm off on an adventure.

RUBEK [*shouts back*]. An adventure in search of what?

MAJA [*comes nearer*]. Life! To replace all those other things.

RUBEK [*mockingly*]. You too, Maja dear?

MAJA. Yes. I've made up a song. It goes like this. [*Sings joyfully.*]
I am free! I am free! I am free!
No longer this prison for me!
I'm as free as a bird! I am free!
I do believe I'm awake—at last.

RUBEK. It might almost appear so.

MAJA [*breathes deep*]. Oh . . . how heavenly it feels to be awake.

RUBEK. Good night, Maja . . . and good luck!

ULFHEIM [*shouts a warning*]. Be quiet, damn you! And keep your fancy phrases to yourself! Can't you see we're going out shooting. . . ?

RUBEK. What will you bring me back from the shoot, Maja?

MAJA. I'll bring you a bird of prey. You can model it. I'll wing one for you.

RUBEK [*with a bitter, scornful laugh*]. Wing it, yes . . . casually. . . . You are very good at that.

MAJA [*tosses her head*]. You just let me look after myself from now on. . . . [*Nods, and laughs mischievously.*] Farewell! And have a nice quiet summer night on the mountain!

RUBEK [*gaily*]. Thank you! And the worst of luck to you and your shoot!

ULFHEIM [*with a guffaw*]. That's more like it!

MAJA [*laughing*]. Thank you, professor, thank you!

[*They have crossed the visible part of the mountain waste, and go out through the birchwood, right.*]

RUBEK [*after a short pause*]. Summer night on the mountain. Yes, what a life *that* would have been.

IRENE [*suddenly, with a wild look in her eyes*]. Would you like a summer night on the mountain? With me?

RUBEK [*opens his arms wide*]. Yes, yes! Come!

IRENE. My love, my lord and master.

RUBEK. Oh, Irene!

IRENE [*smiles, and gropes for the knife; hoarsely*]. It will be merely an episode. . . . [*Quickly whispers.*] Sh! Don't look round, Arnold!

RUBEK [*also quietly*]. What is it?

IRENE. A face, staring at me.

RUBEK [*turns involuntarily*]. Where? [*Starts.*] Ah!

[*The* NUN's *head comes half into view among the bushes on the path down to the right. Her eyes are fixed on* IRENE.]

IRENE [*rises and speaks in a low voice*]. We must part. No, don't get up! Listen to me! You mustn't come with me. [*Bends over him and whispers.*] I'll see you tonight. On the mountain.

RUBEK. You'll come, Irene?

IRENE. Yes, I will come. Wait for me here.

RUBEK [*repeats as in a dream*]. Summer night on the mountain. With you. With you. [*His eyes meet hers.*] Oh Irene, that could have been our life . . . And we let it slip by. . . .

IRENE. We only see what we have missed when . . . [*Breaks off abruptly.*]

RUBEK [*looks questioningly at her*]. When. . . ?

IRENE. When we dead awaken.

RUBEK [*shakes his head sadly*]. And what then do we see?

IRENE. We see that we have never lived.

[*She goes across to the hillside and walks down. The* NUN *makes way for her, and follows.* PROFESSOR RUBEK *remains sitting motionless by the stream.*]

MAJA [*is heard singing joyfully on the mountain side*].

I am free! I am free! I am free!
No longer this prison for me!
I'm as free as a bird! I am free!

ACT THREE

A wild precipitous place high in the mountains, with a sheer drop behind. Snow-covered peaks tower up, right, vanishing into the drifting mist. Left, among a fall of rock, stands an old broken-down cottage. It is early morning. Dawn is breaking. The sun has not yet risen.

MAJA RUBEK comes, flushed and excited, down the rock fall, left. ULFHEIM follows, half angry, half amused, holding her fast by the arm.

MAJA [*tries to tear herself free*]. Let me go! Let me go, I say!

ULFHEIM. Now, now . . . you'll be biting me next, you bad-tempered little vixen.

MAJA [*hits him over the head*]. Let me go, I said! And calm down. . .

ULFHEIM. Not damn well likely!

MAJA. Then I'm not going a step further with you. Do you hear! Not another step!

ULFHEIM. Ah ha! And how will you get away from me up here . . . in the mountains?

MAJA. I'll leap straight over that precipice there, if I have to. . . .

ULFHEIM. And finish up battered and pulped like a dog's dinner . . . all nice and bloody. [*Lets go of her.*] All right, off you go! Over the edge and down, if you feel like it. It's fearsomely steep. Just a narrow path, and that's pretty nigh impassable.

MAJA [*dusting her skirt with her hand and looking at him angrily*]. You're a right one to go out shooting with!

ULFHEIM. Don't you mean: to have a bit of sport with?

MAJA. So you call this sport, eh?

ULFHEIM. I make so bold. This is the kind of sport I like best.

MAJA [*tosses her head*]. Well, I must say! [*After a moment, looks enquiringly at him.*] Why did you let the dogs loose up there?

ULFHEIM [*winks and smiles*]. So that they could go off on a bit of hunting by themselves of course.

MAJA. That's not true! It wasn't for their own sake you let them loose.

ULFHEIM [*still smiling*]. So why did I? Tell me.

MAJA. You did it to get rid of Lars. You said he had to run after them and catch them. And meanwhile . . . Nice thing to do, I must say!

ULFHEIM. And meanwhile . . . ?

MAJA [*curtly*]. Never you mind.

ULFHEIM [*confidentially*]. Lars won't find them. You can be bloody sure of that. He won't come back before time.

MAJA [*looks at him angrily*]. I'm sure he won't.

ULFHEIM [*tries to seize her arm*]. Because Lars . . . knows the way I take my sport, you see.

MAJA [*evades him, and looks him up and down*]. Do you know what you are like, Mr. Ulfheim?

ULFHEIM. I imagine I'm mostly like myself.

MAJA. Absolutely right. You are exactly like a faun.

ULFHEIM. A faun?

MAJA. Precisely.

ULFHEIM. A faun—isn't that some kind of monster. A wood-demon or something?

MAJA. Yes, just like you. With a beard like a goat and legs like a goat. And horns as well.

ULFHEIM. Aye-aye . . . horns as well.

MAJA. A nasty pair of horns, just like you.

ULFHEIM. And you can actually see my horns?

MAJA. I reckon I can see them very distinctly.

ULFHEIM [*takes a dog-leash out of his pocket*]. Then I'd better take you and tie you up.

MAJA. Have you gone mad! Tie me up. . . !

ULFHEIM. If I'm a devil, I might as well behave like one. Well, well! You can see my horns, eh?

MAJA [*soothingly*]. Now, now . . . do behave yourself, Mr. Ulfheim. [*Changing the subject.*] But where's this hunting lodge of yours you talked so much about? It must be somewhere around here, you said.

ULFHEIM [*indicates the cottage*]. There it is, right in front of your eyes.

MAJA [*looks at him*]. That old pigsty there?

ULFHEIM [*laughs into his beard*]. That has housed more than one King's daughter in its day.

MAJA. Was that where that awful man you told me about came to the King's daughter in the form of a bear?

ULFHEIM. The very place, my dear huntress. [*He makes a gesture of invitation with his hand.*] If you would care to step inside. . . .

MAJA. Ugh! I wouldn't set foot . . . Ugh!

ULFHEIM. Oh, two people can nicely while away a summer night pretty comfortably in there. Or a whole summer, if it comes to that.

MAJA. Thank you! But it depends whether you've an appetite for that kind of thing. [*Impatiently.*] But I'm bored now with you and with the whole expedition. I want to go back to the hotel—before people wake.

ULFHEIM. How do you suppose you can get down from here?

MAJA. That's your business. There must be a way down somewhere, that I do know.

ULFHEIM [*points to the background*]. Of course there is, bless you! Of a sort. Just over the edge there. . . .

MAJA. You see! A bit of good will and . . .

ULFHEIM. Just try and see if you dare.

MAJA [*doubtfully*]. You don't think so?

ULFHEIM. Never in this world. Unless I helped you. . . .

MAJA [*uneasily*]. So come and help me then. What else are you here for?

ULFHEIM. Would you like me to carry you on my back. . . ?

MAJA. Rubbish!

ULFHEIM. Or carry you in my arms?

MAJA. Let's not start all that nonsense again!

ULFHEIM [*biting back his anger*]. I did that once to a girl off the streets . . . lifted her up out of the gutter and carried her in my arms. With these hands I carried her. I wanted to carry her through life like that . . . so that she shouldn't ever again bruise her foot against a stone. Her shoes were worn right through when I met her. . . .

MAJA. Yet you lifted her up and carried her in your arms?

ULFHEIM. Lifted her out of the mire and carried her as high and as gently as I knew how. [*With a gruff laugh.*] And you know what thanks I got.

MAJA. No. What?

ULFHEIM [*looks at her, smiles and nods*]. I got these horns. These horns that you can see so distinctly. Isn't that a funny story, my dear lady bear-hunter?

MAJA. Oh yes, quite funny. But I know another story that's even funnier.

ULFHEIM. And how does *that* story go?

MAJA. Like this. Once upon a time there was a silly little girl. She had a father and a mother, but they were rather poor. Then into this life of poverty came a splendid gentleman, and he lifted the little girl up in his arms—just like you—and carried her far, far away. . . .

ULFHEIM. Did she want to be where he was?

MAJA. Yes. Because she was stupid, you see.

ULFHEIM. I'm sure he must have been ever such a nice man.

MAJA. No, he wasn't all that nice, in fact. But he gave her the idea that she was going up with him to the top of the highest mountain where the sun shone ever so bright.

ULFHEIM. So he was a mountaineer, was he? This man?

MAJA. Yes, in his way.

ULFHEIM. So he took this girl up with him . . . ?

MAJA [*tosses her head*]. Huh! Took her up? Oh yes, marvellously, believe you me! No, he tricked her into a cold, damp cage, without sun or fresh air—or so it seemed to her—only gilded walls, and round them a lot of great spooky figures in stone.

ULFHEIM. Served her damn well right!

MAJA. Yes. But its quite a funny story all the same, don't you think?

ULFHEIM [*looks at her for a moment*]. Now just you listen to me, my good . . .

MAJA. Well? What is it now?

ULFHEIM. Couldn't you and I patch something together from our tattered lives?

MAJA. So you fancy starting up in the rag trade?

ULFHEIM. Dammit, I do. Couldn't we try tacking a few of the bits and pieces together . . . and we might be able to make some kind of life out of it?

MAJA. And when that poor little outfit was worn through—what then?

ULFHEIM. Then we'll stand there, free and unafraid. As we really are!

MAJA [*laughs*]. You with your goat's legs, eh?

ULFHEIM. And you with your . . . Well, let it pass!

MAJA. Come! Let's go!

ULFHEIM. Not so fast! Where to?

MAJA. Down to the hotel, of course.

ULFHEIM. And then?

MAJA. Then, nicely and politely, we'll say 'Goodbye. Nice to have met you.'

ULFHEIM. *Can* we part, you and I? Do you really think we can?

U1

MAJA. Well, you didn't tie me down, you know.

ULFHEIM. I can offer you a castle. . . .

MAJA [*points to the hut*]. On the style of *that*?

ULFHEIM. It hasn't collapsed yet.

MAJA. And all the glory of the world perhaps?

ULFHEIM. A castle, I said. . . .

MAJA. No, thank you! I've had enough of castles.

ULFHEIM. And miles of shooting land all round.

MAJA. Are there works of art in this castle?

ULFHEIM [*slowly*]. Actually no. No works of art. But . . .

MAJA [*relieved*]. That's good!

ULFHEIM. Will you come with me, then? All the way?

MAJA. There's a tame bird of prey keeping watch over me.

ULFHEIM [*wildly*]. We'll put a slug in him, Maja! Wing him!

MAJA [*looks at him for a moment, then speaks with determination*]. Then come and carry me down the ravine.

ULFHEIM [*puts his arm round her waist*]. Yes, it's high time! The mist is upon us . . . !

MAJA. Is the path down terribly dangerous?

ULFHEIM. Mountain mist is more so!

[*She tears herself loose, goes across to the edge and looks down, but comes running back.*]

ULFHEIM [*goes across to her and laughs*]. Does it make your head swim?

MAJA [*faintly*]. Yes, it does. But go and look down! Those two climbing up. . . .

ULFHEIM [*goes across and leans over the edge*]. It's only your bird of prey— and his strange lady.

MAJA. Can't we slip past them . . . without them seeing us?

ULFHEIM. Impossible. The path's far too narrow. And there's no other way down.

MAJA [*summoning up courage*]. Oh, well . . . Let's brave it out here!

ULFHEIM. Spoken like a true bear-hunter!

[PROFESSOR RUBEK *and* IRENE *come into sight over the edge of the ravine. He has his plaid over his shoulders, she has a fur cape thrown loosely over her white dress, and a swansdown hood over her head.*]

RUBEK [*still only half visible over the edge*]. Well, Maja! So we meet again!

MAJA [*with an air of confidence*]. At your service! Come on up!

[PROFESSOR RUBEK *climbs up, then gives his hand to* IRENE *who also climbs over the edge.*]

RUBEK [*coldly, to* MAJA]. So you've been on the mountain all night, too? Like us.

MAJA. Yes, I've been out shooting. You gave me leave of absence.

ULFHEIM [*pointing to the ravine*]. Have you come up that path?

RUBEK. As you saw.

ULFHEIM. And the lady, too?

RUBEK. Obviously. [*With a glance at* MAJA.] This lady and I do not intend to follow separate paths from now on.

ULFHEIM. You know it's a death-trap, the way you've come. . . ?

RUBEK. We tried it, anyway. It didn't look too bad to begin with.

ULFHEIM. No, there's nothing very bad about the beginning. But then you can find yourself in an awkward spot where you can't go either forward or back. Then you are stuck, Professor! Pinned to the rock, as we sportsmen say.

RUBEK [*smiles, and looks at him*]. I take it these are intended to be words of wisdom, Mr. Ulfheim?

ULFHEIM. Words of wisdom from me? Not goddam likely! [*Insistently, pointing upwards to the peak.*] But can't you see the storm's right overhead! Don't you hear the wind?

RUBEK [*listens*]. It sounds like the prelude to the day of resurrection.

ULFHEIM. It's the wind blowing from the mountain, man! Look at the clouds rolling up on us, and closing in. They'll soon be all round us like a winding sheet.

IRENE [*starts up*]. Winding sheets. I know about them.

MAJA [*pulling at his arm*]. Let's go down.

ULFHEIM [*to* RUBEK]. I can't cope with more than one. Stay in the hut there . . . while the storm is on. Then I'll send some men up to get you.

IRENE [*in terror*]. To get us! No, no!

ULFHEIM [*roughly*]. To bring you in by force if necessary. This is a matter of life and death. So now you know. [*To* MAJA.] Come on! Trust me, and put yourself in my hands.

MAJA [*clinging to him*]. Just get me down safely in one piece. . . .

ULFHEIM [*begins the descent and shouts to the others*]. Wait in the hut till the men come with ropes to get you.

> [ULFHEIM, *with* MAJA *in his arms, clambers quickly but cautiously down the ravine.*]

IRENE [*looks at* RUBEK *with terror in her eyes*]. Did you hear that, Arnold! Men are coming up here to get me! Many men . . . coming up here. . . .

RUBEK. Calmly now, Irene!

IRENE [*in growing terror*]. And the woman in black . . . she'll come, too. She must have missed me long ago by now. She'll seize hold of me, Arnold . . . and put me in a straitjacket. She's got it with her, in the trunk. I've seen it myself. . . .

RUBEK. Nobody is going to touch you.

IRENE [*with a confused smile*]. No . . . I've got my own way of stopping them.

RUBEK. What is that?

IRENE [*draws the knife*]. This!

RUBEK [*reaches for it*]. A knife. . . !

IRENE. Always, always. Night and day. Even in bed.

RUBEK. Give me that knife, Irene!

IRENE [*puts it away*]. You can't have it. I can quite well find a use for it myself.

RUBEK. Here? What use?

IRENE [*looks steadily at him*]. It was meant for *you*, Arnold.

RUBEK. For me?

IRENE. As we were sitting last night by the Taunitzer See. . . .

RUBEK. The Taunitzer . . . ?

IRENE. Outside the farmhouse. Playing at swans and water-lilies. . . .

RUBEK. What then?

IRENE. And when I heard you say—cold as an icy grave—that I was nothing more than an episode in your life . . .

RUBEK. It was *you* who said it, Irene! Not I.

IRENE [*continues*]. . . . I took out the knife. I was going to plunge it into your back.

RUBEK [*darkly*]. And why didn't you?

IRENE. Because I suddenly realized with horror that you were already dead. . . . Long, long dead.

RUBEK. Dead?

IRENE. Dead. Like me. We sat there by the Taunitzer See, two clammy corpses . . . playing games together.

RUBEK. I don't call that death. But you don't understand me.

IRENE. What has become of that burning desire you battled against when I stood naked before you as the woman risen from the dead?

RUBEK. Our love is not dead, Irene.

IRENE. That love which is of our earthly life—the glorious, marvellous, mysterious life on earth—that love is dead in us both.

RUBEK [*passionately*]. I tell you that love burns as strongly and as passionately in me now as ever it did!

IRENE. And I? Have you forgotten who I am now?

RUBEK. Whoever you are, whatever you are, makes no difference! For me you are the woman of my dreams.

IRENE. I have stood on a pedestal, naked, and shown my body to hundreds of men—after you. . . .

RUBEK. It was *I* who drove you to it . . . blind fool that I was! Setting that dead clay image above the happiness of life and love.

IRENE [*looking down*]. Too late. Too late.

RUBEK. Nothing that has happened since has lowered you one hair's breadth in my eyes.

IRENE [*her head high*]. Nor in mine!

RUBEK. Well, then! We are free! And there is still time for us to live, Irene!

IRENE [*looks sadly at him*]. The desire to live died in me, Arnold. Now I am risen. I search for you, and find you. I then see that you lie dead, and life lies dead . . . just as I am dead.

RUBEK. You are wrong! Life within us and about us still beats as strongly as ever it did before!

IRENE [*smiles and shakes her head*]. As the young woman of your resurrection looks down, she can see all life laid out on its funeral straw.

RUBEK [*throws his arms passionately about her*]. Then let us two dead people live life to the full once more—before we go down into our graves again!

IRENE [*with a cry*]. Arnold!

RUBEK. But not here in this half-darkness! Not here, with this loathsome clammy shroud enveloping us. . . .

IRENE [*rapturously*]. No, no! Up into the glory and splendour of the light. Up to the promised peak!

RUBEK. Up there will we celebrate our wedding feast, Irene—my beloved!

IRENE [*proudly*]. Then the sun can look down upon us, Arnold.

RUBEK. All the power of light can look down upon us. And of the darkness, too. [*Takes her hand*]. Will you come with me now, my bride of grace?

IRENE [*as though transfigured*]. Gladly and willingly, my lord and master.

RUBEK [*drawing her along*]. First through the mists, Irene, and then . . .

IRENE. Yes, through the mists. Then right to the very top of the tower, lit by the rising sun.

[*The mists settle thick over the landscape.* PROFESSOR RUBEK, *holding* IRENE *by the hand, climbs up over the snowfield, right, and soon disappears into the low cloud. Biting winds rage and whine. The* NUN *appears on the rock-fall, left. She stops and gazes round, searchingly, silent.*]

MAJA [*is heard singing happily far down the mountainside.*]
I am free! I am free! I am free!
No longer this prison for me!
I'm as free as a bird! I am free!

[*Suddenly there is a roar as of thunder from high up on the snowfield, which begins to slide and tumble down at terrifying speed.* RUBEK *and* IRENE *can be glimpsed indistinctly as they are caught up and buried by the mass of snow.*]

THE NUN [*utters a shriek, stretches out her arms to them as they fall, and cries out*]. Irene! [*She stands for a moment, silent, then makes the sign of the cross in front of her in space.*] Pax vobiscum!

[*The sound of* MAJA's *singing is heard still further down the mountain.*]

EARLIER DRAFT OF

WHEN WE DEAD AWAKEN

⟨*dated*⟩ 22.2.99

Resurrection Day

⟨*altered to* When the dead awaken
altered again to When we dead awaken⟩

Play in three acts

by

Henrik Ibsen

1899

⟨On half-title page:⟩
Resurrection Day

CHARACTERS

PROFESSOR ARNOLD STUBOW, sculptor

MRS. MAJA STUBOW, his wife

THE SUPERINTENDENT of the Spa

ULFHEIM, a landowner

A WOMAN TRAVELLER

A NUN

SERVANTS, TOURISTS AND CHILDREN

The first act takes place at a seaside resort; the second and third acts in the vicinity of a mountain sanatorium

ACT ONE

*Outside the spa hotel, of which part of the main building can be seen, right.
Open space with trees and flowerbeds. Left, a little pavilion, almost overgrown with ivy and wild vine. A view out over the fjord in the background,
with sailing boats and small islands in the distance. It is a still, hot summer's
morning.*

    PROFESSOR STUBOW *and his wife* MAJA *are sitting after lunch in basket
chairs at a laid table on the lawn in front of the hotel. They are now drinking
champagne and seltzer. The* PROFESSOR *is an elderly distinguished-looking
man, wearing a black velvet jacket but otherwise dressed in light summer
clothes.* MAJA RUBEK *is quite youthful, with a vivacious face and bright
playful eyes,* ⟨inserted later *though she has a slightly weary air.*⟩ *She is
elegantly dressed in travelling clothes.*

MAJA [*sits a while waiting for the* PROFESSOR *to say something*]. Aah . . . !

PROFESSOR STUBOW [*looks up*]. Well, Maja?

MAJA. Listen to the stillness.

STUBOW [*smiles*]. Can you hear it?

MAJA. Hear what?

STUBOW. The stillness.

MAJA. Of course I can.

STUBOW. Well, perhaps you are right, mein Kind. One can actually hear the
stillness.

MAJA. Yes, indeed you can ⟨*altered to* God knows you can.⟩ Particularly when
it's so overwhelming as it is here. . . .

STUBOW. Here at the resort, you mean.

MAJA. I mean everywhere in this country. I grant you there was a fair amount
of noise and activity back there in the town. But then it's supposed to be
something of a big city. At the same time . . .

STUBOW [*searchingly*]. Aren't you in any way glad to be back home again, Maja?

*The draft then continues to the end of Act I with only minor variations from
the final version, of which the following are worthy of note:*

(*a*) *the name* STUBOW *is retained until the third side of folio 6 (p. 247, l. 20); on the fourth side it changes to* STUBECK (*twice*), *then to* STUBEK (*twice*); *then, on the first side of folio 7, it becomes* RUBEK; *on the second side of folio 8 (p. 251, l. 12) it once more reverts to* STUBEK, *then again becomes* RUBEK.

(*b*) 'It can't be more than about four years' (*p. 240, l. 31*) *was originally* 'it can't be more than a year', *and was then altered to* 'it can't be more than a couple of years'.

(*c*) 'Four or five years' (*p. 245, l. 22*) *was originally* 'five or six years'.

(*d*) *the draft lacks the stage directions:* 'Visitors to the spa . . . behind the pavilion (*p. 246*).

(*e*) *the Superintendent is* (*once*) *given the name* BRAGER (*folio 8, p. 250, l. 24*).

The draft of Act I is dated at the end '31.7.99', *to which was later added* 'Fair copied 19.10.99'.

ACT TWO

2.9.99 ⟨in error for 2.8.99?⟩
Fair copied 20.10.99

A sanatorium up in the mountains. A hillock with a stone bench in the foreground on the right. ⟨Inserted in top margin: *A little waterfall descends* [altered to: *divides and tumbles*] *over a steep rocky face* [inserted: *in the foreground*] *and flows smoothly down across the wasteland to the right.*⟩ *A vast expanse of bare treeless landscape stretches away towards a long mountain lake. On the far side of the lake rises a range of mountain peaks, the snow in their crevasses tinged with blue. It is an afternoon in the month of August, near to sunset.*

⟨Inserted: *Some distance away, beyond the stream*⟩ *a group of* ⟨inserted: *small*⟩ *children and some bigger young girls are playing and dancing. Some are dressed in town clothes, others in folk costume. During the following scenes merry laughter and singing can be faintly heard.*

PROFESSOR RUBEK *is sitting up on the bench with a plaid over his shoulders looking* ⟨inserted: *down*⟩ *at the children at play.*

After a short while, MAJA *enters* ⟨inserted: *from among the bushes*⟩, *left, and looks across the wasteland* ⟨altered to: *out*⟩, *shading her eyes with her hand. She is wearing a flat travelling bonnet, a short skirt hitched half-way up her legs, and heavy, laced, calf-length boots. In her hand she carries a long stick.*

MAJA [*at last catches sight of* RUBEK *and goes up to him*]. ⟨Inserted: MAJA [*breathes heavily*]. Oh, I've been looking everywhere for you, R.⟩

RUBEK [*nods casually and asks*]. Have you come down from the sanatorium?

The draft continues to the end of Act II with only minor variations from the final version. It is, however, noteworthy that Irene's reproaches (p. 279) originally took a somewhat different form:

Because you are soft and spineless and full of ⟨*inserted:* complacent⟩ excuses for everything you've ever done or thought. I have known several people of that sort. You have too. ⟨*Inserted:* They were your friends.⟩ So you know very well who I'm referrring to. Recognize yourself in them, Arnold.

When you have ruined a few human destinies, and crippled or killed a soul or two here and there, all to satisfy your own needs, then you emerge into the light of day, all regret and remorse and penitence. . . . And with that the account is paid up and settled.

The end of the Second Act is dated 23.8.99. *Fair copied* 10.11.99.

ACT THREE

*The beginning of Act Three is dated '*25.8.99. *Fair copied* 11.11.99.*' The sentence in the stage directions 'On the left lies a little, half dilapidated cottage' was inserted later. The exchanges between* MAJA *and* ULFHEIM *about the broken-down cottage (p. 289, ll. 7–22) are missing from the draft; clearly they were jotted down on a separate piece of paper and added to the text during fair-copying.*

There are two different versions in manuscript of the final moments of the play: an earlier version which persisted until at least the latter part of September 1899; and a revised version, corresponding in all essentials to the final printed version. The following gives the original version (see p. 293):

RUBEK [*smiles and looks at him*]. I take it these are intended to be words of wisdom, Mr. Ulfheim?

ULFHEIM. Words of wisdom from me? Not damn well likely!

MAJA [*changing the subject*]. Isn't it strange that we four should meet up here in the wild mountains?

RUBEK. You with an eagle hunter and I with [*To* IRENE] . . . Well, who am I with?

IRENE. With a shot eagle.

MAJA. Shot?

IRENE. Winged, Mrs. Rubek.

MAJA. Rubek . . . I think there is something nice and forgiving in the fact of our meeting here for the last time.

RUBEK. Never to meet again. If you feel as I do.

MAJA. More than gladly.

ULFHEIM. Then all's well. I'd have preferred to have snatched her away . . . by force . . . with violence . . . but that's as maybe . . .

MAJA. So I'll say goodbye, Rubek.

RUBEK. I have done you a great wrong. I also took you by force and violence . . .

MAJA. The time you bought me. . . .

RUBEK [*nods*]. . . . Bought you, despite all your bubbling, open-air vitality.

MAJA. And now that you so easily and joyfully release me, it's because you yourself wish to be free.

RUBEK. Yes, I couldn't bear it any longer.

MAJA. If we hadn't been 'united in wedlock', as people call it, you'd have borne it longer.

RUBEK. You too! You too, Maja! Night and day you've regretted it.

ULFHEIM. Don't think about that now. We met here, and we part here. And here we'll have a celebration.

MAJA. Celebration here? Where will you get the champagne from, Mr. Ulfheim?

ULFHEIM. Champagne? Does it have to be champagne?

MAJA. Nothing less will do!

ULFHEIM. Then, by all that's sacred, you shall have it! [*He takes a key out of his pocket, opens the door of the hunting cottage and goes in.*]

MAJA [*watches him*]. Now what is he up to?

RUBEK. He's raking up knives and forks. And glasses. He's preparing a celebration for us.

[ULFHEIM *comes out with tray of cold meats and bottles of wine and puts it down on the stone table.*]

MAJA. What in the world . . . !

ULFHEIM. The company will have to make do with what there is. Actually it was only meant for two. But you are welcome guests. [ULFHEIM *opens a bottle of champagne.* ⟨Inserted later: *Says softly.*] Lars is good. He knows me. Sees to everything.⟩

MAJA [*in a low voice*]. Oh, you low-down criminal!

ULFHEIM. Don't abuse your hunting companion. [*Fills up the glasses.*] Only meant for two, as I said. We men must manage with beer glasses. [*Hands round, and raises his glass.*] Ladies and gentlemen, your health! [*To* MAJA.] What shall we drink to, noble lady?

MAJA. Let us drink to freedom! [*She empties her glass in one.*]

RUBEK. Yes, let's drink to freedom. [*He drinks.*]

IRENE. And a toast to the courageous man who dares to use it. [*She sips the glass and throws the rest on to the ground.*]

ULFHEIM. Thank you for that toast, madam. I accept it for myself. Because I've never lacked the courage to use freedom! [*He empties his glass, and refills all the glasses.*] And now a toast to the pursuit of the new life. I have a castle to offer the one who follows me . . .

MAJA. Not a castle! I don't want one!

ULFHEIM. Might well come to that. Perhaps in a year or two we can whistle for all the rest.

MAJA. Hurrah! Then we are completely free. [*She empties her glass.*]

ULFH. Then all we have left will be the cottage.

MAJA. We can set fire to that. Burn it down any day we like.

ULFHEIM. But live first—live in there!

MAJA. Live the new life, yes!

ULFH. And now we take our leave.

PROF. R. I suppose we'll meet down in the hotel.

ULF. Hardly. I'll be gone by the time you get down.

PROF. R. Are you going with him, Maja?

M. Yes, I'm going with him.

PROF. R. And we'll go deeper into the mountains.

ULF. Shouldn't we warn him?

M. [*struggles a moment with herself*]. No. Let him choose his way himself.

ULFH. [*raises his hat*]. Have a good trip in the mountains.

[*Both parties bid a silent goodbye.* ULFHEIM *and* MAJA *clamber down the rocky cliff in the background.*]

ULFH. Step carefully. We tread the path of death.

M. [*half jocular, half serious*]. You must bear the responsibility for us both.

[*They clamber further down and are lost to view.*]

PROF. R. [*breathes more easily*]. Now I am free! That she should leave me so easily and joyfully!

IRENE. She has wakened.

PROF. R. Wakened?

IRENE. From the deep heavy sleep of life. As she descends into the abyss, so she is borne aloft to the light-filled heights of home . . . without her knowing it.

PROF. R. For me she is dead. So let her live—or rest.

IRENE. Did you not murder her a little every day—living together?

PROF. R. I?

IRENE. Just as you murdered me a little every day? Sucked the blood out of her, too—to feed yourself . . .

PROF. R. Never! I have sinned against you. But never against her. Never against anybody else.

IRENE. Perhaps it was precisely *that* which was death to her.

PROF. R. Nobody else in the world means anything to us. Now we can live completely for each other.

IRENE. Now!

PROF. R. Yes, now. Come, Irene. Before we return home, we will climb to the peak there and look far out over the land and all its glory.

IRENE. Driving clouds are moving over the mountainside.

PROF. R. But the peak towers above them.

IRENE. You want to go up there?

PROF. R. Together with you. Live Resurrection Day and re-create it in a new likeness . . . in your likeness, Irene.

IRENE. In my . . . ?

PROF. R. In yours, just as you are now.

IRENE. And do you know how I am now?

PROF. R. Be as you will. For me you are the one I believe I see in you.

IRENE. I have stood on the revolving platform, ⟨*inserted:* in the light of electric lamps, to thundering fanfares,⟩ naked, and displayed myself to hundreds of men—after you.

PROF. R. I was the one who drove you up on that platform—blind as I was at the time. I the one who set the dead clay image above life's—above love's happiness—Not by a hairsbreadth has it diminished you in my eyes.

IRENE. Not in mine, either. But the desire for life died in me. ⟨*Inserted:* So we are free. And there is still time to live life.⟩ Now I have risen and I see that ⟨*inserted:* you and⟩ life are lying like a corpse ⟨*inserted:* like me⟩. All life is lying on its death straw. [*The clouds slowly sink down like a clammy mist.*] See how the shroud descends over us too! But I will not die all over again, Arnold! Save me! Save me, if you can and will!

PROF. R. Above the mists I glimpse the mountain peak. There it stands glittering in the sunrise. We must go up there . . . through the mists of night up into the light of morning.

[*The mists settle ever more heavily over the landscape.* R. *and* IRENE *descend into the mists and are gradually lost to view. The head of the* NUN, *watching, becomes visible through a break in the mist. High above the sea of mist, the mountain peak shines in the morning sun.*]

21.9.99.

APPENDIX I

LITTLE EYOLF: COMMENTARY

1. Dates of composition
2. Draft manuscripts
3. Some pronouncements of the author
4. Contemporary reception

1. DATES OF COMPOSITION

Predictably, and in line with a pattern of working which (with one major variation) had served him for the previous 16–17 years, Ibsen began to think constructively about a new drama within eight or nine months of publishing the previous one, in the expectation of being able to complete it in not much more than a year. *The Master Builder* had been published in Christiania on 12 December 1892. On 18 Sept. 1893 he confided to Jacob Hegel, his publisher, that he had begun to plan a new drama, which he intended to complete in the course of the coming summer; it was, he added, a great convenience for him now to have a home of his own, and he found it easy to work there. To another correspondent, on 26 January 1894, in reporting an unusually mild winter, he revealed that he was turning over ideas for his new play and hoped to be able, 'as usual', to start work on it in earnest with the approach of spring. On 19 April 1894 he reported a steady progress on the preparatory work of his new play to his publisher, and said he hoped to have it ready 'by the usual time'; he did not dare contemplate taking a summer holiday that year.

The period of more intensive work on the play appears to have set in about mid-June. On 15 June 1894 he wrote a letter to his daughter-in-law Bergliot on her birthday: 'Tomorrow it is of course your birthday. But I cannot come out and bring you greetings in person on this occasion. Yesterday I began in earnest the writing of the dialogue of my new play. And in consequence I am tied to my desk and to my cogitations, and I never feel I can spare time for anything else; and anyway I am no earthly use for anything—other than getting the work completed. It's always been like that for me, as Sigurd [his son] knows well enough.'

A week later, on 22 June 1894, he wrote to Fru Gerda Brandes to reply to a letter which had been lying unanswered on his desk for three months: 'You will know from your husband about my incorrigible weaknesses in all things relating to letter writing. But today I must and will do something about it. For

I have now begun in earnest to write my new play, and I must therefore set about clearing my desk and relieving my conscience as far as possible.'

Ibsen seems then to have worked from about mid-June until 7 August 1894 on this main draft, printed above, pp. 107-49; and followed this, in the period 1–18 September, with further revisions to Act II, perhaps carrying the fair-copying of this Act along with him as he made these revisions. (For a more detailed discussion of the course of this work, see section 2, below.) By the end of the month, the play was almost complete in fair copy. On 1 October he wrote to his publisher that only the last few pages remained to be fair-copied, and that he hoped the final MS. would be delivered within fourteen days. A letter of 14 October to his agent confirmed that the MS. had been despatched the previous day. A small correction to Act III was posted on 31 October.

The play was published in Copenhagen and Christiania on 11 December 1894 in an edition of 10,000 copies; a second edition came on 21 December, and a third on 20 January 1895. Translations in English, French, German, Russian and Dutch were published in the course of 1895; and in Italian in 1897.

2. DRAFT MANUSCRIPTS

One almost complete draft version of the play has survived, together with a further 30 or so sides of notes, mostly in the form of revisions to the dialogue of this main draft. Only one item—an early list of characters—appears to ante-date the main draft. All this draft material is now in the University Library, Oslo (Ms. 1117.4° and 1941.8°). The fair copy sent to the printer is in the Collin Manuscript Collection (no. 262, IV, 4°) of the Royal Library, Copenhagen.

Worked into the closing moments of Act III of the main draft (see p. 147) is a poem which Allmers claims to have written, and which he reads aloud to Rita. This poem (with two slight changes) is the one which Ibsen later described as 'the first preliminary study for *The Master Builder*', and dated 16 March 1892 (see *The Oxford Ibsen*, vol. vii, pp. 520–1). The two changes are: (*a*) in l. 7, the word 'så' (so) is inserted before 'hænder' (happens); and (*b*) in the penultimate line, 'tro' (faith) is replaced by 'ro' (peace).

A. EARLY LIST OF CHARACTERS

 1. *One folded sheet, octavo, of squared paper containing, on the first side, a list of characters; sides 2–4 are blank:*

The characters

Harald Borghejm
Johanne, his wife
Rita, his sister
Alfred, his son, 11 years old
Ejvind Almer, road engineer
Miss Varg, Johanne's aunt

The action takes place on Borghejm's estate by the fjord.

B. MAIN DRAFT AND REVISIONS

1. *Thirty folded sheets, octavo, making 60 leaves in all, numbered 2–22 and 24–32; i.e. in his numbering, Ibsen seems to have omitted no. 23 in error. There is no title page, list of characters, or initial stage directions; and fol. 2 starts a moment or two before the appearance of father and son (here called Hakon Skjoldhejm and Alfred respectively).*

The acts are dated, beginning and end, thus:

Act I		end: 10.7.94
Act II	beg: 11.7.94	end: 24.7.94
Act III	beg: 25.7.94	end: 7.8.94

Added on the manuscript at the beginning of Act II, below the original date, is the further date 1.8.94, which was itself later crossed through.

The manuscript is in a clear and well-formed hand, and is obviously based on earlier drafts which apparently have not survived. A number of alterations were made subsequently on the manuscript itself, but most of the major final revisions were made on separate sheets (see B2–6 below) and incorporated from these into the final fair copy.

2. *One folded sheet of lined paper, octavo, containing revised passages for Act I, written on all four sides. On the first side the sister is called* (E)DITH; *this changes to* (A)STA *for the remaining sides of this item.*

(a) first side
Corresponds substantially to p. 39, l. 19–p. 40, l. 20 of the final version, except that the two characters are identified here as E(dith) *and* R(ita).
(b) second, third, and fourth sides
Correspond substantially to p. 41, l. 22–p. 42, l. 13 and p. 43, l. 17–p. 45, l. 29 of the final version. The sister is now called A(STA). *In this item, the name of the Ratwife is* WARG, *not as in the earlier and later items* VARG. *The stage directions marking* ALLMERS' *initial entrance first read:*

A. Allmers with Eyolf by the hand comes in through the door, left. He is a slim, slight man of 37–38 years old with brown, thick hair but without beard. On his face there is an earnest, pensive expression. The eyes sparkle. Eyolf walks with a crutch under his left arm. His leg is lame. He is short in build, looks delicate, but has big intelligent eyes.

This was subsequently amended on the MS. by insertions, deletions, and revisions to read:

A. Allmers, in a summer suit, with Eyolf by the hand, comes in through the door, left. He is a slim, slightly built man of 36–37 years old, with gentle eyes, brown, thin hair and beard. On his face there is an earnest thoughtful expression. Eyolf walks with a crutch under his left arm. His leg is lame. He is short in build, looks delicate, but has beautiful intelligent eyes.

3. *Two folded sheets of squared paper, octavo, lettered 'a' and 'b', containing further revised passages for Act I. Occupying the four sides of 'a' and most of the first side of 'b' is a passage corresponding substantially to p. 49, l. 24–p. 54, l. 34 and p. 56, l. 25–p. 57, l. 9 of the final version. The characters are here designated as* All(mers), R(ita), *and* A(sta). *On the last side of 'b' are two further lines of dialogue corresponding to p. 65, ll. 2–3.*

4. *Four folded sheets, octavo, numbered 1, 3, 4, and 5 (i.e. fol. 2 seems to have gone astray), containing revised passages which make up most of Act II. Dated 1.9.94 on the first side, and 18.9.94 at the end, on the third side of fol. 5. In sum, these correspond substantially to p. 66, l. 1–p. 70, l. 14 and p. 76, l. 3–p. 88, l. 17 of the final version, the missing fol. 2 doubtless having contained the intervening passage.*

The stage directions for the opening of the Act are less detailed than in the final version:

> A narrow clearing in All. forests down by the shore. Tall old trees on both sides stretch over the area. Down the slope left, a stream tumbles between the rocks. The background is open, with a view across the fjord. A couple of tables with chairs to right and left. It is a gloomy wet day with driving rainclouds. Far out on the fjord there is a shower which partly obscures the landscape.

5. *One folded sheet, octavo, numbered '3', containing a passage of revised dialogue for Act III, corresponding substantially to p. 98, l. 26–p. 103, l. 18 of the final version.*

6. *A single leaf containing* (a) *a revision of the stage directions at the beginning of Act II, corresponding very closely to the final version; and* (b) *three lines of dialogue largely corresponding to p. 70, ll. 20–2 of the final version.*

C. FAIR COPY

47 serially numbered folded sheets, differing from the printed version in only minor respects, the only significant one of which is the change in Rita's age from '30–32 years' in the manuscript fair copy to 'about 30 years' in the printed version.

The progressive change in the names of the characters from the earliest drafts to the final fair copy provides evidence for a rough chronological ordering of the manuscript material. Item A is apparently the oldest surviving document in the genesis of the play. The dating of the three Acts in B 1 then provides a general chronological framework, upon which may be superimposed the evidence of B 2. The full sequence of events relating to the composition of the play is, however, only partially documented by this material, and only approximately ordered by the dates (not all of them unambiguously reliable) which attach to it. Certainly it would be wrong to think of the main draft (2 B 1) as representing the supervention of a dramatic form upon an inspiration already complete and consistent in its details. One is aware of changes not merely in emphasis and direction but also in the simple *donnée* of the dramatic situation— changes not merely between the draft and the final version, but also within the draft itself: for example, the relationship between Asta and Borghejm moves in reverse from an openly declared engagement in Act I and the early part of Act II of the draft to a situation at the end of Act II where there is no more than a suspicion that there might perhaps be 'something between them'.

Many of the more significant (or at least memorable) elements belonging to the final version—the fact of Eyolf's crippling disability, the sexually-charged circumstances that had led to it, the crutch, the transvestite practices of Alfred and Asta when younger, the Asta–Eyolf transferences, the ordeal of Alfred in the mountains—entered the play at a comparatively late stage in its composition. And, inevitably, in many instances these new introductions required careful adjustments to the existing fabric of the play. A reconstruction of the sequence of events might nevertheless suggest the following pattern.

The earliest stage is probably that represented by the list of characters in A 1. Here the ratwife-type figure is related by family ties to the others—she is the wife's aunt—a characteristic which persisted through a number of stages in the play's composition until eventually eliminated. It could also conceivably be significant for this stage of the play that Rita (i.e. the later Asta) should be described as Harald's (i.e. the later Alfred's) *sister*, and not the half-sister of the final version. If it was in fact intended at this stage to be a *full* sibling relationship, this would indicate that the emphasis given to the real nature of the Alfred– Asta relationship came later, with all its other attendant implications; because with a straight brother–sister relationship, it would be virtually impossible to deny or eliminate altogether the element of blood relationship, as happens in the final version. It may not be without significance that, as it stands, the first Act of the main draft (2 B 1) could quite adequately sustain a play based on the conflicting pulls of wife and (full) sister. Only in Act Two of this draft does the action begin to hint at the uncertainties in the relationship.

Act One of this draft then falls into two main parts, with the break coming just over one-third of the way through (between fols. 6 and 7) with an extensive reshuffling of the characters' names (see p. 314). A second change of name for the son (to Eyolf) was made later in Act One; and at the beginning of Act Two (dated by Ibsen 11 July 1894), the names of the two main women characters were switched: the wife changing from Andrea to Rita, the sister changing from Rita to Andrea. The name Asta is not introduced until Act Three of this draft.

Little Eyolf: *characters' names*

Final published version	MS. A1 List of characters	MS. B1: Full draft version Act I fols. 2–6	Act I fols. 7–14	Act II	Act III	MS. B2
Alfred Allmers	Harald Borghejm	Hakon Skjoldhejm	Alfred [Almer]/ Allmer/Allmers/ [Allmers]	Alfred Allmers		A(llmers)
Mrs. Rita Allmers	Johanne	Mrs. Andrea Skjoldhejm	Mrs. Andrea Almer . . . etc.	Mrs. Rita Allmers		R(ita)
Eyolf	Alfred	Alfred	Ejvind/Eyolf	Eyolf		E(yolf)
Miss Asta Allmers	Rita	Rita		Andrea	Asta	Edith/Asta
Borghejm	Ejvind Almer	Berghejm/Borghejm				
Ratwife [Miss Varg]	Miss Varg, Johanne's aunt	Miss Varg/ Aunt Ellen				Warg

Whilst at work on the latter half of Act Two, and before moving on to the draft of Act Three, Ibsen seems to have modified his conception of the play in a number of important respects; and many of the changes and additions he was eventually to make to Acts One and Two at the final revision stage are indirectly anticipated by the shape of this draft version of Act Three. Whether these new developments were ideas that he held in suspense in his mind whilst completing the draft of Act Three, or whether (as is more likely) he jotted down his ideas on loose sheets of paper which were then progressively cast away as the final version took firmer shape, is not of prime significance. What is important is to note that the draft of the Third Act (dated by Ibsen 25 July–7 August 1894) imposed substantial revision upon the existing drafts of Acts One and Two. These changes in their turn brought the need for significant changes in the final revision of Act Three, which indeed was to be in large measure rewritten.

The position of item 2 B 2 in the sequence and in the chronology of events is ambiguous. It contains, on its first side, a change of name for the sister first to '(E)dith' and subsequently to 'A(sta)'. If the name-changes undergone by this character in the course of the drafts was a simple linear progression, the evidence would then seem to put this item between Act Two of the draft (where she is called Andrea) and Act Three (where she is finally called Asta). This would then seem to date it (possibly somewhat implausibly) between 24 and 25 July. It is however conceivable that after having adopted 'Asta' for the purposes of drafting Act Three, Ibsen then briefly played with the idea of a further change to 'Edith,' only to abandon the idea in favour of a return to 'Asta'. If this was the case, it would tend to place this item in time somewhere in mid-August, i.e. after the completion of the draft of Act Three on 7 August, and at a time when it would be natural for Ibsen to begin the full revision of the play, starting again with Act One. This would then be consistent with Ibsen's dating of his revisions to Act Two as 1–18 September (item 2 B 4 above). This might then further suggest that the (deleted) second-dating by Ibsen of Act Two of the main draft was an error: '1.8.94' when he should have written '1.9.94'. It is not otherwise easy to make good sense of this date.

3. SOME PRONOUNCEMENTS OF THE AUTHOR

1. After dinner I had an hour-long conversation with Ibsen who that day was in brilliant mood; ideas and suggestions crackled and sparked, and we disputed so that the feathers flew. I didn't want him to gain the impression that I agreed with everything he said; nevertheless he avowed that if he could have a three-hour conversation with me, with just the two of us there, we would reach agreement. It was mainly marriage we talked about, and divorce, which he defended and I attacked. He is busy again with some more 'tomfoolery'. 'I don't suppose you'll ever read it. You are very virtuous', he said; but I

repudiated any imputation of such idiocy. Then he talked a lot about Suzannah —well, I really must not write up the whole of that conversation; for it was very remarkable.—'To you I can confide all this. I have unbounded confidence in you.' I'd very much like to know whether he has some use for me in his gallery. He told me that in the Tirol he had met a lady 'whom he'd been able to make use of while working on *Hedda Gabler*'. Can a painter work without a model? Can a poet do any different? Papa also had a long conversation with Ibsen about his youthful contemporaries. He talked about Johan Sverdrup— whom he greatly despised. How once he was ill and a friend suggested that it might be serious, and he answered that 'one doesn't die before one has been given the Grand Cross'. Ibsen might well say the same.... (*Conversation with Elise Aubert, 7 Feb. 1894, reported in Sofie Aubert Lindbæk, Årgang 1875, Oslo, 1948, pp. 90–1.*)

2. I had occasion to learn from him that he was working on a new play, of which—as he told me with the conscientiousness usual to him—'three-fifths' were complete. I assumed therefore that this meant the first three acts of a five-act drama. (*Report by Paul Lindau, July 1894, in Nur Erinnerungen, 2nd ed., Stuttgart and Berlin, ii, pp. 380 ff.*)

3. We got in touch today with Dr. Ibsen in connection with these statements [that the Ratwife in *Little Eyolf* had had its origin in Goethe's poem 'Der Ratten-fänger']. We asked the author whether the Ratwife was a reminiscence from his reading of Goethe.

'No, it isn't', answered the poet. 'I don't know Goethe's poem. Of course I know the tale about Hameln. But what I used as a source was a memory from Skien of a person who was called "the Ratwife". She was also called "Auntie". [*Faster* = Father's sister]. Similar figures were known in other places.'

There was also a sort of 'Ratwife' in Bergen, whom the street boys shouted at. This was during the period Dr. Ibsen was a producer at the Bergen Theatre....

The poet paused, as though searching his memory.... 'Yes', he said. 'It's quite possible I took some part of the idea from there.... But, as I said, I distinctly remember the figure from Skien.'

We mentioned that people in town were discussing the casting of the play. Many believed that Herr Fahlstrøm, who had recently been away on study leave, had got the part of Allmers.

'Well, I don't doubt Herr Fahlstrøm's ability to interpret the words. But in the part of Allmers there are places where a lyrical temperament breaks through ... where what lies behind the words can only be understood by the timbre of the voice. So Schrøder and I agreed to put Herr Halvorsen in that part. This casting business is a difficult thing. One often has to be hard to get things the way one wants.... I shall certainly be attending a few of the rehearsals.' (*Interview with Ibsen, 18 Dec. 1894, in Dagbladet.*)

4. I cannot resist the impulse to send you my special thanks for your 'Goethe and Marianne v. Willemer'. I was not acquainted with the episode from his

life which you describe there. Perhaps I did read about it long, long ago in Lewes; but if so, I must have forgotten it again because that relationship had no personal interest for me at the time. Now, by contrast, the matter takes on a different aspect. When I think of the character of Goethe's output in those years, the rebirth of his youth, I feel I could have told he must have been blessed with something as wonderful as meeting this Marianne v. Willemer. Fate, providence, chance really can be rather kind and beneficent powers sometimes. (*Letter of 11 Feb. 1895 to Georg Brandes.*)

4. CONTEMPORARY RECEPTION

The book sales of *Little Eyolf* marked a new high level of commercial success for Ibsen, both on the home market as well as abroad in translation. It is clear from his correspondence that on this occasion he gave a great deal more attention to the problems which his translators and his foreign publishers had to face than he ever had before.

The day following the completion and despatch of the fair copy to his publisher, he was making suitable arrangements for the translation of the work into German, French, and English: 'My son will again be seeing to the German translation,' he wrote to his agent on 14 October 1894, 'and Count Prozor, St. Petersburg, the French, and probably Mr. William Archer the English.' On 24 October he wrote direct to Archer: 'At last my new play is finished and the manuscript delivered to Gyldendal's. I am informing you of this in consequence of my promise this summer and I shall not approach anybody else until I have heard whether you can and will take it upon yourself to see to the translation and the publication of the English edition. If you felt inclined to get in touch with Mr. Gosse and Mr. Heineman [*sic*] it might at least be helpful in avoiding undesirable competition. I will not approach Mr. Heineman myself until you have spoken about the matter and perhaps put forward some other arrangement which I might enter into. The play is in three acts, its theme serious, and is about the same length as *The Master Builder*. If you decide to take it on and can make suitable arrangements, the proofs will be sent to you section by section from Copenhagen, in order that your translation can be printed simultaneously with the original.' Certainly the problems that faced his translators were very much a matter of concern to Ibsen. On 27 October he wrote again to his agent to say that he would be particularly grateful if the translators could have reasonably generous time to carry out their not altogether easy task; at the same time he also hinted at the possibility that the English translation might once again be a joint undertaking by Archer and Edmund Gosse: 'Mr. William Archer's [address is] 40 Queen's Square, London W.C. For the present, however, nothing is to be sent to him, for the negotiations with the publisher are not yet wholly complete. Probably W. Archer and Edmund Gosse will carry out the translation jointly.' This time, however (after the complications with *Hedda Gabler* and *The Master Builder*—see the *Oxford Ibsen*, vol. vii, pp. 507–13 and 535–40), Archer arranged to translate the play for Heinemann without Gosse's collaboration. A letter from Ibsen dated 5 November 1894, clearly in answer to an earlier communication from Archer, said: 'Very many thanks for the monies received. A receipt is enclosed. Equally may I thank you for the arrangement with Mr. Heinemann. I accept his offer and thus regard the contract as concluded. May I nevertheless request that the honorarium be sent direct to me here as soon as the last proofs sheets have arrived from Copenhagen. You will receive the first consignment at about the same time as this letter, and the succeeding sections will follow quickly. The title page and the list of characters will come last. Assured as I am that you will keep the matter confidential, I can inform you that the title of the play is *Little Eyolf*. And to assist you with the translation it can be remarked, since you do not have the list of characters, that Asta Allmers is Alfred Allmers' *half*-sister, the child of the father's second marriage.' A fortnight later he followed this up with an assurance about publication days: 'In answer to your and Mr. Heinemann's telegram I can inform you that there will be no advance of publication date in Copenhagen. The original edition will come out at the same time as the English, just as we agreed. You may now, if you wish, announce the play's title. May I ask you to be my representative in everything which concerns the contract with Heinemann.'

On 26 November he again wrote to his agent: 'Once again I'm afraid I have to be a nuisance to you. May I ask you please to inform my German representative, Dr. Julius Elias, of the date on which it is intended to publish my book in Copenhagen. His address in Matthäikirchstrasse 4, Berlin. And could the same information be sent in good time to W. Archer. In this connection it will be necessary to send as soon as possible 12 unbound copies to W. Heinemann, addressed to 21 Bedford Street, London.' These latter copies were doubtless meant to serve the by now almost routine 'performance' to secure the performing rights in England; the play was given a reading in Norwegian on the stage of the Haymarket Theatre, London, on the morning of 3 December 1894.

By mischance, there was a leak of information about the play in Copenhagen the month before it was published. A Danish author, calling at the printers for his own proofs, had been handed the proofs of the first two Acts of *Little Eyolf* in error; he had then spoken incautiously to a journalist about it, with the consequence that the newspaper *Politiken* printed a somewhat garbled version of this part of the play. Ibsen, who had formed the habit of insisting that his new plays be treated as confidential documents until they were actually published, was furious; and he expressed his anger in interviews published in mid-November in a number of Norwegian newspapers. In the event, however, the leak probably only increased the public appetite for the new work; and the first edition of 10,000 copies was sold out virtually on publication day, 11 December 1894. A second edition, published on 21 December, brought the total to 15,000. And a third edition was necessary within a further month. English, French, and German editions were published virtually simultaneously with the Scandinavian first edition, though with the year 1895 on the title page.

Naturally, the book was widely reviewed in Scandinavia; among the more significant pieces were those by Georg Brandes (in *Verdens Gang*, no. 297, 1894), Nils Kjær (in *Dagbladet*, no. 362, 1894), Nils Vogt (in *Morgenbladet*, no. 695, 1894), Just Bing (in *Morgenbladet*, no. 710, 1894), Herman Bang (in *Aftenbladet*, no. 2594, 1894), and Edvard Brandes (in *Politiken*, no. 348, 1894). The contemporary reception in Scandinavia was in general not marked by any sensitive understanding of what the play was concerned to say.

There was, however, one reader in Norway with an informed sense of the power of the work. The novelist Alexander Kielland wrote to his daughter on 14 December 1894:

'In the midst of all my affliction I have read Ibsen's new book with great pleasure. It terrifies me to think how high he towers above all the others.— Indeed, I have finally come almost to enjoy the fantastic and the unreal elements in his work which are so contrary to my own nature. I find the Ratwife, who gives her attention to those small children who are not loved, both deeper and finer and much more true than Hans Andersen's "Story of a Mother"—which itself nevertheless ranks high. . . . See how this old Satan goes much deeper into our ways and shows that the so highly praised love of parents for children is merely a burden of responsibility and a feeling of jealousy while one has them, and a bad conscience when they are lost. . . . The thing I admire pretty well the most in the smaller details of the play is the fact that, after the scene with the Ratwife, little Eyolf says to his aunt: "Imagine! Now I too have seen the Ratwife." To think that this old apparition can remember that this is precisely the way an experience takes shape in a lad. If you see Ibsen, you must bow three times on my account right down to the ground, but you need not say anything.'

The Christiania première on 15 January 1895 in the presence of the author was in fact not the world première; that distinction was achieved by the production at Berlin's Deutsches Theater on 12 January. The stage success in Scandinavia, though considerable, was nevertheless not commensurate with the book sales; in Christiania it achieved 36 performances in the course of 1895. Following its opening night in Bergen on 21 January, it ran for 11 performances. And a touring company took it to various Norwegian provincial towns in the June of 1895. Copenhagen's Royal Theatre played it on 13 March 1895. Elsewhere in Scandinavia, it was played on 21 January in Helsinki, on 30 January in Gothenburg, and on 14 March in Stockholm.

Milan saw the play performed as early as 22 February 1895; Vienna on 27 February at the Burgtheater; Munich on 22 April; and Paris on 8 May 1895.

It was also played in Dano-Norwegian in Chicago in the spring of that same year.

In London, one of the first to gain first-hand familiarity with the new play was Henry James. In November 1894 Heinemann sent James most of the first two Acts in English translation; and James responded with characteristic enthusiasm:

'My dear Heinemann,
    'I feel as if I couldn't thank you enough for introducing me to Ibsen's prodigious little performance! I return it to you, by the same post conscientiously after two breathless perusals,—which leave me with a yearning as impatient, an appetite as hungry, for the rest, as poor Rita's yearning and appetite are for the missing caresses of her Alfred. Do satisfy me better or more promptly than he satisfied her. The thing is immensely characteristic and immensely—immense. I quite agree with you that it takes hold as nothing else of his has as yet done—it appeals with an immoderate intensity and goes straight as a dose of castor oil! I hope to heaven the thing will reach the London stage: there ought to be no difficulty, if Rita, when she offers herself, can be restricted to a chair, instead of lying on her back on the sofa. Let her *sit*, and the objection vanishes—I mean let her eschew the sofa. Of course I don't know what the rest brings forth—but this act and a half are a pure—or an impure—perfection. If he really carries on the whole play simply with these four people—and at the same high pitch (it's the *pitch* that's so magnificent!) it will be a feat more extraordinary than any he's achieved—it will beat *Ghosts*. Admirable, gallant old man! The success of this would be high! I greatly enjoyed our "lovely luxurious" (as Rita would say) *fin de soirée*, on Monday. [Herbert Beerbohm] Tree is as dewily infantine as Eyolf!
                        Yours truly,
                        Henry James.
'P.S. *Do* remember that I'm on the sofa, with my hair down—and pink lamp shades!'

Then, on 22 November 1894, he wrote no less enthusiastically about the play to Elizabeth Robins, whose reputation as an Ibsen actress was now high:

'Dear Miss Robins
    'Heinemann has lent me the proofs of the 2 first acts of the Play—the ineffable Play—and I can't stay my hand from waving wildly to you! It is indeed immense,—indeed and indeed. It is of a rare perfection—and if 3 keeps up the tremendous pitch of 1 and 2 it will distinctly stand at the tiptop of his achievement. It's a masterpiece and a marvel; and it *must* leap upon the stage. It must leap with *your* legs, moreover—excuse, in an Ibsen connection, the metaphor! The inherent difficulties are there, but they are not insurmountable. They are on the contrary manageable —they are a matter of tact

and emphasis—of art and discretion. The thing will be a big *profane* (i.e. Ibsen and non-Ibsen *both*) success. The part—*the* part is Asta—unless it be the Rat-hound in the Bag! *What* an old woman—and what a Young!—I am to see Mrs. Bell today—but it isn't with her I want to talk of it, but with *you*, when I have gulped Act III.

Yours in convulsions
Henry James.'

Alas for James, the third Act—when he had had a chance of reading it—was a profound disappointment, mainly, one supposes, because the part of Asta (which he had privately marked down for Elizabeth Robins) seemed to fall right away. In a letter to Miss Robins three days later, he confesses that he might have spoken a little too freely about the new play, and that this breach of confidence might perhaps have done some harm. He then goes on:

'I fear, in truth, no harm *can* be done equal to the harm done to the play by its own most disappointing third act. It came to me last night—and has been, to me, a subject of depressed reflection. It seems to me a singular and almost inexplicable drop—dramatically, *representably* speaking; in short strangely and painfully meagre. It has beauty, as you say—but only as far as anything so meagre *can* have it. The worst of it is that it goes back, as it were, on what precedes, and gives a meagreness to that too—makes it less interesting and less significant. He simplifies too much and too suddenly. It doesn't surprise me, indeed—for one had the sense that with his paucity of elements, of figures, he had, in 1 and 2 squeezed out of these things every drop that they would yield; still, at the same time, one dimly expected a sort of miracle—based on the fact that Act 2 carried on the action of Act 1 more than could have been hoped. I don't see the meaning or effect of Borgheim—I don't see the value or final *function* of Asta; that is, I don't in the *presentation* of these things—and it's the presentation that constitutes the play. On the other hand the beauty of the conversations between Allmers and Rita is incontestably even exquisite—and I even think it will give you, or would give you, a great deal to do with Rita. My objection is that I find the solution too simple, too immediate, too much a harking back, and too productive of the sense that there might have been a stronger one. I have just paused to read it over again, and the effect of doing so is to make me feel that an *actress* no doubt (i.e. E.R.) could do an immense deal with Rita. My idea that Asta was to become an active, *the* active agent is of course blighted. Really uttered, *done*, in the gathered northern twilight, with the flag flown and the lights coming out across the fjord, the scene might have a real solemnity of beauty—and perhaps that's all that's required!!—A vulgar material drawback seems to me the shortness—inadequate duration—of the whole thing—and in especial the brevity of this last, reduced to the 2 simple conversations. Still the second conversation *is* lovely: oh yes, it is. You will think I am taking back my "disappointment"! I am not; it is perfectly consistent with my appreciation. The talk between husband and wife is charming—but one listens to it as if it had been a substitute for something else to which one suspects it of being inferior. But the audience may quite possibly prefer the substitute.' (Elizabeth Robins, *Theatre and Friendship*, London, 1932, pp. 157–61.)

When Archer's translation of *Little Eyolf* was published in the second week of December 1894, it was fairly widely reviewed in the English daily and periodical press: see, in particular, a full (though unsigned) review in *Saturday Review*, lxxviii, 15 Dec. 1894, pp. 662 ff., in the course of which a link is suggested between the play and Tolstoy's *Kreuzer Sonata*, and the next day a review by J. T. Grein in the *Sunday Times* of 16 Dec. 1894 (both the above items substantially reprinted in Michael Egan, *Ibsen: the Critical Heritage*, London, 1972, pp. 334–9); W. L. Courtney, 'A note on Ibsen's *Little Eyolf*', in *Fortnightly Review*, lvii, New Series, 1895, pp. 277–84; G. W. Steevens, 'The New Ibsen', in *New Review*, xii, Jan.–Jun. 1895, pp. 39–45, in the course of which it is asserted: '*Little Eyolf* . . . is ruined by a fault of construction. It sets out to consider the case of a husband and wife who, indirectly by their own fault, lose their one crippled child. . . . [Ibsen] faces the situation with penetrating insight and unflinching logic. But, most unluckily for him, this will not make a play.' And, in America: W. M. Payne, '*Little Eyolf*', in *The Dial*, xviii, 1895, pp. 5–6; and W. H. Carpenter, '*Little Eyolf*', in *The Bookman*, iii, 1895, pp. 39–40.

It took nearly two years for the play to reach the London stage. Shaw wrote of its having been 'boycotted'; looking back over the 1894–5 season in the pages of the *Saturday Review* (27 July 1895) to see if there was any moral to be drawn by a manager with enough money at stake to make him anxious to get some guidance for the following season, he suggested: 'To him, as far as I can see, the season has been like Ibsen's plays: the moral is that there is no moral. The outcry against Ibsen has been deferred to carefully. *Little Eyolf* has been boycotted; and none of the older plays have been touched in English, whilst there has been a plentiful supply of what was described the other day, in contradistinction to Ibsen's work, as "the drama that the public likes and the public pays for."' (*Our Theatres in the Nineties*, London, 1932, vol. 1, p. 191.) Eventually it was performed at the Avenue Theatre on 23 Nov. 1896 with Janet Achurch as Rita, Elizabeth Robins as Asta, Mrs. Patrick Campbell as the Ratwife, and Courtenay Thorpe as Allmers. In later life, Elizabeth Robins liked to remember that she had had a hand in this production of *Little Eyolf* 'where Janet Achurch again made an unforgettable impression in the long part of Rita, while Mrs. Patrick Campbell, in the small part of the Rat Wife, gave perhaps the most haunting and perfect piece of poetic acting that stands to her credit'. (*Ibsen and the Actress*, London, 1928, p. 51.)

This was the occasion for Shaw to give the play his extended attention. Observing that London had put off the torture of *Little Eyolf* as one puts off a visit to the dentist, he announced (on 7 November 1896, in a piece entitled 'Ibsen Ahead!') a series of matinée performances at the Avenue Theatre from 23 to 27 November: '. . . The torture tempts us in spite of ourselves; we feel that it must be gone through with; and now, accordingly, comes Miss Hedda Hilda Gabler Wangel Robins, christened Elizabeth, and bids us not only prepare to be tortured, but subscribe to enable her to buy the rack. A monstrous proposition, but one that has been instantly embraced. No sooner was it made than Mrs. Patrick Campbell volunteered for the Ratwife, the smallest part in *Little Eyolf,* consisting of a couple of dozen speeches in the first act only. (Clever Mrs. Pat! it is, between ourselves, the most fascinating page of the play.) Miss Janet Achurch, the original and only Nora Helmer, jumped at the appalling part of Rita, whom nobody else on the stage dare tackle, for all her "gold and green forests". The subscriptions poured in so fast that the rack is now ready, and the executioners are practising so that no pang may miss a moan of its utmost excruciation. Miss Robins herself will play Asta, the sympathetic sister without whom, I verily believe, human nature could not bear this most horrible play.' (*Our Theatres in the Nineties,* London, 1932, vol. ii, p. 240.)

Shaw devoted the whole of his piece in the *Saturday Review* of 28 Nov. 1896 to a consideration of *Little Eyolf*—'an extraordinarily powerful play', he called it—and to its production at the Avenue Theatre. He judged the performance to be a very remarkable one, which, considering the cast, was not surprising: 'When, in a cast of five, you have the three best yet discovered actresses of their generation, you naturally look for something extraordinary.' The part of Rita was the most arduous to play, but Miss Achurch was more than equal to the occasion, even though Shaw's attention was frequently distracted by the virtuosity of the actress's heroics: 'As Rita she produced almost every sound that a big human voice can, from a creak like the opening of a rusty canal lock to a melodious tenor note that the most robust Siegfried might have envied. She looked at one moment like a young well-dressed, very pretty woman: at another she was like a desperate creature just fished dripping out of the river by the Thames Police. Yet another moment, and she was the incarnation of impetuous, ungovernable strength. Her face was sometimes winsome, sometimes listlessly wretched, sometimes like the head of a statue of Victory, sometimes suffused, horrible, threatening, like Bellona or Medusa. She would cross from left to right like a queen, and from right to left with, so to speak, her toes turned in, her hair coming down, and her slippers coming off. A more utter recklessness, not only of fashion, but of beauty, could hardly be imagined. . . .'

Shaw twice saw Mrs. Campbell play the Ratwife: once enchantingly, like a messenger of heaven, supernaturally, beautifully; on the other occasion most disappointingly: '. . . To my unspeakable fury, she amused herself by playing like any melodramatic old woman, a profanation for which, whilst my critical life lasts, never will I forgive her.' As for Elizabeth Robins, the part of Asta did not really extend her; Courtenay Thorpe, in the part of Allmers, played intelligently; C. M. Lowne was miscast as Borghejm; the child playing Eyolf 'was one of the best actors in the company'.

All in all, however, and despite the individual excellences, the production was in Shaw's view an unsatisfactory one. It was essentially a scratch performance, quickly thrown together, and with no prospect of any real continuity. (*Our Theatres in the Nineties*, vol. ii, pp. 256–64.)

Positive though qualified approval was also expressed by Henry James, who confessed that once again he succumbed to the fascination which Ibsen always exerted on him: 'It is simply the acceptance of the small Ibsen *spell*, the surrender of the imagination to his microcosm, his confined but completely constituted world, in which, in every case, the tissue of relations between the parts and the whole is of a closeness so fascinating. The odd thing—I speak of course from the point of view of my particular stall—is that the fascination appears quite independent either of the merit or of the place held by the play in the Ibsen list. The place of *Little Eyolf* is not of the highest, and even in London, on other occasions, the author has had, on the whole, I think, more acting. Yet prompt to the moment the charm descended—as sharp as ever rang the little silver bell.' (*Harper's Weekly*, 23 Jan. 1897, xlv, no. 2092, pp. 134–5, reprinted in *The Scenic Art*, ed. Allan Wade (London, 1949), pp. 288–90.

Most of the initial press criticism was unambiguously hostile: offence was taken at the more explicit sexual references; the symbolism was dismissed as vague; the dramatist's obsession with abnormal mental and physical disease was resented; and the stock anti-Ibsenist epithets were once again paraded: 'gloom and depression', 'patients of a madhouse', 'morbid, melancholy and unwholesome', 'coarseness and vulgarity', 'alternately pathetic and nasty'. A selection of these—including excerpts from the *Pall Mall Gazette*, *The Times*, *Evening Standard*, *Daily News*, *Daily Telegraph*, and *Daily Chronicle* (all of 24 Nov. 1896), and by J. T. Grein from *Sunday Times* (29 Nov.)—are conveniently reprinted in Michael Egan, *Ibsen: the Critical Heritage*, London, 1972, pp. 340–56. Other items worthy of mention include: Frederick Wedmore, 'Little Eyolf', in *Academy*, 1, no. 1282, 28 Nov. 1896, p. 465; H. D. Traill, 'Ibsenism: the craze', in *National Review*, xxviii, 1897, pp. 641–7; Ronald McNeill, 'Ibsenism: *Little Eyolf*', ibid., pp. 648–53; anon., 'Ibsen's *Little Eyolf*' in *The Humanitarian*, x, Jan. 1897, pp. 72–6.

The first five matinées were sold out; and this encouraged certain commercial interests to provide the backing for an extension of the run. But—as Shaw chronicles in his utterly devastating account in the *Saturday Review* for 12 Dec. 1896—this brought changes. The new syndicate, finding the whole thing wrong from the root up, promptly set to work to show how Ibsen really ought to be done:

'The silly Ibsen people had put Miss Achurch, an Ibsenite actress, into the leading part, and Mrs. Patrick Campbell, a fashionable actress, into a minor one. This was soon set right. Miss Achurch was got rid of altogether, and her part transferred to Mrs. Campbell. Miss Robins, though tainted with Ibsenism, was retained, but only, I presume, because, having command of the stage-right in the play, she could not be replaced—say by Miss Maude Millet——without her own consent. . . .

'Mrs. Patrick Campbell has entered thoroughly into the spirit of the alterations. She has seen how unladylike, how disturbing, how full of horror even, the part of Rita Allmers is, acted as Miss Achurch acted it. And she has remedied this with a completeness that leaves nothing to be desired. . . . Mrs. Campbell succeeded wonderfully in eliminating all unpleasantness from the play. She looked charming; and her dresses were beyond reproach: she carried a mortgage on the "gold and green forests" on her back. Her performance was infinitely reassuring and pretty. . . . There was not a taste of nasty jealousy: this Rita tolerated her dear old stupid's preoccupation with Asta and Eyolf and his books as any sensible (or insensible) woman would. Goodness gracious, I thought, what things that evil-minded Miss Achurch did read into this harmless play! And how nicely Mrs. Campbell took the drowning of the child! Just a pretty waving of the fingers, a moderate scream as if she had very nearly walked on a tin tack, and it was all over, without tears, without pain, without more fuss than if she had broken the glass of her watch. . . . The main drawback is that it is impossible not to feel that Mrs. Campbell's Rita, with all her charm, is terribly hampered by the unsuitability of the words Ibsen and Mr. Archer have put into her mouth.' (*Our Theatres in the Nineties*, vol. ii, pp. 271–8.)

Somewhat later, there also appeared A. F. Spender, '*Little Eyolf*—a plea for reticence', in *Dublin Review*, cxx, 1897, pp. 112–25; William Archer, 'The harmonics of *Little Eyolf*', in *The Theatrical 'World' for 1896*, London, 1897, pp. 306–14 and 322–4; and E. R. Russell and P. C. Standing, *Ibsen on his merits*, London, 1897, esp. pp. 120–34.

Little Eyolf was played by the Ibsen Club at the Rehearsal Theatre on 12 November 1911, and again on 2 February 1913. But for its next professional production, London had to wait until the Ibsen centenary year of 1928, when it was played on 3 December, at the Everyman Theatre.

APPENDIX II

JOHN GABRIEL BORKMAN: COMMENTARY

1. Dates of composition
2. Draft manuscripts
3. Some pronouncements of the author
4. Contemporary reception

1. DATES OF COMPOSITION

A measured two years after the publication of *Little Eyolf*, the new Ibsen play appeared in the bookshops. Even Henry James was moved to comment on the astonishing control Ibsen exercised over his creative life: '*John Gabriel Borkman* . . . embodies the very last biennial revolution—a series unfailing in its regularity and as punctual to a day as the will of fate—of the wonderful old man of Christiania.' (*Harper's Weekly*, xlv, 2092, 23 Jan. 1897.) So smoothly, indeed, did the composition of the work go on this occasion that the MS. was ready for the printer with time to spare—time which Ibsen directed should be used to give his translators an opportunity to ponder their work, and to co-ordinate publication dates.

Work on *John Gabriel Borkman* left little residual comment in Ibsen's letters. When on 27 June 1895 he wrote to William Archer, it was to express the—at this period in the cycle—usual hope that he would be writing a new play the following year; but he added that for the present he had no certain plans. By 24 April 1896, however, he was reporting to Georg Brandes that he was 'taken up with preparations for a big new work'. And a week later, on 1 May 1896, in a letter to Archer in which he commented on the advantages to him of the new Bern Copyright Convention, he again referred to the new work: 'Already some time ago I began to occupy myself with preparations for a new drama. It will be fairly long. But I do not give up the hope of having it ready by the usual time. As you may know, Norway recently joined the Bern convention, and those books I may now write will henceforth be protected in all those countries which have already joined the above-mentioned international union. This will clear out of the way many of the difficulties connected with publication in London. But I hope that our relationship in that respect will nevertheless remain unchanged.' On 7 July he wrote to his agent, August Larsen, that he was 'working at full pressure'.

From the evidence of the dates which Ibsen entered on the draft manuscript of the play, at the beginning and end of each Act, it would seem that he was then uninterruptedly at work from 11 July to 18 October 1896, with scarcely any respite. (A letter of 3 October to Georg Brandes tells of his having 'refused to be at home to anybody', because he was working on his new play which he wished to complete as soon as possible.) The MS. datings reveal the following timetable:

(*a*) draft version: 11 July–26 August 1896
　　Act I　:　11 July–24 July
　　Act II　:　25 July–10 August
　　Act III:　11 August–20 August
　　Act IV　21 August–26 August
(*b*) revision and fair copy: 27 August–18 October
　　Act I　:　27 August–15 September
　　Act II　:　16 September –29 September
　　Act III:　30 September–10 October
　　Act IV:　11 October–18 October

This pattern of events is then entirely consistent with the few other references in his correspondence to this work. On 27 July he wrote to his publisher: 'Things are progressing exceptionally quickly and easily with my new play. The more than Mediterranean heat which prevails up here this summer is not preventing me from working uninterruptedly, and it is quite possible that on this occasion I shall be able to send you the manuscript for printing rather earlier than usual.' He wrote again on 6 September: 'I am pleased to be able to tell you that I completed the [draft] manuscript of my new play at the end of last month, and I am now busy on the fair copy which will be available for you in October. The play is in four fairly long Acts, and I think the work may be said to be good and successful.' And on 20 October he sent off the MS. with an accompanying letter: 'Along with this I am sending you the manuscript of my new play. I think we shall both have joy of it. Don't let any light-fingered literary gentlemen get hold of the proofs [a reference to what had happened to *Little Eyolf*], and put the printing in hand at once in the interests of the theatres and the translators.'

The play was published in Copenhagen on 15 December 1896 in an edition of 12,000 copies, the largest edition to date of any Ibsen play. Even so, the demand was so great that a further edition of 3,000 copies was published the same day.

As was now the regular practice in England, an edition of 12 copies of the Norwegian text was published by Heinemann in advance of the official publication day, on 12 December; and this was followed by a 'performance' of the play—necessary for copyright purposes—at the Avenue Theatre on 14 December. Translations of the play into English, German, French, and Russian appeared almost immediately.

2. DRAFT MANUSCRIPTS

None of the preliminary notes and jottings which Ibsen habitually made in the early stages of writing a play has survived in the case of *John Gabriel Borkman*. The bulk of the surviving manuscript material consists of a full working draft of the play (A 1 below); with this are associated two separate short items (A 2 and A 3 below) containing passages of dialogue which were incorporated at a fairly late stage in the play's composition.

A. DRAFT MANUSCRIPT AND REVISION NOTES

1. *Forty-three folded sheets, octavo, numbered 2–44, making 86 leaves in all. There is no title page, and no list of characters; only one and a quarter sides of fol. 44 are written on. The beginning and the end of each Act is double-dated, the first date doubtless referring to the original drafting, and the second to the revision and fair-copying. The dates are: Act I 11.7.96 (27.8.96)–24.7.96 (15.9.96); Act II 25.7.96 (16.9.96)–10.8.96 (29.9.96); Act III 11.8.96 (30.9.96)–20.8.96 (10.10.96); Act IV 21.8.96 (11.10.96)– 26.8.96 (18.10.96).*

The draft was originally written in a generally well-formed hand; to it were then made a number of additions and emendations, many of which are in a rapid hand. It is not always easy to determine in every case whether the alterations were made during the initial drafting or in the course of the later revision; but it is at least clear that the bulk of them were made during this second stage.

Some guide to the dating of these revisions is provided by the pattern of change in the names of the characters (see p. 329).

2. *One folded sheet, octavo, numbered '1', containing on the first side scraps of the dialogue which were eventually incorporated in substance into Act II of the final version: (a) p. 179, l. 26–p. 180, l. 5; (b) p. 184, l. 29–p. 185, l. 9; and (c) p. 185, ll. 20–3. The names of the speakers are omitted on the MS.*

3. *One folded sheet, octavo, containing on the first side scraps of dialogue which were eventually incorporated in substance into Acts III and IV: (a) p. 207, ll. 33–5; (b) p. 227, l. 30–p. 228, l. 2; (c) p. 228, ll. 7–15; and (d) p. 231, ll. 17–19.*

B. THE DRAFT AND THE FINAL TEXT COMPARED

Many of the changes which Ibsen made to the draft version were not of far-reaching significance. Moreover it is not always possible to convey in transla-tion what many of these minor changes embodied. Below is a brief catalogue of some of the more significant changes, with illustrative quotations. (For changes in characters' names, see p. 329.)

John Gabriel Borkman: *characters' names*

Final printed version	Act I			Act II	Act III	Act IV
	fols. 2–3	fols. 4–7	fols. 8–13			
John Gabriel Borkman				Jens/Jens Jørgen/Jens Adolf/J.G./J. Gabriel/Jens Gabriel Borkman	John Borkman	John Gabriel Borkman
Mrs. Gunhild Borkman	Mrs. Ella Renton	Mrs. Gunhild Renton	Mrs. Gunhild Borkman	Mrs. Gunhild Borkman		
Erhart Borkman	[Erhard]	[Erhard]	Erhard Borkman	[Erhard/Erhart]	Erhard/Erhart	[Erhart]
Miss Ella Rentheim	Miss Gunhild Borkenheim	Miss Ella Borkenheim	Miss Ella Rentheim	Miss Ella Rentheim		
Mrs. Fanny Wilton	[Mrs. Wilborg]	[Mrs. Vilborg]	Mrs. Wilton	[Mrs. Wilton]	Mrs. Fanny Wilton	[Mrs. Wilton]
Vilhelm Foldal		[Foldal]		Vilhelm Foldal		Vilhelm Foldal
Frida Foldal			[Frida Foldal]	Frida Foldal	[Frida Foldal]	[Frida Foldal]
Maid	Maid		Maid		Maid/Malene	Maid

1. *The stage setting and the opening moments were less elaborately orchestrated:*

11.7.96
27.8.96

ACT ONE

A sitting-room in the house of MRS. RENTON, *furnished in old-fashioned faded splendour. At the back, an open folding door leads out on to a garden room, with windows and a glass door. Through them is a view to the garden, with slurrying snow. On the side wall, right, a door leads from the hall. Further downstage is a large, old-fashioned iron stove, where a fire is burning. On the left, further back, a smaller door. Forward of it, on the same side, a window. Between this and the door a sofa, and in front of it a table with a cloth over it. By the stove an armchair and an upholstered rocking chair.*

MRS. RENTON *is sitting on the sofa with her crotchet-work. She is an elderly lady, who holds herself stiffly, and has hard impassive features. Her hair is almost white. Delicate transparent hands. Dark dress. A crocheted woollen shawl over her shoulders.*

The MAID *comes in through the hall door with a visiting-card on a small wooden tray.*

MAID. There is a lady outside . . .

MRS. RENTON. Mrs. Wilton, I suppose?

MAID [*approaches*]. No, this lady is a stranger . . .

MRS. RENTON [*picks up the card*]. Let me see . . . [*Reads it and rises quickly.*] Are you sure this is meant for me?

MAID. Yes, I understood it was for you, madam.

MRS. RENTON. Very well. Tell her I am at home.

[*The* MAID *opens the door for the caller and goes out.* MISS BORKENHEIM *comes in, dressed in a black velvet coat. She is older than her sister and resembles her, with traces of past beauty. She still retains her dark, abundant hair.*]

MISS BORKENHEIM [*remains standing just inside the door*]. You look somewhat surprised to see me, Ella.

MRS. RENTON [*stands rigid and unmoving between the sofa and the table*]. Haven't you made a mistake? The bailiff lives in the side wing.

2. *Borkman's prison sentence was originally six and not five years (p. 158, ll. 3–6):*

MRS. RENTON. You don't imagine I ever consort with him? Ever see him? He who had to serve six years. The terrible shame to think of it. For us all! For the whole family!

3. *The draft has no reference to the 'kingly' aspects of Borkman's former life-style (p. 158, l. 25–p. 159, l. 4):*

MRS. RENTON. Yes, always the talk was of having 'to create an impression'. Oh, we created an impression all right. Never by a single word did he tell me about the real state of his affairs.

MISS BORKENHEIM. No, but none of the rest of us had any idea, either.

4. *The history of Ella Rentheim's adoption of Erhart is less circumstantial (p. 160, l. 1–p. 161, l. 2):*

MISS BORKENHEIM. No. I can't say I have.

MRS. RENTON. Then why did you take him and look after him. Why did you pay everything for him when *we* . . . when *I* couldn't any longer. You were lucky, Ella ⟨*sic*⟩. You managed to make sure your money was saved.

MISS BORKENHEIM. Not because of anything I did. I didn't know that the securities in my name had escaped.

MRS. RENTON. Well, I don't understand these things. All I can say is you were lucky. But if it wasn't for the sake of the family, for the line, for the name which attaches to both Erhard and me . . . ? Why make the sacrifices you have made? You must have had some motive.

MISS BORKENHEIM. I wanted to give Erhard every chance of finding happiness in life.

5. *The present of a piano from Ella Rentheim to Borkman was a later addition (p. 165, ll. 12–20):*

MRS. RENTON. And Erhard's arranged for her to study music. She's now quite good—good enough to come and play for him of an evening. Erhard has arranged that, too.

6. *The 'change of name' motif was originally introduced earlier into the action (p. 169, l. 27–p. 170, l. 5):*

MRS. BORKMAN. He believes what is the truth. That you are ashamed of us, despise us. Or perhaps you don't? Didn't you once consider trying to adopt him. To get him to change his name. Call himself Rentheim. Erhard Rentheim.

MISS RENTHEIM. That was when the scandal was at its height. When the case was before the court.

MRS. BORKMAN. Yes, you wanted me to lose my boy, too. Just as I lost everything ... everything else. I was simply to remain behind with the dishonoured name. I alone. For me it was good enough to be called Borkman.

MISS RENTHEIM. I've given up any idea of that now.

MRS. BORKMAN. In any case it wouldn't get you anywhere. For what would then become of his mission! No, thank you. Erhard doesn't need you any longer now. As far as you are concerned, he might as well be dead! And you to him.

MISS RENTHEIM [*bursting out*]. You can say that, Gunhild!

MRS. BORKMAN. He has promised me that. He has solemnly sworn it to me. Now you know.

MISS RENTHEIM [*firmly, decisively*]. We'll see. Now I shall stay here.

7. *The specific reference to 'Danse macabre' is not in the draft (p. 176, l. 29–p. 177, l. 10):*

MRS. BORKMAN [*threateningly, towards her sister*]. You want to part him from me!

MISS RENTHEIM. If only I could, Gunhild!

ERHARD [*twisting as though in pain*]. Oh, I can't stand this any longer. [*Seizes his hat.*] Mother, let me go!

MRS. BORKMAN. Leave your mother! Is that what you want?

8. *The set for Act II, certain details of the personal appearance of the characters, and other elements are different in the draft; furthermore, Borkman's references to mining and his miner's past are of later incorporation:*

25.7.96
16.9.96

ACT TWO

What was formerly the great hall of the Borkman residence. The walls are covered with tapestries, portraying hunting scenes, gods, shepherds and shepherdesses, all in faded colours. On the left, folding doors; forward of that a piano. In the left-hand corner of the rear wall, a tapestry-covered door without surround. In the middle of the wall, right, a desk with books and papers. Forward of this, on the same side, a sofa with tables and chairs. The furniture is restricted to a severely Empire style. From the ceiling hangs a lighted chandelier.

JENS BORKMAN *stands by the piano in front of a music stand, playing the violin.* FRIDA FOLDAL *sits at the instrument and accompanies him.*

BORKMAN *is of medium height, slim, in his sixties. Distinguished appearance, with a firmly cut profile. White hair and smooth-shaven. He is formally dressed in a black suit and a white cravat.* FRIDA FOLDAL *is a seventeen-year-old, pretty, pale girl, with a somewhat tired and strained expression. Inexpensive dark dress.*

They play the final bars of a piece by Beethoven.

BORKMAN [*lowers his violin and remains standing by the music stand*]. That went passably well this evening. You are beginning to get somewhere, Miss Foldal.

FRIDA. Oh, I'm afraid I've had so little practice so far. I am not skilled enough.

BORKMAN. You have the musical fire in you. And to have fire in the mind, that is the decisive thing. Decisive in all walks of life. [*He thumbs through the music.*] Let me see . . . What shall we choose now . . .

FRIDA [*looks at her watch*]. Excuse me, Mr. Borkman . . . but I'm afraid I must go now . . .

BORKMAN. Are you going already?

FRIDA [*gets up*]. Yes, I really must. I have an engagement to play somewhere else this evening.

BORKMAN. Are you to play for dancing there?

FRIDA. Yes, they want to dance after dinner.

BORKMAN [*placing his violin and bow on the piano*]. Do you like playing for dancing? In these private circles?

FRIDA. Yes, when I can get an engagement. I manage to earn a little money that way.

9. *In the draft, Foldal has 'seven' children left at home after Frida has gone, not 'five' (p. 183, l. 15).*

10. *Foldal's offer to read an Act or two of his tragedy to Borkman was a later addition (p. 185, ll. 3–4—and see also 2 A 2 above).*

11. *Erhart is reported in the draft to have been brought up by his aunt 'from the age of ten or eleven', which was changed in the final version to 'from the age of six or seven' (p. 189, l. 16).*

12. *A revision made on the MS. which would have given more information about Foldal's past life was in the event not taken up into the fair copy (p. 190, ll. 5–7):*

BORKMAN. Yes, I do. That's what's stopped you from ever getting on. ⟨*Inserted later*: You wanted to be a poet, so you broke off your studies.⟩ If only you would give up all this business, I could still get you on your feet again, help you to get ahead.

13. *The timing of the events following Borkman's betrayal of Ella is more precisely defined in the draft (p. 196, ll. 11–12):*

MISS RENTHEIM. And that was ten years after you had betrayed me . . . and married Gunhild!

14. *Borkman's arguments at the beginning of Act III justifying his past actions lack in the draft certain of the elements they have in the final version (p. 207, l. 7–p. 208, l. 4):*

BORKMAN. But what they don't know is *why* I did it. Why I *had* to do it. And that is what I want to explain to you.

MRS. BORKMAN. Reasons do not acquit.

BORKMAN. In your own eyes they can.

MRS. BORKMAN. Oh, let's leave this! I've brooded enough on this business.

BORKMAN. So have I. Six years in the cell gave me time for that. And the eight years I've spent in that room upstairs have given me even more. I have conducted a re-trial of the whole case—in my own mind. I have turned every one of my actions inside out and upside down. And the verdict I have reached is this: the only person I have committed any offence against—is myself.

MRS. BORKMAN. Not against me? Not against your son?

BORKMAN. I include you and him in it when I say 'myself'.

MRS. BORKMAN. And what about the hundreds of others—all those people you are supposed to have ruined?

BORKMAN. I had the power. These others didn't concern me.

MRS. BORKMAN. There is something in that.

BORKMAN. Do you think if the others had had the power, they wouldn't have acted exactly as I did?

MRS. BORKMAN. They wouldn't—not most of them.

15. *The precise account, by years, of Borkman's imprisonment in the final version in Act IV was not originally part of the draft (p. 223, l. 30–p. 224, l. 3):*

BORKMAN. It's about time I got a bit of fresh air and exercise again.

FOLDAL. Yes, yes, yes . . .

BORKMAN. But tell me, what do you want me for?

16. *The emphasis given to Foldal's learning of Frida and Ehrhart's departure that very night is lacking in the draft (p. 225, ll. 25–33):*

BORKMAN [*chuckling inwardly*]. Of course, of course.

FOLDAL. Such a nice, warm, loving letter it is, too—let me tell you. Not a trace of contempt for her father. And how refined of her to say goodbye in writing. [*Laughs.*] But of course she won't get away with that!

17. *Following Foldal's departure in Act IV, the draft originally read as follows (cf. p. 227, l. 27–p. 233, l. 27):*

BORKMAN [*stands silently for a moment staring vacantly*]. Goodbye, Vilhelm! It's not the first time in your life you have been run over, my friend.

ELLA RENTHEIM. Please come inside, John!

BORKMAN. It's no use trying that. Haven't I told you . . .

ELLA RENTHEIM. I beg and implore you.

BORKMAN [*in terror, hurries down to the courtyard*]. Never under a roof any more. If I went up to that room now . . . the walls and the ceiling would shrink and crush me . . . crush me like a fly . . .

ELLA RENTHEIM [*goes down to him*]. But where will you go?

BORKMAN. I will go on, and on, and on. Will you go with me, Ella?

ELLA RENTHEIM. I? Now?

BORKMAN. Yes, yes. At once!

ELLA RENTHEIM. But how far?

BORKMAN. As far as I can.

ELLA RENTHEIM. Oh, think what you're doing. A wet winter night like this.

BORKMAN. Aha! The lady is worried about her health, eh? Ah yes . . . it's not altogether robust, is it?

ELLA RENTHEIM. It's your health I'm worried about.

BORKMAN. Ha! ha! A dead man's health! Really you make me laugh, Ella.

[*He walks on.*]

ELLA RENTHEIM [*goes after him*]. What's that you say?

BORKMAN [*walking on*]. A dead man, I say.

ELLA RENTHEIM. I'm going with you, John.

BORKMAN. Yes, we two belong together.

[*They have arrived in among the trees, left. In time they are lost to sight. The house and the courtyard disappear. The landscape slowly changes.*]

ELLA RENTHEIM'S VOICE [*is heard within the forest*]. Where are we going, John?

BORKMAN'S VOICE [*further away*]. Up the winding path.

ELLA RENTHEIM [*still concealed*]. But I can't keep going any more!

BORKMAN [*can be heard nearer*]. Come! Come! We'll soon be at the look-out place.

[*They have arrived at a small clearing in the forest. The mountain side rises steeply above them. To the left, the landscape stretches into the distance, with fjords and distant massed peaks. In the clearing is a dead pine tree with a bench under it. The snow lies deep on the clearing.*

BORKMAN, *followed by* ELLA RENTHEIM, *wades with difficulty through the snow.*]

BORKMAN [*stops by the precipice, left*]. Come here, Ella! I want to show you something.

ELLA RENTHEIM [*by him*]. What do you want to show me, John?

BORKMAN. See how distant the land lies?

ELLA RENTHEIM. Yes, I know it well.

BORKMAN. Can you see the smoke from the steamships out on the fjord?

ELLA RENTHEIM. No.

BORKMAN. I can. They come and they go. They bring with them movement and light. They create well-being in many thousands of homes. That was what I dreamed of achieving.

ELLA RENTHEIM [*softly*]. And it remained a dream.

BORKMAN. Yes. It remained a dream. . . . And listen! The factories at work! It's the night shift. The wheels spinning, the rollers turning . . . round and round. Can you hear it, Ella?

ELLA RENTHEIM. No.

BORKMAN. I can. But all these are merely the outworks to the kingdom, you know!

ELLA RENTHEIM. What kingdom . . . ?

BORKMAN. *My* kingdom. The kingdom I was about to take possession of when . . . when I died.

ELLA RENTHEIM [*softly, shaken*]. Oh, John, John!

BORKMAN. And now it lies there—defenceless, leaderless, exposed to thieving and attack. Ella, you see those distant mountains there—ranging, soaring, towering. That is my vast, my infinite, my inexhaustible kingdom.

ELLA RENTHEIM. But it's an icy blast that blows from that kingdom, John.

BORKMAN. It's a fresh blast to me. Like a greeting from loyal subject spirits. They are the captive millions, the veins of metal reaching out their twisting, sinuous, beckoning arms to me. You want to be freed. And I cannot free you. My son betrayed me. Destroyed all my strength. [*With outstretched arms.*] But let me whisper this to you, here in the stillness of the night. I love you: you who lie in a trance of death in the darkness and the deep. I love you: your life-endowed treasures . . . with all your bright retinue of power and glory.

ELLA RENTHEIM [*in quiet agitation*]. Yes, your love is down there, John. There where it has always been. But up here, in the light of day, there throbbed a warm and living human heart. Beating for you. You broke that heart. Worse . . . oh, ten times worse! You sold it for . . .

BORKMAN [*starts*]. For the kingdom . . . and the power . . . and the glory . . . you mean!

ELLA RENTHEIM. That is what I do mean. I have said once before tonight. You murdered love in the woman who loved you. And whom you loved in return. In so far as you ever could love. [*With uplifted arm.*] I therefore prophesy this, John Gabriel Borkman: you will never collect the price you demanded for this murder. You will never enter into your cold dark kingdom.

BORKMAN [*staggers to the bench and sits down heavily*]. I fear your prophecy is probably right, Ella.

ELLA RENTHEIM [*goes over to him*]. You must not *fear* it, John. It would be the best thing for you.

BORKMAN [*with a cry*]. Ah!

ELLA RENTHEIM. What was it?

BORKMAN [*weakly, sinks back on the bench*]. A hand of ice clutched at my heart.

ELLA RENTHEIM. John!

BORKMAN [*mumbling*]. No. It was a hand of iron.

[*He sinks down on the bench.*]

ELLA RENTHEIM [*tears off her kerchief and covers him with it*]. Lie there. I'll fetch help. [*She goes a few steps to the right, stops and goes back and feels his face. Speaks softly but firmly.*] No. Best so. Best so.

[*She spreads the kerchief more closely about him, and sits down in the snow in front of the bench.* MRS. BORKMAN, *wrapped in an overcoat, enters from the right. In front of her walks the* MAID *carrying a lighted lantern.*]

MAID. Yes, yes, ma'am. Here are footprints.

MRS. BORKMAN. There they are.

ELLA RENTHEIM [*rises*]. Are you looking for us?

MRS. BORKMAN. Yes, what else could I do.

ELLA RENTHEIM [*points*]. There he is, Gunhild.

MRS. BORKMAN. Asleep!

ELLA RENTHEIM. A long sleep, I fear.

MRS. BORKMAN. Ella! [*To the* MAID.] Fetch help. Men and horses.

[*The* MAID *goes out, right.*]

MRS. BORKMAN [*behind the bench*]. The night air has killed him.

ELLA RENTHEIM. So it seems. Don't you want to see him?

MRS. BORKMAN. No, no, no. He couldn't live in the fresh air.

ELLA RENTHEIM [*nods slowly*]. It seems so. The cold has killed him.

MRS. BORKMAN. Ella . . . the cold had killed him long ago.

ELLA RENTHEIM. Us, as well.

MRS. BORKMAN. You are right.

ELLA RENTHEIM. We are three dead people . . . we three here.

MRS. BORKMAN. We are. So we two can surely now join hands, Ella.

ELLA RENTHEIM [*softly*]. Over the third. Yes.

[MRS. BORKMAN, *behind the bench, and* ELLA RENTHEIM, *in front of it, take each other's hands.*]

26.8.96.

18.10.96.

C. FAIR COPY

The fair copy consists of 56 numbered folded sheets, quarto, and is now in the Royal Library, Copenhagen (Collin Manuscript Collection, no. 262 IV 4to).

3. SOME PRONOUNCEMENTS OF THE AUTHOR

I.

Bergmanden

Bergvæg, brist med drøn og brag
for mit tunge hammerslag!
Nedad må jeg vejen bryde,
til jeg hører malmen lyde.

Dybt i fjeldets øde nat
vinker mig den rige skat,—
diamant og ædelstene
mellem guldets røde grene.

Og i dybet er der fred,—
fred og ørk fra evighed;—
bryd mig vejen, tunge hammer,
til det dulgtes hjertekammer!

Engang sad som gut jeg glad
under himlens stjernerad,
trådte vårens blomsterveje,
havde barnefred i eje.

Men jeg glemte dagens pragt
i den midnatsmørke schakt,
glemte liens sus og sange
i min grubes tempelgange.

Dengang først jeg steg herind,
tænkte jeg med skyldfrit sind:
dybets ånder skal mig råde
livets endeløse gåde.—

End har ingen ånd mig lært,
hvad mig tykkedes så sært;
end er ingen stråle runden,
som kan lyse op fra grunden.

Har jeg fejlet? Fører ej
frem til klarhed denne vej?
Lyset blinder jo mit øje,
hvis jeg søger i det høje.

Nej, i dybet må jeg ned;
der er fred fra evighed.
Bryd mig vejen, tunge hammer,
til det dulgtes hjertekammer!—

Hammerslag på hammerslag
indtil livets sidste dag.
Ingen morgenstråle skinner;
ingen håbets sol oprinder.

Rockface, break with boom and roar before my heavy hammer-stroke! I must open up the way below till I hear the ore resound.

Deep in the mountain's desolate night, the rich treasure beckons to me—diamond and precious stone in among the red veins of gold.

And in the depths there is peace—peace and solitude from eternity—break open the way for me, heavy hammer, to the heart chambers of the hidden!

Once as a boy I sat happy beneath the firmament of stars, trod the flower path of Spring, possessed of childhood's peace.

But I forgot the glory of day in that dark as midnight shaft, forgot the sounds and songs of the hillside in the cloisters of my mine.

When I first descended here, I thought with innocent mind: the spirits of the deep will reveal the endless mysteries of life.

Still no spirit has taught me what I deemed so special; still no ray has emerged which can shed light from the depths.

Have I erred? Does this way not lead to clarity? The light blinds my eye if I seek it in the heights.

No, I must down into the depths; there is peace from eternity. Break open the way for me, heavy hammer, to the heart chambers of the hidden!

Hammerblow on hammerblow until life's final day. No ray of morning shines; no sun of hope rises.

Cf. the letter which Edvard Grieg, after reading the play, sent on 27 Dec. 1896 from Austria to Frants Beyer: 'And what about Borkman! It is receiving high praise in the papers here. He knew what he was doing, the Old Man, when he took up the poem of his youth about *The Miner*. That is just the thing for him to dig into.' (*Breve fra Edvard Grieg til Frants Beyer 1872–1907*, Kristiania, 1923, p. 158.)

2. '. . . The old married clerk. In his youth he once wrote a play, which was produced once. Is perpetually polishing it and lives in the illusion he will one day get it published and make his mark. However, he takes no other measures in this respect. Nevertheless counts himself among the country's authors. His wife and children believe blindly in "the play". (Perhaps he is a tutor, not a clerk?)' (*Extract from Ibsen's preliminary notes and jottings to* The Lady from the Sea; *cf.* The Oxford Ibsen, *vol. vii, p. 449*.)

3. I answered your telegram yesterday; and today I have received your letter. And in respect of both these communications I wish to say the following: I am afraid I am not wealthy enough to be able to continue to use Herr Fischer as publisher—which is more or less equivalent to letting him have my books free. With Herr Fischer I have in fact had to pay the greater part of the translator's fees, in that I have had to make over to the translator one-half of the total performing royalties, whilst Herr Fischer himself has paid only a mere bagatelle for the work of translation. My own author fees last time were 1,000 Mark; and in a letter which I received at the same time as your telegram he very generously offers me a whole 200 Mark more! Now, when the work is protected by the Bern Convention! In your telegram the offer is 3,000 Mark; but that is described as the greatest sacrifice—and this is something I have no wish to inflict on Herr Fischer. For comparison let me please inform you what kind of fee Herr Albert Langen in Munich finds himself in a position to offer without it ever occurring to him to speak in terms of a sacrifice. Herr Langen will pay me 5,000 Mark as an author's fee; and the performing royalties will come exclusively to me, since the costs of translation have already been covered by Herr Langen.—After this, I hope you will think it sensible that I cannot in future take upon myself the pecuniary sacrifice of retaining Herr Fischer as publisher.—For further comparison with Herr Fischer's offer may I inform you that my English publisher, Mr. W. Heinemann of London, has paid me the same fee for my two previous plays as Herr Langen is paying now; and now that I am protected by the Convention, he will pay me even more. (*Letter to Julius Elias, 1 Nov. 1896*.)

4. Emanuel Hansen in St. Petersburg, whom perhaps you know, will take over the Russian translation of my new play; may I therefore request that the proofs be sent to him as they become available. He gives his address in St. Peterburg as follows: Ismailofski polk 7 Rota H.18. qu. 2.' (*Letter to August Larsen, 11 Nov. 1896*.)

5. Your kind enquiry I answered yesterday by telegram; so I hope that

matter is now settled.—In the interests of the foreign editions, may I plead that the book should not be published in Copenhagen before 15 December, even if it might be ready a few days earlier. On the other hand, Professor P. Hansen can be allowed to see the play beforehand—on promise of complete confidentiality—something which is of course desirable when considering the movable scene sets. On publication, may I ask for copies of the book to be sent in my name to the head of the Royal Theatre, George Brandes, Mrs. Thoresen, Miss Johanne Krebs, as well as to Miss Bergsøe and Mrs. Blicher Clausen (with tickets enclosed), and finally to your nephew, Herr Karl Larsen, whom I have to thank for so many splendid books. I would also have liked a copy to go to Edvard Brandes, but he is in Paris and I don't know his address there. And then there are the two previously arranged copies to me, which do not need to be bound. (*Letter to August Larsen, 29 Nov. 1896.*)

6. Thank you for your letter!—What Herr Hennings reports in connection with his conversation with me here is rubbish. I told him explicitly, in Schrøder's presence, that there was *no* main role for Mrs. Hennings in my new play; there might however be a minor role. Actually I was thinking of Frida. For Ella I would propose Mrs. Oda Nielsen. Anybody who can play Rita must also be able to play Ella. And she can credibly play twin-sister to Mrs. Eckardt, who of course must play Gunhild.

Your scene painter is very welcome to come and see me, and I shall be at his service in any way I can. There is at the theatre here a very able scene painter, and he will be at Herr Peterson's disposal during his visit here. (*Letter, from Christiania, to Peter Hansen, 17 Dec. 1896.*)

7. I hereby confirm that I have received from August Lindberg the sum of 1,000 kroner as a fee in respect of my play *John Gabriel Borkman*, whereby Herr Lindberg acquires the sole rights for two years to perform the above-mentioned play in the provincial towns of Norway. (*Letter to August Lindberg, 28 Dec. 1896.*)

8. As I remarked in my telegram, I felt I had to conclude from your total silence that the Bergen Theatre did not regard itself as being in a position to produce my new play—an assumption which was all the more justified since the play presents quite unusually difficult problems both in respect of casting and of scenery and stage machinery.—Now there is nothing else for you to do but make contact with Herr Lindberg, who is at present living here, and see if you cannot arrive at some amicable arrangement with him. I am sure this will not be difficult since he for his part requires your premises to be able to perform the play in Bergen. I shall also do what I can, and I hope we can arrange things satisfactorily in the end. (*Letter from Christiania to Olaf Hansson in Bergen, 2 Jan. 1897.*)

9. I enclose herewith an order for 4,400 kroner, and I hope that in the course of the next few days a similar order for 3,600 kroner will arrive from W. Heinemann, London. These two sums, totalling 8,000 kroner, I would like

you to invest well, securely and advantageously, and I rely on your kind advice in this matter. I wrote recently to Herr Hegel about similarly investing the author royalties from the two editions of the book, and I don't want to bother him again; this is why I turn to you in the hope that you will be able to help me in this matter.—The quite extraordinarily handsome format of my new book has given me particular pleasure, and I want to thank you for this as well as for the many copies you have sent me. (*Letter to August Larsen, 10 Jan. 1897.*)

10. Nothing would be nicer for me now than to be able to come to Berlin and be present at the performance of my new play there. But that I fear is altogether impossible. Every day letters and telegrams come streaming in to me which have to be answered immediately. At this present time, therefore, I cannot change my place of residence, particularly since the performance of the play is very soon, and my attendance at the rehearsals is absolutely necessary. I find these matters extremely painful and inconvenient; but, alas, I cannot avoid them. How very different it would be if only I could come and join my friends in Berlin! (*Letter from Christiania to Julius Elias, 16 Jan. 1897.*)

11. 'It is much easier,' he said, 'to write a piece like *Brand* or *Peer Gynt,* in which you can bring in a little of everything, than to carry through a severely logical (*konsekvent*) scheme, like that of *John Gabriel Borkman,* for example. (*In conversation with William Archer; see* Monthly Review, *June 1906, pp. 17–18.*)

12. The main thing is that Mrs. Borkman loves her husband. Initially she was not a hard and evil woman, but a loving wife who had become hard and evil from the disappointments she had suffered. She was disappointed by her husband first in love, then in respect of his genius. It is on this above all that the actress must lay emphasis. If Mrs. Borkman had not loved her husband, she would have forgiven him long ago. Now she waits—in spite of her double disappointment, whose sacrifice she has been—for the sick wolf whose steps she hears every day. Just as he waits for 'the world', so *she* waits for *him.* This emerges clearly from the dialogue; and it is this side of Mrs. Borkman's character that the person interpreting her must above all emphasize. (*An interview with a correspondent of* Kjøbenhavns Aftenblad, *reported in the second, revised, German edition of Henrik Jæger,* Henrik Ibsen, *Dresden and Leipzig, 1897, pp. 277–91.*)

4. CONTEMPORARY RECEPTION

The play was published in book form, simultaneously in Copenhagen, Oslo, and Stockholm, on 15 Dec. 1896 in a first edition of 12,000 copies. A second edition of 3,000 copies was published the same day. Almost immediately there were published translations in English (by William Archer, on 6 Jan. 1897), in German (by Ibsen's son, Sigurd), in French (by Count Prozor, in *Revue de Paris*), and in Russian.

On publication, the play was immediately and widely reviewed both in the

Scandinavian and in the wider European press, by many of the leading critics of the day: in Norway, by Carl Nærup (in *Verdens Gang*, no. 314, 21 Dec. 1896), Nils Vogt (in *Morgenbladet*, no. 787, Dec. 1896), Hans Aanrud (in *Norske Intelligenssedler*, no. 311, 16 Dec. 1896), Christopher Brinchmann (in *Dagbladet*, no. 372, 1896), Vetle Visle (in *Dagbladet*, no. 173, 1897), and Kristofer Randers (in *Aftenposten*, no. 895, 20 Dec. 1896); in Denmark by Georg Brandes, (in *Politiken*, no. 357A, 1896—and also in Christiania's *Verdens Gang*, 19 Dec. 1896), Valdemar Vedel (in *Tilskueren*, 1897, pp. 166–72), and Vilhelm Andersen (in *Illustreret Tidende*, no. 19, 1897, pp. 305 ff.); and in Sweden by Johan Mortensen (in *Nordisk revy*, 1896, ii, pp. 925–33, reprinted in his *Likt och olikt*, Stockholm, 1908, pp. 299–315). For fuller details of these and other items, including leading German and French reviews, see *Samlede Værker*, ix, Copenhagen, 1900, pp. xii–xvii.

On the whole, the tenor of the reviews was respectful, reverential even, rather than wholeheartedly enthusiastic. Carl Nærup's piece in *Verdens Gang* is not untypical:

'I know of no event more proud, more rich, more festive in the hectic, blindly urgent and chaotically confused cultural life of the day than the assured and as it were predetermined appearance of Ibsen's plays. How beneficial, how exhilarating it is to see a man who—proof against the turmoil and cries of the day, independent of the shifts and currents, the fashions and the modes of the moment, and unconcerned by the entire confusion of mutually hostile critics—goes his own way and hammers out into immortal works of art those thoughts and feelings he carries within himself. Everything he has ever written revolves about this one thing: the growth and the development of personality, the never-ceasing battle between the conflicting forces within the Self, from which character is born. No writer in the world has depicted that conflict so insistently, so profoundly and powerfully as he has. It rushes like a breath of youth through Ibsen's new drama.'

In England, the first circumstantial news of the new play began to reach literary and theatrical circles in London in December 1896, mainly (one imagines) through the agency of William Archer, Elizabeth Robins, Henry James, and (possibly) Edmund Gosse. The 'copyright' copies of the play in Norwegian had been published in England on 12 December by Heinemann; the usual 'performance', again for copyright purposes, had taken place at the Avenue Theatre on 14 December. On 19 December, a very full account and assessment of the Norwegian edition, including a detailed report of the plot of the play, appeared in the *Saturday Review*, lxxxii, pp. 654–5:

'*John Gabriel Borkman* is every whit as powerful a piece of composition as any one of its predecessors. . . . Its relations are with an earlier section of

Ibsen's work, that which began with *The Pillars of Society* and seemed to close with *Hedda Gabler*. With the former play, indeed, *John Gabriel Borkman* has a close analogy. It is a far more coherent and concentrated example of dramatic construction, and aims at a higher psychology; it is coloured by that symbolism which has become part of the bones and marrow of Ibsen.'

Henry James also found occasion to express first his private and then his public enthusiasm for the play, which he had been able to read, in part, in a French version published in the *Revue de Paris*, and also seemingly in proof form in English. As early as 18 December 1896 James wrote privately to Elizabeth Robins:

'I am coming to the Avenue tonight and hoping to see you once or twice in the entractes and even, if you can, to drive home with you—or, rather, to *drive* you home; and this is a word of warning to make my application at the Stage door more convenient to you. It is above all an overflow of my exaltation over the 1st 2 Acts of "John-Gabriel" which I have just read in the French of the *Revue de Paris*: an exaltation prepared and confirmed by Mrs. Green's telling me last night of your blessed possession of the play and preparedness to produce it. It is magnificent and Ella Rendheim [*sic*] for you from top to toe and floor to ceiling. She is a part to do *everything* with, a wondrous chance. DO *ask Mrs. Crowe to do Mrs. Borkman*. It seems to me she's for *her*, too. Ah, who will "do" J.- Gabriel? He's immense. What an old boy is our Northern Henry!—he is too delightful—an old darling!' (Elizabeth Robins, *Theatre and Friendship*, London, 1932, pp. 186–7.)

To his Notebooks, three days later, James confided:

'I realize—none too soon—that the *scenic* method is my absolute, my imperative, my only salvation. The *march of an action* is the thing for me to, more and more, attach myself to: it is the only thing that really, for *me*, at least, will *produire* L'ŒUVRE, and L'ŒUVRE is, before God, what I'm going in for. Well, the scenic scheme is the only one that *I* can trust, with my tendencies, to stick to the march of an action. How reading Ibsen's splendid *John Gabriel* a day or two ago (in proof) brought that, FINALLY AND FOREVER, home to me!' (*The Notebooks of Henry James*, ed. F. O. Matthiessen and Kenneth B. Murdoch, N.Y., 1947, p. 263.)

And he followed this up in a report to *Harper's Weekly* on the London theatrical scene, where he expressed the hope that the new play would probably be dealt with more expeditiously by the London managements than *Little Eyolf* which had had to wait two years before reaching the stage:

'It is true that we have at present the promise of all proper quickness in the case of *John Gabriel Borkman*, the four-act piece which embodies the very last biennial revolution—a series unfailing in its regularity and as punctual to a day as the mill of fate—of the wonderful old man of Christiania. Mr. William Archer has just translated it, Mr. Heinemann is about to publish it, and it is shortly to be produced by Miss Robins, who, in England, has rendered Ibsen all the pious service of a priestess of the altar. I have read the play with the sense of a great warming of the critical heart, and I emphasize the prospect because I profess no vagueness as to the fact that it belongs to that very small group of impressions theatrical which—as things appear mainly to be going—denote a calculable comfort.' ('London', in *Harper's Weekly*, xlv, no. 2092, 23 Jan. 1897, pp. 134–5.)

When the Archer translation eventually became available on 6 Jan. 1897— the date of Henry James's anticipatory piece in *Harper's Weekly* being presumably the consequence of transatlantic delays—it was accorded a predictable measure of attention by the London daily and periodical press, including a review by Shaw, 'Ibsen's new play', in *Academy*, li, 1289, 16 Jan. 1897, pp. 67–8, along with unsigned pieces in the *Athenæum*, no. 3612, 1897, p. 519, in *The Speaker*, Jan. 1897, in *The Humanitarian*, x, Feb. 1897, pp. 144–50, and elsewhere.

In America, one of the first and certainly the most influential reviews to appear was that by Henry James, again in *Harper's Weekly* (xlv, no. 2094, 6 Feb. 1897, pp. 78ff.). In it, James confesses that he finds Ibsen 'one of the peculiar pleasures of the day, one of the current strong sensations'. Ibsen's characters he calls 'highly animated abstractions, with the extraordinary, the brilliant property of becoming when represented at once more abstract and more living. . . . The author nevertheless arrives at the dramatist's great goal— he arrives for all his meagreness at intensity. The meagreness, which is after all but an unconscious, an admirable economy, never interferes with that: it plays straight into the hands of his rare mastery of form.'

Other items which appeared in America, then and later, included: Charlotte Porter, 'Ibsen's New Play: *John Gabriel Borkman*', in *Poet Lore*, ix, 1897, pp. 302–6; W. M. Payne, '*John Gabriel Borkman*', in *The Dial*, xxii, 1897, pp. 37–41; W. H. Carpenter, '*John Gabriel Borkman*', in *Bookman*, v, 1897, pp. 157–60; Johannes Reimers, 'Henrik Ibsen's *John Gabriel Borkman*' in *Overland Monthly* (San Francisco), xxx, 1897, pp. 463–5; V. Thompson, '*John Gabriel Borkman*', *National Magazine* (Boston), viii, 1898, p. 120; and C. Porter and H. Clarke, 'Oedipus, Lear and Borkman', in *Poet Lore*, xi, 1899, pp. 116 ff.

Shaw's further piece in *Saturday Review* at the end of January 1897—'The New Ibsen Play', lxxxiii, 30 Jan. 1897, pp. 114–15—was explicitly not a review, but a plea for an early London production: 'The appearance some weeks ago in these columns of a review of the original Norwegian edition of Ibsen's new play, *John Gabriel Borkman*, relieves me from repeating here what I have said elsewhere concerning Mr. William Archer's English version. In fact, the time for reviewing it has gone by: all who care about Ibsen have by this time pounced on the new volume, and ascertained for themselves what it is like. The only point worth discussing now is the play's chances of performance.' His melancholy conclusion, after several pages of head-shaking at the capacity of English stupidity to stave off foreign genius, was that: 'Altogether, the prospects of a speedy performance of *John Gabriel Borkman* are not too promising.' Despite his misgivings, however, the play was performed on 3 May of that year at the Strand Theatre.

Well before the play reached the London stage, however, there had been the usual competitive European rush to be the first to get the new play on the boards; and, on this occasion, the smaller companies and the remoter theatres won easily. (The following brief account collates information to be found in: *Samlede Værker*, ix, Copenhagen, 1900, pp. xv–xvii; *Samlede Verker*, Hundreårsutgave, xii, Oslo, 1963, pp. 32–6; Emil Reich, *Henrik Ibsens Dramen*, 14th ed., Berlin, 1925, pp. 429–30; N. Å. Nilsson, *Ibsen in Russland*, Stockholm, 1958, pp. 97f.)

Discounting the 'performance' on 14 December at the Avenue Theatre, London, the world première seems clearly to have been achieved (several times over, apparently) in Finland: in Helsinki, on 10 January 1897, it is claimed that there were performances of the play at both the Swedish and the Finnish theatres; and another performance, 'at about the same time', in the provincial town of Åbo (Turku). Frankfurt am Main followed on 16 Jan., with a production which won general acclaim from both critics and public. In Copenhagen, on 17 Jan., a private performance was given, for members only, by the Copenhagen Workers Independent Theatre. The Norwegian première took place in the provincial town of Drammen, performed by August Lindberg's (part-Swedish and part-Norwegian) company which had acquired the performing rights of the play outside Christiania; for this occasion, the theatre was reported 'sold out', helped in part by the fact that a special train was run from Christiania for enthusiasts who wished to see this first performance of the new Ibsen play. In the course of the following week this same company gave further performances in Larvik, Skien (Ibsen's birthplace), Tønsberg, Moss, Fredrikstad, and Fredrikshald. In Bergen, after negotiation with Lindberg and an appeal to Ibsen himself, and final arbitration by Christian Michelsen (then chairman of the theatre, later Prime Minister), the play was performed by the resident company on 19 February.

The capital city, Christiania—where the play had been under rehearsal since 7 Jan., with Ibsen sometimes in attendance—first saw the play on 25 Jan. Ibsen was there in person on the first night, and was warmly applauded. (See Sigurd Bødtker, *Kristiania-premièrer gjennem 30 aar* (Kristiania, 1923), vol. 1, pp. 13–17.) The same evening also marked the first performance in Stockholm, at the Vasa Theatre, in a translation by Gustav af Geijerstam. The Deutsches Theater in Berlin followed on 29 Jan.; and before the month was out, on 31 Jan., it had also been performed at Copenhagen's Royal Theatre; there, despite

Ibsen's express advice to the contrary (see above, p. 342), the part of Ella Rentheim was in fact taken by Mrs. Hennings. A performance of the play, sometime in January, is also reported to have taken place in Rotterdam. Thus, within about six weeks of the play's publication, it had been played in the capital cities of Denmark, Norway, Sweden, Finland, and Germany, and altogether in something like fifteen different towns in six different countries.

One of the attendant features of the productions in these weeks was the compulsion felt by certain theatre managements to point up what they supposed might be an ulterior meaning in the play by giving a distinctive and recognizable kind of make-up to Borkman. The impulse for this doubtless came from an allegation, which gained currency not only in the Scandinavian but also in the German and English press, that a violent quarrel had broken out between Ibsen and Bjørnson 'because the latter has seen in the relationship between Borkman and Hinkel an allusion to his own conflict with the late Prime Minister Richter, and that he considers these allusions to be so malicious that he intends to startle the world with a vehement attack on Ibsen' (see the Copenhagen newspaper *Politiken*, 28 Jan. 1897). To this rumour, Ibsen himself issued a formal statement—published in the same issue of *Politiken*—that 'he firmly and solemnly denies having made allusion to Bjørnson', and that furthermore 'he declares he never makes allusion to particular persons in his plays'. For the production in Drammen, Borkman (as played by Lindberg) was reported to have been made up 'strikingly like' Johan Sverdrup (President of the Storting, 1871–84); in Berlin, he was seemingly made up in a way reminiscent of both Bjørnson and Ibsen; and in Copenhagen the likeness was more specifically to Ibsen himself.

In the course of 1897, the play was seen in a great many German provincial cities: Hamburg (Feb.), Meiningen, Breslau, Cologne (26 Mar.), Munich (27 Mar.), Bonn (9 Apr.), Nuremberg (23 Apr.), Stuttgart (3 Oct.). On 11 Mar. it was played by the German theatre in Prague; and the same month it was also played in Graz. Vienna had to wait until 31 May 1900 for its first performance. In Paris there were private performances in the house of Mme Aubernon de Nerville on 23 and 24 Mar. 1897; and the Théâtre de l'Œuvre produced it later in the year on 8 Nov. (subsequently taking it to Brussels on 5 Nov. 1898, and to Ostend in Aug. 1899). For an account of the play's reception in France, see A. Dikka Reque, *Trois auteurs dramatiques scandinaves devant la critique française 1889–1901* (Paris, 1930), pp. 187 ff.; and Francisque Sarcey, *Quarante ans de théâtre* (Paris, 1902), pp. 370 ff. In New York, the opening of the Criterion Independent Theatre on 18 Nov. 1897 was marked by a production of the play. Italy first saw it in October 1898 in Bologna, and on 11 Jan. 1899 in Rome. Moscow had to wait until 19 Nov. 1904; but when the play did somewhat belatedly arrive, its quality together with the interpretation and production it received were given warm praise from the critics, who were clearly impressed by the theatre's technical virtuosity during the closing scenes where the garden dissolves into forest and mountain.

In London, despite Shaw's misgivings in the matter, the play was in fact not greatly delayed in reaching the stage. It was produced by the New Century Theatre group at the Strand Theatre on 3 May 1897, with Elizabeth Robins as Ella Rentheim, Genevieve Ward as Gunhild Borkman, W. H. Vernon as Borkman, Martin Harvey as Erhart, Mrs. Beerbohn Tree as Mrs. Wilton, James Welch as Foldal, and Dora Barton as Frida. The casting of Genevieve Ward as Mrs. Borkman was—as Elizabeth Robins later admitted—a mistake: 'Just so "right" as they [i.e. Janet Achurch and Mrs. Patrick Campbell] were in *Little Eyolf,* just so wrong was my old friend Miss Genevieve Ward as the wife of John Gabriel Borkman in the play of that name. Miss Ward was a fine example (especially in Shakespeare parts) of the actress of the old school. She had found appreciation the round world over; but nothing would induce her to listen to Ibsen's promptings. Her ears were full of the stage directions of all the Sydney Grundys of the last fifty years. It was instructive, if infuriating, to see how her refusal to take her cue from her new author—how the need she seemed to feel to show a sense of humour and tragedy superior to Ibsen's— affected disastrously not only herself but others.' (*Ibsen and the Actress,* London, 1928, pp. 51f.) This finds corroboration in Shaw's notice of the production: 'The truth is, her tragic style, derived from Ristori, was not made for Ibsen.'

Shaw's was, not unexpectedly, the most substantial critical piece prompted by this occasion (in *Saturday Review,* lxxxiii, 8 May 1897, pp. 507–9, reprinted in *Our Theatres in the Nineties,* vol. iii, London, 1932, pp. 122 ff.). He was clearly disappointed, less by the play than by the production, finding serious deficiencies or misinterpretations in all the leading parts, and pronouncing only the playing of Mrs. Wilton and Frida successful. He was dismissively scornful of the set, which he called shabby: '. . . I beg the New Century Theatre, when the next Ibsen play is ready for mounting, to apply to me for assistance. If I have a ten-pound note, they shall have it: if not, I can at least lend them a couple of decent chairs.' He was also seriously critical of W. H. Vernon's stage manage- ment. 'On the whole,' he concluded, 'a rather disappointing performance of a play which cannot be read without forming expectations which are perhaps unreasonable, but are certainly inevitable.'

Of the wide coverage given by the London press to this performance, Michael Egan usefully reprints, in whole or in extract (in *Ibsen, the Critical Heritage,* London, 1972, pp. 366–74), the following pieces: 'H.W.M.' in the *Daily Chronicle,* 4 May; an unsigned notice (by Clement Scott) in the *Daily Telegraph,* 4 May; and unsigned notices in *Era,* 8 May, *Lloyd's Weekly News,* 8 May, and *The People,* 9 May. Reference can also usefully be made to: 'G.S.S.' in *Academy,* li, no. 1305, 8 May 1897, p. 503; an unsigned notice in *Theatre,* xxix N.S., 1 June 1897, pp. 335–7; William Archer, 'The Last Ibsen Play: *John Gabriel Borkman.* A technical study' in *Progressive Review,* ii, June 1897, pp. 242–5; Archer's piece on '*John Gabriel Borkman*' in *The Theatrical World for 1897* (London, 1898), pp. 121–3; and E. R. Russell and P. C. Standing, *Ibsen on his Merits* (London, 1897), pp. 169 ff.

Archer's translation came under attack in an article in *The Speaker* (10 July 1897), the general charge being that 'Ibsen's beautifully polished style is hastily thrown into the rough and ready "dialogue" of the English stage'. This drew a reply from Archer which was published in the next issue of the periodical. It also left a small residue in the form of an exchange of letters between Archer and Gilbert Murray, whose attention Archer had drawn to the affair (see C. Archer, *William Archer*, London, 1931, pp. 224–7).

Although the anti-Ibsenist critics found this play also gloomy, tedious, lifeless, pretentious, boring, depressing, dull and wearisome, they nevertheless on this occasion found less than usual to take offence at. One passage did, however, cause some concern: at the point where Mrs. Wilton comments that Frida will be there for Erhart 'to fall back on' when she (Mrs. Wilton) has tired of him, or he of her—'a single sentence which Ibsen purism might do well, we think, to evade, since it can only be cynically interpreted', as the otherwise strongly pro-Ibsenist piece in the *Saturday Review* of 19 Dec. 1896 put it. This sentence, it seems, was indeed cut out by the censor when the play was performed in Frankfurt on 16 Jan. 1897. Sir Edward Russell (*Ibsen on his Merits*, ed. cit., p. 175) most typically voiced the outrage some people felt: '... A lady of very light character, though not previously actually of ill life, takes away a young girl with her in eloping, and suggests that she will serve for her own lover to fall back upon when tired of her. This is terribly foul, and surely not less foolish; for what woman would say such a thing, even if we can conceive a woman feeling it? A suggestion such as this is more offensive than passages of supposed indelicacy which have been objected to in some of the other plays.'

APPENDIX III

WHEN WE DEAD AWAKEN: COMMENTARY

1. Dates of composition
2. Draft manuscripts
3. Some pronouncements of the author
4. Contemporary reception

1. DATES OF COMPOSITION

For the greater part of the last quarter of the nineteenth century, Ibsen had taken pride in having a new play ready every second year for the Christmas book market. Since 1877, the biennial rhythm had been broken only once, when his anger at the critics' reception of *Ghosts* in 1881 had provoked him into publishing *An Enemy of the People* after an interval of only one year instead of two. Thereupon the next seven plays, from *The Wild Duck* (1884) to *John Gabriel Borkman* (1896), had followed the biennial pattern. In 1897, in the earliest stages of the composition of his new play, Ibsen clearly hoped to hold to the usual interval between works; it soon became apparent, however, that on this occasion there was going to be some slippage.

On 3 June 1897 he reported to Georg Brandes: 'For the rest, I live on in solitude here [in Christiania] planning some new dramatic thing. But I cannot see clearly yet what it is going to be.' Ten days later, on 13 June 1897, he wrote to his wife (who was in Monsummaro) to say that his plans for a new play had begun to 'sprout'; he could already sense the basic mood, but so far he could only see one of the characters, but the others (he felt) would doubtless emerge. On 2 July 1897 he again wrote to Suzannah: 'I am extremely well. . . . And I have begun turning over a new play in my mind. In this connection I have extended my daily walks, and every day I walk first to Skillebæk and back—and then down into town; and I thrive splendidly on this.' Close on a year later, on 29 May 1898, he wrote to his German editor, Julius Elias, in the sad realization that on this occasion he was not going to be able to sustain his usual publication rhythm: 'I have, as you know, been occupied over the last year by so many extraordinary things that it is extremely doubtful whether I shall be able this time to get my projected play ready by the usual time; and in any case I shall not be able to deliver it in time for a German edition to be arranged for this year. . . . I had never thought of having my so-called "Memoirs" ready in the very near future.'

There had indeed been many things to interrupt him. First there had been the proposal to bring out a big collected edition of his works in German, which he mentions in the letter of 2 July 1897 to his wife (referred to above): 'I am now greatly active with correspondence about the new German edition which will fill nine thick volumes.' Shortly afterwards came the plan to publish a Norwegian collected edition. Both these undertakings caused him much work —getting hold of and re-reading his earlier works—and involved him in a considerable amount of correspondence. Celebrations to mark his 70th birthday, on 20 March 1898, brought a large number of public and private engagements, including banquets in his honour in Copenhagen and Stockholm as well as in Christiania, with many associated interviews. He also had speeches to prepare and give (see pp. 358–63).

He began turning over in his mind plans for a new and different kind of book which would, he felt, take him away from dramatic composition for perhaps a year. In the speech he made at the Christiania banquet (23 March 1898) he announced that he had been thinking of writing a book about his own life and work:

'A book that will link my life and my authorship together into an illuminating whole. Because I think I have now reached an age of sufficient maturity to be allowed to enjoy a bit of a breathing space . . . take a year's holiday. Because such a book would indeed be a holiday by comparison with the exacting and exhausting work of dramatic composition. And I have never really had a holiday since I left Norway 34 years ago. I think I might need it now.'

'But, ladies and gentlemen, you must not therefore think that I am finally intending to lay down my dramatist's pen. No, I intend to hold on to it, and keep going to the very end. In fact I still have various pieces of tomfoolery in stock which up to now I have not yet found occasion to give expression to. Only when I've got them off my back will it be time to call a halt.'

The summer of 1898 was again full of interruptions for him. The German collected edition was claiming more and more of his time, and his impatience with his German editors was beginning to show as early as April 1898 in his correspondence with them. A short letter to Rosa Fittinghoff of 7 July makes a wry reference to what he was having to endure: 'This July I have two German literary men with me daily; they have come in connection with the new German edition of my books. (One of these gentlemen is sitting here with me in my room as I write this—can't you see this by the form of this letter?)'

To another correspondent, on 26 July 1898, he wrote: 'For months now my German translator Dr. Morgenstern has been staying out at Nordstrand, busy on *Love's Comedy*, *Brand* and *Peer Gynt*. And in this connection long daily "Fragebogen" hang threateningly over my head. Moreover my English translator, Mr. William Archer, has announced his arrival one of these days.' To William Archer, in conversation, Ibsen announced that he had put aside the idea of writing an autobiography, and was now maturing the scheme of a new drama. ' "I have turned the characters out to grass," he said. "I hope they will fatten." ' (William Archer, 'Ibsen as I knew him', in *The Monthly Review*, no. 69, xxiii, 3 June 1906, p. 18.)

On 29 August 1898 an irritable letter to the German editor, requesting that a stop be put to the further despatch of any proofs of the German edition of *The Vikings at Helgeland*, 'for this would be too disturbing to what I am at present engaged on', might conceivably be seen either as an oblique reference to his new drama or to his autobiographical work. (Earlier, on 29 May 1898, he had after all written to this same correspondent that he had never thought of having his so-called 'Memoirs' ready in the very near future.) It was not until after the turn of the year, on 13 February 1899, that Ibsen could be found making positive reference to the fact of his working on a new drama. On that day he wrote to Jacob Hegel: 'I have now begun work in earnest on my new play, and I have confident hopes of having it ready by the usual time, later in the autumn.'

A folded sheet of preliminary notes and jottings (see A 1 below) is dated 20 February 1899. The title page of the main extant draft manuscript (see B 1 below) is dated 22 February 1899. And two days later, on 24 February 1899, he again reported to Hegel: 'I am working daily on my new play and hope to have the manuscript ready considerably earlier than usual so that printing can be done more leisurely than usual.'

Work on the play does not appear, however, to have reached a peak of intensity until the months of July, August, and the first half of September 1899. The draft manuscript was originally dated thus: end of Act I 31 July; beginning of Act II 2 September (presumably in error for 2 August); end of Act II 23 August; beginning of Act III 25 August; end of Act III 21 September 1899. Corroboration for this chronology is found in Ibsen's correspondence of this period. On 7 July 1899 he reported to the German critic Roman Woerner that he was much occupied, and working steadily at his new play. On 23 July he promised his publisher that he would send the manuscript of his new play 'in 2–3 months'. On 27 July he reported to another correspondent, Ludvig Bergh, that he was 'uninterruptedly occupied' on his new work. On 25 August, writing to Herr and Fru Thommessen, he excused himself from accepting an invitation on the grounds that he was in the middle of a new work and 'dare not interrupt the thread of thought'. On 3 September he declined another invitation—this time from the librarian J. B. Halvorsen—for the reason that interruptions over the previous few days had drained his strength; and he insisted that he must now begin again on his new work which he had found himself compelled to neglect for the previous week.

Fair copying, including the final revisions, must presumably have begun after the above draft of Act III was complete (21 September), for the end of Act I has a further annotation: 'Fair copied 19 October 1899'; the beginning and end of the fair copying of Act II are similarly dated 20 October and 10 November 1899 respectively; and of Act III 11 November and 21 November 1899.

On 20 November he sent off a telegram to his publishers announcing that his new play was ready and that the MS. for the printer would be sent off in two days' time. On 22 November 1899 he followed this up with a letter expressing the hope that the work could be published for Christmas; on this occasion he did not feel the need to insist on the title of the new book being kept secret. On 24 November he wrote to William Archer: 'I am pleased to inform you that the manuscript of my new three-act play went off to Gyldendal some days ago; proofs will in time be sent to you from there. The title of the play is *When We Dead Awaken*. Please be so good as to inform Mr. Heinemann.'

The setting and the printing of the new work went swiftly. On 3 December 1899 Ibsen thanked August Larsen for the 'astonishing speed' at which the printing of the new work had gone ahead. On 9 December his correspondence shows that the final set of proofs had reached him.

The play was published in Copenhagen on 19 December 1899, in an edition of 12,000 copies.

2. DRAFT MANUSCRIPTS

A number of preliminary notes, a list of characters, and other jottings have survived, along with a full working manuscript of the play in draft form; these are all now in the University Library, Oslo. The fair copy is in the Royal Library, Copenhagen.

A. PRELIMINARY NOTES AND JOTTINGS

1. *One folded sheet, quarto, dated in top right-hand corner of first side '20.2.99'; the fourth side is blank.*

(*a*) *the first side*

20.2.99

Notes and jottings

The first act takes place in summer. Elegant spa on the sea coast.
Second act at a sanatorium up in the mountains.
Third act among glaciers and precipices on the descent to the west.
He is a sculptor. Elderly. Famous. Newly married. Returning from honeymoon. Has taken her 'up on a high mountain and shown her all the glory of the world'. And thus he has won her. She is young, fair and joyful. Both are radiantly happy. Now he means to begin to enjoy life.
Then it happens that at the spa he meets 'the earlier one'. The forgotten one. She who has never forgotten. Dressed in white. Accompanied by her

nurse. Was of a wealthy family. Left her home and ran away with him—the young, poor, unknown rising artist. Became his model. Then she broke with everything and left him. Since then has been married to another man and divorced again. Then married again. He committed suicide. All this occurred abroad.

(b) *the second side*

Characters in the play

The spa doctor, a youngish, intelligent man.

The superintendent at the spa. Fussy. Goes among the visitors and carries gossip from one to the other.

The gossipy woman from the capital city. Considered to be enormously entertaining among the spa visitors. Malicious from thoughtlessness.

Many visitors to the spa with their *children*

A servant in the spa hotel

Waitresses

The mountain sportsman

⟨There is here inserted a thumbnail pen-and-ink sketch of the setting.⟩

Stubow. Rambow.

Professor Erik Stubow, famous sculptor

(c) *the third side*

Scene sequence:

Stubow and Maja

Those present and the Superintendent

Those present and the strange white-clad lady with her nurse. Into the pavilion.

Those present, the woman from the capital city and other ladies.

The ladies leave after a short scene.

The mountain sportsman comes with servant and dogs from the steamer.

The servant and the dogs off, right.

Stubow, Maja, Mountain sportsman and the Superintendent.

Mountain sportsman and Maja off, right.

The strange lady from left.

The Superintendent goes into the hotel.

The lady and Stubow alone. Conversation.

Maja comes. The lady leaves.

Stubow and Maja want to leave for the mountain sanatorium.

In this country it is only the mountains that give an echo, not the people.

B.   WORKING DRAFT

1. *A complete working draft of the play on 32 numbered folios or folded sheets, quarto, making a total of 64 leaves; the last three sides of folio*

Z1

no. 32 are blank. The first side of folio no. 1 is a title page which originally read:

Resurrection Day
Play in three acts

by
Henrik Ibsen
1899

The original title was then deleted and replaced by
'When the dead awake', *itself later amended to* 'When we dead awake.'
The third side of folio no. 1 repeated the original title: ' Resurrection Day'.

The fourth side contained a list of characters (see p. 299). Act One begins on the first side of folio no. 2.

An account of this draft version, with translations of those sections that differ significantly from the final version, is given on pp. 299–307.

In addition to the date on the title page, the Acts are dated at the beginning and end as follows:

End of Act I:		31.7.99
	Fair Copy	19.10.99
Beg. of Act II:		2.9.99 ⟨in error for 2.8.99?⟩
	Fair Copy	20.10.99
End of Act II:		23.8.99
	Fair Copy	10.11.99
Beg. of Act III:		25.8.99
	Fair Copy	11.11.99
End of Act III:		21.9.99
	Fair Copy	21.11.99

A number of other notes, drafts, and emendations were made during the work on the play, some on the draft itself and some on separate folios or on loose sheets of paper. The more significant are listed in 2 and 3 below.

2. A revised ending, corresponding closely to the final version, was contained on two folios or folded sheets, numbered 30 and 31, and one single sheet, numbered 32, quarto, and interleaved with the last three folios of B 1 above. Only one third of the first side of no. 32 is written on, and the final annotation reads: 'Finished 21.11.99'.

3. One loose sheet, octavo, containing on one side scraps of draft dialogue for Act I (see pp. 255–7), and on the other some notes relating to Acts I and II.

a) *first side*

He was a diplomat, a high Russian ⟨*altered to* Bulgarian⟩ diplomat.

I sent him mad, insane, incurably insane. Really funny whilst it was being
led up to. I used to laugh inwardly. If I had anything within.

And that was Herr v. Satow.

No, my second husband was called Satow. He was a Russian.

And where is he now.

Him I killed.

Killed!

Killed with a fine sharp knife which I took to bed with me.

⟨*Inserted:*

Don't believe you

Can well believe it⟩

Have you never had children

Yes, many children

Where are they now

I killed them.

Now you are lying Irene. ⟨*Inserted:*

All this.⟩

Killed them ⟨*inserted:* really and truly murdered them⟩ as soon as they
came into the world. ⟨*Inserted:* Long long ago⟩

One after the other.

Religious worries?

No, I've never . . .

There are strings within you which have snapped.

Doubtless that always happens when a person dies.

(*b*) *second side*

Firs[t] famous through Irene. Then he wishes to live and enjoy his youth
over again with a second person. So he re-fashions the sculpture as a group.
Irene becomes a subsidiary figure in that which made him famous.

First a single statue; then a group. Then she left.

Our life was not two people's

What was it then

Only the artist's and the model's

2nd act

Children playing on the mountain side

Professor Rubek sits on the bench and looks at the game.

Fru Maja comes looking for him. Scene between them ⟨*crossed out:* The
hunter fetches . . .⟩

Irene comes with a group of children across the mountain side.

The bear hunter comes and fetches Fru Maja.

Irene and Rubek. Big scene.

Something has got locked in for me

Taken the key

⟨*There follow three lines written with the paper turned the other way up:*⟩
  When we dead awaken
  Yes, what will we see then?
  We will see that we have never lived.

3. SOME PRONOUNCEMENTS OF THE AUTHOR

A. *Public statements on the occasion of his 70th birthday, March–May 1898*

I.   19 Mar. 1898

The scene is the Travellers' Lounge of the Grand Hotel.

It is a spring day . . . in a week in which the sun shines warm for the first time. It is about twelve o'clock in the morning.

Over by the window on the extreme left of the Travellers' Lounge, and facing the happy ebb and flow of people, sits a dignified old man, elegantly and formally dressed, with luxuriant white hair, with sharp eyes behind polished spectacles and mouth tightly compressed, staring half-dreaming in front of him. . . . It is Henrik Ibsen.

. . . We go into the Travellers' Lounge to the old poet. We bow and greet each other; and the world-famous seventy-year-old man, whose birthday it is, half rises in friendly fashion, removes his silk hat and gloves from the leather chair beside him, and we sit by the window in the spring sunshine.

He begins at once in the friendliest way to chat; and we ask him how he is, and how things have been with him recently.

'I am always well,' answers Henrik Ibsen. 'I have never been ill, never for a single day in my life. I have never consulted a doctor. I have never had a prescription. And all this despite the fact that I have often been in a fever-infected climate and exposed to disease.'

We compliment him, and proceed: 'How are things going with your next work? Have you done much work on it?'

'Oh, I have made a number of notes and jottings. By that I mean nothing yet which I want to use, but rather things which will be helpful later, stimulate thought and bring out what is right. I haven't done more than that.

'When will the new book come out?'

'It isn't very easy to say. I am now taken up with so many other things . . . these big German and Danish editions of my works.'

'The final proofs?'

'No, far from it. I don't read proofs. But I have to look through my books again to see whether any mistakes have found their way into them. I have never read my own books myself.'

'Haven't read your own books!'

'No.' He smiles. 'When I have completed a new book, I never look at it again. I immediately begin on something new.'

'What is your new book going to be about?'

It was obvious Henrik Ibsen did not like that question. But he did answer; and I feel I can say that Herr Ibsen's next book will presumably be *a commentary* [*et ræsonnerende Værk*] *on his collected works* and a biography—an account of what he has experienced and lived through. A work in which he will indicate how his dramas hang together, and how they have all been created to a distinct plan.... (*Part of an interview by Hans Tostrup, printed in* Ørebladet, *19 Mar. 1898.*)

2. *To my readers.*

When my publisher was kind enough to propose a collected edition of my literary works, chronologically ordered, I at once realized the great advantage an undertaking of this kind would offer for a better understanding of the works.

As my output progressed, so new generations have grown up over the years, and I have often had occasion to remark with regret that their familiarity with my more recent books was considerably more intimate than with the older ones. Consequently there has occurred a disjunction in the minds of these readers between the mutual interrelation among these works; and to this I attribute no small part of the strange, deficient and misleading interpretations which my more recent works have been subjected to in so many quarters.

Only by conceiving and accepting my entire output as a coherent, continuous unity will one be receptive to the impression the individual parts were intended to convey.

In brief, my appeal to the reader is that he will not put any play to one side for the time being, will not temporarily skip over anything, but will take possession of these works—by reading them and experiencing them—in the same order in which I wrote them. Kristiania, March 1898. Henrik Ibsen (*Preface to the Norwegian edition of his* Samlede Værker.)

3. Gentlemen! I haven't many words which I want to say after this homage, partly because my voice is not up to it, partly for other reasons.

But I ask one thing: Were any gentlemen present in the theatre yesterday to see a play that treated of a man who was terrified of youth?

That was a man who was in some way akin to me.

However I am not afraid of youth. I have never been afraid of youth. I knew that it would come and beat upon the door. It came, and I greet it now with joy.

All I wish to do now is express the wish that the many young and talented people in this crowd may also enjoy their jubilee.

I would so very much like to be present. I would not shut my door. I would so gladly take part in it.

I cannot say more. Sincere thanks! A thousand thanks! (*Speech to student torchlight procession in Christiania, 22 Mar. 1898.*)

4. As I struck just now on my glass for silence, everything became so quiet. Expectant. Or so it seemed to me. But if people were waiting for me to reply exhaustively to all the warm and friendly words which have been addressed to me tonight they are mistaken. For those words I can only express my most heartfelt thanks in the most general of terms. And likewise for all the homage and honour which has been shown to me here today.

Or perhaps people were expecting me to make a little speech about my books? That I could not bring myself to do. For then I would have to bring my whole life into it. And that alone would make a huge thick book in itself.

Apart from that . . . I am in fact thinking of *writing* such a book now. A book that will link my life and my authorship together into an illuminating whole. Because I think I have now reached an age of sufficient maturity to be allowed to enjoy a bit of a breathing space . . . take a year's holiday. Because such a book would indeed be a holiday by comparison with the exacting and exhausting work of dramatic composition. And I have never really had a holiday since I left Norway 34 years ago. I think I might need it now.

But, ladies and gentlemen, you must not therefore think that I am finally intending to lay down my dramatist's pen. No, I intend to hold on to it, and keep going to the very end. In fact I still have various pieces of tomfoolery in stock which up to now I have not yet found occasion to give expression to. Only when I've got them off my back will it be time to call a halt. And how easy it will be to call a halt then in contrast to the time when I was only just starting. How empty and silent all things were about one then! How one's fellow combatants stood then, scattered, isolated, without mutual support, without any inter-relatedness! Many's the time it seemed to me as though, when I was away, I had never really been there. Nor my work.

But *now*! There are people around one everywhere. Young confident forces have joined the scene. *They* have no need any longer to write for a narrow circle. *They* have a public to talk to, a whole community to direct their thoughts and feelings to. Whether they meet opposition or support . . . is much the same. It is only closed ears, rejection, which is evil. That is something I have felt.

I sincerely regret that I have made such little personal contact in this country with many of those who will continue the work. Not because I would have wanted, in the event, to exert any pressures, but because I wished to achieve a deeper understanding myself. In particular I would have used this closer relationship to remove a misconception which has in many ways been an obstacle to me—the idea that the rare experience which destiny has given me of achieving fame and a reputation in many countries represents some sheer unalloyed kind of happiness. And I have found warm and understanding hearts out there too. That above all.

But that genuine inner happiness—that is no chance discovery, no simple gift. It must be earned at a price that may often seem rather excessive. And *that* is the real thing: he who has won a home for himself out there in many countries . . . feels in his inmost self to be nowhere completely at home—even in his native land, scarcely.

Yet perhaps that may come. And I shall look to this evening as a starting point.

For *here* I glimpse something which is like a coming together. *Here* all attitudes, all divergent opinions have found themselves able to congregate round the one thing. Here I no longer have the painful feeling of being regarded as a poet belonging to one party only. Of one side or the other. A poet must have his entire people around him . . . either in support or in opposition. And then the collective ideas can progress towards greater goals and higher aims. That is my hope and my belief!

Therefore, ladies and gentlemen, I beg you to accept my most heartfelt thanks for all your kindness! (*Speech at a banquet in Christiania, 23 Mar. 1898.*)

5. Thank you. My most sincere and heartfelt thanks for this great ovation. I have over many years longed to meet the youth of Denmark again. But I never dreamed that the meeting would be so festive. Thank you, my dear young friends. (*Speech to a student torchlight procession, 31 Mar. 1898.*)

6. Professor Hansen's speech has confused me, and upset my reply. I must now improvise, and I beg your kind forbearance. Today is April 1st. That same day in the year 1864 I came to Copenhagen for the first time. That is now 34 years ago. Remember the date and the year. I travelled south, through Germany and Austria, and passed through the Alps on 9 May. Clouds hung over the high mountains like great dark curtains, and we drove in under these and through the tunnel, and suddenly found ourselves at Mira Mara where the beauty of the South—a strangely light gleam shining like white marble—suddenly manifested itself to me and left its stamp on all my later output, even though not everything in it was beauty.

This feeling of having escaped from the dark into the light, from the mists and through a tunnel into the sunlight—this feeling I had again the other day as I looked down the length of Öresund. After which I found here these loyal Danish eyes. I feel that these two journeys took on an intimate relationship, and for this I express to you my most heartfelt thanks. (*Speech at a banquet in Copenhagen, 1 April 1898. In fact, Ibsen's chronology is inaccurate in some details: he had been in Copenhagen earlier in 1852 when on a study tour following his appointment to the Bergen theatre; and in 1864, his journey through Copenhagen was several days later than the date he gives.*)

7. Ladies and Gentlemen! I want to thank you most warmly for this evening. It has been a peculiar feeling for me to be present here. I don't know that I have ever belonged to any association; and I rather believe that this is the first time ever that I have been present at a meeting of one. It is true that there is in Christiania an association which is of much the same nature as this one; but

there I am a member merely for appearance' sake and for a number of reasons never take part in its meetings. Here I find myself for the first time in such an association, and that is therefore something quite new for me. An association isn't really anything for me. And in one particular sense, it might seem that an association is one of the last things appropriate for authors; for they must go their own errant ways . . . as errant, indeed, as they could ever wish, if they are to fulfil their life's mission. (*Loud applause.*) Yet I do think that an association like this one may nevertheless in certain matters have a proper task to perform. Real cultural tasks. One of these tasks is for authors to join together to guard against threats from without, something which can often be very necessary. And then there is a second task which I consider no less important, and which I cannot refrain from emphasizing here. It is alas the case that dramatic works have to be translated; but the Scandinavian peoples—and I really cannot give up my old idea of a united Scandinavia as a cultural entity—couldn't they perhaps agree to avoid as far as possible reading each other in translation. Anything read in translation must always run the risk of being in greater or lesser degree misunderstood; for translators are unfortunately all too often somewhat lacking in understanding. I believe that if we were to read each other in the original language, we would achieve a very much more intimate and profound understanding of the content. To work for an improvement in this respect is one of the finest tasks of this association. Finally, may I be allowed to say that I always enjoy being here in Sweden. I find here an old-established culture, built on a strong tradition, stronger than in many other countries, and which goes deeper than many people think. Also I have met here so many good and trusty people. Such people I do not easily forget, once I have got to know them.

I shall always retain an unforgettable memory of this evening and of all those who have shown me the honour of coming along to join me. My heartfelt thanks. (*Speech at the banquet of the Swedish Authors Association, Stockholm, 11 Apr. 1898.*)

8. Gentlemen! To me it seems like a dream, this visit of mine here in Stockholm. And indeed it is a dream. The first figure to meet me in this dream was His Majesty the King himself. He bestowed upon me the greatest honour it was possible to accord me. I was astonished—I who had come to express my gratitude was given still more to be grateful for. Then I was invited to this brilliant gathering, representative of so many walks of life. When His Majesty awarded me this honour, I saw it as a kind of extravagant royal gesture. And this present occasion is somewhat similar. The homage you have paid me I do not regard as a personal homage. In it I see an acknowledgement of literature as a cultural force, underwritten by the Swedish nation. And you can well imagine how I am affected by this. My life has shaped itself like some long, long Passion Week. And now, as I stand here in the real, great Passion Week, my life is transformed into a saga tale. I, the aged dramatist, see my life trans-

formed into a poem, a fairy tale. For me it is a transformation into a midsummer night's dream. Thank you, thank you for that transformation. (*Speech at a city banquet in Stockholm, 13 Apr. 1898.*)

9. I am not a member of the Women's Rights Association. Nothing I have written has come from any deliberately tendentious intent. I have been more the poet and less the social philosopher than people generally seem inclined to believe. I thank you for your toast, but I must disclaim the honour of having consciously worked for Women's Rights. I am not even very clear what Women's Rights are, in fact. For me it has always been a matter of individual rights. And if one reads my books attentively, one will see that. Certainly it is desirable to solve the woman problem, alongside the rest; but that has not been the whole purpose. My task has been *to depict people.* Admittedly, whenever *that* has in some degree struck home, the reader interposes his or her own feelings and sentiments. These are then ascribed to the writer; but that is not how it is. People nicely and happily re-vamp things to accord with their own personality. Not only those who write but also those who read are poets. They are co-poets. They are often more poetical than the writer himself.

Allow me then, with these modifications, to thank you for the toast you have proposed to me. For I of course recognize that women have a great task to do, particularly in those fields in which this association is active. I wish to express my thanks by proposing a toast to the Women's Rights Association, and wishing it good fortune and success.

I have always seen as one of my tasks that of bettering our country and of raising the level of the people. Two factors apply here: it is up to the *mothers,* by slow and unremitting work, to awake a conscious feeling of *culture* and *discipline.* This must be created in the individual before the country can be advanced. It is the women who must solve the human problem. Solve it as mothers. And only in this way can they do it. Here lies a great task for women. My thanks and best wishes to the Women's Rights Association! (*Speech at a banquet of the Norwegian Women's Rights Association, 26 May 1898.*)

B.   *Other comments*

10. Dearest Miss Rosa, You are more than kind to send me that little blue flower—*die blaue Blume* which is so full of meaning and is so rarely found or won.—And thank you for thinking of me and of 11 April last year. That day is one I shall never forget. Be assured of that!—Your letters live in a special little place in my writing desk, and when I go to work in the morning, I always look in on them in their little place and give a greeting to Rosa. Sincere wishes. H.I. (*Letter of 17 Apr. 1899 to Rosa Fittinghoff, a young girl whom he had met the previous year in Stockholm. 11 April may be in error for 16 April, on which day she was one of a group of folk dancers who entertained Ibsen and who was later presented to him.*)

11. . . . I cherish the hope that, when the time comes, Herr Christian Morgenstern will take over the translation of my new play. He is a highly gifted, genuine poet. . . . Moreover he is completely familiar with the Norwegian language, an advantage which I was not fortunate enough to find in many of my German translators. . . . (*Letter of May 1899 to Julius Elias, printed in German translation in Michael Bauer,* Christian Morgensterns Leben und Werk, *Munich, 1938, p. 113.*)

12. It was true, he said, that he had for a time entertained some idea of writing a sort of literary autobiography—an account of the external circumstances, and the conditions of thought and feeling, that had generated each of his works. The upshot would have been—so he believed, at any rate—a demonstration of the continuity and consistency of his process of development. But he had put the idea aside, and was now (1898) maturing the scheme of a new drama. 'I have turned the characters out to grass,' he said. 'I hope they will fatten.' In 1899 he told me that the play was nearly finished, and that he thought of calling it *A Dramatic Epilogue*—a sort of summing-up, I understood him to imply, of the work of his later life. That play was—alas!—*When We Dead Awaken*. (*Interviews with William Archer in 1898 and 1899, reported in 'Ibsen as I knew him', in* The Monthly Review, *no. 69, xxiii, 3 June 1906, pp. 1–19.*)

13. One of our contributors met Dr. Ibsen yesterday on his morning walk, and told him of the significance which [the newspaper] *Politiken* had read into the word 'Epilogue'. 'That interpretation is too hasty,' answered Dr. Ibsen. 'The designation "Epilogue" does not relate to any such idea on my part. What I intended in this connection by "Epilogue" is merely to indicate that the play forms the epilogue to that series of my dramas which begins with *A Doll's House* and which is now completed with *When We Dead Awaken*. This last work belongs to those experiences I have wished to describe in the series as a whole. This forms a unity, an entity, and it is with this I am now finished. If after this,' the poet continued, 'I write anything else, everything will be in a completely different context, perhaps also in a different form.'

'Are you possibly referring to the autobiographical work there has been some mention of at times, Dr. Ibsen?'

'No, I am not. The idea of writing something of that sort I've given up . . . like so many other ideas.' (*Interview in* Verdens Gang, *12 Dec. 1899.*)

14. I cannot let myself in for some kind of bourgeois explanation of what I meant to say. Irene's allusions might reasonably be regarded as a sort of 'Wahrheit und Dichtung'.

On *my* list of characters it says 'A lady traveller'; in the German edition this is 'improved' to read 'Irene'. It is impossible that my excellent, sensitive and understanding translator can be guilty of that. It must be the printer or one of his people. I hope a watchful eye can be kept on him in future.—The 1,000 abortive copies of volume 9 will I hope be pulped.

It is fortunate for the people concerned that the hysterical paroxysms in the

Fischer circle [i.e. the German publisher] are now over, so that I may hope to be spared any more telegrams in that legalistic style which Herr Fischer's lawyer and others thought it fit to send me.

It is presumably superfluous to add that I have never had any thought of signing any contract with Herr Albert Langen concerning my new play. For this reason I did not answer the threatening letters. (*Letter of 3 Jan. 1900 to Julius Elias, editor of the German edition of Ibsen's works.*)

15. Dear Gunnar Heiberg, You were right, and I was wrong. I have looked it up in my notes. Irene is about 40 years old. (*Letter of Feb. 1900; see also Heiberg's account, in* Aftenposten, *no. 250, Feb. 1900, of a conversation he had with Ibsen about Irene's age:*

He answered: 'Irene has to be 28 years old.'

'That is impossible,' I said.

He regarded me, looked me up and down, and said quietly and crushingly: 'Yes, you know better.'

'Yes, I do,' I answered. And I set it all out how Irene must be at least 40 years old. . . .

'Irene has to be 28 years old,' interrupted Ibsen. 'And why do you ask if you know so well already.'

He left crossly.

The next day I got a letter from him. . . .)

16. How far I shall come in writing any new drama, I do not know; but if I can keep the physical and mental powers I still enjoy, I don't suppose I shall be able to keep away from the old battlefields for very long. But in that case I'll be turning up with new weapons and new equipment.

Fundamentally you are right when you say that the series which is completed with the epilogue actually began with *The Master Builder*. But I don't want to go into things any deeper than that. I leave all commentary and interpretation to you. (*Letter of 5 Mar. 1900 to Moritz Prozor, his French translator.*)

17. I should have written long ago to thank you for your kind letter of 4 April. But since the middle of March I have been unwell (though not confined to my bed) and my doctor has forbidden me to use pen and ink. For the time being that is now over, and I have been given permission to write short letters to my closest friends, and this permission I am now availing myself of.

First let me thank you for the most recent purchase of bonds, which was very much to my advantage—and, after that, because you reminded me that my last play is not included in the contract for the collected works. This play can therefore appear later, either separately or in some other framework or other, after we have discussed things further. Most acceptable for me would be to see an arrangement whereby *When We Dead Awaken* was taken in as a concluding item to the collected works, where it organically belongs as a finale for that series. (*Letter of 30 Apr. 1900 to August Larsen.*)

4. CONTEMPORARY RECEPTION

The play was published from Copenhagen on 19 December 1899, in a first edition of 12,000 copies. Because Denmark had not yet subscribed to the Berne convention, the name of the German publisher, Samuel Fischer, also appeared on the title page in order to assure the copyright in Germany: *Når vi døde vågner. En dramatisk epilog i tre akter af Henrik Ibsen. København. Berlin.* 1899. The first edition was sold out before publication day, and a second edition appeared almost immediately on 22 December 1899. An edition of 12 copies, identical to the above save for the entry 'W. Heinemann, London' on the title page, was published in England on 19 December 1899 in order to assure the English copyright. (Despite these precautions, this was still not sufficient to secure the American copyright; and Ibsen was forced to make special arrangements with William Archer and Mr. Heinemann, which involved his accepting a reduced fee; cf. translation of a letter from Ibsen to Archer, 28 Jan. 1900, in C. Archer, *William Archer,* London, 1931, pp. 262–3.) William Archer's own translation of the play into English was published on 22 March 1900: *When We Dead Awaken. A dramatic epilogue in three acts. Translated by William Archer.* London, 1900. Count Prozor's French translation, *Quand nous nous réveillons d'entre les morts,* first appeared in the pages of *La Revue de Paris,* vii, i (Jan.–Feb., 1900), pp. 5–53, and was published in volume form later that same year. Christian Morgenstern's German translation appeared in vol. ix of *Henrik Ibsens sämtliche Werke* (Berlin, [Dec.] 1899), and also in a separate edition. Before 1900 was out, the play had also been published in Italian, Russian, and Polish translation.

Already, before publication day, a measure of controversy had attached to the play. As early as 9 December it was known not only that the title of the play was to be 'When we dead awaken', but also that the author had designated it 'a dramatic epilogue'. This immediately gave rise to speculation as to whether this indicated that Ibsen was now finished with writing drama. This Ibsen was quick to deny; and in an interview, published in the Norwegian newspaper *Verdens Gang* on 12 December, he insisted that this appellation meant no more than an indication that this play served to conclude the series of dramas that had begun twenty years earlier with *A Doll's House* (see above, p. 364).

When the play was published it called forth a large number of reviews, both inside and outside Scandinavia. It was, however, rarely met with any real understanding from the critics.

In Norway, the most impressive response in the daily press was that of *Verdens Gang:* on 20 December 1899 (no. 374) it had a piece by Carl Nærup; on 22 December (no. 375) by Gunnar Heiberg; on 28 December (no. 380) by Georg Brandes; and these it followed with a piece by Christian Collin on 5 April 1900 (no. 87). For Carl Nærup, it was a bizarre work of genius, the peculiar charm of which was its mood of anguish and its fantastic lyricism; for Gunnar

Heiberg it was a drama of two people who experienced love for each other, but at different times; and Georg Brandes pointed out that, although the characters are living, they do not live a simple earthly existence but at a higher level, grander, emblematically: 'They are superior beings who, whatever they may say, always retain something ineffable.' The published drama was also reviewed inside Norway in *Aftenposten, Dagbladet, Morgenbladet* and other Christiania papers, as well as in the press of Bergen, Trondheim, Christiansand, Stavanger, and elsewhere. (An exhaustive list is to be found in Halvdan Koht's introduction to Ibsen's *Samlede Værker,* vol. x, Copenhagen, 1902, pp. viii–xiv.)

In Denmark, Edvard Brandes was quick to claim the work as a masterpiece (*Politiken,* 20 Dec. 1899, no. 354), adding that in it Ibsen was declaring that there was only one god, Eros, and the poet was his prophet. Valdemar Vedel (in *Tilskueren,* 1900, pp. 81–6) thought otherwise: he thought of Ibsen's more recent works as 'children of old age', and *When We Dead Awaken* was no exception. These works were sensitive and penetrating, he thought, but somewhat wan and faded.

Among the very many ephemeral pieces in Germany that greeted the publication of the play in book form, one or two have more lasting value: Max Dreszler, 'Was ist Leben nach Ibsens dramatischem Epilog', in *Preussische Jahrbücher,* cii, 1900, pp. 231–45; Alfred Kerr, 'Epilog' (1 Feb. 1900), reprinted in *Das neue Drama* (Berlin, 1905); Max Lorenz, 'Wenn wir Toten erwachen', in *Preussische Jahrbücher,* xcix, 1900, pp. 300–8; and Helene Zimpel, 'Ibsen-Studien', in *Nord und Süd,* xxvi, 103, Dec. 1902, pp. 343–61. In France, one might select P. G. la Chesnais (signed Peer Eketræ), 'Le génie et le bonheur dans l'œuvre d'Ibsen', in *Mercure de France,* xxxiii, Feb. 1900, pp. 391–404; and Henri Bérenger, article in *La Revue et Revue des Revues,* xxxv, 1900, p. 429.

In Britain, there was—with the notable exception of James Joyce's published article and Bernard Shaw's privately expressed views—a notable lack of enthusiasm for *When We Dead Awaken* at the time of its publication. William Archer felt considerable embarrassment at having to translate it—an embarrassment he did not attempt to conceal when he wrote to his brother Charles on 14 Dec. 1899 (in Charles Archer, *William Archer,* London, 1931, pp. 261–2):

'... Well, here's a cheerful end to the century! And to cheer you up a little more, I send a hurried line to say that at last the Old Man *is* an old man, and the new play is a sad fiasco. It is a mere hash up of fifty old ideas (going as far back as Peer Gynt and Den Grönklaedte [i.e. the Woman in Green]) and is utterly without dramatic fibre. Furthermore it is scabrous to a degree—if it weren't like deserting the Old Man, 'pon my soul I'd let some one else translate it. Of course it is not at all wonderful that a man of 71 should write such a piece, but it is wonderful that the man who wrote this should have written *Borkman* only three years earlier. The first act disappointed me greatly, though, on a second reading, I thought rather better of it. There are flashes of the old fire in it, though scarcely any new material, and no dramatic action even foreshadowed. But the second act merely repeats the first (almost word for word in long passages), and the third is wild without being effective. It is a caricature of Ibsen, and a triumph for the heathen, who will declare (wrongly) that it is indecent, and (rightly) that it is mad. The N.C.T. [i.e. New Century Theatre] can't possibly touch it, and I can scarcely believe that anyone else will—though it is on the cards that Shaw may declare it his masterpiece, and the Charringtons do it on a Sunday evening. Good Lord! how I wish I either had it translated or hadn't to translate it. So the old man goes out with the century! It is sörgeligt [sad]; but after all, how many men have had such an innings!'

Problems also arose about the timing and the terms of the English translation. Heinemann, clearly in difficulties about keeping to the date originally agreed for publication, seems to have asked for the Copenhagen publication date to be put back. A telegram from Ibsen to Archer, dated 15 December, reads: 'Impossible now to change publication of the original. Mr. Heineman [*sic*] has never made any similar demand before. Must arrange things as best he can.' This intransigence seems to have stung Heinemann into cutting the agreed fee to half; whereupon, on 16 December, an angry Ibsen wrote to Archer:

'I have received the enclosed telegram via Gyldendal. I am not accepting any *half*-fees from Mr. Heinemann. Instead I present him with the *whole* fee which he can keep on condition that in future I am spared any connection with him. Be so very good as to inform him of this, and forgive me for burdening you with this disagreeable commission.'

Enclosed with this letter was a copy of a telegram from Heinemann to Gyldendal, dated 12[?].12.1899, which reads: 'In that case inform Ibsen that I pay only half fee. Heinemann.' The bitter exchanges continued all through January, with Archer playing the uncomfortable intermediary. On 8 January 1900, Ibsen wrote to Archer:

'My son has passed your letter to me, from which I can see that Mr. Heinemann would much prefer to be relieved of his obligations as publisher of my new play. Neither Hegel [Ibsen's publisher] nor I have anything to reproach ourselves for. It was quite impossible to meet Mr. Heinemann's wholly unexpected demand for a postponement. Meanwhile the English edition must not be delayed. May I ask you therefore to be so good as to take the thing into your own hands on my behalf and either reach a new agreement with Mr. Heinemann or with some other publisher for a fee immediately payable—in other words not a percentage on sales.'

Archer's reply, delayed as it was by his absence from London, has survived only in the form of a typed carbon copy:

'20 January 1900

'Dear Dr. Ibsen [i.e. Sigurd]

'I have been absent from London for some days, else I should probably have been able to send an earlier answer to your Father's letter of January 8th.

'On my communicating its terms to Mr. Heinemann, he wrote me as follows: "I propose to you the following terms: namely—that I pay £100 for the English right, and a nominal fee, say £20 for the authorization in America—£120 in all; it being quite understood that as there is no copyright in America, Dr. Ibsen authorizes only your translation and the edition arranged for by me."

'On receiving this letter, which is dated January the 12th, I wrote to two other publishers, Mr. Grant Richards and Mr. Duckworth, whom I knew to be interested in dramatic literature, and therefore most likely to take up the matter, asking them what they were prepared to pay for the English copyright and stageright, warning them that the proposal must be for a sum down and not for a percentage. Mr. Grant Richards's answer I enclose; as you will see, it is very far from satisfactory. Mr. Duckworth writes from the Engadin that he is much interested in the suggestion but can make no offer until his return to London next week.

'That is how the matter now stands. I am inclined to advise acceptance of Mr. Heinemann's offer. The play is really worth more to him than to others, because he holds the copyright of all the earlier plays that *are* copyright, and can thus issue them in a uniform edition. I do not think it at all likely that any other publishers will offer more. Should Mr. Duckworth, on his return, make a larger offer, I will at once let you know; but so far as my own judgement goes I should think Mr. Heinemann's offer the most advantageous that we are at all likely to get.'

To this Ibsen responded on 28 January by indicating his acceptance of Heinemann's terms as Archer had reported them:

'I am very grateful for your letter to my son which he has passed to me. I feel very strongly that your translation should be published as soon as possible, and as I very much want to see an end to the unfortunate misunderstanding with Mr. Heinemann I hereby declare myself ready to accept his offer of a total of £120 for the whole thing, and with this I regard the matter as closed. Gyldendal's nevertheless regard themselves as completely without blame in the difficulties which have arisen. It would therefore be hurtful both for Hegel and for his manager if they should learn anything of the reduction in the fees which I have had to agree to for the English and American edition. To avoid this may I ask that Mr. Heinemann's cheque this time might be sent to me personally here in Kristiania, and not as on similar occasions earlier to Gyldendal's in Copenhagen; then nobody there need know anything about the changed terms. Dear Mr. Archer—it is truly most disagreeable for me when I think of all the trouble this business has caused you. Happily it is presumably all over now, and I am now longing and looking forward to seeing these latest human creations of mine in English dress.'

Archer's views did not change greatly with the years; and his introduction to vol. XI of the *Collected Works*, published in 1907, held very much to the same line:

   'As the last great confession, so to speak, of a great artist, the Epilogue will always be read with interest. It contains, moreover, many flashes of the old genius, many strokes of the old incommunicable magic. One may say with perfect sincerity that there is more fascination in the dregs of Ibsen's mind than in the "first sprightly running" of more commonplace talents. But to his sane admirers the interest of the play must always be melancholy, because it is purely pathological. To deny this is, in my opinion, to cast a slur over all the poet's previous work, and in great measure to justify the criticisms of his most violent detractors. For *When We Dead Awaken* is very like the sort of play that haunted the "anti-Ibsenite" imagination in the year 1893 or thereabouts. It is a piece of self-caricature, a series of echoes from all the earlier plays, an exaggeration of manner to the pitch of mannerism.'

Edmund Gosse shared Archer's estimate of the play as a work of senility; and later, in his *Henrik Ibsen* (London, 1907, pp. 223–5), he put this view very forthrightly:

   '. . . It is impossible to deny that, whether in the study or on the boards, it proved a disappointment. It displayed, especially in its later acts, many obvious signs of the weakness incident on old age. . . . There was certainly in the whole conception a cloudiness, an ineffectuality, which was very little like anything that Ibsen had displayed before. The moral of the piece was vague, the evolution of it incoherent, and indeed in many places it seemed a parody of his earlier manner. Not Mr. Anstey Guthrie's inimitable scenes in *Mr. Punch's [Pocket] Ibsen* were more preposterous than almost all the appearances of Irene after the first act of *When We Dead Awaken*. . . . [It] is the production of a very tired old man, whose physical powers were declining.'

Bernard Shaw in no way shared this view of the play as a piece of senility. On 21 Feb. 1900, a postcard from him to William Archer contained the declaration: 'By the way, the Ibsen play [*When We Dead Awaken*] is powerful, and *frightfully* moral. The best review I have seen is in the last *Speaker*. It *must* be played.' And when in time he added a chapter on Ibsen's later plays for the second edition of *The Quintessence of Ibsenism* (London, 1913), he flatly contradicted Archer and Gosse: 'The simplicity and brevity of the story is so obvious, and the enormous scope of the conception so difficult to comprehend, that many of Ibsen's most devoted admirers failed to do it justice. They knew that he was a man of seventy, and were prepossessed with the belief that at such an age his powers must be falling off. . . . There is no falling off here in Ibsen. . . . It shews no decay of Ibsen's highest qualities; his magic is nowhere more potent.'

The most positive and prophetic voice proved, however, to be that of the young James Joyce, who at the age of eighteen contributed an article on *When We Dead Awaken* entitled 'Ibsen's New Drama' to *Fortnightly Review*, lxvii NS, 1 Apr. 1900, pp. 575–90. This offered by far the fullest analysis in English of the play in these years, and concluded with the suggestion that '. . . *When We Dead Awaken* may rank with the greatest of the author's work— if, indeed, it be not the greatest'. When on 16 April 1900 Ibsen belatedly wrote to thank Archer for sending him a copy of the English edition of the play, he also remarked on the Joyce article:

'I should have thanked you long ago for *Wehn* [sic] *We Dead Awaken*, but for five weeks I have been ill and my doctor has forbidden me to write during all that time. The English edition looks splendid and distinguished in every respect and I have found it fairly easy to read and understand most of it; but I am inclined to believe that the book has been difficult to translate. I have also read—or rather, spelled out—a review by Mr. James Joyce in *Fortnightly Review*, which is very benevolent and which I really would have liked to thank the author for if only I were competent in the language.'

Archer must have passed on Ibsen's remarks to Joyce without delay, for on 28 April Joyce replied from Dublin to Archer:

'13 Richmond Avenue
Fairview, Dublin
April 28, 1900

'Dear Sir,
'I wish to thank you for your kindness in writing to me. I am a young Irishman, eighteen years old, and the words of Ibsen I shall keep in my heart all my life.
Faithfully Yours
Jas. Joyce

William Archer Esq.
Southampton Row
London'

Other slighter reviews of the play in Archer's translation included: an unsigned piece, 'The Husk of Technique', in *Academy*, lviii, 1458, 14 Apr. 1900, pp. 307–8; an unsigned review in *Athenæum*, no. 3780, 7 Apr. 1900, pp. 442–3; an unsigned review in *The Humanitarian*, xvi, May 1900, pp. 373–7. And in America: W. M. Payne, 'When We Dead Awaken', in *The Dial* (Chicago), xxviii, 1900, pp. 109–13; a piece signed 'A.M.' in *The Bookman* (N.Y.), May 1900, pp. 283 ff.; and an anonymous review in *Nation*, 1900, pp. 70–94.

When it came to staging the play, there was the (by then) familiar international scramble among the theatres of Europe to be the first to put it on. Disregarding those occasions which were essentially readings—like the morning 'performance' at the Haymarket Theatre, London, on 16 Dec. 1899, when Elizabeth Robins took the part of Irene, and H. L. Braekstad and his wife read Rubek and Maja—the race was won by the Hoftheater in Stuttgart with a first night on 26 Jan. 1900. It was quickly followed, before the month was out, by Stettin (Dr. Heine's Travelling 'Ibsen Theater') on 27 Jan., by Copenhagen (Royal Theatre) on 28 Jan., by Breslau (Lobetheater) and Halle on 29 Jan., and by Helsinki (the Swedish Theatre, performed in Swedish translation) also on 29 Jan. 1900.

In Norway, Ibsen had already been the subject of some hostile press comment for having agreed to let Copenhagen's Royal Theatre take precedence over Christiania's newly established National Theatre in the matter of timing. The Christiania first night on 6 Feb., nine days later than Copenhagen, was no great theatrical success. The author was not himself present on the first night to give it a sense of occasion; it was generally agreed that the two main women's roles— with Mrs. Ragna Wettergren playing Irene, and Mrs. Johanne Dybwad playing Maja—had been badly cast, despite the fact that this casting had been done to meet Ibsen's express wishes; and the stage set was also in some ways sadly deficient. The National Theatre ran the play for no more than eleven performances, the last being on 19 March 1900. See also the account by A. Edmund Spender, *Two winters in Norway* [i.e. 1900/1], London, 1902, pp. 142–64: 'Actors and dramatists', in the course of which he comments:

> '*When the Dead Awake* . . . is one of Ibsen's most incomprehensible plays. Yet with much that is gruesome and painful, it contains scenes of commanding power and brilliancy. . . . Too much cannot be said in praise of Fru Dybwad's quick changing of disposition from grave to coquetting, or of Fru Ragna Wettergreen's [*sic*] awakening from her catalepsy of all emotion. Mr. Egil Eide, as Professor Rubek, had a peculiarly difficult part to play: he was conscious of his limits, and hardly added another feather to his fame by his perpetual clinging to his stony seat and swaying of his body to and fro like a galley slave in chains; it would be well if he could show himself more at his ease at times, so as to relieve the constant tension of his part. For scenery nothing could be finer than the filed snowclad mountain peaks that stood out against a stormy sky, whilst the shadows of clouds passed over their untrodden glory and completed a picture which was vividly real.'

It was not performed again at this theatre until the 1933–4 season, and again in 1934–5, with the same actor, Egil Eide, in the part of Rubek as had played it in 1900.

Elsewhere in Scandinavia, it was played (in Swedish) in Åbo, Finland, on 2 Feb.; and on 14 Feb. in Stockholm at the Swedish theatre, with August Lindberg in the part of Rubek.

If the reception given to the play in Scandinavia had been only lukewarm, Germany made the play peculiarly its own; it was astonishingly widely played in many different German cities, and in its German version it also reached other parts of Europe well beyond the frontiers of Germany proper. Following the January performances, listed above, at Stuttgart, Stettin, Breslau, and Halle, the spread of the play was rapid: 3 Feb. at the Stadttheater, Frankfurt am Main; 9 Feb. in Oppeln; 13 Feb. at the Alte Theater in Leipzig, and again at the same city's Neues Theater on 19 Feb; 18 Feb. in Posen. The following month there were productions at the Deutsches Theater in Berlin (17 Mar.), in Wiesbaden (27 Mar.), and in Nuremberg, Bielefeld, Minden, and Mannheim. Hamburg saw the play in November 1900 at the Stadttheater; Dresden on 10 Jan. 1901 at the Hoftheater; and Cologne on 25 March 1902 at the Residenztheater. Estimates of the number of performances of the play in Germany during the early months vary from '215 up to March 1901' (Philip Stein, *Henrik Ibsen: Zur Bühnengeschichte seiner Dichtungen*, Berlin, 1901, pp. 48–52) to 'almost 200 in the first half of 1900'(Emil Reich, *Henrik Ibsens Dramen*, 14th ed. Berlin, 1925, p. 448).

Additionally, there were performances in German (either by resident or by travelling companies) as follows: in March 1900 in Zurich; in April 1900 in Graz; and by Gustav Lindemann's travelling company in May 1901 in Cracow and other Polish cities, and in November 1901 in Sofia. Vienna, however, had to wait until 20 March 1904 for its first performance at the Deutsches Volkstheater.

In Russia, a first performance of the play in Kharkov on 11 Oct. 1900 was followed by a production at the Art Theatre, Moscow, on 28 Nov. 1900, directed by Nemirovich-Danchenko. This was the third Ibsen play to be put on at the Art Theatre since its foundation in 1898: *Hedda Gabler* on 19 Feb. 1899; *An Enemy of the People* on 24 Oct. 1900, with Stanislavsky both directing and playing the part of Stockman; then *When We Dead Awaken*. As part of his extremely thorough preparations for the production of this last play, Nemirovich-Danchenko sent his assistant to Norway in the summer of 1900 to make full notes of details of costumes, scenery, and props. In the event, although *An Enemy of the People* had been a huge success, and a personal triumph for Stanislavsky both as actor and producer, *When We Dead Awaken* was coolly received. Work on the production left behind a valuable residue, however: a lively and detailed exchange of correspondence from the summer of 1900 between Stanislavsky and Nemirovich-Danchenko on the problems of staging the play (see V. J. Nemirovich-Danchenko, *Izbrannye pis'ma*, Moscow, 1954; and Martin Nag, *Ibsen i russisk åndsliv*, Oslo, 1967); and an article from the pen of Nemirovich-Danchenko (in *Russkaya mysl'*, 1900, 9, pp. 183 ff.) in which he discusses the concept of 'realism' as the key to Ibsen, even in such a play as *When We Dead Awaken*. (See an account, in German, of this article in N. Å. Nilsson, *Ibsen in Russland*, Stockholm, 1958, pp. 78 ff.). The following year, the play was performed at the New Theatre, St. Petersburg, with Lydia Yavorskaya in the part of Irene.

There was a performance of the play in Italian at the Manzoni Theatre in Milan on 2 May 1900. Astonishingly, Paris had to wait for many more years before it saw a production of the play.

By contrast with the German theatre, the British and American theatre gave only tardy recognition to the play. The first professional production was not until 26 Jan. 1903 by the Stage Society at the Imperial Theatre, London, with G. S. Titheradge as Rubek, Henrietta Watson as Irene, Mabel Hackney as Maja, and Laurence Irving as Ulfheim. Max Beerbohm, who, as Bernard Shaw's successor as dramatic critic of the *Saturday Review*, reviewed the production ('Ibsen's "Epilogue"', xcv, 7 Feb. 1903, pp. 168–9), was clearly unimpressed and dismissed it as 'an old man's work': 'The meaning may not be profound, and the symbolism may be a trifle crude; but there is no other possible objection to them. From first to last the play is as clear as it can be. If anything, it is too clear: there is too much expression of its meaning. The characters express, in varying terms, the same thoughts and the same feelings over and over again. There is not really enough in them to fill an evening bill. Nor can we wonder, remembering that this is the latest and last play of a very old man.'

Ibsen: the Critical Heritage, ed. Michael Egan (London, 1972), pp. 391–404, reprints a useful selection of the London critical reaction to this 1903 production, including Beerbohm's notice, together with extracts from unsigned notices appearing in *Daily Telegraph* (26 Jan.), *Daily Chronicle* (27 Jan.), *The Times* (27 Jan.), *Sunday Times* (1 Feb.), *Lloyd's Weekly News* (1 Feb.), *Referee* (1 Feb.), and a pseudonymous notice by 'Momus' in *Gentlewoman* (7 Feb.). To these may be added a further anonymous notice in *Athenæum*, no. 3927, 31 Jan. 1903, pp. 155–6.

Although there were non-professional performances of the play by the Ibsen Club at the Ibsen Studio on 5 June 1910 and on 17 Dec. 1911, London had to wait long years before it saw another professional production: at the Torch Theatre, on 18 Nov. 1938, with Wilfrid Grantham as Rubek, Iris Baker as Maja, Katherine Morley as Irene, William Hutchison as Ulfheim, and Patrick Gover as the Superintendent.

In America it was first played in Danish on 11 Feb. 1900 at the Scandia Hall, Chicago. The first performance in English was on 7 March 1905 at the Knicker-bocker Theatre, New York, with Frederick Lewis as Rubek and Forence Kahn as Irene.

APPENDIX IV

IBSEN PRODUCTIONS IN ENGLISH

1. Principal London productions
2. B.B.C. radio productions
3. Television productions in Britain

1. PRINCIPAL LONDON PRODUCTIONS (1889-1974)

The earliest performance of Ibsen in English was of *Pillars of Society*, on this occasion entitled 'Quicksands', at the Gaiety Theatre on 15 December 1880. (The first performance of an Ibsen play in America was of a very free adaptation of *A Doll's House*, on this occasion entitled 'The Child Wife', at the Grand Opera House, Milwaukee, on 2 June 1882; *A Doll's House* was played in Louisville, Kentucky, on 7 December 1883.)

On 3 March 1884 'Breaking a Butterfly', based on *A Doll's House*, was performed at the Princes Theatre; and in March 1885 a charity performance of 'Nora' (i.e. *A Doll's House*) was given in London by 'The Scribblers' Dramatic Society'. (In the spring of 1886 there was a performance of 'Phantoms', i.e. *Ghosts*, at the Columbia Theatre, Chicago.)

1889 *A Doll's House*, 7 June, Novelty; *Pillars of Society*, 17 July, Opera Comique.

1891 *A Doll's House*, Jan., Terry's; *Rosmersholm*, 23 Feb., Vaudeville; *Ghosts*, 13 March, Royalty; *Hedda Gabler*, 20 April, Vaudeville; *The Lady from the Sea*, 11 May, Terry's; *A Doll's House*, 2 June, Criterion.

1892 *A Doll's House*, 19 April, Avenue.

1893 *Ghosts*, 27 Jan., Royalty; *The Master Builder*, 20 Feb., Trafalgar Square; *Hedda Gabler*, *Rosmersholm*, and *The Master Builder*, 29 May–10 June, Opera Comique; *An Enemy of the People*, 14 June, Haymarket; *A Doll's House*, June, Lyric, in Italian.

1894 *The Wild Duck*, 4 May, Royalty.

1895 *Rosmersholm* and *Solness* [i.e. *The Master Builder*], 25–30 March, Opera Comique, in French.

1896 **Little Eyolf**, 23 Nov., Avenue, with Courtenay Thorpe as Allmers, Elizabeth Robins as Asta, Janet Achurch (later replaced by Mrs. Patrick Campbell) as Rita, Mrs. Patrick Campbell (later replaced by Florence Farr) as the Ratwife.

1897 **John Gabriel Borkman**, 3 May, Strand, with W. H. Vernon as Borkman, Genevieve Ward as Mrs. Borkman, Martin Harvey as Erhart, Elizabeth Robins as Ella, and Mrs. Beerbohm Tree as Mrs. Wilton; *A Doll's House*, 10 May, Globe; *The Wild Duck*, 17 May, Globe; *Ghosts*, 24 June, Independent Theatre, Queen's Gate Hall.

1900 *The League of Youth*, 25 Feb., Vaudeville.

1901 *Pillars of Society*, 15 May, Garrick, prod. by Stage Society.

1902 *The Lady from the Sea*, 7 May, Royalty.

1903 **When We Dead Awaken**, 26 Jan., Imperial, prod. by the Stage Society, with G. S. Titheradge as Rubek, Henrietta Watson as Irene, Mabel Hackney as Maja, Laurence Irving as Ulfheim; *The Vikings at Helgeland*, 21 April, Imperial; *Hedda Gabler*, 7 Oct.

1905 *Die Wildente* [*The Wild Duck*], 8 March, Great Queen Street, in German; *The Wild Duck*, 17 Oct., Court; *An Enemy of the People*, 2 Nov., His Majesty's.

1906 *Lady Inger*, 28 Jan., Stage Society.

1907 *Hedda Gabler*, 5 March, Court; *The Master Builder*, 17 Sept., Bijou Theatre.

1908 *Rosmersholm*, 10 Feb., Terry's.

1909 *The Master Builder*, 16 March, Court; *An Enemy of the People*, 30 April, His Majesty's; *Hedda Gabler*, Dec., His Majesty's.

1910 **John Gabriel Borkman**, 25 Oct., Court, with Franklin Dyall as Borkman, Rosina Filippi as Mrs. Borkman, Emily Luck as Ella Rentheim, Donald Calthrop as Erhart, Amy Ravenscroft as Mrs. Wilton, Campbell Cargill as Foldal, and Cathleen Nesbitt as Frida.

1911 *The Wild Duck*, 8 Jan., Ibsen Studio; **John Gabriel Borkman**, 26 Jan., Court, with James Hearn as Borkman, Rosina Filippi as Mrs. Borkman, Emily Luck as Ella Rentheim, Owen Nares as Erhart, Cathleen Nesbitt as Mrs. Wilton, Campbell Cargill as Foldal, and Benvenuta Filippi as Frida; *A Doll's House*, 14 Feb., Royalty; *Peer Gynt*, 26 Feb., Rehearsal Theatre; *The Master Builder*, 28 March, Little; *The Lady from the Sea*, 9 April, Ibsen Studio; *Peer Gynt*, 30 April, Rehearsal Theatre; *Ghosts*, 14 May, Ibsen Studio; *Hedda Gabler*, 27 May, Kingsway; *Olaf Liljekrans*, 18 June, Rehearsal Theatre; **Little Eyolf**, 12 Nov., Ibsen Studio; **When We Dead Waken**, 17 Dec., Rehearsal Theatre.

1912 *Rosmersholm*, 28 May, Little; *The Hero's Mound*, 30 May, Clavier Hall; *Brand*, 11 Nov., Court; *Hedda Gabler*, 26 Nov., Clavier Hall.

1913 **Little Eyolf**, 2 Feb., Ibsen Studio; *The Pretenders*, 13 Feb., Haymarket; *The Master Builder*, 9 March, *The Lady from the Sea*, 30 March, and *Peer Gynt*, 27 April, all Ibsen Studio; *The Wild Duck*, 1 Dec., St James's; **When We Dead Awaken**, 2 Dec., Cosmopolis, with Rathmell Wilson as Rubek, Pax Robertson as Maja.

1914 *Ghosts*, 26 April, Court, revived 14 July, Haymarket.

1917   *Ghosts*, 28 April, Kingsway; *Rosmersholm*, 5 June, St. Martin's; *Ghosts*, 6 Nov., St James's.

1918   *The Master Builder*, 13 May, Court.

1921   *St. John's Night*, 1 May, Chelsea; *A Doll's House*, 11 July, Everyman; *The MasterBuilder*, 27 Nov., Chelsea; **John Gabriel Borkman**, 6 Dec., Everyman, with Franklin Dyall as Borkman, Maud Jolliffe as Ella Rentheim, Jean Cadell as Mrs. Borkman, Richard Bird as Erhart, Mary Merrall as Mrs. Wilton, Joseph A. Dodd as Foldal, and Henzie Raeburn as Frida.

1922   *Peer Gynt*, 6 March, Old Vic; *Hedda Gabler*, 22 May, Everyman.

1923   'La Donna del Mare' (*The Lady from the Sea*), 7 June, New Oxford; 'Spettri' (*Ghosts*), 12 June, New Oxford.

1925   *The Lady from the Sea*, 2 Feb., Lyric; *The Wild Duck*, 30 June, Everyman; *Ghosts*, 13 Oct., Everyman; *A Doll's House*, 20 Nov., Playhouse.

1926   *Hedda Gabler*, 31 Jan., Gate; *Pillars of Society*, 13 July, Everyman, transferred to Royalty, 5 Aug.; *Rosmersholm*, 30 Sept., Kingsway.

1928   *Hedda Gabler*, 12 March, Everyman; *A Doll's House*, 20 March, Kingsway; *An Enemy of the People*, 26 March, Wyndham's; *Ghosts*, 27 March, Wyndham's; *The Master Builder*, 11 June, 'Q' Theatre; *The Vikings at Helgeland*, 1 Oct., Old Vic; *The Master Builder*, 4 Oct., Everyman; **John Gabriel Borkman**, 15 Oct., 'Q' Theatre, with Victor Lewisohn as Borkman, Mrs. Patrick Campbell as Ella Rentheim, Nancy Price as Mrs. Borkman, Terence de Marney as Erhart, Nancy Pawley as Mrs. Wilton, H. O. Nicholson as Foldal, and Primrose Morgan as Frida; *The Lady from the Sea*, 4 Nov., Apollo; **Little Eyolf**, 3 Dec., Everyman, with Rupert Harvey as Allmers, Moyna MacGill as Asta, Mary Merrall as Rita, Betty Brunton as Eyolf, Nancy Price as the Ratwife, and Tristan Rawson as Borghejm.

1930   *A Doll's House*, 20 March, Arts, transferred to Criterion, 14 April; *Ghosts*, 19 April, Everyman; *The Wild Duck*, 9 Oct., Everyman; **Little Eyolf**, 15 Oct., Arts, with Ernest Milton as Allmers, Dorothy Holmes-Gore as Asta, Jean Forbes-Robertson as Rita, Peter Penrose as Eyolf, Marie Ault as the Ratwife, Robert Speaight as Borghejm.

1931   *Hedda Gabler*, 17 March, Arts; *The Master Builder*, 19 Nov., Duchess.

1932   *Peer Gynt*, 18 Oct., Gate.

1933   *Maison de Poupée*, 22 Feb., Arts; *Ghosts*, 26 March, Arts.

1934   *A Doll's House*, 4 March, Arts; *The Master Builder*, 15 April, Westminster; *An Enemy of the People*, 1 Oct. Embassy.

1935   *Ghosts*, 19 July, Little; *Peer Gynt*, 23 Sept., Old Vic; **John Gabriel Borkman**, 21 Oct., Grafton, with Clephan Bell as Borkman.

1936   *Catiline*, 27 Jan., Croydon Rep., transferred 18 Feb. to Royalty; *A Doll's House*, 2 March, Criterion; *Rosmersholm*, 5 March, Criterion; *Hedda Gabler*, 9 March, Criterion; *The Master Builder*, 12 March, Criterion; *Peer Gynt*, 5 May, Sadler's Wells; *The Wild Duck*, 3 Nov., Westminster.

1937   *Ghosts*, 8 Nov., Vaudeville.

1938   **When We Dead Awaken**, 18 Nov., Torch, with Wilfrid Grantham as Rubek, Iris Baker as Maja, Patrick Gover as the Inspector, William Hutchison as Ulfhejm, Katherine Morley as Irene, and Flora Brandon as the Nun.

1939   'Nora' [i.e. *A Doll's House*], 3 Feb., Duke of York's; *An Enemy of the People*, 21 Feb., Old Vic.

1940   *Ghosts*, 30 May, Duchess.

1942   *Hedda Gabler*, 30 Sept., Mercury; revived 16 March 1943.

1943   *Ghosts*, 25 June, Duke of York's; *The Master Builder*, 29 June, Westminster.

1944   *Peer Gynt*, 31 Aug., New.

1945   **When We Dead Awaken**, 17 March, Chanticleer, with Laurence Payne as Rubek, Sheila Burrell as Maja; **Little Eyolf**, 12 June, Embassy, with Walter Hudd as Allmers, Lydia Sherwood as Rita, Helen Burns as Asta, Hilda Schroder as Eyolf, Betty Potter as the Ratwife, and Julian Randall as Borghejm; *A Doll's House*, 11 July, Arts; *Rosmersholm*, 18 Aug. Torch.

1946   *A Doll's House*, 17 Jan., Winter Garden; *The Lady from the Sea*, 13 March, Arts.

1947   *The Master Builder*, 1 Jan., Arts; *Lady Inger of Ostraat*, 26 March, Gateway; *The Wild Duck*, 31 Oct., Torch.

1948   *The Master Builder*, 14 May, Westminster; *Rosmersholm*, 8 July, Arts; *The Wild Duck*, 3 Nov., St Martin's.

1950   **John Gabriel Borkman**, 1 March, Arts, with Frederick Valk as Borkman, Louise Hampton as Mrs. Borkman, Cicely Paget-Bowman as Ella Rentheim, Lyndon Brook as Erhart, Elaine Wodson as Mrs. Wilton, Scott Harrald as Foldal, and Patricia Gilder as Frida; *Rosmersholm*, 22 Aug., St Martin's.

1951   *Hedda Gabler*, 17 Jan., Arts; *Ghosts*, 12 June, Embassy.

1953   *A Doll's House*, 8 Sept., Lyric, Hammersmith.

1954   *Hedda Gabler*, 8 Sept., Lyric, Hammersmith, transferred 29 Nov. to Westminster.

1955   *The Wild Duck*, 21 Dec., Saville.

1958   **Little Eyolf**, 11 March, Lyric, Hammersmith, with Robert Eddison as Allmers, Barbara Clegg as Asta, Heather Chasen as Rita, John Hall as Eyolf, Selma Vaz Dias as the Ratwife, Michael David as Borghejm; *Ghosts*, 12 Nov., Old Vic.

1959   *Brand*, 8 April, Lyric, Hammersmith; *Rosmersholm*, 18 Nov., Royal Court, transferred 5 Jan. 1960 to Comedy.

1961   **John Gabriel Borkman**, 16 Feb., Mermaid, with Bernard Miles as Borkman, Freda Jackson as Mrs. Borkman, and Josephine Wilson as Ella Rentheim; *The Lady from the Sea*, 15 March, Queen's.

1962   *Peer Gynt*, 26 Sept., Old Vic; *The Master Builder*, 19 Nov., Ashcroft Theatre, Croydon, transferred 4 Dec. to New Arts.

1963   *A Doll's House*, 29 Nov., Unity; **John Gabriel Borkman**, 4 Dec., Duchess, with Donald Wolfit as Borkman, Flora Robson as Mrs. Borkman, Margaret Rawlings as Ella Rentheim, Delphi Lawrence as Mrs. Wilton, Patrick Mower as Erhart, and Karen Fernald as Frida.

1964   *Hedda Gabler*, 12 Feb., Arts; Brand, 21 April, Questors Theatre; **When We Dead Awaken**, 29 May, Tower, with Donald Goffin as Rubek; *The Master Builder*, 9 June, Old Vic.

1967   *Ghosts*, 14 June, Aldwych.

1968   *Hedda Gabler*, 3 June, Aldwych (in Swedish).

1970   *Hedda Gabler*, 29 June, Cambridge; *The Wild Duck*, 10 Nov., Criterion.

1971   *The Lady from the Sea*, 30 April, Greenwich.

1972   *Hedda Gabler*, 28 June, Royal Court; *A Doll's House*, 1 Nov., Greenwich.

1973   *A Doll's House*, 20 Feb., Criterion; *Rosmersholm*, 17 May, Greenwich; *The Wild Duck*, 28 May, Aldwych (in Swedish).

1974   *Ghosts*, 17 Jan., Greenwich.

2. B.B.C. RADIO PRODUCTIONS (1928–1974)

1928   *The Master Builder*, 19 and 20 March.

1933   *The Wild Duck*, 31 May, recorded repeat 2 June.

1934   *Ghosts*, 16 Jan., rec. rpt. 18 Jan.

1937   *Ghosts*, 9 Dec., rec. rpt. 10 Dec.

1938   *The Master Builder*, 24 April.

1939   *A Doll's House*, 8 Dec.

1941   *An Enemy of the People*, 20 April.

1942   *The Master Builder*, 27 Sept.

1943   *The Wild Duck*, 17 May.

1944   *An Enemy of the People*, 30 Jan.; *Ghosts*, 18 Dec.

1945   *The Wild Duck*, 3 Sept.; *Hedda Gabler*, 26 Nov.

1946   **John Gabriel Borkman**, 12 Aug., rec. rpt. 20 Nov., with Franklin Dyall as Borkman, Cathleen Nesbitt as Gunhild Borkman.

1947   *A Doll's House*, 12 May, rec. rpt. 27 May; *Rosmersholm*, 1 Dec., rec. rpt. 8 Dec.

1948   *The Master Builder*, 24 May.

1949   *The Wild Duck*, 23 May; *Brand*, 11 Dec., rec. rpt. 16 Dec.

1950   *Pillars of Society*, 1 Jan., rec. rpt. 4 Jan; *An Enemy of the People*, 9 Jan.; *A Doll's House*, 15 Jan., rec. rpt. 18 Jan.; *Ghosts*, 6 Feb., rec. rpt. 10 Feb.; *An Enemy of the People*, 26 Feb., rec. rpt. 1 March; *The Wild Duck*, 9 April, rec. rpt. 12 April; *Rosmersholm*, 23 April, rec. rpt. 26 April;

The Master Builder, 7 May, rec. rpt. 10 May; **John Gabriel Borkman**, 21 and 27 May, rec. rpts. of original production of 12 Aug. 1946; **When We Dead Wake**, 6 June, rec. rpt. 8 June, with Valentine Dyall as Rubek and Catherine Lacey as Irene; *Hedda Gabler*, 6 Nov., rec. rpt. 12 Nov; *The Lady from the Sea*, 10 Dec., rec. rpt. 13 Dec., again rpt. 3 Jan. 1951.

1951   *A Doll's House*, 24 Jan.; *An Enemy of the People*, rec. rpt. of the production of 26 Feb. 1950; *The Master Builder*, 31 May, rec. rpt. of production of 7 May 1950; **When We Dead Wake**, 17 June, rec. rpt. of production of 6 June 1950; *Ghosts*, 10 Sept.

1952   *The Lady from the Sea*, 22 Sept.; *Hedda Gabler*, 26 Nov., rec. rpt. 1 Dec.

1953   **John Gabriel Borkman**, 11 May, rec. rpt. of production of 12 Aug. 1946; *Emperor and Galilean*, 17 May, rec. rpt. 19 May; *Rosmersholm*, 24 Aug., rec. rpt. 6 Sept.

1954   *Brand*, rec. rpt. of original production of 11 Dec. 1949; *The Wild Duck*, 30 July, rec. rpt. of original production of 9 April 1950; *The Wild Duck*, 6 Sept., rec. rpt., of original production of 23 May 1949.

1955   *The Master Builder*, 14 March; *The Wild Duck*, 10 April, rec. rpts. 12 April and 21 June; *An Enemy of the People*, 20 April, rec. rpt. 25 April.

1956   **Little Eyolf**, 12 Feb., rec. rpts. 17 Feb. and 23 June, with Maxine Audley as Rita and Richard Hurndall as Allmers; *An Enemy of the People*, 23 May, rec. rpt. of original production of 26 Feb. 1950; **John Gabriel Borkman**, 28 May, with Stephen Murray as Borkman and Beatrix Lehmann as Gunhild Borkman; *Pillars of the Community*, a modern Scots version, 2 July; *Brand*, 30 Dec.

1957   *Brand*, 4 Jan. and 5 March, rec. rpts. of original production of 30 Dec. 1956; *An Enemy of the People*, 16 March; *Ghosts*, 4 July, rec. rpts. 6 July and 30 Oct.; *Hedda Gabler*, 11 Nov.

1958   *Hedda Gabler*, 20 Jan., rec. rpt. of original production of 11 Nov. 1957.

1959   *Rosmersholm*, 4 Jan.; *A Doll's House*, 3 July, rec. rpt. 19 July; *Peer Gynt*, 30 Dec.

1960   *Pillars of Society*, 30 May; *The Wild Duck*, 30 Sept.; *The Lady from the Sea*, 7 Nov.

1961   *The Wild Duck*, 5 March, rec. rpt. 3 May; *The Lady from the Sea*. 1 Sept., rec. rpt. 15 Sept.

1962   *Rosmersholm*, 17 Jan.; *The Lady from the Sea*, 1 June, rec. rpt. of production of 5 March 1961; *Rosmersholm*, 27 Aug.; *Pillars of Society*, 28 Sept.

1963   *Brand*, 29 April; *Peer Gynt*, 9 June; *Pillars of Society*, 17 Sept.

1964   *A Public Menace* (i.e. *An Enemy of the People*) 21 Sept.; *The Pretenders*, 23 Oct.

1965   *A Doll's House*, 23 May, rec. rpt. 18 June; *The Wild Duck*, 27 Sept.; *Hedda Gabler*, 17 Oct., rec. rpt. of production of 7 Nov. 1957; **Little**

Eyolf, 5 Nov., rec. rpt. 23 Nov., with Marius Goring as Allmers, Mary Wimbush as Rita, and Prunella Scales as Asta.

1966 **John Gabriel Borkman**, 22 April, with Donald Wolfit as Borkman, Beatrix Lehmann as Gunhild, and Nicholas Edmett as Erhart.

1968 *Ghosts*, 22 Jan.; *Hedda Gabler*, 11 Dec.

1969 **When We Dead Awaken**, 8 Aug., with Ralph Richardson as Rubek, Irene Worth as Irene, and Barbara Jefford as Maja.

1971 *An Enemy of the People*, 22 March; *Brand*, 12 Dec.

1974 **John Gabriel Borkman**, 4 Aug., with Ralph Richardson as Borkman, Irene Worth as Ella, Sylvia Coleridge as Gunhild.

3. TELEVISION PRODUCTIONS IN BRITAIN (1947–1974)

(a) B.B.C.

1947 *Rosmersholm*, 17 July, rpt. 18 July.

1950 *The Master Builder*, 2 May; *An Enemy of the People*, 3 Dec., rpt. 5 Dec.

1951 *Ghosts*, 18 March, rpt. 22 March.

1952 *The Wild Duck*, 2 March, rpt. 6 March; *A Doll's House*, 4 Nov.

1953 *The Lady from the Sea*, 10 May, rpt. 14 May.

1954 *Peer Gynt*, Part I, 31 Oct., Part II, 4 Nov.

1956 *A Doll's House*, 24 May; *Pillars of Society*, 25 Nov.

1958 *The Master Builder*, 23 Feb.; *The Lady from the Sea*, 24 Aug.

1959 *Brand*, 11 Aug.

1961 *An Enemy of the People*, in three instalments on 17, 24, and 31 Jan.

1962 *Ghosts*, 26 Jan.; *Hedda Gabler*, 28 Dec.

1963 **Little Eyolf**, 18 Dec., with James Maxwell as Allmers, Avril Elgar as Asta, and Dilys Hamlett as Rita.

1965 *Rosmersholm*, 26 Sept.

1968 *Ghosts*, 17 March.

1970 **When We Dead Awaken**, 12 Feb., with Alexander Knox as Rubek, Wendy Hiller as Irene, Irene Hamilton as Maja, and Brian Cox as Ulfhejm.

1971 *The Wild Duck*, 21 March.

1972 *Peer Gynt*, 26 Sept.; *Hedda Gabler*, 20 Oct.

1974 *The Lady from the Sea*, 5 March.

(b) I.T.V.

1957 *The Wild Duck*, 30 Jan.; *An Enemy of the People*, 20 March; *Hedda Gabler*, 29 May.

1958 **John Gabriel Borkman**, 19 Nov., with Laurence Olivier as Borkman, Pamela Brown as Ella Rentheim, Irene Worth as Gunhild Borkman, George Relph as Foldal, and Maxine Audley as Mrs. Wilton.

1961 *A Doll's House*, 31 Oct.; *The Wild Duck*, 12 Dec.

1970 *A Doll's House*, 17 Jan.

SELECT BIBLIOGRAPHY

(a) bibliographies
(b) biographies
(c) translations
(d) works of criticism

(a) BIBLIOGRAPHIES

Extensive bibliographical information is to be found in J. B. Halvorsen, *Norsk Forfatter–Lexikon 1814–1880*, vol. 3 (Christiania, 1892), pp. 1–89; Hjalmar Pettersen, *Henrik Ibsen 1828–1928, bedømt af Samtid og Eftertid* (Oslo, 1928); Reidar Øksnevad, *Norsk litteraturhistorisk bibliografi 1900–1945* (Oslo, 1951), pp. 163–222, and *Norsk litteraturhistorisk bibliografi 1946–1955* (Oslo, 1958), pp. 51–59; Ingrid Tedford, *Ibsen Bibliography 1928–57, Norsk bibliografisk bibliotek*, vol. 20 (Oslo, Bergen, 1961); and in the annual bibliographies of the *Ibsen-Årbok*, 1952 ff. Other bibliographical data, with particular emphasis on Ibsen's reception and standing in the English-speaking world, may be found in: Miriam A. Franc, *Ibsen in England* (Boston, U.S.A., 1919); Carl Burchardt, *Norwegian Life and Literature* (London, 1920), pp. 208–11; I. T. E. Firkins, *Henrik Ibsen: a bibliography of criticism and biography* (New York, 1921); Annette Andersen, 'Ibsen in America', in *Scandinavian Studies and Notes*, 14 (1937), pp. 65–109 and 115–55; and Brian W. Downs, 'Anglo-Norwegian literary relations 1867–1900', in *Modern Language Review*, xlvii, 4, Oct. 1952, pp. 449–94. For his reception in other countries, see: W. H. Eller, *Ibsen in Germany 1870–1900* (Boston, U.S.A., 1918); F. Meyen, *Ibsen-Bibliographie* (Brunswick, 1928); Wictor Hahn, *Henryk Ibsen w Polsce* (Lublin, 1929); B. A. Meuleman, *Ibsen en Nederland* (The Hague, 1931); H. Gregersen, *Ibsen and Spain* (Cambridge, Mass., 1936); Olav K. Lundeberg, 'Ibsen in France', *Scandinavian Studies and Notes*, 8 (1924–5), pp. 93–107; Kela Nyholm, 'Henrik Ibsen paa den franske Scene', in *Ibsen-Årbok 1957–59* (Skien, 1959), pp. 7–78; K. K. T. Wais, *Henrik Ibsens Wirkung in Spanien, Frankreich, Italien* (Brunswick, 1933); and N. Å. Nilsson, *Ibsen in Russland* (Stockholm, 1958).

(b) BIOGRAPHIES

Biographies available in English are: Henrik Jæger, *The Life of Henrik Ibsen*, tr. Clara Bell, with the verse done into English . . . by Edmund Gosse (London, 1890); Edmund Gosse, *Ibsen* (London, 1907); Adolph E. Zucker, *Ibsen the*

Master Builder (London, 1929); Theodore Jorgenson, *Henrik Ibsen: a study in art and personality* (Northfield, Minn., 1945); Bergliot Ibsen, *The Three Ibsens: memories of Henrik, Suzannah and Sigurd Ibsen*, tr. G. Schjelderup (London, 1951); Michael Meyer, *Henrik Ibsen*, 3 vols. (London, 1967–71); Hans Heiberg, *Ibsen: A Portrait of the Artist*, trans. Joan Tate (London, 1969); Halvdan Koht, *Life of Ibsen* (New York, 1971).

(c) TRANSLATIONS

Collected editions

The Pillars of Society, and other plays. [*The Pillars of Society*, tr. William Archer; *Ghosts*, tr. William Archer; *An Enemy of Society*, tr. Mrs. Eleanor Marx-Aveling.] Introduction by Havelock Ellis. (The Camelot Classics, London, 1888.)

Ibsen's Prose Dramas, ed. William Archer. Authorized English editions, 5 vols. (Walter Scott, London, 1890–1.) Vol. 1: *The League of Youth*, tr. William Archer; *The Pillars of Society*, tr. William Archer; *A Doll's House*, tr. William Archer. Vol. 2: *Ghosts*, tr. William Archer; *An Enemy of the People*, tr. Mrs. E. Marx-Aveling; *The Wild Duck*, tr. Mrs. F. E. Archer. Vol. 3: *Lady Inger of Ostråt*, tr. Charles Archer; *The Vikings at Helgeland*, tr. William Archer; *The Pretenders*, tr. William Archer. Vol. 4: *Emperor and Galilean*, tr. William Archer (based on an earlier translation by Catherine Ray). Vol. 5: *Rosmersholm*, tr. Charles Archer; *The Lady from the Sea*, tr. Mrs. F. E. Archer; *Hedda Gabler*, tr. William Archer.

The Prose Dramas of Henrik Ibsen, ed. Edmund Gosse. Lovell's Series of Foreign Literature. 3 vols. (New York and London, 1890.) Vol. 1: *A Doll's House, Pillars of Society, Ghosts*, all tr. William Archer; *Rosmersholm*, tr. M. Carmichael. Vol. 2: *The Lady from the Sea*, tr. Clara Bell; *An Enemy of Society*, tr. William Archer; *The Wild Duck*, tr. Mrs. E. Marx-Aveling; *The Young Men's League*, tr. Henry Carstarphen. Vol. 3: *Hedda Gabler*, tr. William Archer, with Preface by Edmund Gosse.

The Collected Works of Henrik Ibsen. Copyright edition. Revised and edited by William Archer. 12 vols. (Heinemann, London, 1906 ff.) Vol. 1 (1908): *Lady Inger of Ostråt*, tr. Charles Archer; *The Feast at Solhoug*, tr. William Archer and Mary Morison; *Love's Comedy*, tr. C. H. Herford. Vol. 2 (1906): *The Vikings at Helgeland*, tr. William Archer; *The Pretenders*, tr. William Archer. Vol. 3 (1906): *Brand*, tr. C. H. Herford. Vol. 4 (1907): *Peer Gynt*, tr. William and Charles Archer. Vol. 5 (1907): *Emperor and Galilean*, tr. William Archer. Vol. 6 (1906): *The League of Youth*, tr. William Archer; *Pillars of Society*, tr. William Archer. Vol. 7 (1907): *A Doll's House*, tr. William Archer; *Ghosts*, tr. William Archer. Vol. 8 (1907): *An Enemy of the People*, tr. Mrs. E. Marx-Aveling; *The Wild Duck*, tr. Mrs. F. E. Archer. Vol. 9 (1907): *Rosmersholm*, tr. Charles Archer; *The Lady from the Sea*, tr. Mrs. F. E. Archer. Vol. 10 (1907): *Hedda Gabler*, tr. Edmund Gosse and William Archer; *The Master Builder*, tr. Edmund Gosse and William Archer. Vol. 11 (1907):

Little Eyolf, tr. William Archer; *John Gabriel Borkman*, tr. William Archer; *When We Dead Awaken*, tr. William Archer. Vol. 12 (1912): *From Ibsen's Workshop*. Notes, scenarios, and drafts of modern plays, tr. A. G. Chater.

Early Plays, tr. Anders Orbeck (Amer.-Scand. Foundation, New York, 1921, and O.U.P., London, 1922): *Catiline; The Warrior's Barrow; Olaf Liljekrans*.

Everyman's Library (1910 ff.): *Lady Inger of Ostraat, Love's Comedy*, [and] *The League of Youth*, tr. R. Farquharson Sharp (1915); *Brand*, tr. F. E. Garrett, with an introduction by P. H. Wicksteed (1915), re-issued with a new introduction by Brain W. Downs (1961); *Peer Gynt*, tr. R. Farquharson Sharp (1921); *The Pretenders, Pillars of Society*, [and] *Rosmersholm*, tr. R. Farquharson Sharp (1913); *A Doll's House, The Wild Duck*, [and] *The Lady from the Sea*, tr. R. Farquharson Sharp and Mrs. E. Marx-Aveling (1910); *Ghosts, The Warriors at Helgeland*, [and] *An Enemy of the People*, tr. R. Farquharson Sharp (1911); *Hedda Gabler, The Master Builder, John Gabriel Borkman*, tr. Eva Le Gallienne and Norman Ginsbury, intr. Brian W. Downs (1966).

Penguin volumes (1950 ff.): *Peer Gynt*, tr. Peter Watts; *A Doll's House, and other plays* [*The League of Youth, The Lady from the Sea*], tr. Peter Watts; *Ghosts, and other plays* [*A Public Enemy, When We Dead Wake*], tr. Peter Watts; *The Master Builder, and other plays* [*Rosmersholm, Little Eyolf, John Gabriel Borkman*], tr. Una Ellis-Fermor; *Hedda Gabler, and other plays* [*Pillars of the Community, The Wild Duck*], tr. Una Ellis-Fermor.

The Plays of Ibsen, tr. Michael Meyer (Rupert Hart-Davis, London, 1960 ff.): *The Pretenders; Brand; Peer Gynt; Pillars of Society; A Doll's House; Ghosts; An Enemy of the People; The Wild Duck; Rosmersholm; The Lady from the Sea; Hedda Gabler; The Master Builder; Little Eyolf; John Gabriel Borkman; When We Dead Awaken*.

Six Plays by Henrik Ibsen, tr. Eva Le Gallienne (Modern Library, New York, 1957): *A Doll's House; Ghosts; An Enemy of the People; Rosmersholm; Hedda Gabler; The Master Builder*.

Signet Classics: *Peer Gynt*, tr. Rolf Fjelde (New York, 1965); *Four Major Plays*, vols. 1 and 2, trans. Rolf Fjelde (New York, 1965 and 1970)—Vol. 1: *A Doll's House, The Wild Duck, Hedda Gabler, The Master Builder;* Vol. 2: *Ghosts, An Enemy of the People, The Lady from the Sea, John Gabriel Borkman*.

Bantam Classics: *Last plays of Henrik Ibsen*, tr. Arvid Paulson (New York, 1962) [*Rosmersholm; Hedda Gabler; The Master Builder; John Gabriel Borkman; When We Dead Awaken*].

Letters, articles, and speeches

The Correspondence of Henrik Ibsen, ed. Mary Morison (London, 1905).

Speeches and New Letters, tr. Arne Kildal, with bibliographical index (Boston, 1910, and London, 1911).

Ibsen: Letters and Speeches, ed. Evert Sprinchorn (New York, 1964, and London, 1965).

The standard German edition of the works is: *Henrik Ibsens sämtliche Werke in deutscher Sprache*. Durchgesehen und eingeleitet von Georg Brandes, Julius Elias, Paul Schlenther, 10 vols. (Berlin, 1898 ff.)

The standard French edition of the works is: *Œuvres complètes*, traduits par P. G. la Chesnais, 16 vols. (Paris, 1914–45.)

(d) WORKS OF CRITICISM

(i) general studies, in English, arranged chronologically

Edmund Gosse, *Studies in the Literature of Northern Europe* (London, 1879), pp. 35–69.

Georg Brandes, *Eminent Authors of the Nineteenth Century*, tr. Rasmus B. Anderson (New York, 1886), pp. 405–60.

Havelock Ellis, *The New Spirit* (London, 1890), pp. 133–73.

George Bernard Shaw, *The Quintessence of Ibsenism* (London, 1891)—second edition 'completed to the death of Ibsen', London, 1913.

Philip H. Wicksteed, *Four lectures on Henrik Ibsen dealing chiefly with his metrical works* (London, 1892).

F. Anstey [i.e. Thomas Anstey Guthrie], *Mr. Punch's Pocket Ibsen*. A collection of some of the master's best-known dramas. Condensed, revised, and slightly rearranged for the benefit of the earnest student (London, 1893).

'Zanoni' [pseud.], *Ibsen and the Drama* (London, [? 1894]).

H. H. Boyesen, *A Commentary on the Works of Henrik Ibsen* (London, 1894).

Edward Russell, *Ibsen*. A lecture delivered at University College, Liverpool, 26 Jan. 1894 (Liverpool, 1894).

George Bernard Shaw, *Our Theatres in the Nineties*. 3 vols. (London, 1932)—being dramatic criticisms contributed week by week to *The Saturday Review* from Jan. 1895 to May 1898.

Henry James, *The Scenic Art*, ed. Allan Wade (London, 1949), pp. 243–60, 286–94—including: 'On the occasion of Hedda Gabler', *New Review*, June 1891; 'The Master Builder', *Pall Mall Gazette*, 17 Feb. 1893; 'Little Eyolf', 'John Gabriel Borkman', *Harper's Weekly*, 23 Jan., 6 Feb., 1897.

Edward Russell and Percy Cross Standing, *Ibsen on his merits* (London, 1897).

Georg Brandes, *Henrik Ibsen, Bjørnstjerne Bjørnson. Critical studies* (London, 1899.)

Max Beerbohm, *Around Theatres* (London, 1953)—being dramatic criticisms May 1898–April 1910, including; 'An hypocrisy in play-going' [on *Hedda Gabler* played in Italian, Oct. 1903], pp. 277–81; 'Ibsen' [an obituary, May 1906], pp. 432–6; 'A memorable performance' [on *Rosmersholm*, Feb. 1908], pp. 497–501.

James Joyce, 'Ibsen's New Drama' [i.e. *When We Dead Awaken*], *Fortnightly Review*, lxvii NS, 1 Apr. 1900, pp. 575–90.

James Huneker, *Iconoclasts: a book of dramatists* (London, 1905), pp. 1–138.

Arthur Symons, *Figures of Several Centuries* (London, 1916), pp. 222–67: 'Henrik Ibsen', written 1906.

Jeanette Lee, *The Ibsen Secret*. A key to the prose dramas of Henrik Ibsen (London, 1907).

Haldane Macfall, *Ibsen: the man, his art and his significance* (London, 1907).

G. Saintsbury, *The Later Nineteenth Century* (London, 1907), pp. 307–26.

G. A. Mounsey, *The Life Work of Hendrik Ibsen from the Russian of Merejkowski* (n.d. [? 1908]).

J. Moses Montrose, *Henrik Ibsen: the man and his plays* (New York, 1908).

James Huneker, *Egoists: a book of supermen* (London, 1909), pp. 317–39.

Edward Dowden, *Essays, modern and Elizabethan* (London, 1910), pp. 26–60.

Archibald Henderson, *Interpreters of life and the modern spirit* (London, 1911), pp. 157–283.

Otto Heller, *Henrik Ibsen: plays and problems* (New York, 1912).

R. Ellis Roberts, *Henrik Ibsen: a critical study* (London, 1912).

Henry Rose, *Henrik Ibsen: poet, mystic and moralist* (London, 1913).

William Archer, 'The true greatness of Ibsen', a lecture delivered at University College, London. *Edda*, xii, 1919, pp. 175–91.

Carl Burchardt, *Norwegian life and literature* (London, 1920).

Storm Jameson, *Modern Drama in Europe* (London, 1920).

Janko Lavrin, *Ibsen and his creation*. A psycho-critical study (London, 1921).

T. M. Campbell, *Hebbel, Ibsen and the analytical exposition* (Heidelberg, 1922).

Illit Grøndahl and Ola Raknes, *Chapters in Norwegian Literature* (London, 1923), pp. 186–215.

Basil King, 'Ibsen and Emile Bardach', *Century Magazine* (New York), 1923: Oct. pp. 803–15, Nov. pp. 83–92.

Benedetto Croce, *European Literature in the Nineteenth Century* (London, 1924), pp. 326–43.

Hermann J. Weigand, *The modern Ibsen: a reconsideration* (New York, 1925).

Paul Henry Grumman, *Henrik Ibsen: an introduction to his life and works* (New York, 1928).

Elizabeth Robins, *Ibsen and the actress* (London, 1928).

Bonamy Dobrée, *The Lamp and the Lute* (Oxford, 1929), pp. 1–20.

Harley Granville-Barker, 'The coming of Ibsen', in *The Eighteen Eighties, Essays by Fellows of the Royal Society of Literature*, ed. Walter de la Mare (Cambridge, 1930), pp. 159–96.

J. G. Robertson, *Essays and addresses on literature* (London, 1935), pp. 147–226.

A. Anstensen. *The Proverb in Ibsen* (Columbia U.P. and London, 1935).

E. M. Forster, *Abinger Harvest* (London, 1936), including chapter on 'Ibsen the Romantic'.

Theodore Jorgenson, *Henrik Ibsen: a study in art and personality* (Northfield, Minn., 1945).

Ronald Peacock, *The Poet in the Theatre* (London, 1946), pp. 65–71.

Brian W. Downs, *Ibsen: the intellectual background* (Cambridge, 1946).

Barrett H. Clark and George Freedley, *A History of Modern Drama* (New York and London, 1947), pp. 1–20—chapter by Alrik Gustafson.

Eric Bentley, *The Modern Theatre* (London, 1948), pp. 64–90 and *passim*.

M. C. Bradbrook, *Ibsen the Norwegian* (London, 1948).

P. F. D. Tennant, *Ibsen's Dramatic Technique* (Cambridge, 1948).

Alan Reynolds Thompson, *The Dry Mock* (Berkeley, Cal., 1948), pp. 197–244: 'Ibsen'.

Francis Fergusson, *The Idea of a Theatre* (Princeton U.P. and London, 1949)—with special reference to *Ghosts*.

Brian W. Downs, *A study of six plays by Ibsen* (Cambridge, 1950).

Janko Lavrin, *Ibsen: an approach* (London, 1950).

Raymond Williams, *Drama from Ibsen to Eliot* (London, 1952); 2nd rev. ed. *Drama from Ibsen to Brecht* (London, 1969).

John Northam, *Ibsen's Dramatic Method: a study of the prose dramas* (London, 1953).

G. K. Chesterton, *A Handful of Authors* (London, 1953), pp. 134–58: 'Henrik Ibsen', articles written in 1906 and 1928.

J. T. Farrell, *Reflections at Fifty, and other essays* (New York, 1954), pp. 66–96: 'Joyce and Ibsen'.

Francis Bull, *Ibsen: the man and the dramatist*. Taylorian Lecture (Oxford, 1954).

Eric Bentley, *In search of theatre* (London, 1954), pp. 365–80.

Eva Le Gallienne, *Hedda Gabler*, A preface . . . with a new translation (London, 1955), and *The Master Builder*, a translation . . . with a prefatory study (London, 1955).

T. R. Henn, *The Harvest of Tragedy* (London, 1956), pp. 172–88: 'A Note on Ibsen'.

J. W. McFarlane, *Ibsen and the Temper of Norwegian Literature* (London, 1960).

Una Ellis-Fermor, *Shakespeare the Dramatist* (London, 1961): chap. on 'Ibsen and Shakespeare as dramatic artists'.

J. Setterquist, *Ibsen and the beginnings of Anglo-Irish drama* (Harvard U.P., 1961).

Kenneth Muir, *Last Periods of Shakespeare, Racine and Ibsen* (Liverpool U.P., 1962).

F. L. Lucas, *The Drama of Ibsen and Strindberg* (London, 1962).

G. Wilson Knight, *Ibsen* (Edinburgh, 1962).

J. W. McFarlane (ed.), *Discussions of Ibsen* (Boston, U.S.A., 1962)—essays by various hands.

M. J. Valency, *The flower and the castle* (New York, 1964).

R. Brustein, *The Theatre of Revolt* (New York, 1964, and London, 1965), pp. 35–84: 'Henrik Ibsen'.

Rolf Fjelde (ed.), *Twentieth-century views on Ibsen* (New York, 1965)—essays by various hands.

John Northam, *Dividing Worlds* [on *The Tempest* and *Rosmersholm*] (Kristian-sand, 1965).

Daniel Haakonsen (ed.), *Contemporary Approaches to Ibsen*, no. 1, Ibsen Year-book, vol. 8 (Oslo, 1966).

B. W. Downs, *Modern Norwegian Literature 1860–1918* (Cambridge U.P., 1966), pp. 43–64 and 116–32.

Raymond Williams, *Modern Tragedy* (London, 1966).

David Grene, *Reality and the Heroic Pattern: Last plays of Ibsen, Shakespeare and Sophocles* (Chicago, 1967).

Bernard de B. Nicol, *Varieties of Dramatic Experience* (London, 1969), pp. 153–72.

J. W. McFarlane (ed.), *Henrik Ibsen*. Penguin critical anthology (London, 1970).

Orley J. Holtan, *Mythic Patterns in Ibsen's Last Plays* (Minneapolis, 1970).

Daniel Haakonsen (ed.), *Contemporary Approaches to Ibsen*, no. 2, Ibsen Year-book, vol. 11 (Oslo, 1971).

Martin Esslin, *Reflections: Essays on Modern Theatre* (New York, 1971), pp. 27–45: 'Henrik Ibsen'.

Michael Egan (ed.), *Ibsen: the Critical Heritage* (London, 1972).

Ronald Gaskell, *Drama and Reality: the European Theatre since Ibsen* (London, 1972), pp. 75–93.

James Hurt, *Catiline's Dream: an essay on Ibsen's plays* (Illinois, 1972).

Charles R. Lyons, *Henrik Ibsen: the Divided Consciousness* (Southern Illinois U.P., 1972).

John Northam, *Ibsen: a critical study* (Cambridge, 1973).

(ii) other studies in English of the plays in this volume (extra to those items mentioned in the Appendices, pp. 317–25, 343–50, and 366–74) include

Sverre Arestad, 'Ibsen's portrayal of the artist' in *Edda*, lx, June 1960, pp. 86–100; '*Little Eyolf* and human responsibility' in *Scandinavian Studies*, xxxii, Aug. 1960, pp. 140–52; '*When We Dead Awaken* reconsidered' in *Scandinavian Studies*, xxx, 1958, pp. 117–30; Edvard Beyer, '*When We Dead Awaken*' in *Ibsen-Årbok 1970–71*, no. 11 (Oslo, 1971), pp. 26–41—identical with Daniel Haakonsen, *Contemporary Approaches to Ibsen*, no. 2, mentioned above; Harold F. Brooks, '*Pygmalion* and *When We Dead Awaken*' in *Notes and Queries*, 1960, pp. 469–71; Paul Henry Grumman, 'Ibsen's symbolism in *The Master Builder* and *When We Dead Awaken*' in *Nebraska University Studies* (Lincoln, Neb.), x, 1910, pp. 235–41; James E. Kerens, ' "Kindermord" and will in *Little Eyolf*' in *Modern Drama: Essays in Criticism*, ed. T. Bogard and W. I. Oliver (New York, 1965), pp. 192–208; Charles R. Lyons, 'The Function of Dream and Reality in *John Gabriel Borkman*' in *Scandinavian Studies*, xlv, 1973, no. 4; Robert Raphael, 'From *Hedda Gabler* to *When We Dead Awaken*: the quest for self-realisation' in *Scandinavian Studies*, xxxvi, 1964, pp. 34–47; T. B.

Thompson, 'Ibsen's *When We Dead Awaken*' in *Poet Lore*, xx, May 1909, pp. 201–17.

(iii) of the secondary literature in languages other than English, the following items dealing particularly with the last plays may be found useful:

Asbjørn Aarseth, 'Holdning og struktur i *Lille Eyolf*' in *Edda*, lxvi, 1966, pp. 260–9; and '*Når vi døde vågner:* myte og symbolikk' in *Ibsen på festspillscenen* (Bergen, 1969), pp. 65–78; Herman Anker, '*Når vi døde vågner:* Ibsens dramatiske epilog' in *Edda*, lvi, 1956, pp. 178–219; and 'Ibsens skyggeskikkelser' in *Nordisk Tidskrift*, xxxii, 1956, pp. 185–93; Harald Beyer, *Nietzsche og Norden*, 2 vols. (Bergen, 1962); Håkon Bjørn-Hansen, 'Menneskenes livsoppgaver i Henrik Ibsens nåtidsdramaer from *Samfundets støtter* til *Når vi døde vågner*' in *Ibsen-Årbok 1960–62* (Skien, 1962), pp. 93–185; Oddlaug Bringe, 'Henrik Ibsen: *Lille Eyolf*', Oslo Univ. thesis (hovedoppgave), 1968, typescript; Per Tore Dalen, 'Bilde, symbol og myte i *Lille Eyolf*', Oslo Univ. thesis (hovedoppgave), 1971, typescript; Kjersti Ericsson, '*Lille Eyolf* og familiemyten' in *Samtiden*, lxxxi, 1, 1972; Pavel Fraenkl, 'Tabu og drama i *Når vi døde vågner*' in *Nordisk Tidskrift*, xliv, 1967, pp. 340–63; Gudrun Gvåle, '*Når vi døde vågner*' in *Ibsen-Årbok 1968–69* (Oslo, 1969), pp. 23–37; Daniel Haakonsen, *Henrik Ibsens realisme* (Oslo, 1957), with chap. on *John Gabriel Borkman*; Fredrik J. Haslund, 'Ibsens diktning avgir stadig nye signaler: en struktur-analyse av *John Gabriel Borkman*' in *Forskningsnytt*, vii, 1972; Alf Kjellen, '*John Gabriel Borkman*—ensamhetens tragedi', in *Ord och Bild*, lxviii, 1959, pp. 27–38; Borghild Krane, 'Bergmannen og *John Gabriel Borkman*' in *Ibsen-Årbok, 1967* (Oslo, 1967), pp. 14–26; Fritz Paul, *Symbol und Mythos: Studien zum Spätwerk Henrik Ibsens* (Munich, 1969)—esp. pp. 128–46: 'Symbol und Mythos in *Når vi døde vågner*'; Erik Østerud, '*Når vi døde vågner* på mytologisk bakgrunn' in *Ibsen-Årbok 1963–64* (Oslo, 1964), pp. 72–97; Peter Simonsen, 'Om *Hedda Gabler*, *Lille Eyolf* og Lord Byron', in *Edda*, lxii, 1962, pp. 176–84; Yngvar Ustvedt, 'Professor Rubek og Henrik Ibsen' in *Edda*, lxvii, 1967, pp. 272–87.